GPU Zen

GPU Zen

Advanced Rendering Techniques

Edited by Wolfgang Engel

BLACK CAT PUBLISHING

Black Cat Publishing Inc.
Encinitas, CA

Editorial, Sales, and Customer Service Office

Black Cat Publishing Inc.
144 West D Street Suite 204
Encinitas, CA 92009
http://www.black-cat.pub/

ISBN 13: 978-0-9988228-9-1

Printed in the United States of America
12 11 10 09 08 10 9 8 7 6 5 4 3 2 1

Contents

Preface

This book—like its predecessors—is created with the target of helping readers to better achieve their goals.

I would like to thank Alice Peters for collecting and editing the articles and for creating the beautiful layout. I would also like to thank Carsten Dachsbacher, Chris Oat, Eric Haines, Mark Chatfield, and Wessam Bahnassi, all of whom worked hard to finish this book. Eric Haines wants to thank Jim Susinno (anonymously) for reviewing the two VR articles.

I would also like to thank Jean-Normand Bucci from Eidos Montreal for giving us permission to use the images from *Deus Ex*.

—Wolfgang Engel

I Geometry Manipulation

In this section we explore graphics algorithms that deal with the processing of 3D geometric data. The two articles presented here are ultimately optimization techniques that are interesting, in part, because they make clever performance trade-offs between the CPU and the GPU.

Our first article is "Attributed Vertex Clouds" by Willy Scheibel, Stefan Buschmann, Matthias Trapp, and Jürgen Döllner in which a system for compactly representing and procedurally rendering large numbers of primitive shapes and polygonal meshes is described. This method trades some GPU computation for very fast CPU processing of complex arrangements of instanced 3D shapes. The system presented has immediate applications in data visualization, but could also be leveraged for use in other kinds of programs that exploit instanced geometry.

The second article is "Rendering Convex Occluders with Inner Conservative Rasterization" by Marcus Svensson and Emil Persson. Here, the authors present an inner-conservative software rasterization and occlusion system that can be used to test for visibility of objects prior to rendering them. By investing some CPU cycles towards occlusion testing, great savings can be had in avoiding wasted draw calls and needless GPU processing of non-visible geometry.

I would like to thank the authors of both articles for sharing their work and I hope that you, the reader, find these articles as interesting and exciting as I do!

—Christopher Oat

1

Attributed Vertex Clouds

Willy Scheibel, Stefan Buschmann,
Matthias Trapp, and Jürgen Döllner

1.1 Introduction

In current computer graphics applications, large 3D scenes that consist of *polygonal geometries*, such as triangle meshes, are rendered. Using state-of-the-art techniques, this geometry is often represented on the GPU using vertex and index buffers, as well as additional auxiliary data, such as textures or uniform buffers [Riccio and Lilley 2013]. It is usually loaded or generated on the CPU and transferred to the GPU for efficient rendering using the programmable rendering pipeline. For polygonal meshes of arbitrary complexity, the described approach is indispensable. However, there are several types of simpler geometries (e.g., cuboids, spheres, tubes, or splats) that can be generated procedurally. For scenes that consist of a large number of such geometries, which are parameterized individually and potentially need to be updated regularly, another approach for representing and rendering these geometries may be beneficial.

In the following, we present an efficient data representation and rendering concept for such geometries, denoted as *attributed vertex clouds* (AVCs). Using this approach, geometry is generated on the GPU during execution of the programmable rendering pipeline. Instead of the actual geometry, an AVC contains a set of vertices that describe the target geometry. Each vertex is used as the argument for a function that procedurally generates the target geometry. This function is called a *transfer function*, and it is implemented using shader programs and therefore executed as part of the rendering process.

This approach allows for compact geometry representation and results in reduced memory footprints in comparison to traditional representations. Also, AVCs can be rendered using a single draw call, improving rendering performance. By shifting geometry generation to the GPU, the resulting *volatile* geometry can be controlled flexibly, i.e., its position, parameterization, and even the type of geometry can be modified without requiring state changes or uploading new data to the GPU. Furthermore, the concept is easy to implement and integrate into existing rendering systems, either as part of or in addition to other rendering approaches.

1.2 Concept

An *attributed vertex cloud* consists of a number of vertices, each of which describes one instance of the target geometry. A single vertex can thereby contain either a parameterized description of the geometry [Overvoorde 2014] (e.g., a cuboid can be specified by center point, extent, and orientation), or more generally an arbitrary data point, which by some function can be transformed into the desired geometry parameterization. For each vertex, a *transfer function* is applied, that converts the vertex into a parameterized description of the target geometry. This function determines the type and configuration of the target geometry based mainly on the input vertex, but the transfer function can also take into account other parameters such as global configuration, camera position, or interaction states. Finally, a geometry generation function is invoked with the selected parameters, creating the actual geometry [Kemen 2012] which is then rasterized and rendered to the screen.
The AVC concept (see Figure 1.1) consists of the following elements:

Attribute Vertex Cloud. The AVC is a vertex buffer that contains a set of data points which are rendered as the geometry of a scene. Each vertex thereby represents one instance of the target geometry and provides all relevant

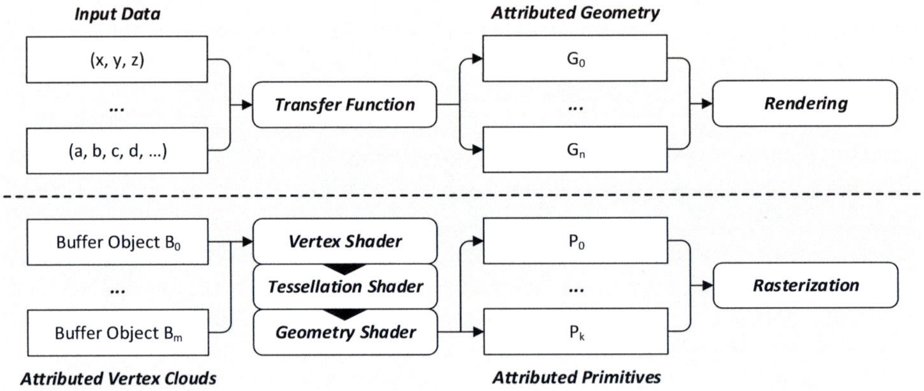

Figure 1.1. Concept overview of attributed vertex clouds. Data points with arbitrary attributes are passed to a transfer function that creates attributed geometry (attributed vertices arranged in primitives). More specific, one data point of an attributed vertex cloud is passed through the programmable rendering pipeline and transformed into attributed vertices and primitives.

attributes needed to select and configure the target geometry. However, the actual definition of one vertex may vary widely depending on the use case. A vertex can already contain a detailed configuration of the geometry (e.g., it may describe a cube by its center position, extents, orientation, and color). In other use cases, a vertex may contain a data point of the target domain (e.g., a tracking point in a movement trajectory, consisting of the current geo-location, speed, and acceleration) or compressed attributes [Purnomo et al. 2005]. The AVC is represented on the GPU as a vertex array buffer, consisting of several vertex attributes. It may also reference other buffers by index. This can be used to represent shared data between vertices, such as *per-group*, *per-batch*, or *global* attributes.

Transfer Function. The transfer function selects the configuration of the output geometry for each vertex. It is usually implemented in either the vertex or the geometry shader, taking a data point of the AVC as input and creating a geometry configuration vector as its output. The transfer function can depend not only on the values of the vertex itself, but also on other parameters that can be used to influence the target geometry. For example, the current camera position can be used to determine the distance from the camera to the geometry that is about to be rendered. Based on that distance, the type and style of the generated geometry can be altered. This enables the implementation of level-of-detail and, to a certain degree, level-of-abstraction techniques. Further, interaction and navigation states (e.g., interactive filtering or selection by the user) can be applied to parameterize geometry generation. Also, global configuration parameters specified by the user can be taken into account, allowing the user to control or parameterize the generated geometry (e.g., select geometry types, provide size factors or constraints, etc.).

Geometry Generation. In the last step, the actual geometry is generated according to the configuration previously selected by the transfer function. This is usually implemented using tessellation and geometry shaders. Due to practical considerations, the implementations of transfer function and geometry generation can sometimes be merged into one. Depending on the use case, different types of geometries can be emitted for each individual vertex. Where applicable, vertices may also be culled [Rákos 2010]. If such dynamic geometry generation is used, we suggest to separate the draw calls to one geometry type per batch for optimized performance.

1.3 Applications for Attributed Vertex Clouds

As described above, data layout of the vertices, complexity of the transfer function, and implementation of the geometry generation vary with the specific use case in which *attributed vertex clouds* are applied. They also depend on the level of interactivity intended for the target application. For our examples, the transfer function and geometry generation implementations are distributed over vertex, tessellation, and geometry shader stages.

In the following, we present a number of use cases and explain the different implementations of AVCs in these contexts. Also, we provide a comparison of the proposed AVC approaches with an implementation of the same example using hardware instancing techniques. To illustrate the general concept, we present block worlds. As examples from the visualization domain, cuboids, arcs, polygons, and trajectories are described. All examples presented in this section can be accessed as code and executable with the provided demos.[1] They are based on OpenGL 4.0 and GLSL as the shading language; some are compatible with OpenGL 3.2.

1.3.1 Block Worlds

The scene of our example block world contains equally-sized blocks of differing types that are arranged in a regular, three-dimensional grid. Conceptually, each grid cell may contain a block; thus, a block can be identified through its position in the grid. Each block type is visually distinguishable through a different texture that is applied on its surface.

An implementation using hardware instancing [Carucci and Studios 2005] prepares a triangle strip with normalized positions and normal-vectors. Per-instance data passes the block position in the grid and the type to the rendering pipeline. During the vertex shader stage (Listing 1.1), each vertex is converted into actual world space coordinates using the normalized positions, the block position in the grid, and the size of each block (passed as uniform). The normalized positions and the triangle normal-vectors are also passed to the fragment shader to compute texture coordinates and perform texture lookup and shading. To encode the same scene as an attributed vertex cloud, we use one vertex per block. The vertex contains the block position in the grid and its type. During the vertex shader execution (Listing 1.2), the center of the block is computed by the position in the grid and the size of each block (passed as uniform). In the geometry shader (Listing 1.3), the center and the size of each block is used to compute the corners and emit the triangle strip for the rasterization. This triangle strip has normal-vectors and normalized positions attached and is thus usable for the same fragment shader.

[1] Hosted on https://github.com/hpicgs/attributedvertexclouds.

```
uniform mat4 viewProjection;
uniform float blockSize;
in vec3  in_vertex; // instancing template
in vec3  in_normal; // instancing template
in ivec4 in_positionAndType; // per instance data
flat out vec3 g_normal;
flat out int  g_type;
out vec3 g_localCoord;

void main() {
    gl_Position = viewProjection
        * vec4((in_vertex + vec3(in_positionAndType.xyz)) * blockSize, 1.0);

    g_normal = in_normal;
    g_type = in_positionAndType.w;
    g_localCoord = in_vertex * 2.0;
}
```

Listing 1.1. Block world vertex shader using hardware instancing. The per-instance data is packed into a single input.

```
in ivec4 in_positionAndType; // per instance data
out int v_type;

void main() {
    gl_Position = vec4(in_positionAndType.xyz, 1.0);

    v_type = in_positionAndType.w;
}
```

Listing 1.2. Block world vertex shader using AVCs. The per-instance data is packed into a single input.

```
layout (points) in;
layout (triangle_strip, max_vertices = 14) out;
uniform mat4 viewProjection;
uniform float blockSize;
in int v_type[];
flat out vec3 g_normal;
flat out int g_type;
out vec3 g_localCoord;

void emit(in vec3 position, in vec3 normal, in vec3 localCoord) {
    gl_Position = viewProjection * vec4(position, 1.0);
    g_normal = normal;
    g_type = v_type[0];
    g_localCoord = localCoord;
    EmitVertex();
}

void main() {
    vec3 center = gl_in[0].gl_Position.xyz * blockSize;
    vec3 llf = center - vec3(blockSize) / vec3(2.0);
    vec3 urb = center + vec3(blockSize) / vec3(2.0);

```

```
    emit(vec3(llf.x, urb.y, llf.z), POSITIVE_Y, vec3(-1.0,  1.0, -1.0));
    emit(vec3(llf.x, urb.y, urb.z), POSITIVE_Y, vec3(-1.0,  1.0,  1.0));
    emit(vec3(urb.x, urb.y, llf.z), POSITIVE_Y, vec3( 1.0,  1.0, -1.0));
    emit(vec3(urb.x, urb.y, urb.z), POSITIVE_Y, vec3( 1.0,  1.0,  1.0));
    emit(vec3(urb.x, llf.y, urb.z), POSITIVE_X, vec3( 1.0, -1.0,  1.0));
    emit(vec3(llf.x, urb.y, urb.z), POSITIVE_Z, vec3(-1.0,  1.0,  1.0));
    emit(vec3(llf.x, llf.y, urb.z), POSITIVE_Z, vec3(-1.0, -1.0,  1.0));
    emit(vec3(llf.x, urb.y, llf.z), NEGATIVE_X, vec3(-1.0,  1.0, -1.0));
    emit(vec3(llf.x, llf.y, llf.z), NEGATIVE_X, vec3(-1.0, -1.0, -1.0));
    emit(vec3(urb.x, urb.y, llf.z), NEGATIVE_Z, vec3( 1.0,  1.0, -1.0));
    emit(vec3(urb.x, llf.y, llf.z), NEGATIVE_Z, vec3( 1.0, -1.0, -1.0));
    emit(vec3(urb.x, llf.y, urb.z), POSITIVE_X, vec3( 1.0, -1.0,  1.0));
    emit(vec3(llf.x, llf.y, llf.z), NEGATIVE_Y, vec3(-1.0, -1.0, -1.0));
    emit(vec3(llf.x, llf.y, urb.z), NEGATIVE_Y, vec3(-1.0, -1.0,  1.0));
    EndPrimitive();
}
```

Listing 1.3. Block world geometry shader using AVCs. The 14 emitted vertices build a full block triangle strip.

When comparing the instancing implementation to the AVC implementation, the main difference is encoding and application of the cube template. Using hardware instancing, the geometry is encoded using a vertex buffer that is input to the vertex shader stage. Using AVCs, the geometry is generated during the geometry shader stage. This results in fewer attributes passing the vertex shader stage.

1.3.2 Colored Cuboids

When using cuboids for rendering (e.g., for rectangular treemaps [Trapp et al. 2013]), these cuboids may contain a position, an extent, and a color. The color is typically encoded as a scalar value that is converted to a color using a gradient.

Similar to the blocks of a block world, an instancing implementation provides a cuboid triangle strip with normalized positions and normal-vectors (refer to the vertex shader in Listing 1.4). However, the actual position, extent, and color value are per-instance data. The color is computed using a texture lookup during the vertex shader stage. The inputs for the rasterization are the triangle strip with the attached color and normal-vector attributes.

The same scene encoded in an AVC would use the same per-instance data with adjusted vertex shader (Listing 1.5), since the target geometry is generated during the geometry shader stage (Listing 1.6). Therefore, the provided position and extent attributes are used to compute the eight corners of the cuboid and a triangle strip is emitted containing the vertex positions and the attached normal-vectors and color attributes (Figure 1.2).

```
uniform mat4 viewProjection;
in vec3  in_vertex; // instancing template
in vec3  in_normal; // instancing template
in vec3  in_position; // per instance data
in vec3  in_extent; // per instance data
in float in_colorValue; // per instance data
uniform sampler1D gradient;
flat out vec3 g_color;
flat out vec3 g_normal;

void main() {
    gl_Position = viewProjection * vec4(in_vertex * in_extent + in_position, 1.0);
    g_color = texture(gradient, in_colorValue).rgb;
    g_normal = in_normal;
}
```

Listing 1.4. Cuboids vertex shader using hardware instancing.

```
layout (points) in;
layout (triangle_strip, max_vertices = 14) out;
uniform mat4 viewProjection;
in vec3 v_extent[];
in vec3 v_color[];
in float v_height[];
flat out vec3 g_color;
flat out vec3 g_normal;

// Emits a vertex with given position and normal
void emit(in vec3 position, in vec3 normal);

void main() {
    vec3 center = gl_in[0].gl_Position.xyz;
    vec3 halfExtent = vec3(v_extent[0].x, v_height[0], v_extent[0].y) / vec3(2.0);
    vec3 llf = center - halfExtent;
    vec3 urb = center + halfExtent;
```

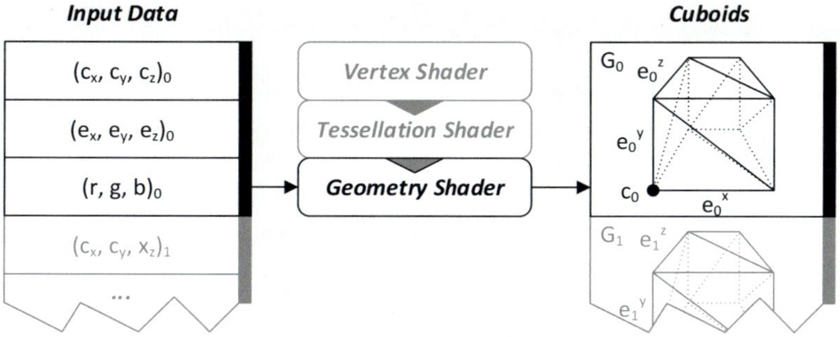

Figure 1.2. Concept of generating cuboids from an AVC. The center, extent, and color of each attributed vertex is used to emit one triangle strip with attached normal-vectors and colors.

```
in vec3  in_position; // per instance data
in vec3  in_extent; // per instance data
in float in_colorValue; // per instance data
uniform sampler1D gradient;
out vec3 v_extent;
out vec3 v_color;

void main() {
    gl_Position = vec4(in_position, 1.0);
    v_extent = in_extent;
    v_color = texture(gradient, in_colorValue).rgb;
    v_height = in_heightRange.y;
}
```

Listing 1.5. Cuboids vertex shader using AVCs.

```

    emit(vec3(llf.x, urb.y, llf.z), POSITIVE_Y);
    // ...
    // analoguous to geometry shader of the block world
    // ...
    emit(vec3(llf.x, llf.y, urb.z), NEGATIVE_Y);
    EndPrimitive();
}
```

Listing 1.6. Cuboids vertex shader using AVCs. The emitted triangle strip is created analoguous to the block world but without the local coordinates.

1.3.3 Colored Polygons

A polygon is a two-dimensional geometry type that has a number of vertices larger than two. In visualization, this geometry type is often extruded into the third dimension using the same polygon as bottom and top face, assigning a uniform height and adding side faces. To encode such a geometry in a single vertex is not feasible since the number of vertices of the polygon may differ between different polygons. However, we propose an approach that stores a polygon using two buffers. The first buffer contains attributes that are common for the vertices of a single polygon (e.g., height, center, color value). The second buffer contains each vertex of the polygon with its two-dimensional position (the third dimension is stored as a common attribute in the first buffer) and a reference to the polygon for the attribute fetching. The order of vertices in this buffer is relevant: adjacent vertices in the buffer have to be adjacent vertices

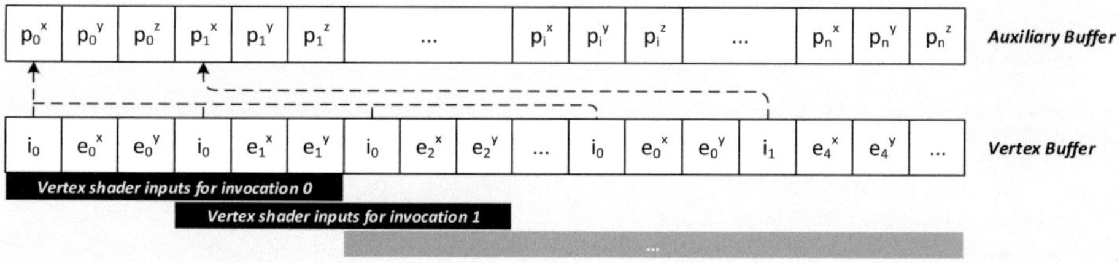

Figure 1.3. Polygon AVC buffer layout and vertex shader input management. One vertex shader invocation consumes two adjacent vertices as input but advances by just one vertex for the next vertex shader invocation.

in the polygon. To allow a closed looping over the vertices, we repeat the first vertex as the last one (Figure 1.3).

With this structure, the AVC can be rendered using the second buffer as vertex array buffer and the first buffer as auxiliary buffer that is accessed during the programmable rendering pipeline. We configure the vertex pulling stage to fetch two adjacent vertices from the buffer (handled as one vertex, refer to Listing 1.7), but advance only by one vertex for the next invocation (Figure 1.3). This way, we have access to the current and the next vertex and the common polygon data during the geometry generation which enables us to generate a polygon-*wedge* (Listing 1.8). To handle a pipeline start with two different referenced polygons for the two vertices we stop the pipeline during the geometry shader stage. By looping over the complete list of vertices, all wedges of the polygon are generated and, as a result, the full polygon is rasterized (see Figure 1.4).

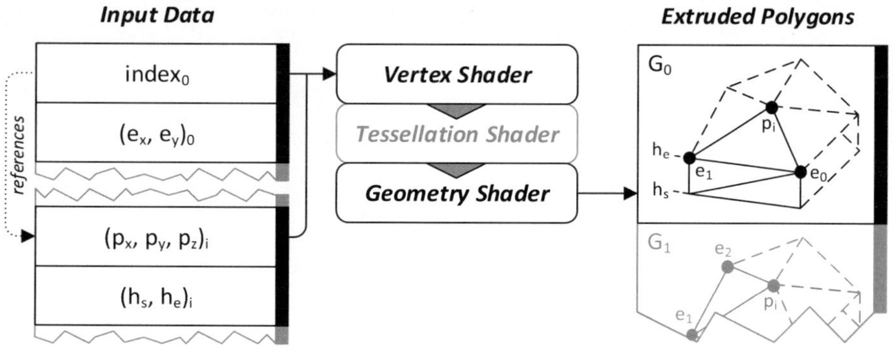

Figure 1.4. Concept of generating polygon-wedges from an AVC. One wedge is built up from the top and bottom triangle and the side face.

```
in vec2 in_start;
in int in_startIndex;
in vec2 in_end;
in int in_endIndex;
out vec2 v_start;
out vec2 v_end;
out int v_index;

void main() {
    v_start = in_start;
    v_end = in_end;
    v_index = in_startIndex == in_endIndex ? in_startIndex : -1;
}
```

Listing 1.7. Polygon vertex shader using AVCs. The index of the referenced polygon is checked to detect erroneuos wedge combinations and omit them in the geometry shader.

```
layout (points) in;
layout (triangle_strip, max_vertices = 6) out;

uniform mat4 viewProjection;
uniform samplerBuffer centerAndHeights;
uniform samplerBuffer colorValues;
uniform sampler1D gradient;
in vec2 v_start[];
in vec2 v_end[];
in int v_index[];
flat out vec3 g_color;
flat out vec3 g_normal;

// Emits a vertex with given position and normal
void emit(in vec3 pos, in vec3 n, in vec3 color);

void main() {
    // Discard erroneous polygons wedge combination
    if (v_index[0] < 0) return;

    vec4 centerAndHeight = texelFetch(centerAndHeights, v_index[0]).rgba;
    vec3 color = texture(gradient, texelFetch(colorValues, v_index[0]).r).rgb;
    vec3 cBottom = vec3(centerAndHeight.r, centerAndHeight.b, centerAndHeight.g);
    vec3 sBottom = vec3(v_start[0].x, centerAndHeight.b, v_start[0].y);
    vec3 eBottom = vec3(v_end[0].x, centerAndHeight.b, v_end[0].y);
    vec3 cTop = vec3(centerAndHeight.r, centerAndHeight.a, centerAndHeight.g);
    vec3 sTop = vec3(v_start[0].x, centerAndHeight.a, v_start[0].y);
    vec3 eTop = vec3(v_end[0].x, centerAndHeight.a, v_end[0].y);
    vec3 normal = cross(eBottom - sBottom, UP);

    emit(cBottom, NEGATIVE_Y, color);
    emit(sBottom, NEGATIVE_Y, color);
    emit(eBottom, NEGATIVE_Y, color);
    emit(sTop, normal, color);
    emit(eTop, normal, color);
    emit(cTop, POSITIVE_Y, color);
    EndPrimitive();
}
```

Listing 1.8. Polygon geometry shader using AVCs to generate one polygon wedge.

1.3.4 Colored Arcs

An arc is typically used in visualization, e.g., for sunburst views of file systems. Such an arc can be represented using its center, inner and outer radii, the height range, and a color value. Storing this information in an AVC, we can generate a solid geometry that connects the side faces of the arc directly. However, a rendering should regard the conceptually round nature of an arc. As a GPU rasterizes planar primitives, the state-of-the-art solution is a subdivision of the curved surface to produce planar surfaces that are arranged in a curve. This can be performed using the tessellation shader stage. The result is a set of arc segments with different angle-ranges, which the geometry shader can use to generate the target geometry (Figure 1.5).

Tessellation Control Shader. The output of the tessellation control shader is the degree to which the input geometry should be tessellated. Additionally, user-defined attributes (per-vertex and per-patch) can be specified and passed to the evaluation shader. We use this shader to tessellate two vertices (conceptually a line, refer to Listing 1.9) with the start and end angles as per-vertex attributes and the remaining ones as per-patch attributes. The use of both outer tessellation levels enables greater amounts of subdivision of the arcs. With this configuration, the tessellator produces a set of subdivided lines.

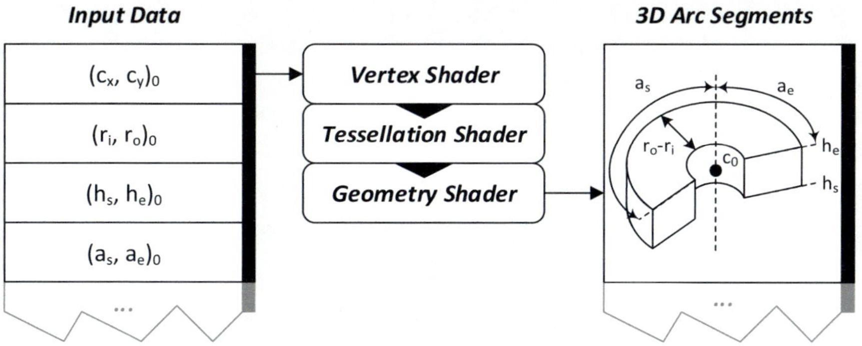

Figure 1.5. Concept of rendering arcs using an AVC. The tessellation shader creates arc lines that are extruded to arc segments using a geometry shader.

```
layout (vertices = 2) out;

in Segment {
    vec2 angleRange;
    vec2 radiusRange;
    vec2 center;
    vec2 heightRange;
    vec3 color;
    int tessellationCount;
} segment[];

out float angle[];

patch out Attributes {
    vec2 radiusRange;
    vec2 center;
    vec2 heightRange;
    vec3 color;
} attributes;

void main() {
    angle[gl_InvocationID] = segment[0].angleRange[gl_InvocationID==0?0:1];

    if (gl_InvocationID == 0) {
        float sqrtTesslevel =
            clamp(ceil(sqrt(segment[0].tessellationCount)), 2.0, 64.0);
        gl_TessLevelOuter[0] = sqrtTesslevel;
        gl_TessLevelOuter[1] = sqrtTesslevel;

        attributes.radiusRange = segment[0].radiusRange;
        attributes.center = segment[0].center;
        attributes.heightRange = segment[0].heightRange;
        attributes.color = segment[0].color;
    }
}
```

Listing 1.9. Arcs tessellation control shader using AVCs. A minimum of two tessellation levels ensures that one segment cannot be both a left and right end.

Tessellation Evaluation Shader. This set of subdivided lines is reinterpreted as the start and end angles of an arc segment, interpolating the per-vertex angles of the prior shader. The per-patch attributes are assigned to each vertex of the resulting lines. Additionally, the first and last vertex of the full arc are flagged to allow the geometry shader to generate additional side-faces (Listing 1.10).

```
layout (isolines, equal_spacing) in;

in float angle[];

patch in Attributes {
    vec2 radiusRange;
    vec2 center;
    vec2 heightRange;
    vec3 color;
} attributes;

out Vertex {
```

```
    float angle;
    vec2 radiusRange;
    vec2 center;
    vec2 heightRange;
    vec3 color;
    bool hasSide;
} vertex;

void main() {
    float pos = (gl_TessCoord.x + gl_TessCoord.y * gl_TessLevelOuter[0])
        / float(gl_TessLevelOuter[0]);

    vertex.angle = mix(angle[0], angle[1], pos);
    vertex.radiusRange = attributes.radiusRange;
    vertex.center = attributes.center;
    vertex.heightRange = attributes.heightRange;
    vertex.color = attributes.color;
    float threshold = 1.0/(gl_TessLevelOuter[0]*gl_TessLevelOuter[1]);
    vertex.hasSide = pos<threshold || pos>1.0-threshold;
}
```

Listing 1.10. Arcs tessellation evaluation shader using AVCs. The position of the generated vertex is projected and used to subdivide the arc segment. It is also used to determine which vertices have side faces.

Geometry Shader. The geometry shader generates the arc segment target geometry. The start and end arc angles, inner and outer radii, as well as the lower and upper height values are used to compute the eight vertices of the arc segment (Listing 1.11). Depending on the `hasSide` property, the required faces are generated and emitted.

```
layout (lines) in;
layout (triangle_strip, max_vertices = 12) out;

in Vertex {
    float angle;
    vec2 radiusRange;
    vec2 center;
    vec2 heightRange;
    vec3 color;
    bool hasSide;
} v[];

uniform mat4 viewProjection;
flat out vec3 g_color;
flat out vec3 g_normal;

// Emits a vertex with given position and normal
void emit(in vec3 position, in vec3 normal);

vec3 circlePoint(in float angle, in float radius, in float height) {
    return vec3(sin(angle), height, cos(angle))
        * vec3(radius, 1.0, radius)
        + vec3(v[0].center.x, 0.0, v[0].center.y);
}

void main() {
    vec3 A = circlePoint(v[0].angle, v[0].radiusRange.x, v[0].heightRange.x);
    vec3 B = circlePoint(v[1].angle, v[0].radiusRange.x, v[0].heightRange.x);
    vec3 C = circlePoint(v[1].angle, v[0].radiusRange.y, v[0].heightRange.x);
    vec3 D = circlePoint(v[0].angle, v[0].radiusRange.y, v[0].heightRange.x);
```

```
    vec3 E = circlePoint(v[0].angle, v[0].radiusRange.x, v[0].heightRange.y);
    vec3 F = circlePoint(v[1].angle, v[0].radiusRange.x, v[0].heightRange.y);
    vec3 G = circlePoint(v[1].angle, v[0].radiusRange.y, v[0].heightRange.y);
    vec3 H = circlePoint(v[0].angle, v[0].radiusRange.y, v[0].heightRange.y);

    vec3 top = vec3(0.0, 1.0, 0.0);
    vec3 bottom = vec3(0.0, -1.0, 0.0);
    vec3 left = normalize(cross(E-A, D-A));
    vec3 right = normalize(cross(F-B, C-B));
    vec3 front = normalize(cross(B-A, E-A));
    vec3 back = -front;

    if (v[1].hasSide) {
        emit(B, right);
        emit(F, right);
    }
    emit(C, right);
    emit(G, right);
    emit(H, back);
    emit(F, top);
    emit(E, top);
    emit(B, front);
    emit(A, front);
    emit(C, bottom);
    emit(D, bottom);
    emit(H, back);
    if (v[0].hasSide) {
        emit(A, left);
        emit(E, left);
    }

    EndPrimitive();
}
```

Listing 1.11. Arcs geometry shader using AVCs. The code emits a triangle strip with six full rectangles forming a distorted cuboid. As it is impossible for both vertices of the input line to have the hasSide flag set, the maximum number of emitted vertices is 12 nevertheless.

1.3.5 Trajectories

For an information visualization example, we describe the application of AVCs to a visualization of movement trajectories [Buschmann et al. 2015]. A trajectory consists of a number of connected tracking points, each of which contains the current position, a time stamp, and additional attributes, such as the current speed or acceleration.

An interactive visualization of trajectories can be helpful, for example, for developing analysis and decision support systems. In such a system, one task is to explore large data sets of trajectories, represented by plain lines for simplicity.

Subsequently, trajectories can be selected to examine their movements in more detail. They are highlighted and displayed more prominently, for example, as extruded tubes. As a final step of analysis, users might want to examine the attributes of individual tracking points. This can be achieved by rendering them using individual spheres, and mapping color and radius to express attribute values.

The described use case can be implemented using AVCs as follows. The vertex buffer contains the nodes with their attributes and a reference to the the associated trajectory. In contrast to previous examples, a vertex does not directly describe the target geometry, but contains a mere data point which is transformed into a geometry later. In the tessellation and geometry shaders, the type of geometry is selected based on three factors: data attributes, distance to the camera, and interaction state. Unselected trajectories that are far away from the camera will be transformed into plain lines. Highlighted trajectories are transformed into tubes, and for selected trajectories, nodes are transformed into individual spheres for attribute visualization. The current speed is mapped onto the color, while acceleration is mapped onto the radius.

To render the trajectories, a similar approach to the polygon rendering can be used. However, the vertex shader has three vertices as input, where the first and the third are used to check for the trajectory reference and the target geometry type. With these additional inputs, the tessellation and geometry shader for the currently processed trajectory node can generate geometry while taking the adjacent trajectory node geometries into account (Figure 1.6). The use of the tessellation shader stages allows for a curved appearance of the tube representation of trajectory nodes (refer to arc rendering with AVCs).

Due to the reduced memory footprints of AVCs, large numbers of trajectories can be rendered simultaneously. Also, the visualization is highly configurable

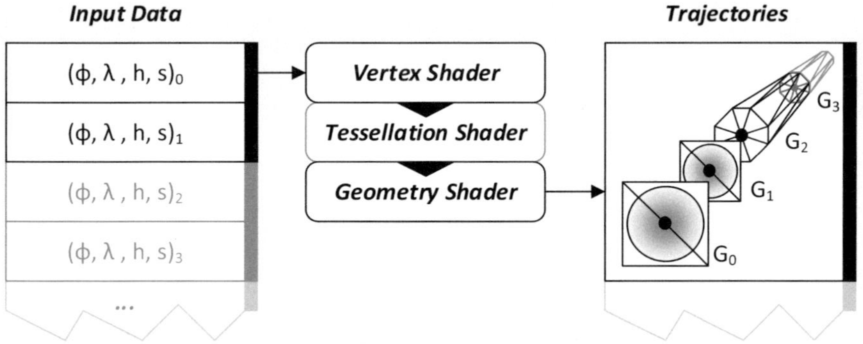

Figure 1.6. Concept of rendering trajectories using an AVC. Each data point gets tessellated and converted into splats, spheres, or tubes, depending on user input.

without requiring any buffer updates. Therefore, it can be controlled by user interaction, e.g., by merely modifying uniform shader variables which control the geometry generation.

1.4 Evaluation

AVCs can improve the rendering of several types of geometry in terms of GPU memory usage, rendering and update performance. Therefore, we compare AVCs to alternative geometry representations and rendering pipelines for the same target geometry, namely full triangles lists (triangles), triangle strips, and hardware instancing using vertex attribute divisors (instancing). Specifically, evaluation is focused on the memory footprint of the geometry, the geometry processing performance, and the overall rendering performance.

Test Setup. Our test setup for the presented performance measurements is a Ubuntu 14.04 machine with a GeForce GTX 980 running at 1430 MHz maximum clock and 4GB VRAM. We used the official Nvidia driver version 355.06. During the tests, the application ran in full-screen mode with the native resolution of the monitor (1920 × 1200 pixels). The test scenes are block worlds with different numbers of blocks, ranging from 4096 (grid size of 16) to 10^6 (grid size of 100).

Memory Footprint. To encode a block of a block world with a fixed size but differing type and position in a 3D grid, each of the four geometry representations have a differing space consumption on the graphics card (Table 1.1). The triangles representation requires 36 vertices per block with the position in the grid, a normal-vector, and the block type as attributes (40 bytes per vertex, 1440 bytes per block). The triangle strip representation requires the same per-vertex attributes but uses 14 vertices to encode the full block (40 bytes per vertex, 560 bytes per block). The instancing representation uses one triangle strip as instancing geometry (containing normalized vertex positions and normal-vectors) and passes the actual position in the grid and the block type as per-instance data (336 byte static data and 16 byte per-instance data, resulting in 16 byte

Technique	Static Data	Vertices	Blocksize	10^6 blocks
Triangles	$\perp$	36	1440 byte	1373 MiB
Triangle Strip	$\perp$	14	560 byte	534 MiB
Instancing	336 byte	1	16 byte	15 MiB
AVC	$\perp$	1	16 byte	15 MiB

Table 1.1. Memory consumption of different block world geometry representations. Each technique is compared with regard to the required static data size, the number of vertices to encode one block, the resulting memory size of one block, and a projection of the memory consumption of a block world with 10^6 blocks.

Technique	Vertex Shader Stage	Geometry Shader Stage	Rasterizer Stage
Triangles	10	$\perp$	11
Triangle Strip	10	$\perp$	11
Instancing	10	$\perp$	11
AVC	4	5	11

Table 1.2. Input component count of the used stages of the programmable rendering pipeline for the block world scene (e.g., a three-dimensional position has a component count of three).

per block). An AVC uses the same amount of per-instance data, but doesn't require the instancing geometry in memory as it is encoded in the geometry shader (16 byte per-vertex data, 16 byte per block). Although the instancing and the AVC representation share a small memory footprint of the geometry, the passed data through the programmable rendering pipeline differs (Table 1.2).

Rasterization Performance. To assess the overall performance of an application that renders the same scene (e.g., a block world) with different memory representations and rendering approaches, we use frames-per-second as a measure. We measured the time to render 1000 full frames (same viewpoint, disabled vertical synchronization, disabled postprocessing, enabled rasterizer). Our measurements indicate that AVCs render faster in each scenario with up to doubled frames-per-second (Figure 1.7). The other techniques perform equally well for reasonable-sized block worlds. We measure similar results for the cuboids demo scenes, but there is a bigger variation within the other techniques. Since render-

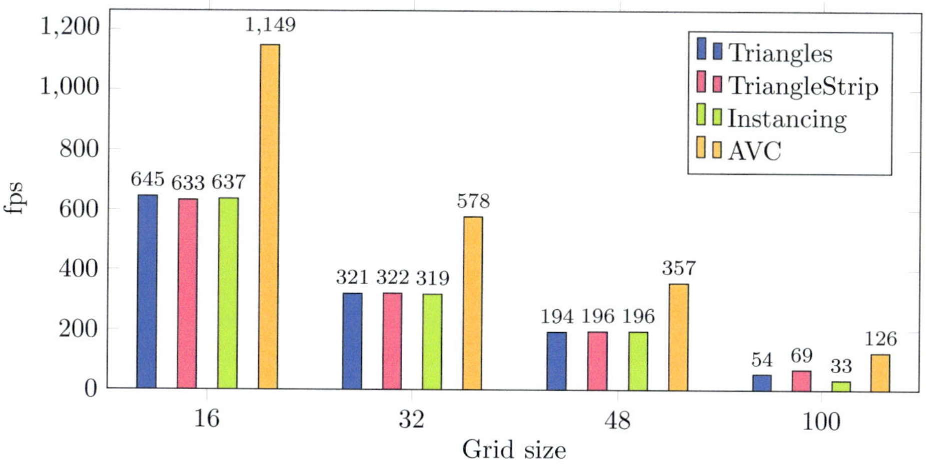

Figure 1.7. Frames per second comparison of block world implementations with different number of blocks.

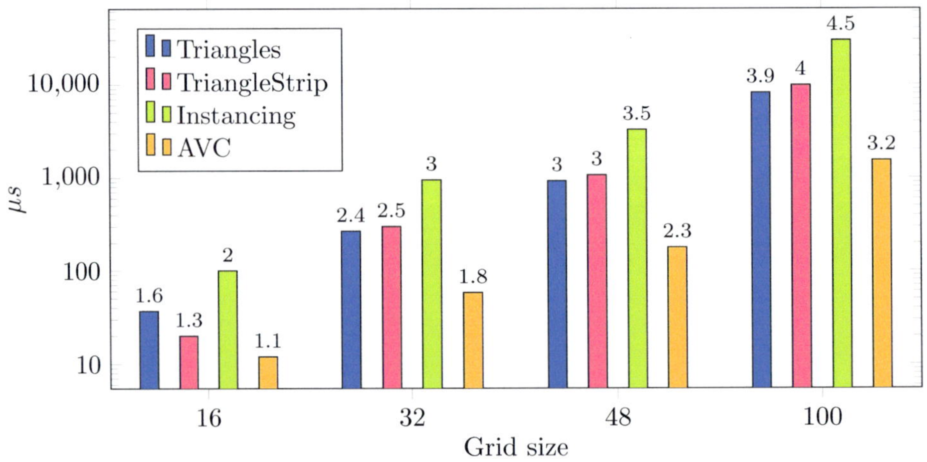

Figure 1.8. Geometry processing performance comparison of block world implementations with different number of blocks (logarithmic scale).

ing a full frame requires additional work by both CPU and GPU that is equal between all techniques, we additionally measured the geometry processing in isolation.

Geometry Processing Performance. In order to measure the timings for the GPU to process the geometry and prepare the rasterization inputs, we disable the rasterizer and measure the time required for the draw call using query objects (Figure 1.8). We measured a significantly smaller processing time for the AVC technique and highly differing times for the other techniques where instancing performs worst. Although the times differ they, seem to have only a small impact on the overall rendering performance (Figure 1.7). The results we measured for the cuboids scene were almost identical.

1.5 Conclusions

We propose attributed vertex clouds (AVC) as an efficient alternative to store geometry of simple gestalt for representation, rendering, and processing on the GPU. The concept utilizes attribute buffers that describe a target geometry. The attributes are processed and converted into the target geometry during the execution of the programmable rendering pipeline. The general concept has various potentials for rendering techniques and engines, since AVCs can be used in combination with explicit geometry representations. The main hardware requirement of this technique is a GPU with a programmable rendering pipeline that includes a geometry shader stage. A tessellation stage can be used to enhance the results. Performance measurements and comparisons using a block world test scene show a significant performance improvement on consumer hardware compared to explicit geometric representations and hardware instancing. With the compact memory representation of an AVC, attribute updates via GPGPU processing or buffer updates can be performed in the data domain instead of the target geometry domain.

The concept of attributed vertex clouds can be applied in general for all rendering techniques and domains in which image synthesis relies on large amounts of simple, parameterizable geometry. This includes games (e.g., block-worlds, vegetation rendering, sprite engines, particle systems), interactive visualization systems [Scheibel et al. 2016] (e.g., information visualization, or scientific visualization), as well as generic rendering components (e.g., text rendering). Further improvement of this technique is a generalized rendering pipeline with reoccurring stages to enable further tessellation of the instantiated geometry.

Acknowledgements

This work was funded by the German Federal Ministry of Education and Research (BMBF) in the InnoProfile Transfer research group "4DnD-Vis" (http://www.4dndvis.de/) and BIMAP (http://www.bimap-project.de).

Bibliography

Buschmann, S., Trapp, M., and Döllner, J. 2015. Animated visualization of spatial–temporal trajectory data for air-traffic analysis. *The Visual Computer*, 1–11.

Carucci, F., and Studios, L. 2005. Inside geometry instancing. In *GPU Gems 2*, M. Pharr and R. Fernando, Eds. Addison-Wesley Professional, 47–67.

Kemen, B., 2012. Procedural grass rendering. URL: http://outerra.blogspot.de/2012/05/procedural-grass-rendering.html.

Overvoorde, A., 2014. Geometry shaders. URL: https://open.gl/geometry.

Purnomo, B., Bilodeau, J., Cohen, J. D., and Kumar, S. 2005. Hardware-compatible vertex compression using quantization and simplification. In *Proceedings of the ACM SIGGRAPH/EUROGRAPHICS Conference on Graphics Hardware*, ACM, New York, 53–61.

Rákos, D., 2010. Instance culling using geometry shaders. URL: http://rastergrid.com/blog/2010/02/instance-culling-using-geometry-shaders.

Riccio, C., and Lilley, S. 2013. Introducing the programmable vertex pulling rendering pipeline. In *GPU Pro 4: Advanced Rendering Techniques*, W. Engel, Ed. CRC Press, Boca Raton, FL, 21–37.

Scheibel, W., Trapp, M., and Döllner, J. 2016. Interactive revision exploration using small multiples of software maps. In *Proc. of IVAPP*, scitepress, vol. 3, 131–138.

Trapp, M., Schmechel, S., and Döllner, J. 2013. Interactive rendering of complex 3D-treemaps. In *Proc. of GRAPP*, 165–175.

2

I

Rendering Convex Occluders with Inner Conservative Rasterization

Marcus Svensson and Emil Persson

2.1 Introduction

Scenes in modern 3D games contain highly detailed geometry. Sending large amounts of scene geometry through the rendering pipeline can become expensive, even when it does not end up as rasterized pixels on the screen. Occlusion culling is an important step to prevent non-visible parts of a scene from being rendered. By identifying occluded parts of a scene and excluding them from rendering, a lot of unnecessary GPU work can be avoided.

Many occlusion algorithms have to cope with balancing performance and accuracy. While it is desirable to accurately identify all occluded parts of a scene, settling with a rough estimate is often more beneficial for the overall performance. Algorithms that rely on a depth buffer can benefit from performing the culling at a lower resolution than the resolution of the screen. Using a lower resolution may result in less accurate culling, but can increase the performance of the occlusion algorithm. Rendering occluders using standard rasterization at a lower resolution would end up rasterizing pixels that are only partially covered at the fullscreen resolution. That could potentially result in false occlusion, which is not desirable.

A solution proposed by Andersson [2009] and Collin [2011] is to manually shrink the occluder meshes by one pixel. This puts a bigger workload on the artists and can be tricky to get right. The artists must take both view distance and perspective projection into consideration, which likely results in overly conservative occluder meshes. Another approach, recently used by Haar et al. [2015], is to render the occluders at fullscreen resolution and conservatively downsample the depth buffer into the lower resolution. This approach does not require any additional work from the artists, but is likely more expensive. There is also a risk of losing depth information during the successive downsampling. When two resolutions do not align, partially covered samples must be gathered, which makes the results overly conservative. Silvennoinen [2012] proposes a solution where the depth buffer is first upsampled to the next multiple of 2^N in each dimension before performing the downsampling. This minimizes the risk of losing depth information during the downsampling as the dimensions are always evenly divisible by two. However, performing the upsampling is likely costly.

This chapter presents an algorithm for rendering convex-shaped meshes with inner conservative rasterization. Unlike standard rasterization, where pixels are rasterized if their center is covered, inner conservative rasterization only includes pixels that are fully covered. Previous work on inner conservative rasterization operate on a primitive basis and can therefore not be applied on the footprint of a mesh. This problem is addressed by applying inner conservative rasterization on the entire mesh instead of on individual primitives. The algorithm is primarily targeted towards occluders, but could potentially have other use cases as well.

2.2 Algorithm

2.2.1 Overview

Inner conservative rasterization has previously been implemented in software by Hasselgren et al. [2005] and in hardware, as a part of the DirectX 12 API [Yeung 2014]. These implementations rasterize pixels that are fully covered by the footprint of an overlapping primitive. Pixels that are fully covered by multiple primitives are not rasterized, which results in gaps between rasterized primitives. The gaps can be eliminated by applying inner conservative rasterization to the silhouette edges and standard rasterization to the interior edges. An illustration of this can be seen in Figure 2.1. The problem with previous techniques is that pixels that are not covered by the mesh footprint are rasterized if their center is overlapped by a primitive that is not part of the silhouette. An illustration of the problem can be viewed in Figure 2.2. The algorithm presented here will attempt to solve this by applying inner conservative rasterization on a mesh basis instead of a primitive basis.

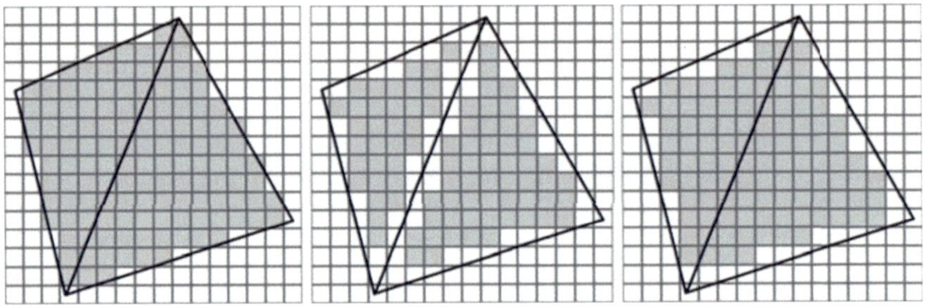

Figure 2.1. Left: two triangles are rendered using standard rasterization. Notice how some pixels are partially outside the outline of the triangles. Middle: the same triangles are rendered using inner conservative rasterization on a primitive basis. Now all pixels are within the outline of the triangles, but there is a gap running between them. Right: the triangles are rendered by applying inner conservative rasterization to the silhouette edges and standard rasterization to the remaining edges. All pixels are now within the outline of the triangles.

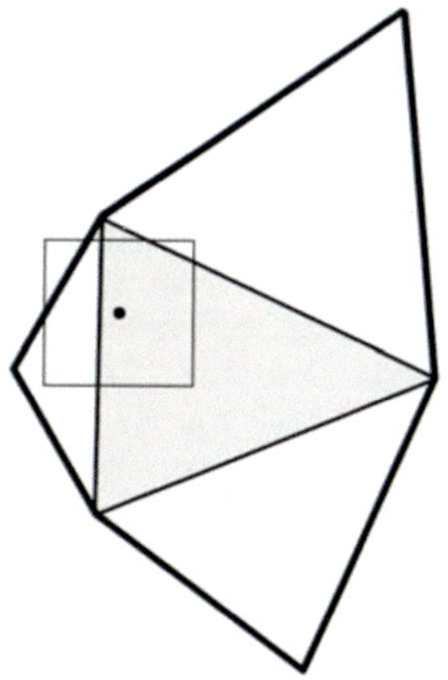

Figure 2.2. An illustration of the problem that occur when applying inner conservative rasterization on a primitive basis. Assume that inner conservative rasterization is applied to the silhouette edges and that standard rasterization is used for the rest. The pixel is partially outside the mesh and should not be rasterized. However, as the pixel is covered by a primitive that is not part of the silhouette, it is still included.

The algorithm is divided into two separate shader passes. The first one is a compute shader pass where the silhouette edges of all meshes are extracted and stored in a global buffer. The global buffer is then passed on to the second shader pass where the meshes are rendered. In the pixel shader, the area of each rasterized pixel is tested against all extracted silhouette edges of the overlapping occluder. If a silhouette edge is intersecting the pixel area, the pixel is not fully covered and is discarded. The remaining pixels are fully covered by the mesh footprint and are output from the pixel shader.

2.2.2 Limitations

The way that silhouette edges are extracted limits the algorithm to only convex-shaped meshes. This is due to the fact that silhouette edges are applied in screen space. If a concave-shaped mesh were used, there would be a risk of detecting silhouette edges that are not part of the outline. These silhouette edges would then appear as gaps across the rasterized mesh, which would render anything behind them visible.

The complexity of the meshes used is another limitation. Meshes with high polygon counts are likely to produce a large number of silhouette edges. Since a pixel is tested against all silhouette edges of an overlapping mesh, the cost of the algorithm will become more expensive as more silhouette edges are tested. The algorithm is therefore best suited for meshes with simple shapes like boxes, cylinders, and spheres, that do not require a high number of polygons.

Another concern is that gaps may appear between neighboring rasterized meshes. A solution for this is to extend nearby occluders into each other so the pixels in between are fully covered by both.

2.2.3 Implementation

Silhouette Edge Extraction. The first step of the algorithm is finding the triangle edges that form the silhouette outline of a mesh footprint. This step takes place before the actual rendering in a separate compute shader pass.

The algorithm works similarly to existing silhouette edge-detection algorithms [Marshall 2001]. It starts off by comparing each triangle against its three adjacent neighbors. If the surface normal of the triangle faces the viewer and the surface normal of the neighbor faces away from the viewer, the shared vertices form a silhouette edge. Listing 2.1 shows the function for determining whether a triangle faces the viewer. When a silhouette edge is found, it is culled against the frustum. By culling non-visible silhouette edges, unnecessary computations in the pixel shader are avoided.

```
bool IsTriangleFrontFacingWS( float3 t_0, float3 t_1,
                              float3 t_2, float3 eye )
{
    float3 center = ( t_0 + t_1 + t_2 ) / 3.0;
    float3 view_direction = normalize( center - eye );
    float3 normal = normalize( cross( t_1 - t_0, t_2 - t_0 ) );
    return dot( view_direction, normal ) >= 0.0;
}
```

Listing 2.1. A function that determines whether a triangle is facing the viewer. All positions are in world space coordinates.

Simply representing a silhouette edge as two endpoints would require more memory than necessary. By calculating the linear equation $y = mx + b$ that goes through both endpoints, the edge can be represented by the constants m and b. As the algorithm is limited to convex-shaped occluder meshes, the line will never touch anything but the silhouette edge. Storing the edge as line constants instead of endpoints halves the memory cost and reduces the number of computations per pixel in the depth rendering pass.

Two buffers are used for storing silhouette edge data: one for keeping track of the number of silhouette edges per instance and one for storing the line constants of each silhouette edge. The maximum number of silhouette edges per instance must be established beforehand so that a sufficient amount of memory can be allocated. This number varies depending on the mesh used, but it is usually quite easy to determine for a convex shape. A box, for example, can have a maximum of six silhouette edges.

Before the silhouette edge extraction starts, the silhouette edge count buffer is reset by setting all instance counters to zero. When a silhouette edge passes the intersection test, the algorithm increments the instance counter by one and uses the original value as an offset to the silhouette edge buffer. The incrementing is performed using atomic operations, which will ensure that the original value is unique for each thread that calls it. Listing 2.2 shows the function that is used for storing the silhouette edges.

```
cbuffer Constants : register( b0 )
{
    uint g_SilhouetteEdgeBufferOffset;
};
RWStructuredBuffer<float2>
    g_SilhouetteEdgeBuffer : register( u0 );
RWByteAddressBuffer
    g_SilhouetteEdgeCountBuffer : register( u1 );

```

```
void StoreSilhouetteEdge( uint instance_index,
                          float m, float b )
{
    uint count, offset =
        instance_index * g_SilhouetteEdgeBufferOffset;
    g_SilhouetteEdgeCountBuffer.InterlockedAdd(
        instance_index * 4, 1, count );
    g_SilhouetteEdgeBuffer[ offset + count ] = float2( m, b );
}
```

Listing 2.2. A function that stores a silhouette edge as the constants m and b in the linear equation $y = mx + b$ in a global buffer.

Depth Rendering. The second step of the algorithm is to render the occluders to the depth buffer. The pixel area of each rasterized pixel is tested against all generated silhouette edges of the overlapping occluder. If a silhouette edge is intersecting the pixel area, the pixel is not fully covered and is discarded. Listing 2.3 shows the code snippet used for determining whether a pixel is fully covered. The remaining pixels are fully covered by the mesh footprint and are output from the pixel shader.

```
cbuffer Constants : register( b0 )
{
    uint g_SilhouetteEdgeBufferOffset;
};
StructuredBuffer< float2 >
    g_SilhouetteEdgeBuffer : register( t0 );
StructuredBuffer< uint >
    g_SilhouetteEdgeCountBuffer : register( t1 );

bool IsPixelFullyCovered( float2 position,
                          uint instance_index )
{
    float4 rect = float4(
        position - float2( 0.5, 0.5 ),
        position + float2( 0.5, 0.5 ) );

    uint count =
        g_SilhouetteEdgeCountBuffer[ instance_index ];
    uint offset =
        instance_index * g_SilhouetteEdgeBufferOffset;
    [ loop ]
    for ( uint i = 0; i < count; ++i )
    {
        float2 edge = g_SilhouetteEdgeBuffer[ offset + i ];

        float y_0 = edge.x * rect.x + edge.y;
        float y_1 = edge.x * rect.z + edge.y;

        float min_y = min( y_0, y_1 );
        float max_y = max( y_0, y_1 );

        if ( rect.y <= max_y && min_y <= rect.w )
            return false;
    }

    return true;
}
```

Listing 2.3. A code snippet for determining whether a pixel is fully covered by the mesh footprint. All calculations are done in the pixel shader and are in screen space coordinates.

Reversed Depth. The depth buffer is reversed to achieve an even distribution of floating-point precision. Since floating-point values have more precision closer to 0 than they do closer to 1, it is more beneficial to set the near plane to 1 and the far plane to 0 rather than the other way around. Persson [2012] proposes a simple solution to achieve this by flipping the near plane and the far plane in the projection matrix.

Conservative Depth. In order to achieve conservatively correct results, the depth value of each pixel should be the farthest depth value found in the pixel cell. Hasselgren et al. [2005] describes a method for calculating the farthest depth value based on the plane of the overlapping primitive. By sending a ray through the pixel corner in the direction of the primitive normal, the farthest depth value can be found in the intersection point between the ray and the plane of the primitive. The method is not completely conservatively correct as a pixel may be partially overlapped by other primitives that are even farther away. However, it ended up being the best alternative, and it has proven reliable in most non-extreme cases. An alternative would be to use the farthest depth value of the entire occluder in all overlapped pixels. The depth value could be computed during the silhouette edge extraction with little extra effort, and the results would be completely conservatively correct. The problem is that the results would suffer from being overly conservative, which is why this method was not used.

2.2.4 Performance

Figure 2.3 shows how the algorithm performs in relation to standard rasterization. The performance is measured on a scene by Kuah [Kuah 2016] where occluders have been placed manually. A total of 49 occluders are rendered, 44 of which are boxes and five of which are cylinders. The cube mesh consists of 12 triangles and the cylinder mesh of 64 triangles.

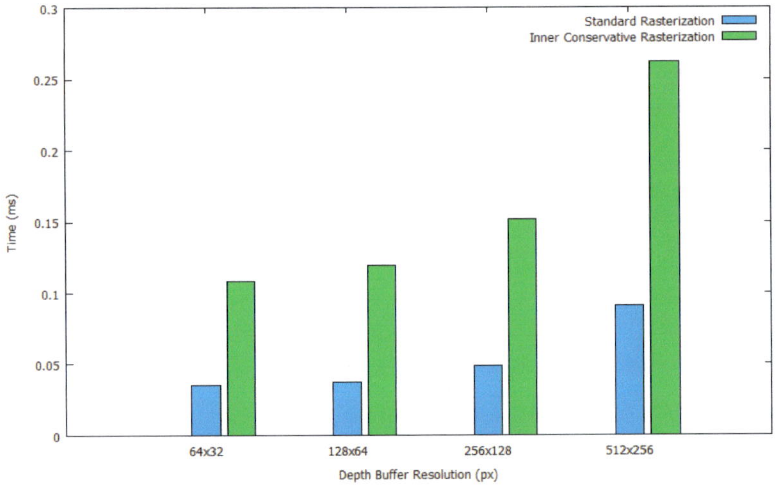

Figure 2.3. Timings for rendering the same set of occluders using the proposed algorithm and standard rasterization. Lower results are better.

The measurements are performed on a computer system with an Intel Core i5-6300HQ running at 2.3 GHz, an Intel HD Graphics 530 (driver version 15.40.26.4474) and 8 GB DDR4 SDRAM running at 2133 MHz. The operating system used is Windows 10 64-bit and the rendering API used is DirectX 12. The compute pass that extracts the silhouette edges uses a block size of $32 \times 1 \times 1$.

2.3 Conclusions and Future Work

An algorithm has been presented for rendering convex-shaped meshes so that all rasterized pixels are fully covered. The algorithm differs from existing alternatives by rasterizing the exact inner conservative footprint of a mesh. This produces accurate results within a reasonable amount of time.

In its current state, the algorithm is lacking in some areas and needs further development to be viable for general use. The risk of gaps appearing between neighboring rasterized occluders is considered the biggest issue as that affects culling efficiency. While the issue can be dealt with to some extent by extending nearby occluders into each other, it is hardly optimal as it adds complexity to the occluder placement process. A potential solution would be to align silhouette edges of neighboring occluders, but that would also require changing how silhouette edges are assigned. Finding a workaround for this issue would be the next step for future development.

Bibliography

ANDERSSON, J. 2009. Parallel graphics in frostbite - current and future. ACM, New York, SIGGRAPH '09 Course. URL: http://s09.idav.ucdavis.edu/talks/04-JAndersson-ParallelFrostbite-Siggraph09.pdf.

COLLIN, D. 2011. Culling the battlefield. GDC '11. URL: http://www.gdcvault.com/play/1014492/Culling-the-Battlefield-Data-Oriented.

HAAR, U., AND AALTONEN, S. 2015. GPU-driven rendering pipelines. In *SIGGRAPH '15: Advances in Real-Time Rendering in Games*. URL: http://advances.realtimerendering.com/s2015/aaltonenhaar_siggraph2015_combined_final_footer_220dpi.pdf.

HASSELGREN, J., AKENINE-MÖLLER, T., AND OHLSSON, L. 2005. Conservative rasterization. In *GPU Gems 2: Programming Techniques for High-Performance Graphics and General-Purpose Computation*, M. Pharr, Ed. Addison-Wesley, Reading, MA, 677–690.

KUAH, K., 2016. Software occlusion culling. URL: https://software.intel.com/en-us/articles/software-occlusion-culling.

MARSHALL, C. S. 2001. Cartoon rendering: Real-time silhouette edge detection and rendering. In *Game Programming Gems 2*, M. DeLoura, Ed. Charles River Media, Boston, MA, 436–443.

PERSSON, E. 2012. Creating vast game worlds - experiences from avalanche studios. In *ACM SIGGRAPH 2012 Talks*, ACM, New York, NY, USA. URL: http://www.humus.name/Articles/Persson_CreatingVastGameWorlds.pdf.

Silvennoinen, A. 2012. Chasing shadows. *Game Developer Magazine 19*, 2, 49–53. URL: http://twvideo01.ubm-us.net/o1/vault/GD_Mag_Archives/GDM_February_2012.pdf.

Yeung, A., 2014. DirectX: Evolving Microsoft's Graphics Platform. URL: https://channel9.msdn.com/Blogs/DirectX-Developer-Blog/DirectX-Evolving-Microsoft-s-Graphics-Platform.

II
Lighting

Where there is light, there is also shadow. And, in a positive sense, this also holds for this chapter of *GPU Zen*.

Louis Bavoil and Holger Gruen describe their approach to rendering stable indirect illumination computed from reflective shadow maps, which is either very expensive—or using noticeable subsampling with all its consequences. More specifically, their method applies deinterleaved texturing in order to support wide filter kernels to blur subsampled images while being cache efficient. The indirect lighting for the final image is obtained from a well-designed and real-time capable cascade of blurring stages with deinterleaved and reassembled subresults.

Nathan Hoobler, Andrei Tatarinov, and Alex Dunn render participating media effects using extruded light volumes—a technique which is used in the NVIDIA Gameworks volumetric lighting library. It is suited for rendering physically-based participating media effects and is compatible with existing rendering pipelines. The key idea is to reuse the shadow map rendered for a light source and extrude the mesh enclosing the lit regions using tessellation hardware. Having this mesh, the full scattering integral along a view ray decomposes into a sum of integrals which can be (more) easily computed, and they show you how.

—Carsten Dachsbacher

II
1

Stable Indirect Illumination

Holger Gruen and Louis Bavoil

1.1 Introduction

This chapter describes how to achieve visually stable indirect illumination at fast frame rates while using a wide sparse filter kernel to sample incoming light from a reflective shadow map (RSM) [Dachsbacher and Stamminger 2005]. The computed indirect illumination is stable even when the viewing direction or position of the observer camera change slowly and also for dynamic scenes.

Our approach is to use deinterleaved texturing (see [Bavoil 2014] and [Segovia et al. 2006] to support sparse and wide filter kernels while being cache efficient. We blur deinterlaved indirect illumination sub-results before reassembling a full resolution result to precondition a smooth result. Finally, the full resolution indirect illumination result is blurred again to hide any remaining structured artifacts.

Sampling the pixels of reflective shadow maps (RSMs) [Dachsbacher and Stamminger 2005] as light sources leads to approximate real-time indirect illumination since these pixels are the sources for the first bounce of light. In order to generate results that are visually stable even with slowly changing view conditions and with dynamic scenes, sampling from a wide filter kernel with many taps is a necessity. These wide filter kernels usually make RSM-based indirect illumination costly, and thus they are usually too slow for games that target high frame rates. Gruen [Gruen 2011] and others have used moderately wide but sparse filter kernels and moderately-sized RSMs to achieve fast running times. Unfortunately, even with these approaches, the wide filter kernels needed for higher resolution RSMs still lead to too low performance.

One possible solution to this problem is to lower the cost by using a small subset of taps that are applied in a round-robin manner over a number of frames. The results of the last frames are reused along with the current frames result and get combined by a temporal filter (see, for example, [Herzog et al. 2010]). In this chapter we do not explore this idea but rather look into another way to make filtering cheaper. Nevertheless, our technique is orthogonal to temporal anti-aliasing techniques like SMAA (see [Jimenez et al. 2012]).

It is usually desirable to render the RSM and the normal shadow map in just one pass over the scene geometry for every light source. The reason for this is that framerates become more easily CPU-limited or geometry-rendering limited if additional full scene passes are needed. As a consequence, the resolution of RSMs that are fed into the lighting stages increases since high shadow map resolutions have become pervasive in games.

Bavoil [2014] and Segovia et al. [2006] have introduced deinterleaved texturing (DT) which uses and evolves the concept of interleaved sampling [Keller and Heidrich 2001] to increase the cache efficiency and performance of large sparse filter kernels.

We adopt DT to significantly reduce RSM filtering time. Yet, even after applying an approximate bi-lateral filter on the results of DT filtering, the computed indirect illumination is not stable when used with a slowly moving camera or dynamic scene elements. The reason for this is that the filter kernel is sparse, and this leads to undersampling of moving scene parts.

Our solution to make the computed indirect illumination stable is to apply cross bilateral blurring to the deinterleaved subresults (of indirect illumination). Then, reassembling these blurred subimages generates a full resolution image that is well-conditioned enough to be visually stable after another full resolution cross bilateral blurring pass.

The remainder of this chapter presents the steps to implement this combination of subimage blurring and DT.

1.2 Deinterleaved Texturing for RSM Sampling

Bavoil [2014] describes the details of using DT in the context of a screen space ambient occlusion technique. In order to adapt DT to our purpose for RSM sampling, we need to not only deinterleave the G-buffer, but also the RSM. Figure 1.1 shows how both the G-buffer and the RSM get deinterleaved by applying 2×2 DT. After the deinterleaving operations are completed, we compute indi-

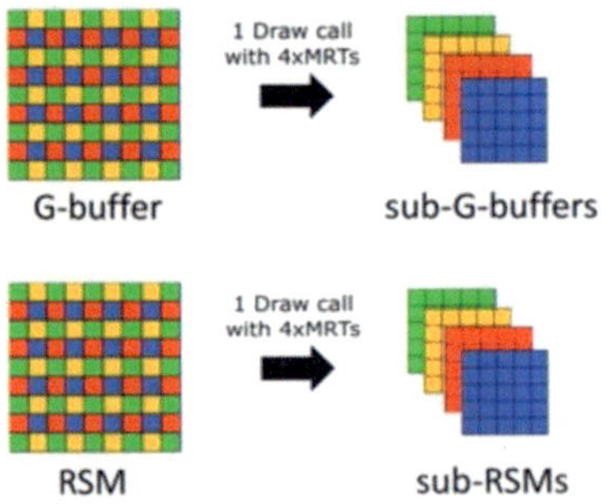

Figure 1.1. G-Buffer and RSM deinterleaving.

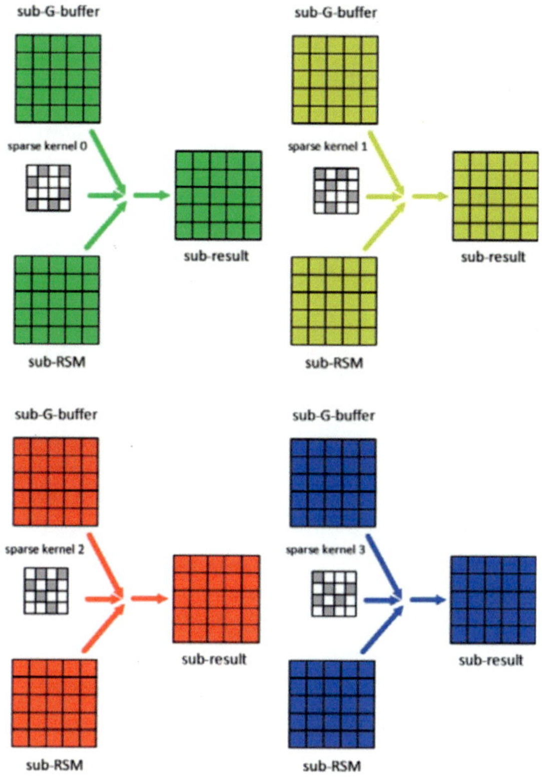

Figure 1.2. Generating low-res deinterleaved indirect illumination buffers.

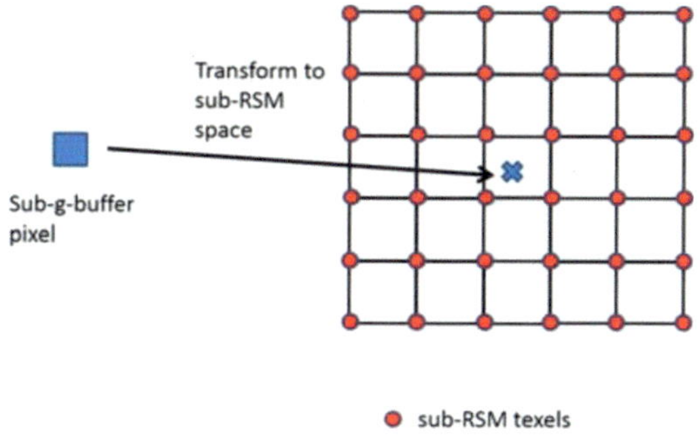

Figure 1.3. Transforming G-buffer pixel position to sub-RSM space.

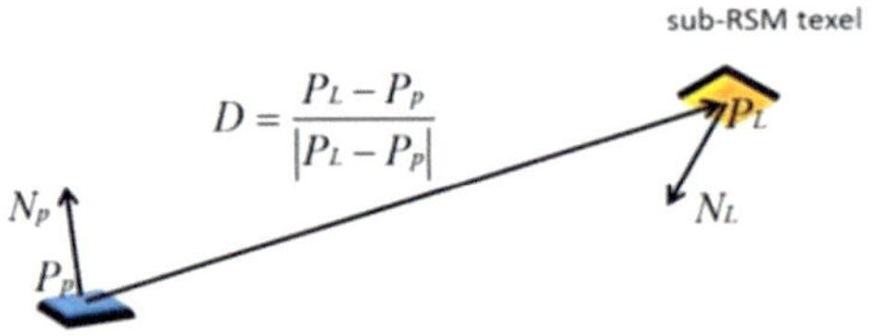

Figure 1.4. Computing the light a RSM pixel sheds on a G-buffer pixel.

rect illumination for each 2×2 sub-G-buffer–sized sub-result buffer (see Figure 1.2). We sample from exactly one sub-RSM for each sub-result. As in Bavoil's work [Bavoil 2014], we keep the sampling pattern constant for each sub-RSM.

Note that another benefit of using DT is that using a sparse RSM filter footprint in $N \times N$ deinterleaved texture space is comparable to a filter footprint that is N times as wide and high in normal (interleaved) texture space.

We implemented this RSM-DT approach in a sample application that uses the algorithms from [Gruen 2011] and applies them to each sub-RSM in turn.

For each pixel of each sub-G-buffer, we transform the three-dimensional position stored in the pixel to sub-RSM texture space as shown in Figure 1.3. Then, for each sample that is taken from the sub-RSM, we compute the radiant intensity based on its flux Φ_{P_L} that it emits towards the current sub-G-buffer pixel, using the visibility-unaware formula given in Equation (1.1) (see Figure 1.4). We approximate the overall irradiance at P_P by accumulating over a sparse filter footprint in each sub-RSM.

$$\text{Contribution } P_L = \frac{\text{saturate}(N_P \cdot D) \cdot \text{saturate}(N_L \cdot -D)}{|P_L - P_P|^2} \cdot \Phi_{P_L} \tag{1.1}$$

After computing all indirect illumination sub-results, we need to reassemble a full resolution indirect illumination result as required by DT; this is shown in Figure 1.5.

We chose to compute the indirect illumination at a resolution which is half of the width and half of the height of the G-buffer. Before the creation of the

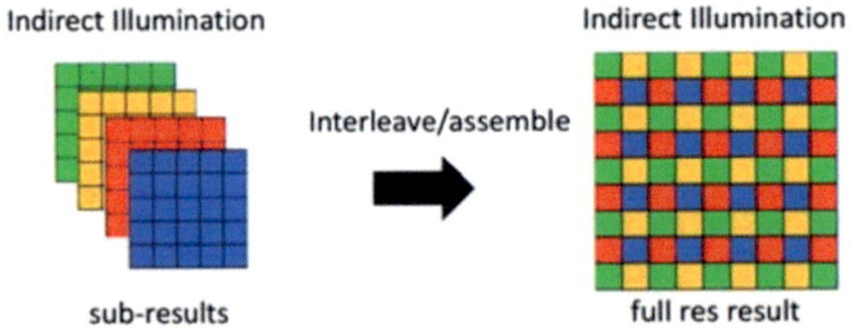

Figure 1.5. Reassembling the full resolution indirect illumination result.

final result, we use bilateral upsampling [Sloan et al. 2007] to scale the indirect illumination up to the full G-buffer resolution.

For the well-known Sponza scene, with a 1024×1024 RSM as an input, using DT, and a sparse filter with 128 taps (and a width of 128 pixels), the steps described above produce pictures like the one shown in the screenshot in Figure 1.6. Note that this screenshot is the raw result without applying any filtering or smoothing. The results are not visually pleasing and reveal the sparseness of the filter. Also, one can observe popping and flickering illumination with a moving camera and dynamic scene elements.

Since a full indirect-illumination simulation includes more than just the first bounce of light, it creates a much smoother result. Inspired by other image-space techniques, we perform a cross bi-lateral blur to approximate multiple localized bounces of light. The cross bi-lateral blur uses weights that use difference in camera depth and in per-pixel normal to avoid blurring across edges, sharp corners, and normal discontinuities. The final result is shown in the screenshot in Figure 1.7.

The screenshot in Figure 1.7 still shows blotches that reveal the structure of the sparse filter. Also, the indirect illumination is not stable when the camera moves, and one can observe flickering. Despite these unsatisfactory visual results, we would still like to present performance numbers for this intermedi-

Figure 1.6. Reassembled and cross bi-laterally upsampled full resolution indirect illumination for 4×4 DT.

Figure 1.7. Smooth but blotchy indirect illumination for the same scene as in Figure 1.6.

ate result. As Table 1.1 shows, the DT implementation clearly outperforms the standard implementation for the jittered sparse sample pattern chosen in our implementation. Note that the timings shown in Table 1.1 are measured for our technique running on pre-rendered data and do not include the costs for rendering the G-buffer or the RSM. DT does offer more than just speed benefits in the context of RSM sampling—it also unlocks the ability to work with deinterleaved sub-results as described below.

Technique	1920×1200	
	NVIDIA GTX 1070	Radeon RX 480
non DT	≈ 4.6 ms	≈ 7.5 ms
DT	≈ 3 ms	≈ 4.6 ms

Table 1.1. Performance of DT vs non-DT.

1.3 Adding Sub-image Blurs

We note that the indirect illumination sub-results (see Figure 1.2) look noisy in themselves because of the sparse filter kernels that are used to compute them. One next logical step is to try to remove the structured artifacts from the sub-results by bilaterally blurring these sub-images before reassembling them.

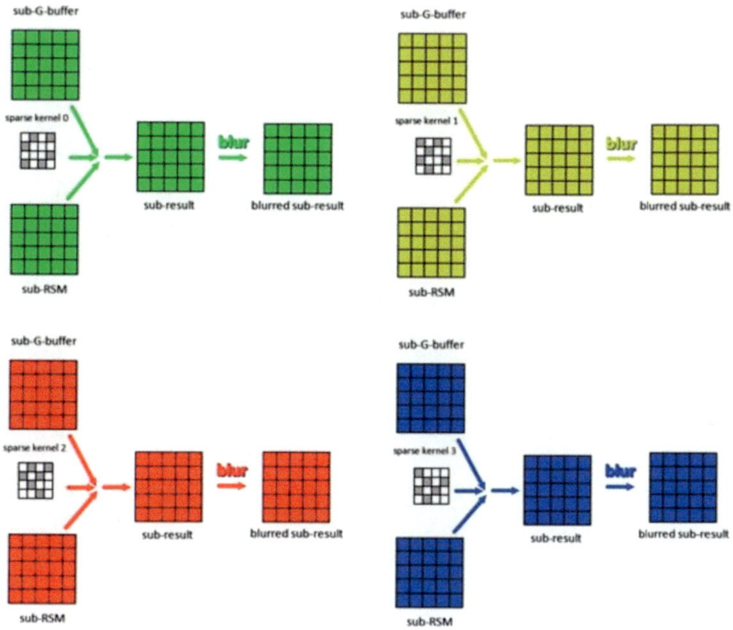

Figure 1.8. Blurring sub-results for 2 × 2 DT.

Therefore, we insert a blurring step right after computing each indirect illumination sub-result as shown in Figure 1.8. And then, instead of the direct results, we reassemble the blurred sub-results as shown in Figure 1.9.

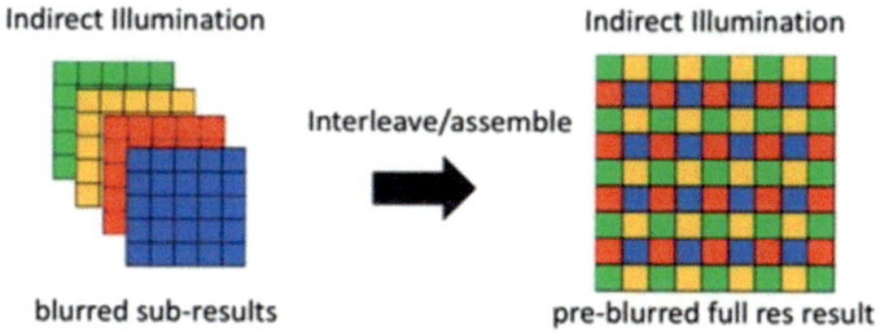

Figure 1.9. Reassembling blurred sub-results.

We now take a look at the results of this changed rendering pipeline in the screenshot in Figure 1.10. The screenshot looks a lot more ordered than the results in Figure 1.6, but it still shows structured artifacts. Turning on a final full resolution cross bi-lateral blur for the reassembled image, however, yields smooth indirect illumination as shown in the screenshot in Figure 1.11.

Testing this new combination of sub-image and full resolution blurs shows that no noticeable flickering or popping remains if one moves the camera through the scene or if dynamic objects appear in the scene.

Figure 1.10. Reassembled blurred sub-results.

Figure 1.11. Stable indirect illumination.

1.4 Results

Our work shows that the use of DT allows the use of filter footprints that are wide enough to capture a wide spread of indirect illumination and to still produce the fast frame rates needed by computer games.

Combining DT and sub-image blurring does finally produce indirect illumination that is visually smooth and stable in the presence of moving or animated objects and for changing light and camera conditions.

Timings have been measured on contemporary GPUs and are given in Table 1.2. Note that the timings shown in Table 1.2 are again measured using pre-rendered data and do not include the costs for rendering the G-buffer or the RSM.

1920 × 1200	
NVIDIA GTX 1070	Radeon RX 480
≈ 3.1 ms	≈ 5.2 ms
≈ 3 ms	≈ 4.6 ms

Table 1.2. Performance of combined DT and sub-blurring..

The screen shots in Figures 1.12 and 1.13 have been taken from a full demo application and show the Sponza scene without, respectively, with indirect illumination computed by the technique described in this chapter.

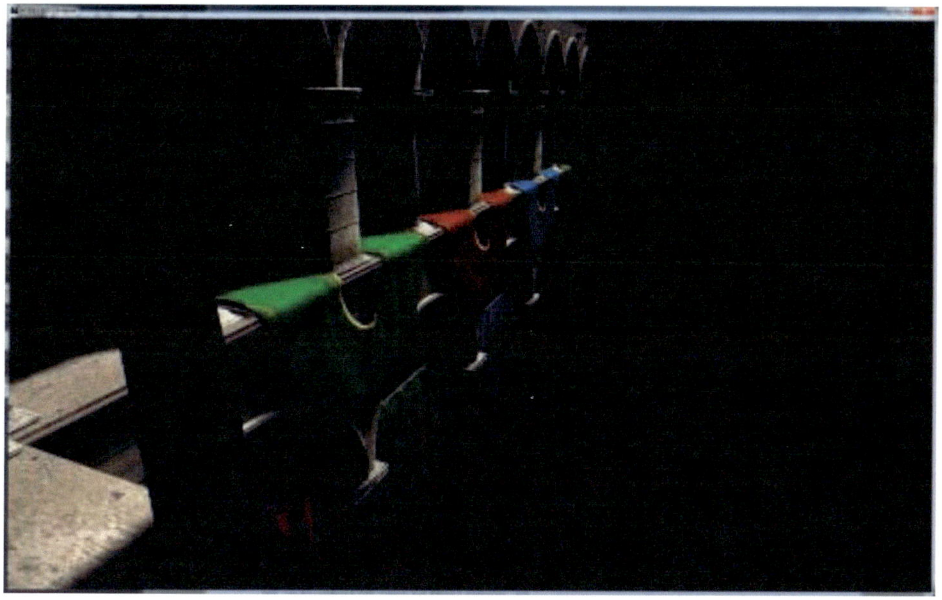

Figure 1.12. Sponza without indirect illumination.

Figure 1.13. Sponza with indirect illumination.

Bibliography

BAVOIL, L. 2014. Deinterleaved texturing for cache-efficient interleaved sampling. Tech. rep., NVIDIA. URL: https://developer.nvidia.com/sites/default/files/akamai/gameworks/samples/DeinterleavedTexturing.pdf.

DACHSBACHER, C., AND STAMMINGER, M. 2005. Reflective shadow maps. In *Proceedings of the 2005 Symposium on Interactive 3D Graphics and Games*, ACM, New York, I3D '05, 203–231. URL: http://doi.acm.org/10.1145/1053427.1053460.

GRUEN, H. 2011. Real-time one-bounce indirect illumination and shadows using ray tracing. In *GPU Pro 2*, W. Engel, Ed. A K Peters/CRC Press 2011, Natick, MA, 159–172.

HERZOG, R., EISEMANN, E., MYSZKOWSKI, K., AND SEIDEL, H.-P. 2010. Spatio-temporal upsampling on the gpu. In *Proceedings of the 2010 ACM SIGGRAPH Symposium on Interactive 3D Graphics and Games*, ACM, New York, I3D '10, 91–98. URL: http://doi.acm.org/10.1145/1730804.1730819.

JIMENEZ, J., ECHEVARRIA, J. I., SOUSA, T., AND GUTIERREZ, D. 2012. SMAA: Enhanced subpixel morphological antialiasing. *Comput. Graph. Forum 31*, 2pt1, 355–364. URL: http://dx.doi.org/10.1111/j.1467-8659.2012.03014.x.

KELLER, A., AND HEIDRICH, W. 2001. Interleaved sampling. In *Proceedings of the 12th Eurographics Workshop on Rendering Techniques*, Springer-Verlag, London, 269–276. URL: http://dl.acm.org/citation.cfm?id=647653.732285.

Segovia, B., Iehl, J. C., Mitanchey, R., and Péroche, B. 2006. Non-interleaved deferred shading of interleaved sample patterns. In *Proceedings of the 21st ACM SIGGRAPH/EUROGRAPHICS Symposium on Graphics Hardware*, ACM, New York, GH '06, 53–60. URL: http://doi.acm.org/10.1145/1283900.1283909.

Sloan, P.-P., Govindaraju, N. K., Nowrouzezahrai, D., and Snyder, J. 2007. Image-based proxy accumulation for real-time soft global illumination. In *Proceedings of the 15th Pacific Conference on Computer Graphics and Applications*, IEEE Computer Society, Washington, DC, PG '07, 97–105. URL: http://dx.doi.org/10.1109/PG.2007.35.

II

2

Participating Media Using Extruded Light Volumes

Nathan Hoobler, Andrei Tatarinov, and Alex Dunn

2.1 Introduction

Over the last few years, there has been a dramatic up-tick in the variety and fidelity of physically-based phenomenon modeled in real-time rendering engines. These technological advances have significantly increased the quality and dramatic impact of the scenes rendered; however, while much attention has been spent on how light interacts with the surfaces of various objects within the scene, the atmosphere within which the scene resides has been largely ignored—or at best, hastily approximated.

Simulating all of the phenomena involved in even local atmospheric scattering is a daunting proposition, however. Not only does it have the inherent complexities of the general global illumination problem (of which it is a subset), but it has the additional complexity that every single point in space can be seen simultaneously as an occluder, a receiver, and an emitter (through multiple scattering events). There are established techniques for resolving so-called participating media effects, but they are often either inefficient, inaccurate, or otherwise unsuited for a dynamic real-time environment.

In this chapter we explain the techniques used in the NVIDIA Gameworks volumetric lighting library to address these issues and provide flexible, dramatic, physically-based participating media effects in a manner compatible with existing rendering pipelines. We start by discussing the physical foundations of what we want to accomplish and explore the prior and state-of-the-art work on the subject. We then talk about our approach by explaining how it is applied using a uniform, directional light (the simplest case), followed by discussing what extensions to the technique are necessary to support local (omnidirectional and spot) lights. After the basic algorithm is explained, we discuss some special-case optimizations to gracefully trade image quality for performance if needed. Finally, we provide some practical performance numbers and discuss issues one would want to be aware of when implementing this technique into an existing rendering engine.

2.2 Background

2.2.1 Light Transport Overview

In physically-based rendering, the image displayed to the user is made up of pixels whose value corresponds to the the instantaneous rate of photons arriving at the view plane at the position corresponding to the pixel over the solid angle subtended by that pixel [Pharr and Humphreys 2004]. The image is generated by solving for the *radiative transfer* from light sources through the scene to the viewer. This was first explored in [Chandrasekhar 1960] and has since been refined and expanded to account for more sophisticated optical phenomenon.

In most renderers, this value is computed by determining where a ray passing through the pixel would intersect the scene and then solving for the radiance reflected in that direction (L_O) based on the radiance emitted from that point (L_e) and radiance reflected towards the viewer (L_s) from all possible incident directions (L_i over the hemisphere Ω). This gives us what is known as the *rendering equation* [Kajiya 1986]:

$$L_O(x, \omega_O) = L_e(x, \omega_O) + \int_{\Omega} f_r(x, \omega_i, \omega_O) L_i(x, \omega_i)(\omega_i \cdot \hat{n}) d\omega \qquad (2.1)$$

Note that we assume a specific wavelength and point in time in Equation (2.1), eliminating the λ and t terms for brevity. For tristimulus rendering, we can evaluate the equation for each color component separately.

The real world, however, is not defined by a set of lights and reflective surfaces sitting within a vacuum; rather, most scenes exist within an atmosphere made up of various (seemingly invisible) components which absorb and scatter energy just like opaque objects. Since the participating medium absorbs and scatters photons that move through it, the radiance is attenuated based on how far it has traveled (both from the light source to the scene, and from the scene to the viewer). The probability with which an interaction between a photon and a particle takes place is called the extinction coefficient. Since an interaction can be either an absorption or a scattering event, the *extinction coefficient* (σ_{ex}) is the sum of the absorption and scattering probabilities (σ_a and σ_s). It is important to note, however, that scattering can also add to the radiance flowing through a given ray, since photons crossing the ray from any other direction and at any point along the ray can be scattered in the given ray's direction. This phenomenon (see Figure 2.1) is called *in-scattering*.

Transmittance (T) is the ratio of power transmitted along a given path (Φ_t) to the power entering the medium along that path (Φ_i). The probability of a photon

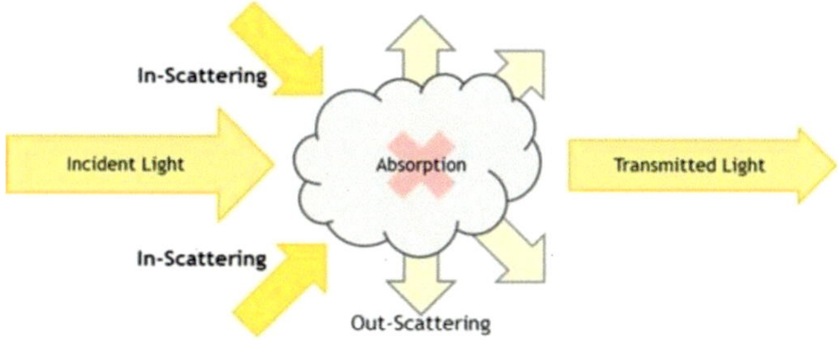

Figure 2.1. Scattering at a single point in space. Transmitted light is the result of incident light in the view direction attenuated by absorption and out-scattering, as well as in-scattered light that gets scattered out in the direction of the viewer.

being absorbed or scattered as it travels through a given medium was described previously using the extinction coefficient, and, indeed, the transmittance along a straight path of length l through a homogenous medium is related to the extinction factor using the Beer-Lambert Law [Lambert 1760, Beer 1852]:

$$T = \frac{\Phi_t}{\Phi_i} = e^{-\sigma_{ex} l}$$

The *phase function* $\rho(v)$ determines how the scattered light is distributed around the scattering point. For most atmospheric effects, it can be expressed as a function of the dot-product between the incident light direction ω_i and the output direction of interest ω_0 (commonly abbreviated as v). Different medium components may scatter light differently based on their size, shape, or other properties, resulting in different underlying functions. These functions (or their intensity) may also vary with wavelength (as with Rayleigh scattering).

An atmospheric medium is often comprised of multiple different elements in varying amounts: very small particles like oxygen and nitrogen molecules which produce Rayleigh scattering, larger suspended particles like water vapor which cause Mie scattering, and elements like dust and smoke which might both scatter and absorb. Though we can simply add together the extinction coefficients of these components to compute transmission,

$$\sigma_{ex}(x) = \sigma_\alpha(x) + \sum_n^k \sigma_n(x),$$

we need to separate scattering and absorption properly to compute the composite phase function:

$$\rho(x, v) = \frac{e^{-\sigma_{ex}}}{\sigma_{ex}(x)} \sum_n^k [\sigma_n(x)\rho_n(v)]$$

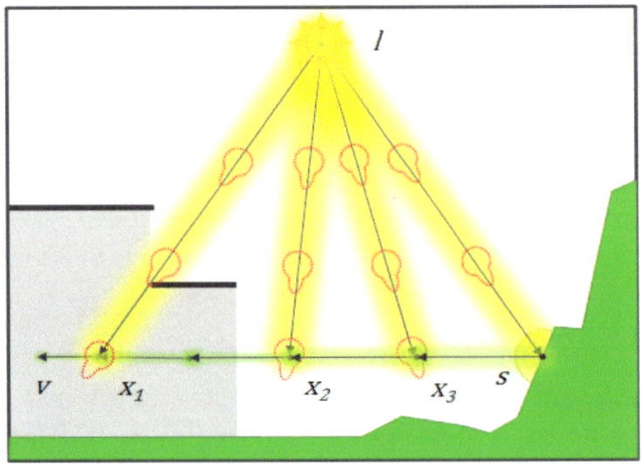

Figure 2.2. In-scattering at points x_1, x_2, and x_3 along the path from s to v.

The in-scattering component L_s (see Figure 2.2) is defined as

$$L_s(x, \omega_0) = \int_\Omega L_i(x, \omega_i)\rho(x, \omega_0 \cdot \omega_i)d\omega$$

By taking into account both extinction and in-scattering, we have worked backwards from the rendering equation to what is essentially the radiative transfer equation discussed by [Chandrasekhar 1960]. Radiance given along a ray ω starting at viewpoint v and intersecting the scene at s is

$$L_p(v, s, \omega) = T(v, s)L_0(s, \omega) + \int_v^s T(v, x)L_s(x, \omega)dx$$

This expands to a fairly large expression; however, if we make a few assumptions then it becomes much simpler. First, we only account for single scattering events, which reduces the integral inside $L_s()$ to evaluating in a single direction (which we then expand to the sum of scattering contribution from all valid lights). Second, we assume that the medium is locally homogenous (uniform density of components within the scale of the scene being rendered) removing the integrals inside the transmission computation and allows for some factors to be further simplified. The incoming radiance $L_i()$ in the scattering term is replaced by $v_l(x)$ (a binary visibility function between light l and point x) and $L_l(x)$ (the attenuated radiance from light l at point x). Expanded, the resulting lighting equation for computing radiance through a pixel in a homogenous medium accounting for single scattering yields

$$\begin{aligned} L_p(v, s, \omega) &= e^{-\sigma_{ex}||\vec{vs}||}L_0(s, \omega) \\ &\quad + \sum_l^{\text{lights}} \int_v^s e^{-\sigma_{ex}||\vec{vs}||}V_l(x)L_l(x)\rho(\omega \cdot \vec{xl})dx \end{aligned} \tag{2.2}$$

In plain terms, Equation (2.2) states that the light at each pixel should equal the light reflected from the scene that gets transmitted through the medium to the viewer plus all the light in-scattered towards the viewer and transmitted through the medium at every point along the ray's path to the scene from every light which might affect that path.

2.2.2 Extruded Light Volumes

In contrast to classic volumetric lighting solutions like ray-marching and slice-based approaches that perform numerical integration of the radiance equation along the view direction of each pixel, our approach relies on direct integrability of the radiance equation which, given the assumptions above, allows us to perform calculations at much lower rates. Instead, we use a version of the technique proposed in [Wyman and Ramsey 2008] and extended by [Billeter et al. 2010] which allows us to only concern ourselves with evaluating the in-scattering integral at points where the light's visibility changes (i.e., at points where the ray enters or leaves a shadowed region). This approach eliminates many of the aliasing and over-sampling issues inherent to naive slicing or ray-marching and allows for volumetric effects to be computed at or very close to the native resolution of the rendering, providing for crisp shadow lines that would not otherwise be possible.

Details. In general, our technique is very similar to that discussed in [Billeter et al. 2010]. Instead of summing discrete integrals evaluated at predetermined points along the view ray, this geometry-based approach exploits the fact that the full integral along the view ray can be expressed as the sum of the integrals along that ray from the eye to all light-shadow transitions minus the sum of the integrals from the eye to all shadow-light transitions. These transitions are found by using a light volume to define the visible hull of light in the scene.

This light volume corresponds to an enclosed mesh that contains all the sections of the world that are visible from the light's point of view (or alternatively, all points in the world from which the light source is visible). This is in some ways equivalent to the silhouette meshes used to render stencil shadows. Instead of relying on actual occluder geometry information (and all the other difficulties that come with generating silhouette meshes), we use a technique similar to that described in [McCool 2000] and extract the mesh using information from a shadow map that was already rendered for the light source. This method is again similar to that used in [Billeter et al. 2010]; however, there are a few differences.

Once we have a light volume mesh, we render it from the viewer's perspective, evaluating the airlight integral at each shaded sample and additively blending either its positive or negative value to an accumulation buffer (see Figure 2.3). This again is very similar to [Billeter et al. 2010] except that we make use of the stencil buffer to allow us to use depth testing without generating "holes" in the

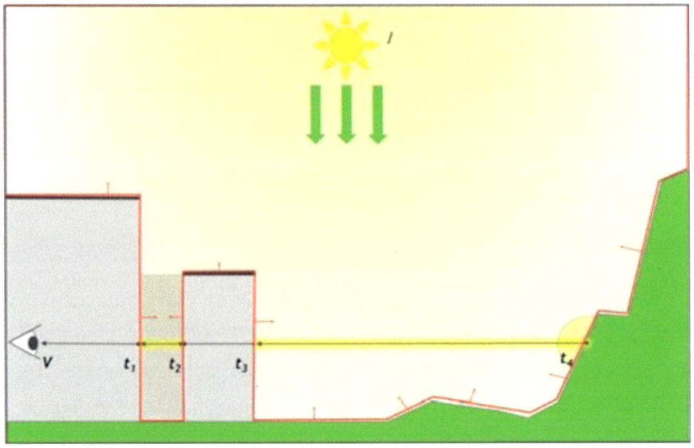

Figure 2.3. Mesh representation of directional light volume in a typical game scene. Lighting contribution comes from sections of the arrow which are illuminated by direct light from the sun.

accumulated data where the mesh interpenetrates the scene. This is explained in more depth in Section 2.3.1.

First, instead of using geometry shaders feeding back into one another, we use hardware tessellation functionality to generate the mesh. To match the depth information in the shadow map, we simply use the shadow map in the displacement shader as a displacement map to offset the vertices so that they fit the bounds of the volume correctly.

Second, instead of using edge filters on the shadow map data to adjust mesh tessellation we use a simple "target feature size" technique. This is fairly common in adaptive hardware tessellation and is described at a high level in [Dudash 2012]. Section 2.3.1 gives an in-depth description of the way we calculate tessellation levels for control quads of the light volume.

Within the pixel shader itself, the direct integrability of the radiance function allows us to evaluate the entire segment of a view vector in a single go, without having to step through it. Such calculations are usually performed as the definite integral for each visible segment of a view ray; however, as calculating segment intervals for each fragment ahead of time would not be practical, an association is made to simplify things. One can say that the sum of all visible line segments on any given view ray is equal to the sum of the line segments that are composed of the points for the viewer ($[v]t = 0$) and the visible light hull intersections (t_i), where those intersections with planar normals that have a positive dot product with the view normal, are added to the total sum (and conversely those without are subtracted). See Figure 2.4 for an example of how this works.

Since knowing all intersection points ahead of time is not practical, an association is made for all $t = 0$, where only the current intersection point (t_i) is

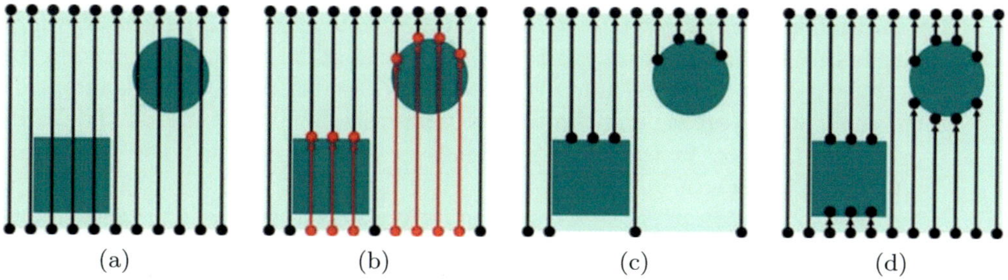

Figure 2.4. Integration intervals seen from the shadow-map point of view. Rendering the volume back-to-front, (a) integrals for the front faces of the furthermost part of the volume are taken with a positive sign, (b) back faces of a volume produced by objects are subtracted, (c) result of subtraction, (d) integrals for the front faces of objects are added with a positive sign

known:

$$\sum_{i=1}^{t_n}\left(\int_{t_{i-1}}^{t_i} f(t)dt\right) \Rightarrow \sum_{i=0}^{t_n}\left(\left(\int_0^{t_i} f(t)dt\right)\cdot\left(\frac{v_{\text{norm}}\cdot t_{i_{\text{norm}}}}{|v_{\text{norm}}\cdot t_{i_{\text{norm}}}|}\right)\right)$$

2.3 Directional Lights

Directional light sources (lights that are extremely far away from the viewer relative to the scale of the scene being rendered) provide the most straightforward scenario for the geometry-based approach. This is because the distance assumption allows us to ignore varying light direction (as all rays will be approximately parallel) and distance attenuation (as all points within the scene will be approximately equidistant to the source). In addition to the assumptions mentioned previously, restricting the simulation to single scattering within a homogenous medium, these assumptions allow for further simplification of our radiance transfer function (Equation (2.2)).

2.3.1 Implementation

The approach described in Section 2.2.2 can be implemented on a wide range of graphics hardware, with a minimal required feature supported to be vertex texture fetch. On more modern GPUs, tessellation can be used in order to achieve better computational efficiency by generating additional geometric detail procedurally within the rendering pipeline. Let's take a look at the basic implementation of our approach using DirectX 9-level hardware and the ways it can be improved using features available in modern generation GPUs.

To reconstruct the light frustum on the GPU, all that is needed is a pretessellated unit square mesh and a shadow-map (a depth buffer rendered using an orthogonal projection camera associated with a directional light source). The degree of tessellation corresponds to the fineness of detail from the shadow map that the resulting mesh is able to capture. Each vertex of the mesh is mapped to the shadow-map space, and the corresponding shadow-map value at the vertex's projected location in the shadow map is used to reconstruct the world-space position of this vertex.

Each invocation of pixel shader used to render the light volume calculates the radiance transfer integral on the interval from the viewer's position to the world-space position of the pixel being rendered. The buffer used to accumulate the scattering results can be of an arbitrary resolution, as long as it is easily mapped to the full framebuffer. As is discussed in Sections 2.5 and 2.6, downsampling can be used for substantial performance gains.

Setup. Before accumulating volumetric lighting, several preparation steps must be performed. First, a depth buffer has to be copied and downsampled if rendering to a resolution lower than the framebuffer resolution. This operation has to be done only once per frame. To guarantee good performance when calculating the integrals for the light volume, a lookup table encoding the scattering phase function is also generated.

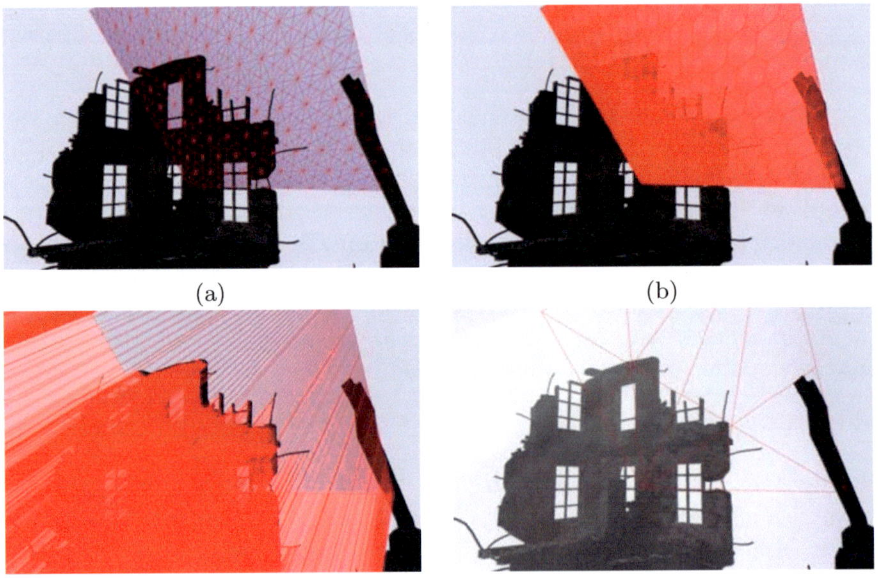

(a) (b) (c) (d)

Figure 2.5. Images showing the various stages of rendering: (a) pre-tessellated plane associated with near clipping plane of shadow-map camera; (b) fully tessellated plane; (c) vertices of a plane extruded based on shadow map; (d) cap is rendered to make a closed volume.

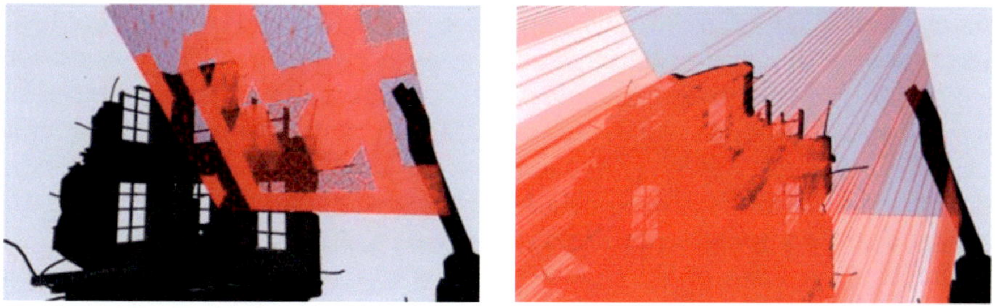

(a) (b)

Figure 2.6. Content-dependent tessellation level: (a) plane tessellated according to shadow-map contents; (b) vertices of a plane extruded based on the shadow-map.

Light Volume Rendering. To render the light volume, a grid, or a pre-tessellated quad, has to be rendered that is aligned with shadow-map camera's near clipping plane. Depending on the GPU capabilities, hardware tessellation can be used to generate the fine-grained mesh on the fly instead of storing all the pre-tessellated vertices in the video memory. In this case, a pre-tessellated mesh consisting of control quads should be rendered, as shown in Figure 2.5. To build a closed volume that is required to correctly evaluate the light equation, an additional quad has to be rendered at the light volume base after the extrusion is complete.

As mentioned in Section 2.3.1, we use adaptive tessellation to render the light volume efficiently (see Figure 2.6). We start by specifying a target size (in pixels) which we would like to make every edge in the rendered mesh match when rendered. By using a screen-space target, we maintain a constant (and ideally imperceptible) degree of error in the mesh fit, without over-tessellating and providing too much detail where it is unneeded. To adapt this method to our use case, we begin by looking at each control patch and determining the closest possible distance between the viewer and the rectangular prism resulting from projecting that patch to the far plane of the light view projection (this will be zero if the viewer is within the volume covered by the patch). Based on the distance calculated, we then compute the number of subdivisions required so that the diameter of a sphere circumscribing each subdivision will match our target feature size (up to a maximum tessellation factor). The result is that the volume mesh gets more tessellated for patches near the camera, but then falls off quickly as distance increases. It should be noted that there is potential room for significant improvement by incorporating some data-dependent adaptation as well—for example by pre-filtering the shadow map to determine the maximum amount of detail within a given patch (as is done by [Billeter et al. 2010]).

In order to produce the correct results, the number of front faces affecting each pixel should match the number of back faces (or be one larger if the viewer is inside the lit volume). If they do not match for whatever reason, the result will either be incorrectly over bright, or over dark (and possibly even negative).

This may seem like a trivial requirement; however, it is a very real problem for several reasons. Since the shadow map we use is an imperfect representation of the scene (in contrast to using the actual scene geometry), there are often cases where the reconstructed volume does not precisely match the scene geometry, and portions of the light volume interpenetrate the world geometry. Having a depth test cull light shafts that are occluded by geometry is generally a good thing and significantly improves performance; however, due to this imprecision, some portions of front faces of the volume (that contribute to the lighting equation with a positive sign) fail the depth test, while their corresponding back faces (which contribute to the lighting equation with a negative sign) are still rendered, resulting in visual artifacts.

One way to prevent these artifacts is to disable the hardware depth test and perform manual depth comparison for every pixel of the light volume (as is done in [Billeter et al. 2010]. If the pixel is behind the scene geometry (depth test fails), its depth is adjusted to precisely match the depth of the scene. All the portions of light volume that should have been correctly culled by a depth test are now snapped to the scene geometry—the integrals for them are still calculated with positive and negative signs, and since these integrals are exactly the same, there is no contribution to the lighting equation. There is, however, a significant waste in such calculations.

If there were some method of counting the number of front and back faces that intersect a given pixel, this could be easily fixed. Fortunately, the stencil buffer provides exactly that functionality. During light volume rendering, the stencil state is configured to increment the stencil value for front faces and decrement it for back faces. For the cases when the camera is inside the volume, a full-screen quad is rendered at the far clipping plane to emulate a back face (which also closes the volume for views that do not intersect the tessellated plane). When light-volume rendering is complete, values in the stencil buffer less than an initial reference point mark pixels that have missing front faces. A final full-screen pass is then performed on those pixels (using the stencil test that is configured to filter only these fragments) that reads from the depth buffer and calculates the missing integrals from the front faces that have been culled by the depth test.

Resolve and Apply. As a final step, rendered light volume is composited with the contents of a framebuffer. Since light volume is commonly rendered to a smaller resolution buffer, an upsampling pass is required. An edge-preserving bilateral upsampling generally suits the purpose, but there may be better content-specific solutions. If the internal buffer is utilizing MSAA, then a resolve pass is done beforehand. Finally, the results are applied to the framebuffer. Since we have to account for both in-scattering (which is added to the target pixel) and out-scattering/extinction (which is used to modulate the target pixel we take advantage of dual-source blending to accomplish this in a single pass with one composite blend function:

$$\text{Dest}_{\text{RGB}} = \text{Src0}_{\text{RGB}} + \text{Src1}_{\text{RGB}} \times \text{Target}_{\text{RGB}}$$

2.3.2 Source Code

The bulk of the interesting work for this algorithm is done in the domain and pixel shaders bound when rendering the volume. The domain shader (Listing 2.1) shows how a point on the tessellated far plane of the light's view volume is mapped to a shadow-map coordinate, and then how that coordinate is used to re-project into world-space to determine the vertex position for the volume. To support cascaded shadow maps, the shader begins with the coarsest cascade provided and then proceeds to map the light-space position to each progressively finer cascade coverage area. By proceeding from coarse to fine in this manner, we end up with a sample from the most detailed map which covers the specified coordinate.

The pixel shader (Listing 2.2) shows what a basic version of the pixel shader would look like. Because directional lights can be analytically calculated, the shader simply determines the distance from the viewer and then evaluates the integral at that point. The sign of the result is then negated depending on whether the geometry is front- or back-facing.

```
[domain("quad")]
PS_POLYGONAL_INPUT main
    (
        HS_POLYGONAL_CONSTANT_DATA_OUTPUT input,
        float2 uv : SV_DOMAINLOCATION,
        const OutputPatch<HS_POLYGONAL_CONTROL_POINT_OUTPUT, 4> Patch
    )
{
    PS_POLYGONAL_INPUT output = (PS_POLYGONAL_INPUT)0;

    float3 vClipIn1 = lerp(Patch[0].vClipPos.xyz, Patch[1].vClipPos.xyz, uv.x);
    float3 vClipIn2 = lerp(Patch[3].vClipPos.xyz, Patch[2].vClipPos.xyz, uv.x);
    float3 vClipIn = lerp(vClipIn1, vClipIn2, uv.y);

    float4 vPos1 = lerp(Patch[0].vWorldPos, Patch[1].vWorldPos, uv.x);
    float4 vPos2 = lerp(Patch[3].vWorldPos, Patch[2].vWorldPos, uv.x);
    float4 vWorldPos = lerp(vPos1, vPos2, uv.y);

    if (all(abs(vClipIn.xy) < EDGE_FACTOR))
    {
        int iCascade = -1;
        float4 vClipPos = float4(0,0,0,1);

        [unroll]
        for (int i = COARSE_CASCADE; i >= 0; --i)
        {
            // Try to refetch from finer cascade
            float4 vClipPosCascade = mul( g_mLightProj[i], vWorldPos );
            vClipPosCascade *= 1.f / vClipPosCascade.w;
            if (all(abs(vClipPosCascade.xy) < 1.0f))
            {
                float2 vTex = float2(0.5*vClipPosCascade.x+0.5,
                                     -0.5*vClipPosCascade.y+0.5);
```

```
                float depthSample = SampleShadowMap( vTex, i );
                if (depthSample < 1.0f)
                {
                    vClipPos.xy = vClipPosCascade.xy;
                    vClipPos.z = depthSample;
                    iCascade = i;
                }
            }
        }

        if (iCascade >= 0)
        {
            vWorldPos = mul( g_mLightProjInv[iCascade], float4(vClipPos.xyz, 1) );
            vWorldPos *= 1.0f / vWorldPos.w;
            vWorldPos.xyz = g_vEyePosition + (1.0f-g_fBias)
                                                *(vWorldPos.xyz-g_vEyePosition);
        }
    }
    else
    {
        vWorldPos = mul(g_mLightToWorld, float4(vClipIn.xy, 1, 1));
        vWorldPos *= 1.0f / vWorldPos.w;
    }

    output.vWorldPos = vWorldPos;
    output.vPos = mul( g_mViewProj, output.vWorldPos );
    return output;
}
```

Listing 2.1. A function that determines whether a triangle is facing the viewer. A domain shader, performing cascade-aware reprojection from shadow space to world space for a light volume hull.

```
float4 main
    (
     PS_POLYGONAL_INPUT pi,
        bool bIsFrontFace : SV_ISFRONTFACE
    ) : SV_TARGET
{
    float fSign = 0;
    float4 vWorldPos = float4(0, 0, 0, 1);
    float eye_dist = 0;
    float3 vV = float3(0, 0, 0);

        fSign = bIsFrontFace ? 1.0f : -1.0f;
        vWorldPos = pi.vWorldPos;
        eye_dist = length(vWorldPos.xyz - g_vEyePosition.xyz);
        vV = (vWorldPos.xyz - g_vEyePosition.xyz) / eye_dist;

    float3 vL = g_vLightDir.xyz;
        float3 integral = Integrate_SimpleDirectional(eye_dist, vV, vL);

    return float4(fSign*integral*g_vLightIntensity.rgb, 0);
}
```

Listing 2.2. A front and backface aware pixel shader rendering directional lights.

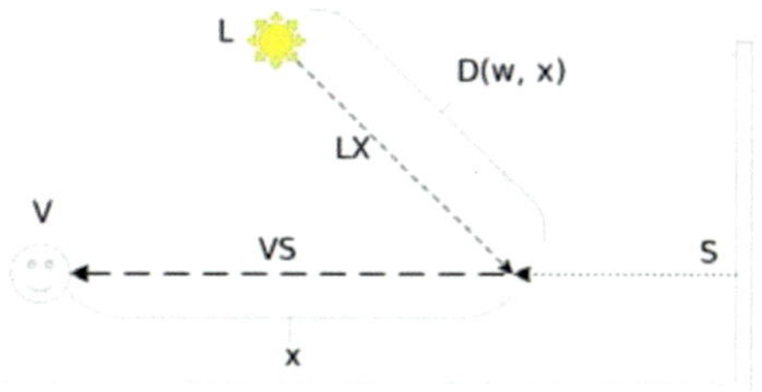

Figure 2.7. Overview of light propagation from a local source.

2.4 Local Lights

Local lights—where the light source is close enough to the scene that its relative distance and direction changes meaningfully across the view region—require more complicated calculations than simple directional lights; however, they can be modeled with a similar approach as that used for directional lights (see Figure 2.7). In this chapter we look at two types of light that fit into that category: omnidirectional lights (where light is emitted equi-radially in each direction from a singular point in space, such as point lights) and spot lights (where light emitted from a single point in space has a projective component along a major axis). When dealing with local lights, some of the assumptions made when calculating a volumetric lighting term for directional lights must be thrown out the window.

2.4.1 Omnidirectional Lights

Omnidirectional lights are immediately more challenging than directional lights, because we can no longer assume that the radiant flux is constant throughout the scene. Directional lights are assumed to be far enough away that the scene subtends a very small solid angle relative to the emitter. In addition to letting us treat all rays as being parallel (the most commonly considered property), omnidirectional lights also allow us to assume that any difference in light-world distance between two parts of the scene is negligible compared to the absolute distance. This in turn lets us ignore distance attenuation (or rather, pre-factor it into the light's intensity and treat it as a constant).

For light sources that exist within the scene these assumptions no longer hold true, so we have to factor an attenuation term into our lighting equation. There is also the added complication of the phase function. With directional lights, the incident light vector is constant, i.e., the angle between the view direction and light direction does not vary. However, since the light source is relatively close to the viewer, it is likely that the angle between the vector to the light $\vec{LW}$ and to the viewer $\vec{VW}$ will change substantially over the length of the view ray. This means that we cannot pull the phase function out of the integral like we were able to with directional lights.

These added complications combine to mean that the simple integral which we were able to evaluate analytically for directional lights now has no (convenient) analytical solution. For ray-marching approaches, this is not a problem since they are numerically integrating the results already; however, our approach requires evaluating a continuous integral from 0 to the render depth at each point along the ray that an extruded volume edge might intersect. While it is possible to evaluate the integral in the pixel shader numerically, this is potentially wasteful if pixels are intersected by multiple faces of the extruded volume. Precomputing the integral ahead of time and then storing it in a lookup table amortizes this cost, but that can be expensive itself given the large parameter space. By exploiting properties of the lights and the scene, however, this lookup table is reduced to a very manageable size and becomes an easy win for performance.

Math. Recall our original single in-scattering integral, expanded to account for omnidirectional lights:

$$L_{\text{inscatter}}(L, V, \vec{\omega}, d) = \int_0^d E_{\vec{LW}}(L, V, \vec{\omega}, x)\rho(\vec{LW} \cdot \vec{VW})T(x)dx$$

where

$$\begin{aligned} W(x) &= V + x\vec{\omega} \\ E_{\vec{LW}}(L, V, \vec{\omega}, x) &= L_0 A\left(||\vec{LW}||\right) T\left(||\vec{LW}||\right) \end{aligned} \tag{2.3}$$

and $T(x)$ is the transmittance from point x to the eye, and $A(x)$ is the attenuation factor (described below).

Using trigonometry we can define the light-world distance at a given distance along the view vector ($D(x)$) and the dot product of the light-world and world-view vectors at a given distance along the view vector ($\phi(x)$):

$$\begin{aligned} D(X) &= ||V + x\vec{\omega} - L|| = \sqrt{||\vec{VL}||^2 + 2x(\vec{VL} \cdot \omega) + x^2} \\ \phi(x) &= \frac{x^2 + D(x)^2 - ||\vec{VL}||^2}{2xD(x)} \end{aligned}$$

Substituting those into the Equation (2.3) gives us the modified integral:

$$L_{\text{inscatter}}(L, V, \vec{\omega}, d) = \int_0^d L_0 A\left(D(x)\right) \rho(\phi(x)) e^{(-\sigma_{ex}(x + D(x)))}$$

This integral is, unfortunately, not trivially solvable analytically. However, We see that $D(x)$ and $\phi(x)$ rely on the distance x and the light position, viewer position, and view direction. Furthermore, the view direction $\vec{\omega}$ does not actually matter—it depends just on the dot product between it and the light-viewer vector $\vec{LV}$. Since L and V are constant for a given frame, this reduces our integral to a function of two parameters: $L_{\text{inscatter}}(\vec{\omega}, d)$. With only two parameters, numerical integration becomes a readily feasible solution. We take advantage of this and compute a 2D lookup table parameterized over $(d, \vec{\omega} \cdot \vec{LV})$ by computing the differential value at each coordinate in the table and then doing a prefix sum across each row to find the integral as d increases. During the subsequent volume rendering pass, we simply sample this lookup texture for the proper d and $(\vec{\omega} \cdot \vec{LV})$ values for the fragment and use that as our integral.

It should be noted that there is significant work in the area of finding solutions to the airlight integral which are either made analytic via some assumptions, or which take advantage of sophisticated refactoring and approximation of the terms within the integral to produce an accurate function that could be evaluated analytically (rather than the numerical technique described above). Most notable is [Sun et al. 2005] (which is used in [Billeter et al. 2010]) and [Pegoraro et al. 2011]. We opted for the numerical approach used here because of its relative simplicity and robustness, and because it did not create significant additional artifacts or cost; however, it's quite possible these closed-form techniques could be applied here instead. One potential issue, however, is that since our method relies on the sum and difference of different sample points along the integral, numerical stability can be a tremendous concern (especially for scenes with a high degree of depth complexity in the volume shadows).

Implementation. Omnidirectional light volume rendering has three stages: generating the pre-integrated look-up table, rendering the tessellated volume mesh, and finally doing a "filler" pass to account for any gaps due to volume-world mesh mismatches.

The lookup texture (see Figure 2.8) is generated in two compute shader passes (shown in Listing 2.3). In the first pass, the instantaneous value (representing the

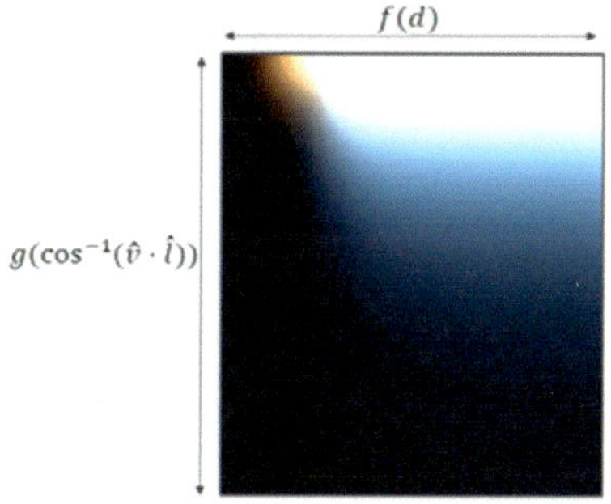

Figure 2.8. Lookup texture used to improve calculation efficiency at runtime. The eye-world depth and angle between the view direction and the eye-light direction are used for the u- and v-coordinates after passing through mapping functions to minimize quantization artifacts.

light reaching the viewer from scattering just at that location) is computed for each sample using geometry derived from the sample's location within the table. The u-coordinate (horizontal) is mapped to the distance of the sample point from the viewer. The v-coordinate (vertical) is mapped to the angle between the view direction of the ray in question and the vector from the viewer towards the light source. Both of these coordinates are transformed to maximize the utilization of the table. The distance is re-mapped to cover only the range from the nearest potential intersection point of the volume to the furthest intersection point, which provides improvements where the viewer is outside of the volume in question. The v-coordinate is derived from a nonlinear mapping of the angle, so as to maximize precision where $\vec{V} \cdot \vec{L}$ is close to zero. Once the instantaneous values within a dispatch group are calculated, a prefix sum of each row within the (32-thread wide) block is performed to produce a partial sum for the block. This is done in the first pass because there is a greater number of work groups in flight, meaning that the cost of this sum is more readily parallelized than if it were all done in the second pass.

The second stage consists of another compute shader pass which marches across all the rows of the table in parallel in 32-entry steps. This pass simply reads the values from the previous stage for that section of the row, offsets them by the total of all entries already processed, and then writes them out again. This produces the final integral across each row, increasing monotonically with distance from the viewer.

As a final optimization, we take advantage of the unused bits in the alpha channel to store a scale factor based on the lighting parameters. The scale factor is used to remap the actual integral to more fully use the floating-point range available. Other options, such as manually packing bits were explored, but that would result in being unable to use texture interpolation when the table is later sampled as well as additional unpacking overhead.

```
static const uint LUT_DEPTH_RES = 256;
static const uint LUT_WDOTV_RES = 512;

float4 PackLut(float3 v, float s)
{
    float log_s = log2(s);
    return float4(v/s, log_s);
}

float3 UnpackLut(float4 v)
{
    float s = exp2(v.a);
    return v.rgb*s;
}

[numthreads( BLOCK_SIZE.x, BLOCK_SIZE.y, 1 )]
void ComputeLUT_FirstPass
    (
        uint3 gthreadID : SV_GroupThreadID,
        uint2 dispatchID : SV_DispatchThreadID,
        uint2 groupID : SV_GroupID
    )
{
    uint idx = gthreadID.y*BLOCK_SIZE.x + gthreadID.x;
```

```
    float2 coord = float2(dispatchID) / float2(LUT_DEPTH_RES-1, LUT_WDOTV_RES-1);

    // Non-linear mapping of Y coordinate to cosine of angle with eye-light vector
    float cos_WV = 2*coord.y*coord.y-1;

    float3 vW = g_vEyePosition - g_vLightPos;
    float Wsqr = dot(vW, vW);
    float W_length = sqrt(Wsqr);
    float t0 = max(0.0f, W_length-g_fLightZFar);
    float t_range = g_fLightZFar + W_length - t0;
    float t = t0 + coord.x*t_range;

    float WdotV = cos_WV*W_length;
    float Dsqr = max(Wsqr+2*WdotV*t+t*t, 0.0f);
    float D = sqrt(Dsqr);
    float cos_phi = (t>0 && D>0) ? (t*t + Dsqr - Wsqr) / (2 * t*D) : cos_WV;
    float3 extinction = exp(-g_vSigmaExtinction*(D+t));
    float3 phase_factor = GetPhaseFactor(tPhaseLUT, -cos_phi);
    float attenuation = AttenuationFunc(D);
    float3 inscatter = phase_factor*attenuation*extinction;

    // Scale by dT because we are doing quadrature
    inscatter *= t_range / float(LUT_DEPTH_RES);

    inscatter = inscatter / g_vScatterPower;
    sAccum_P[idx] = inscatter;

    // Prefix-sum across the rows in this block
    [unroll]
    for (uint d=1; d<32; d = d<<1)
    {
        if (gthreadID.x >= d)
        {
            sAccum_P[idx] += sAccum_P[idx - d];
        }
    }

    static const float LUT_SCALE = 32.0f / 32768.0f;
    rwLightLUT_P[dispatchID] = PackLut(sAccum_P[idx], LUT_SCALE);
}

[numthreads( BLOCK_SIZE.x, BLOCK_SIZE.y, 1 )]
void ComputeLUT_SecondPass
    (
        uint3 gthreadID : SV_GroupThreadID,
        uint3 dispatchID : SV_DispatchThreadID,
        uint2 groupID : SV_GroupID
    )
{
    uint t_offset = 0;

    if (gthreadID.x == 0)
    {
        sOffset[gthreadID.y] = 0..xxx;
    }

    [unroll]
    for (uint t = 0; t < LUT_DEPTH_RES; t += BLOCK_SIZE.x)
    {
        uint2 tc = dispatchID.xy + uint2(t, 0);
        float4 s = 0..xxxx;
        s = tLightLUT_P[tc];

        float3 v = UnpackLut(s) + sOffset[gthreadID.y];
        if (gthreadID.x == (BLOCK_SIZE.x-1))
```

```
        {
            sOffset[gthreadID.y] = v;
        }
        s.a *= exp2(s.a) * LUT_DEPTH_RES/32;
        rwLightLUT_P[tc] = PackLut(v, s.a);
    }
}
```

Listing 2.3. Omnidirectional light lookup table generation. ComputeLUT_FirstPass computes the local differential and then performs a prefix-sum across the rows covered by the thread group. ComputeLUT_SecondPass then marches across the rows of the table to compute the full integral. Values are scaled to floating point precision usage.

After the lookup table is calculated, the mesh for the volume is rendered. Just as in the directional lighting case, tessellation is used to map the base mesh to the volume covered by the actual light-source using the shadow map information provided; however, in this case the base mesh is not a tessellated plane, but a unit cube centered on the light source with six tessellated faces. The resulting vertices of the shape have their distances from the light source computed based on samples from the shadow map. Once tessellated, the resulting geometry is then run through a pixel shader outputting the positive or negative integral based on distance and facing direction. This integral is computed from the previously generated look-up table using the mapping depicted in Listing 2.4. Transforms on the coordinates and values are used to maximize limited resolution and bit precision.

```

float GetLutCoord_X(float t, float light_dist)
{
    float t0 = max(0.0f, light_dist-g_fLightZFar);
    float t_range = g_fLightZFar + light_dist - t0;
    return max(0, (t-t0)) / t_range;
}

float GetLutCoord_Y(float cos_theta)
{
    return sqrt(0.5*cos_theta+0.5);
}

float3 SampleLut(Texture2D tex, float2 tc)
{
    float4 s = tex.SampleLevel(sBilinear, tc, 0);
    return g_vLightIntensity.rgb*g_vScatterPower*s.rgb*exp2(s.a);
}

float3 Integrate_Omni(float eye_dist, float3 vW, float3 vV)
{
    float light_dist = length(vW);
    vW = vW / light_dist;
    float2 tc;
    tc.x = GetLutCoord_X(eye_dist, light_dist);
    tc.y = GetLutCoord_Y(dot(vW, vV));
    return g_vScatterPower * SampleLut(tLightLUT_P, tc);
}
```

Listing 2.4. Omnidirectional light sampling code. Integrate_Omni computes the integral at eye_dist along direction vV, with vW being the vector from the viewer to the light source.

Finally, a full-screen pass is run which uses a stencil buffer populated during the volume rendering pass to fill in areas where the mesh interpenetrated the geometry due to shadow-map precision errors, resulting in an uneven number of front and back faces.

Other Considerations.

Attenuation function: The radiance from a local light source attenuates as the receiver moves away from the light, due to the energy being spread across an increasingly large solid angle. For point light sources, this follows the inverse square law:

$$A_{\text{point}}(d) = \frac{1}{d^2}$$

The falloff is a function of the emissive area of the light source, meaning that lights with physical shapes (such as a sphere) will have different falloff behavior. For example, the attenuation at distance d for a sphere light of radius r, for example, has been shown [Madams 2011] to closely match

$$A_{\text{sphere}}(d) = \frac{1}{1 + \frac{2}{r}d + \frac{1}{r^2}d^2}$$

For the purposes of generality and artist flexibility, the attenuation function thus usually takes the form of an inverse quadratic with specified constant, linear, and quadratic weights:

$$A(d) = \frac{1}{k_c + k_l d + k_q d^2}$$

Shadow/visibility map: Unlike directional lights, omnidirectional light visibility cannot be adequately represented by a view frustum depth map (i.e., a conventional shadow-map). There are several methods for representing shadows for these lights, but two of the most popular are cube-map shadows and dual-paraboloid projections. Supporting these is fairly straightforward, as it mainly just requires a branch in the tessellation domain shader to use the proper code path when looking up the desired tessellation depth.

Mesh topology: Much like with the shadow map, the single tessellated-plane approach used for directional lights will not work for omnidirectional lights. Instead, we use a tessellated cube mesh where the vertex distances from the cube's center are all normalized, forming a sort of rounded "cube-sphere" (with the light origin located at the cube center). When the vertices are tessellated, we look up the appropriate depth for the direction to that vertex from the center point. This is convenient, because it allows for a more unified code base between different light types (since the control mesh shape is still a series of quad grids). Other control mesh geometries, such as a geodesic, might have some advantages here; however, the results from this simple approach seem quite satisfactory.

2.4.2 Spotlights

Spotlights can be described as local lights which behave like omnidirectional lights except that they only illuminate a narrow cone surrounding a specific direction from the light source. Because they are local to the scene, they have the same complications as omnidirectional lights; however, the additional constraint of a spotlight direction and falloff angle/function relative to that direction make the situation significantly more complicated to solve.

Math. Spotlights can be treated as omnidirectional lights with an additional falloff attenuation factor. For a spotlight at L with a central direction $\vec{v}$, a maximum falloff angle ϕ, and a falloff power of n_f, this factor is defined for a world position x as

$$A_s(x) = \left(\frac{\alpha(x) - \beta}{1 - \beta}\right)^{n_f}$$

where α and β are, respectively, the cosines of the spotlight direction and direction to the world position, or the maximum falloff angle:

$$\alpha(x) = \vec{v} \cdot \frac{x \vec{-} L}{||x - L||}$$
$$\beta = \cos(\phi)$$

If we pull out the per-frame and per-pixel constant terms discussed for omnidirectional lights,

$$L_{\text{inscatter}}(\vec{\omega}, d) = L_0 \int_0^d A_s\left(W(\vec{\omega}, x)\right) A_d\left(D(\vec{\omega}, x)\right) T\left(D(\vec{\omega}, x) + x\right) \rho(\vec{\omega}, x) dx \tag{2.4}$$

This additional constraint means that we would have expand to three dimensions the pre-integrated 2D lookup used with omnidirectional lights. This is feasible, but would potentially be much more costly in both computation time and memory bandwidth. Instead, we note that the integral in Equation (2.4) is just the spotlight attenuation factor $A_s(\vec{\omega}, x)$ multiplied by the corresponding omnidirectional light lookup (which can be expressed in two dimensions). If we expand and regroup the expression, we get the following:

$$\alpha(\vec{\omega}, x) = \frac{\vec{v} \cdot (V - L) + x\vec{v} \cdot \vec{\omega}}{D(\vec{\omega}, x)}$$

$$L_{\text{inscatter}}(\vec{\omega}, d) = L_0 \int_0^d \left(\frac{\frac{\vec{v} \cdot L\vec{V} + x\vec{v} \cdot \vec{\omega}}{D(\vec{\omega}, x)} - \beta}{1 - \beta}\right)^{n_f} L_p(\vec{\omega}, x) dx$$

Unfortunately, the falloff exponent n_f seems to make this irreducible. However, we note that the falloff power is generally of secondary importance to the appearance of a spotlight, and since its value usually lies in the range $[\frac{1}{2}, 2]$, we can approximate it by setting $n_f = 1$ and achieve plausible results. This eliminates the power term and lets us pull out additional constants:

$$\begin{aligned}L_{\text{inscatter}}(\vec{\omega}, d) &= \frac{L_0}{1-\beta} \int_0^d \left(\frac{\vec{v} \cdot \vec{LV}}{D(\vec{\omega}, x)} + \frac{x\vec{v} \cdot \vec{\omega}}{D(\vec{\omega}, x)} - \beta \right) L_p(\vec{\omega}, x) dx \\ &= \frac{L_0}{1-\beta} \left[(\vec{v} \cdot \vec{LV}) \int_0^d \frac{1}{D(\vec{\omega}, x)} L_p(\vec{\omega}, x) dx + (\vec{v} \cdot \vec{\omega}) \right. \\ &\quad \left. + \int_0^d \frac{x}{D(\vec{\omega}, x)} L_p(\vec{\omega}, x) dx - \beta \int_0^d L_p(\vec{\omega}, x) dx \right]\end{aligned}$$

By refactoring the integral this way, we reduce our previous three-dimensional lookup to the sum of three two-dimensional lookups (which will scale much better in cost) with all per-pixel varying components pulled outside the integral. Note that we can still support a more general solution with a more expensive code path for arbitrary values of n_f.

Implementation. The lookup table generation is exactly as with an omnidirectional light, except that two additional integrals are also output to separate maps. This gives us three maps in total:

$$\begin{aligned}\text{LUT}_1(\cos(\theta), d) &= \int_0^d L_p(\vec{\omega}, x) dx \\ \text{LUT}_2(\cos(\theta), d) &= \int_0^d \frac{x}{D(\vec{\omega}, x)} L_p(\vec{\omega}, x) dx \\ \text{LUT}_3(\cos(\theta), d) &= \frac{1}{D(\vec{\omega}, x)} L_p(\vec{\omega}, x) dx\end{aligned}$$

In the pixel shader, these three textures are sampled and combined, weighted based on the geometry of the scene and ray that pixel corresponds to

$$\begin{aligned}L_{\text{inscatter}}(\vec{\omega}, d) = \frac{L_0}{1-\beta} &\left[(\vec{v} \cdot \vec{LV}) \text{LUT}_1(\vec{\omega} \cdot \vec{LV}, d) \right. \\ &\left. + (\vec{v} \cdot \vec{\omega}) \text{LUT}_2(\vec{\omega} \cdot \vec{LV}, d) - \beta \text{LUT}_3(\vec{\omega} \cdot \vec{LV}, d) \right]\end{aligned}$$

Once the lookups are generated, a full-screen pre-pass computes the near/far intersection points of the pixel rays with the cone defining the spotlight, as well as other geometric values, such as the dot product between the ray direction and light axis (Listing 2.5). This is done as a pre-pass rather than in the pixel shader during volume rendering, both to reduce shading work for scenes with high occluder complexity and to reduce sources of numerical instability by removing the potential for fragment-to-fragment shading differences to propagate into noticeable noise.

```

uint4 main
    (
        PS_POLYGONAL_INPUT pi,
        uint sampleID : SV_SAMPLEINDEX,
        bool bIsFrontFace : SV_ISFRONTFACE
    ) : SV_TARGET
{
    float4 vWorldPos = pi.vWorldPos;
    float eye_dist = length(vWorldPos.xyz - g_vEyePosition.xyz);
    float3 vV = (vWorldPos.xyz - g_vEyePosition.xyz) / eye_dist;
    float3 vL = g_vLightDir.xyz;
    float3 vW = g_vEyePosition.xyz - g_vLightPos.xyz;
    float light_dist = length(vW);
    float WdotL = dot(vW, vL);
    float VdotL = dot(vV, vL);
    float t0=0, t1=1;

    if (IntersectCone(t0, t1, eye_dist, g_fLightFalloffAngle, vW, vV, vL, WdotL, VdotL))
    {
        t1 = min(t1, eye_dist);
        float WdotV_norm = dot(vW/light_dist, vV);
        return uint4(f32tof16(t0), f32tof16(t1),
                     0.5*(1+WdotV_norm)*MAX_UINT16, 0.5*(1+VdotL)*MAX_UINT16);
    }
    else
    {
        return uint4(0, 0, 0, 0);
    }
}
```

Listing 2.5. Pre-computing per-pixel ray-cone intersection parameters.

After all the lookup textures are complete, the volume itself is rendered. For spotlights, a single tessellated plane is rendered, just as with directional lights, then shaded to reconstruct the integral (Listing 2.6). Since the volume of a spotlight is finite and likely to only cover a small part of the scene (as opposed to a directional light, which would reach all the way to the far plane) the sides of the frustum enclosing the spotlight must also be rendered and shaded. Since the volume itself is actually a cone, the frustum shape is just used to generate pixel fragments for shading: the actual ray-cone intersections previously computed are used for the actual depth values. Finally, a stencil-based fill-in pass is done as with previous methods.

```

float3 Integrate_Spotlight(float eye_dist, float4 bounds, float3 vW, float3 vV,
                           float3 vL)
{
    float3 integral = 0..xxx;
    float VdotW_norm = bounds.z;
    float VdotL = bounds.w;
    float WdotL = dot(vW, vL);

    float t = min(bounds.y, max(bounds.x, eye_dist));

    if (FALLOFFMODE == FALLOFFMODE_NONE)
    {
        float light_dist = length(vW);
```

```
        float2 tc = float2( GetLutCoord_X(t, light_dist), GetLutCoord_Y(VdotW_norm) );
        integral = SampleLut(tLightLUT_P, tc);
        if (bounds.x > 0)
        {
            tc.x = GetLutCoord_X(bounds.x, light_dist);
            integral -= SampleLut(tLightLUT_P, tc);
        }
    }
    else if (FALLOFFMODE == FALLOFFMODE_FIXED)
    {
        float light_dist = length(vW);
        float2 tc = float2( GetLutCoord_X(t, light_dist), GetLutCoord_Y(VdotW_norm) );
        integral = WdotL*SampleLut(tLightLUT_S1, tc)
                       + VdotL*SampleLut(tLightLUT_S2, tc)
                       - g_fLightFalloffAngle*SampleLut(tLightLUT_P, tc);
        if (bounds.x > 0)
        {
            tc.x = GetLutCoord_X(bounds.x, light_dist);
            integral -= WdotL*SampleLut(tLightLUT_S1, tc)
                          + VdotL*SampleLut(tLightLUT_S2, tc)
                          - g_fLightFalloffAngle*SampleLut(tLightLUT_P, tc);
        }
        integral = integral/(1-g_fLightFalloffAngle);
    }
    return integral;
}
```

Listing 2.6. Function inside the pixel shader for computing the spotlight integral. Note that there is a special-case mode for no angular falloff – in this case, the spotlight integral can be evaluated essentially the same as an omnidirectional light for slightly cheaper.

Other Considerations. Unlike omnidirectional lights, spotlights can reuse most of the same volume rendering pathway as directional lights because they are restricted to a narrow range of angles, and thus the volume and visibility can be represented by a view frustum shadow map satisfactorily.

Since the viewer is likely to be able to see the illuminated volume from outside, however, we must take the additional step of rendering the frustum "cap" (the non-tessellated face) rather than applying a full-screen pass as we do for directional lights. In order to deal with the fact that our frustum exists outside the defined space of the integral (i.e., outside the maximum falloff angle) we bound the d value to analytically computed ray-cone intersection points for the view ray and spotlight volume.

2.5 Additional Optimizations

2.5.1 Downsampling and MSAA

There are no barriers to computing the volumetric lighting contribution at a lower resolution than the final framebuffer, provided the scene's depth buffer is reasonably approximated. In practice, running at one-half–dimensional resolution (one-quarter the number of pixels) of the framebuffer provides a substantial performance improvement with little or no noticeable image degradation, even with trivial upsampling.

Furthermore, although we may evaluate the volumetric lighting at a lower pixel resolution, we can take advantage of the fact that we have a higher-resolution source depth buffer and use MSAA depth and accumulation buffers internally. By populating the downsampled-but-MSAA depth buffer with information from the higher-resolution source, we can greatly improve performance with aggressive downsampling but still preserve some of the sharpness at feature edges.

2.5.2 Temporal Antialiasing

Since the effect itself is physically stable, temporal antialiasing can be used to improve quality during the upsample-and-composite pass. Note that we have to be careful about flicker induced by jitter of the base framebuffer, since down-sampling would magnify any flicker to a larger footprint than the final full-frame filtering pass could handle. Doing temporal antialiasing internally reduces that, as well as smoothing out flicker induced by small occluders that may alternate in and out of visibility in the down-sampled depth due to under-sampling.

2.6 Results

2.6.1 Performance

Table 2.1 contains performance numbers from a sample application, with costs broken down for different light types at each step in the algorithm. These measurements were taken on a GeForce GTX 1080 rendering a scene to a 1440p framebuffer. Internally, the volumetric lighting system was running at half resolution (i.e., one-quarter of the total number of pixels) but at 2× MSAA to hide artifacts.

The "Setup and Downsampling" stage simply clears the internal buffers, generates the phase function look-up texture, and makes a copy of the scene depth buffer at the appropriate down-sample and MSAA settings. Thus, it is fairly inexpensive, varying minorly with resolution/downsampling level.

Light Type	Setup	LUT Generation	Volume Rendering	Resolve and Composite	Total Time
Directional	0.09 ms	N/A	0.35 ms	1.28 ms	1.72 ms
Spot	0.09 ms	0.09 ms	0.82 ms	1.24 ms	2.24 ms
Omnidirectional	0.09 ms	0.03 ms	0.94 ms	1.24 ms	2.30 ms

Table 2.1. Performance of various light types on a GTX 1080 at 1440p resolution, using a half-resolution internal buffer at 2 × MSAA. The look-up textures for the omnidirectional and spot lights were 256 × 512.

The "LUT Generation" stage performs the per-light look-up texture generation for omnidirectional and spot lights (it is not done for directional lights). This will be done once per light and should have a constant cost for the light type (more expensive for spot lights than omnidirectional ones).

The "Volume Rendering" stage does the necessary per-light setup and then renders the volume mesh for the light into the scene to accumulate the lighting.

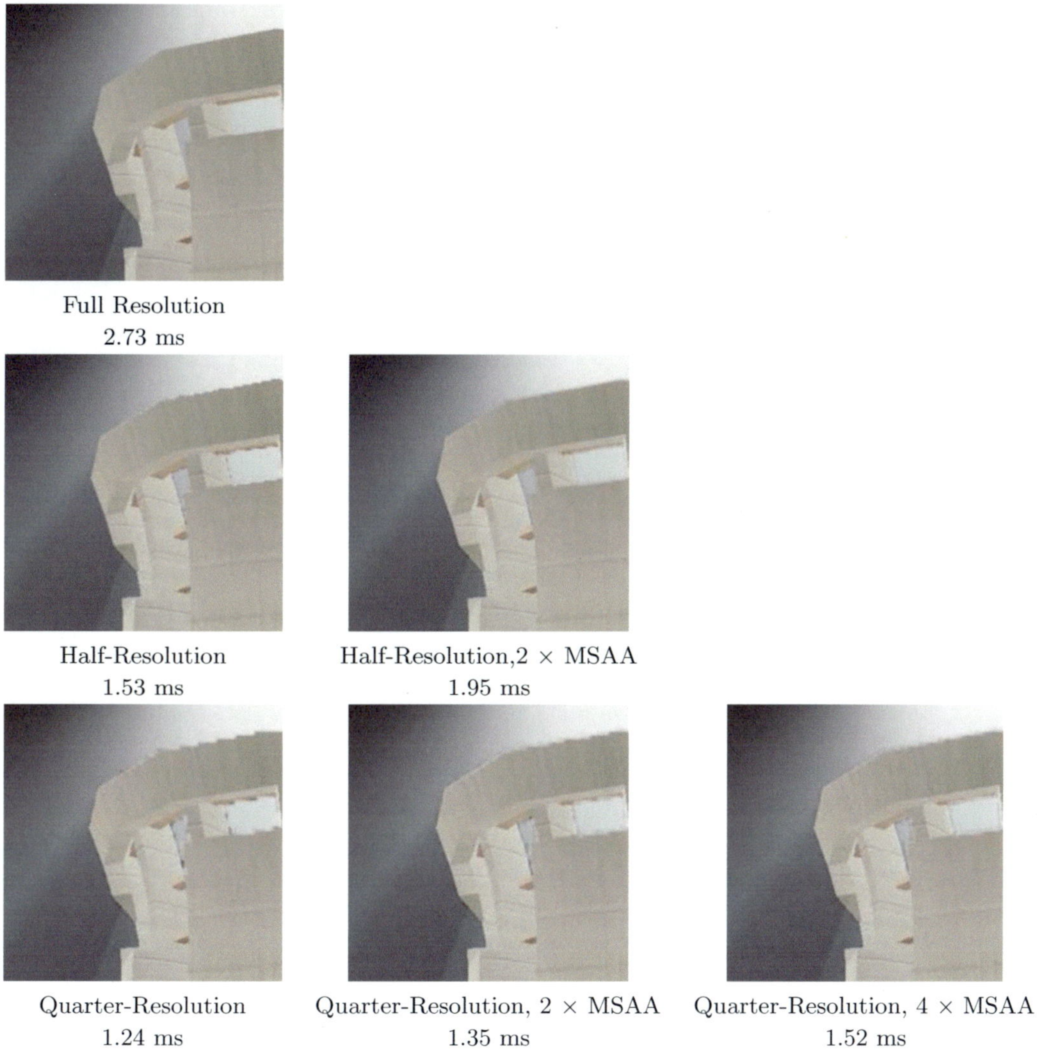

Figure 2.9. Comparison images for a scene rendered with different down-sampling and MSAA settings. Performance numbers are at 1440p base resolution on a GTX 1080.

This happens once for every light in the scene. This cost will tend to vary with the total fill-rate of the rendered volume: simple volumes with a large screen-space coverage and complex volumes with a small screen footprint will tend to be cheaper, while volumes with a lot of overlapping depth complexity (such as due to high-frequency occluders) will tend to be more expensive. Because of this, performance can in some cases be very view-dependant depending on the orientation of the light and camera.

Finally, the "Resolve and Composite" stage resolves any MSAA or temporal sampling (if needed) to a single output buffer and then up-samples that and composites it with the rendered scene. This cost will vary greatly with the native framebuffer resolution and requested down-sampling and MSAA settings; however, even though more aggressive down-sampling tends to increase cost here, that cost is usually offset by much greater savings in the volume-rendering pass. One can think of this as trading off image quality for better average performance and more bounded worst-case performance.

Using MSAA for the internal downsampled depth and accumulation buffers provides substantial image quality benefits for modest additional cost. In Figure 2.9, we show the same section of a frame illuminated with a volumetric spotlight using full-, half-, and quarter-framebuffer resolution internally with 1, 2, and 4 MSAA samples per pixel. As can be seen looking at the non-MSAA cases, the effect is very susceptible to aliasing around the areas where the light volumes intersect scene geometry, or at the edge of sharp volumetric shadows (despite the volumetric light itself being fairly low frequency). By using MSAA depth, we preserve much of the higher resolution detail without additional shading costs, recovering much of the quality lost when moving down in resolution.

With a one-half framebuffer resolution at 2 × MSAA, we produce what is arguably comparable quality to the full-resolution effect roughly 30% faster. The improvements begin to strain at one-quarter resolution, but even the 2×- and 4 ×-MSAA cases show dramatic improvements in quality for modest increases in performance. Additionally, even though the quarter-resolution 4 × MSAA-case may look roughly similar in both quality and cost as the half-resolution case, this cost is balanced differently: at lower resolution and higher MSAA level, more of the workload happens in the static-cost sections (internal buffer resolve) rather than the view-dependant ones (volume rendering) than an equivalent-quality set of settings at a higher resolution. This provides for better overall framerate consistency as it reduces the cost of "worst-case" scenes.

2.6.2 Examples

Figures 2.10, 2.11 and 2.12 each show examples of this technique being put to use in published games. The images from *Fallout 4* (Figure 2.10) show how different light and media settings can create distinct moods within the same scene. Figure 2.11 shows how the technique can be used for both subtle effects, such as showing light dappling through trees, as well as in more dramatic scenes

Figure 2.10. Scenes from *Fallout 4* showing the final image (left) and the contribution from the volumetric lighting (right).

like light streaming into a dusty room. Finally, Figure 2.12 shows how the atmospheric lighting can be used to either magnify the apparent brightness of an intense source like the sun or to add an impression of directionality to a scene that might otherwise seem too hazy and uniform such as a foggy moon-lit night.

Figure 2.11. Screenshots from *Far Cry 4*, showing both indoor and outdoor scenes.

Figure 2.12. Screenshots from *Assassin's Creed IV Black Flag*, showing volumetric lighting from the sun during daytime (left) and from the moon during nighttime (right).

2.7 Summary

2.7.1 Strengths and Weaknesses

While the technique presented in this chapter does rely on certain assumptions about the scene, these assumptions are generally not onerous and we still produce a result that is both plausible and evocative, and at a level of performance comparable or better than other state-of-the-art techniques.

Since the volume extrusion technique uses light-view information, we are able to account for occluders that lie outside the view frustum. This allows for an entire class of media and scattering effects which are not realizable with screen-space techniques and which would be costly to render at high quality for ray-marching techniques.

The main advantage, however, is that this method provides a highly efficient form of importance sampling. Unlike other numerical integration-based approaches, this technique will only evaluate the minimum number of steps per pixel required to realize the shadows that cross that pixel's path. This allows for much better best- and average-case performance, allowing the volumetric lighting to be computed at much higher resolution. In practice, the system is able to produce good results with acceptable performance for samples with 4×4, 2×2, and even 1×1 framebuffer pixel footprints. This is $4\times$–$64\times$ sharper than modern ray-marching or voxel-based approaches for similar performance. Additionally, since the workload is dominated primarily by how much each light's volume overlaps the view frustum, this technique is able to render scenes with a large number of visible volumetric casters with minimal additional cost (provided they do not overlap significantly). This makes it readily compatible with modern light-dense deferred and clustered renderers.

Due to the homogenous media assumption, the extruded-volume approach as presented is not able to account for phenomena like ground fog and transient dust clouds, nor is it able to be extended to a full-sky simulation including clouds, etc. Some of these factors (like ground fog and the exponential density distribution of atmospheric particles) could be accounted for by creating analytical models and including them in the integrals being solved. However, ultimately the "interval-integration" technique this algorithm exploits assumes that the visibility function is binary and that we have a continuous integral from $[0, \max Z]$ to reference. Scene components which cannot be expressed analytically (such as arbitrary dust clouds) must somehow be incorporated into this integral, requiring something closer to the general numerical integration approaches used by other methods such as ray marching and froxels.

2.7.2 Practical Considerations

Shadow-Map Consistency. Since the extruded volume is derived explicitly from a shadow map, artifacts will be very noticeable if the objects rendered to the shadow map do not correspond to the scene. In general, these are all situations that would cause problems for normal shadows as well; however, often these issues might go unnoticed because the problematic occluder is not in the same view as the receiver, and so a user might not notice the incongruity. Since volumetric lighting effectively turns the entire light path into a receiver, every occluder now has a potential receiver immediately adjacent to it, making any such error immediately detectable.

Virtual Reality. With the dawn of virtual reality, there's a fresh need for rendering techniques that do not rely on a single view-perspective in order to function correctly. Typically, this means screen-space techniques do not work so well in VR—and, as such, the commonly used radial-blur–based technique for rendering volumetric light rays [Mitchell 2005] is no longer a good fit, as the effect begins to break down when extreme differences in parallax are present between two stereoscopic views. As the method presented in this chapter is physically stable in worldspace—and has no screenspace component—it can be rendered to a HMD output without any artifacts present.

2.7.3 Sample Code

Source code for a reference implementation of the technique in this chapter is available at https://github.com/NVIDIAGameWorks/VolumetricLighting.

Access to this sample requires that the user be logged into a GitHub account, and that the user agree to the GameWorks EULA by registering their account with the NVIDIA Registered Developer program: https://developer.nvidia.com/programs/gamedev/register.

Bibliography

BEER, A. 1852. Bestimmung der absorption des rothen lichts in farbigen flssigkeiten (determination of the absorption of red light in colored liquids). *Annalen der Physik und Chemie 86*, 78–88.

BILLETER, M., SINTORN, E., AND ASSARSSON, U. 2010. Real time volumetric shadows using polygonal light volumes. In *Proceedings of the Conference on High Performance Graphics*, Eurographics Association, Aire-la-Ville, Switzerland, HPG '10, 39–45.

CHANDRASEKHAR, S. 1960. *Radiative Transfer.* Dover Publications Inc. (reprint Oxford University Press), New York.

DUDASH, B., 2012. Dynamic hardware tessellation basics. URL: https://developer.nvidia.com/content/dynamic-hardware-tessellation-basics.

KAJIYA, J. T. 1986. The rendering equation. *SIGGRAPH Comput. Graph. 20*, 4, 143–150.

LAMBERT, J. H. 1760. *Photometria sive de mensura et gradibus luminis, colorum et umbrae (Photometry, or, On the measure and gradations of light, colors, and shade).* Eberhardt Klett, Augsburg, Germany.

MADAMS, T., 2011. Light attenuation. URL: https://imdoingitwrong.wordpress.com/2011/01/31/light-attenuation/.

MCCOOL, M. 2000. Shadow volume reconstruction from depth maps. *ACM Trans. Graph. 19*, 1, 1–26.

MITCHELL, K. 2005. Volumetric light scattering as a post-process. In *GPU Gems 3*, H. Nguyen, Ed. Addison-Wesley Professional, Reading, MA. URL: http://http.developer.nvidia.com/GPUGems3/gpugems3_ch13.html.

PEGORARO, V., SCHOTT, M., AND SLUSALLEK, P. 2011. A mathematical framework for efficient closed-form single scattering. In *Proceedings of Graphics Interface 2011*, Canadian Human-Computer Communications Society, Waterloo, Ontario, Canada, GI '11, 151–158.

PHARR, M., AND HUMPHREYS, G. 2004. *Physically Based Rendering: From Theory to Implementation.* Morgan Kaufmann, San Francisco.

SUN, B., RAMAMOORTHI, R., NARASIMHAN, S. G., AND NAYAR, S. K. 2005. A practical analytic single scattering model for real time rendering. *ACM Trans. Graph. 24*, 3, 1040–1049.

WYMAN, C., AND RAMSEY, S. 2008. Interactive volumetric shadows in participating media with single-scattering. In *IEEE Symposium on Interactive Ray Tracing, 2008*, IEEE Computer, Los Alamitos, CA, 87–92.

III Rendering

Real-time rendering is an exciting and challenging field. It spans many disciplines and is limited by real-time constraints and a diverse hardware ecosystem ranging from mobile to high-end PCs and virtual reality (VR) displays.

The field is constantly evolving and new techniques are being developed that expand the boundaries of what was previously considered possible to do in real-time. It really is an exciting time to be in this industry and the articles in this section are a reflection of its diverse nature.

"Deferred+: Next-Gen Culling and Rendering for Dawn Engine" by Hawar Doghramachi and Jean-Normand Bucci presents a very in-depth description of a GPU-based culling and rendering system that is capable of handling complex scenes in real time. In addition, the authors cover many of the practical issues and tradeoffs made during development along with a detailed performance comparison with clustered forward rendering. This is a must-read for anyone considering or interested in a GPU-based approach to culling and rendering.

"Programmable Per-pixel Sample Placement with Conservative Rasterizer" by Rahul P. Sathe describes a novel use of the new conservative rasterization capabilities of modern graphics hardware to generate unique sample locations within a pixel. The chapter covers the issues encountered with clipped triangles using this approach and discusses the application of the technique to foveated rendering in VR.

"Mobile Toon Shading" by Felipe Lira, Flávio Villalva, Jesus Sosa, Kléverson Paixão and Teófilo Dutra presents an approach to non-photorealistic rendering (NPR). NPR is interesting in the sense that challenges are generally artistic rather than technical in nature. The authors discuss the evolution of their artistic style and the implementation of their chosen techniques. In addition, they have provided a Unity project so that the reader can see the final results from the combination of their techniques.

"High Quality GPU-efficient Image Detail Manipulation" by Kin-Ming Wong and Tien-Tsin Wong describes a new edge-preserving filter named the "Sub-window Variance Filter" and its application to image detail manipulation. The results are compelling, and the authors provide a full sample application with source code so you can see for yourself.

"Profiling and Optimizing WebGL Applications Using Google Chrome" by Gareth Morgan covers profiling and optimization of WebGL applications focusing on the profiling tools available in the Google Chrome web browser. The article also provides a brief history of WebGL along with several optimization case studies.

"Linear-Light Shading with Linearly Transformed Cosines" by Eric Heitz and Stephen Hill extends their previous work on real-time area-light shading of polygonal light sources with a faster approximation for *linear* (line-shaped) lights. The article covers the mathematics in detail along with concise shader listings. The authors have also provided a WebGL demo application which showcases their technique.

I hope that you enjoy reading these articles and that you find them useful in your own research and projects, either directly or through any inspiration or ideas they provide.

—Mark Chatfield

1

III

Deferred+: Next-Gen Culling and Rendering for the Dawn Engine

Hawar Doghramachi and Jean-Normand Bucci

1.1 Introduction

We present a comprehensive system for culling and rendering complex scenes in real time that we developed internally for future use in the Dawn Engine. This was one of several research projects done by the Eidos-Montréal R&D team, named Labs, but the system is not used in the game *Deus Ex: Mankind Divided.* The main goal of our research was to develop a system that could satisfy the growing demands on visual fidelity and runtime performance, but one that would remain compatible with traditional game assets and allow for fast iteration times during game production.

Our culling system combines the low latency and low overhead of a hierarchical depth buffer-based approach [Hill and Collin 2011] with the pixel accuracy of conventional GPU hardware occlusion queries. It efficiently culls highly dynamic, complex environments while maintaining compatibility with standard mesh assets. Our rendering system uses a practical approach to the idea of deferred texturing [Reed 2014] and efficiently supports highly diverse and complex materials while using conventional texture assets. Both parts of the proposed system make use of new graphics capabilities available with DirectX 12, most notably enhanced indirect rendering and the new shader resource binding model.

1.2 Overview

For real-time rendering applications like video games, it is crucial to employ an efficient occlusion culling system in order to be able to render large environments while ensuring high interactive frame rates. Traditional CPU-based culling systems, for example portal culling, fail to support dynamic, complex, alpha-tested occluders, and they are, therefore, not well-suited for such environments. Our culling system is partially based on the ideas presented by [Haar and Aaltonen 2015], where the depth buffer from the previous frame is used to acquire an initial visibility, and potential false negatives are retested with the updated depth buffer from the current frame. In this way, we avoid rendering dedicated occlusion geometry, which may be difficult to generate; for example, natural environments. However, instead of using a hierarchical depth buffer-based approach, a concept is utilized in the spirit of [Kubisch and Tavenrath 2014] that relies on the early depth-stencil testing capability of modern consumer graphics hardware. The main idea is to rasterize the boundaries of the occludees with the dedicated graphics hardware using a down-sampled and re-projected depth buffer from the prior frame. By forcing the associated pixel-shader to use early depth-stencil testing, only visible fragments mark in a common GPU buffer, at a location unique for each mesh instance, that the corresponding instance is visible. In comparison to a hierarchical depth buffer-based approach, this provides significantly higher culling efficiency with non-clustered, standard mesh assets. A subsequent compute shader generates, from the acquired visibility information, the data which is used later on for indirect rendering. As proposed by [Haar and Aaltonen 2015], occluded objects are retested with the updated depth buffer from the current frame to avoid missing false negatives.

For modern games, it is also important to utilize a rendering system that can handle increasingly complex mesh geometry and realistic surface materials. Forward rendering systems support high material diversity, but they either suffer from overdraw or require a depth pre-pass, which can be expensive for meshes with high triangle counts, GPU hardware tessellation, alpha-testing, or vertex-shader skinning. Deferred rendering systems manage to run efficiently without a depth pre-pass, but only support a limited range of materials and, therefore, often require additional forward rendering for more diverse materials. Our practical approach to deferred texturing combines the strengths of both rendering systems by supporting a high material diversity while only performing a single geometry pass. We go one step further than traditional deferred rendering and completely decouple geometry from materials and lighting. In an initial geometry pass, all mesh instances that pass the GPU culling stage are rendered indirectly, and their vertex attributes are written, compressed, into a set of geometry buffers. No material-specific operations and texture fetches are done (except for alpha testing and certain kinds of GPU hardware-tessellation techniques). A subsequent full-screen pass transfers a material ID from the geometry buffers into a 16-bit depth buffer. Finally, in the shading pass for each material, a screen-space rectangle is rendered that encloses the boundaries of all visible meshes. The depth of the rectangle vertices is set to a value that corresponds to the currently processed material ID and uses early depth-stencil testing to reject pixels from other materials. All standard materials that use the same shader and resource-binding layout are rendered in a single pass via dynamically indexed textures. At this point, material-specific rendering and lighting (e.g., tiled [M. Billeter and Assarsson 2013] or clustered [Olsson et al. 2012]) are done simultaneously.

1.3 Implementation

In the following sections, each step of the system will be described in detail. The explanations are assuming the use of DirectX 12, but the system could be also implemented with OpenGL or Vulkan. No graphics hardware specific assumptions are made and the supplied shader code is hardware agnostic.

1.3.1 Culling

The culling part of the system can be subdivided into two passes, each consisting of several distinct steps (Figure 1.1). We decided to use instancing instead of a flattened mesh list. Even though draw calls will be generated on the GPU, internal tests showed that instancing, paired with a compacted indirect draw buffer, reduced GPU times for rendering geometry into the geometry buffers by approximately 45%.

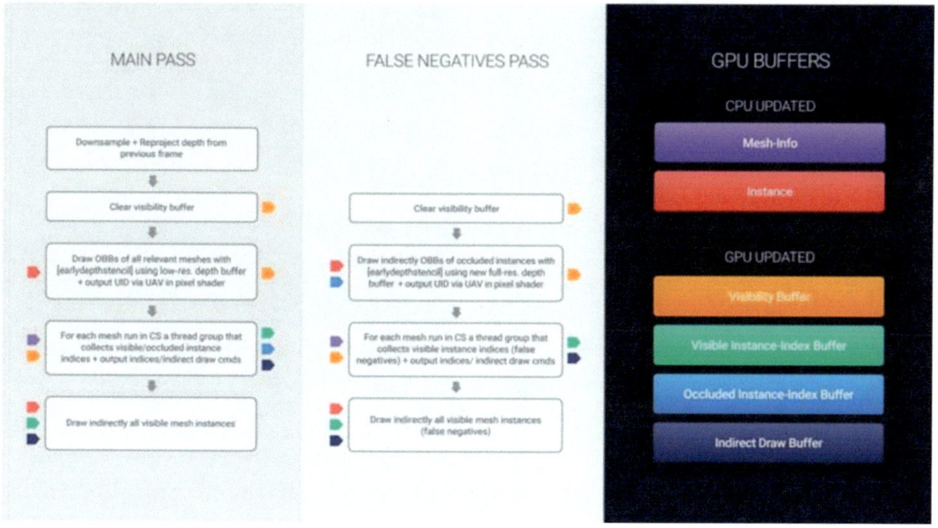

Figure 1.1. Overview of each step involved in the culling system. Grey blocks on the left side represent each culling step, blocks on the right side illustrate the required GPU resources. Arrows on the left side of each culling step represent input data, arrows on the right side output data. The colors match with those of the corresponding GPU buffers.

Main pass. The first pass acquires an initial visibility and can be subdivided into 5 distinct steps.

Depth buffer down-sampling and re-projection. In order to accelerate the algorithm, the depth buffer from the previous frame is first down-sampled to quarter resolution by taking, conservatively, the maximum value of 4 × 4 pixel areas. We found further down-sampling of the depth buffer did not provide any notable performance improvement and deteriorated culling efficiency. Since large planar objects can cause false self-occlusion, the down-sampled depth buffer is re-projected to the current frame. This is done by scattering the re-projected depth values to new pixel locations via atomic max operations on an unordered access view (UAV). Unfortunately, at high camera motion this produces holes that significantly lower culling efficiency. To close such holes, the re-projected depth values are additionally written to the currently processed pixel locations. Large re-projected depth values behind the camera can be an additional source of holes; in that case we use the non-re-projected depth from the last frame. In this way, high culling efficiency can be achieved even under high camera motion while false self-occlusion is significantly reduced (Figure 1.2).

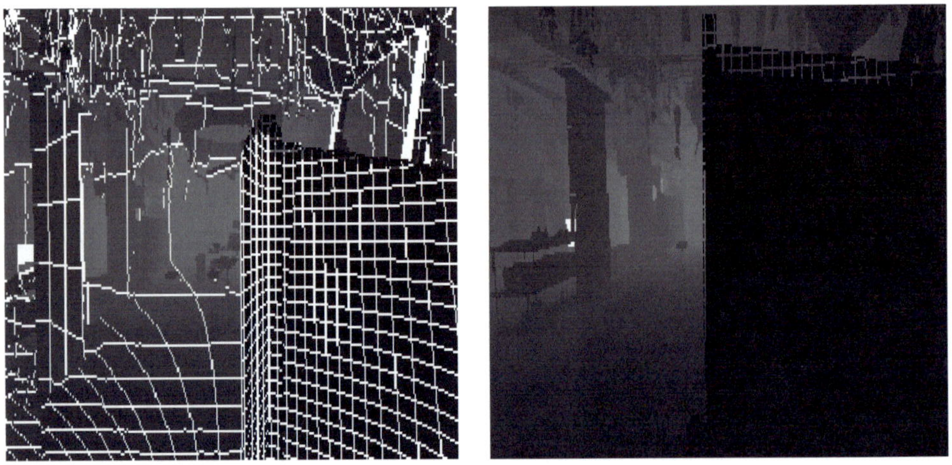

Figure 1.2. The left image shows the down-sampled, re-projected depth buffer from the last frame with many holes, significantly deteriorating culling efficiency. The right image shows how the proposed measures close such holes.

Listing 1.1 shows the HLSL code for a compute shader that down-samples and re-projects the depth buffer from the last frame. Since UAVs are not supported on depth buffers, the down-sampled and re-projected depth values are first written into a color buffer and then copied into the final depth buffer.

```
[numthreads(REPROJECT_THREAD_GROUP_SIZE, REPROJECT_THREAD_GROUP_SIZE, 1)]
void main(uint3 dispatchThreadID : SV_DispatchThreadID)
{
  if((dispatchThreadID.x < (uint(SCREEN_WIDTH)/4)) && (dispatchThreadID.y <
     (uint(SCREEN_HEIGHT)/4)))
  {
    const float2 screenSize = float2(SCREEN_WIDTH/4.0f, SCREEN_HEIGHT/4.0f);
    float2 texCoords = (float2(dispatchThreadID.xy) + float2(0.5f, 0.5f))/screenSize;

    const float offsetX = 1.0f/SCREEN_WIDTH;
    const float offsetY = 1.0f/SCREEN_HEIGHT;

    // down-sample depth (gather and max operations can be replaced by using a max
    // sampler if device supports MinMaxFiltering)
    float4 depthValues00 = depthMap.GatherRed(depthMapSampler, texCoords +
                           float2(-offsetX, -offsetY));
    float depth = max( max( max(depthValues00.x, depthValues00.y), depthValues00.z ),
                       depthValues00.w);

    float4 depthValues10 = depthMap.GatherRed(depthMapSampler, texCoords +
                           float2(offsetX, -offsetY));
    depth = max( max( max( max(depthValues10.x, depthValues10.y), depthValues10.z ),
                 depthValues10.w), depth);

    float4 depthValues01 = depthMap.GatherRed(depthMapSampler, texCoords +
                           float2(-offsetX, offsetY));
    depth = max( max( max( max(depthValues01.x, depthValues01.y), depthValues01.z ),
                 depthValues01.w), depth);

    float4 depthValues11 = depthMap.GatherRed(depthMapSampler, texCoords +
                           float2(offsetX, offsetY));
    depth = max( max( max( max(depthValues11.x, depthValues11.y), depthValues11.z ),
                 depthValues11.w), depth);

    // reconstruct world-space position of last frame from down-sampled depth
    float4 lastProjPosition = float4(texCoords, depth, 1.0f);
    lastProjPosition.xy = (lastProjPosition.xy * 2.0f) - 1.0f;
    lastProjPosition.y = -lastProjPosition.y;
    float4 position = mul(cameraCB.lastInvViewProjMatrix, lastProjPosition);
    position /= position.w;

    // calculate projected position of current frame
    float4 projPosition = mul(cameraCB.viewProjMatrix, position);
    projPosition.xyz /= projPosition.w;
    projPosition.y = -projPosition.y;
    projPosition.xy = (projPosition.xy*0.5f) + 0.5f;
    int2 outputPos = int2(saturate(projPosition.xy) * screenSize);

    // prevent output of large depth values behind camera
    float depthF = (projPosition.w < 0.0f) ? depth : projPosition.z;

    // Convert depth into UINT for atomic max operation. Since bound color buffer is
    // initialized to zero, first invert depth, perform atomic max, and then
    // invert depth back when copied into final depth buffer.
    uint invDepth = asuint(saturate(1.0f - depthF));

    // write re-projected depth to new location
    InterlockedMax(depthTexture[outputPos], invDepth);

    // write re-projected depth to current location to handle holes from re-projection
    InterlockedMax(depthTexture[dispatchThreadID.xy], invDepth);
  }
}
```

Listing 1.1. Compute shader for down-sampling and re-projecting depth buffer from last frame.

Clear visibility buffer. The visibility buffer is a global structured buffer that is used to keep track of the visibility of all processed mesh instances. We avoid atomic memory operations in the next step by using a 32-bit UINT for each mesh instance in the visibility buffer. This leaves 31 bits per entry unused; however, even a visibility buffer that can handle one million mesh instances will consume only 4 MB of GPU memory, which results in a very good performance-memory trade-off. The entries of the visibility buffer are cleared to zero either by using the dedicated UAV clear API of DirectX 12 or by manually running a simple compute shader over the buffer.

Fill visibility buffer. In this step the oriented bounding boxes (OBBs) of all mesh instances, that passed frustum culling on the CPU, are rendered in a single indexed instanced draw call using the down-sampled, re-projected depth buffer from the previous step for depth testing. The associated pixel shader is flagged with [earlydepthstencil] so that only passed fragments will write, with the help of an UAV, to the unique mesh instance location in the visibility buffer. By avoiding atomic operations and ROPs, fast execution times can be achieved. Listing 1.2 shows the vertex and pixel shader for filling the visibility buffer.

```
// vertex shader
VS_Output main(uint vertexID: SV_VertexID, uint instanceID: SV_InstanceID)
{
  VS_Output output;

  output.occludeeID = instanceID;

  // generate unit cube position
  float3 position = float3(((vertexID & 0x4) == 0) ? -1.0f : 1.0f,
                           ((vertexID & 0x2) == 0) ? -1.0f : 1.0f,
                           ((vertexID & 0x1) == 0) ? -1.0f : 1.0f);

  matrix instanceMatrix = instanceBuffer[output.occludeeID];
  float4 positionWS = mul(instanceMatrix, float4(position, 1.0f));
  output.position = mul(cameraCB.viewProjMatrix, positionWS);

  // When camera is inside the bounding box, it is possible that the bounding box is
  // fully occluded even when the object itself is visible. Therefore, bounding box
  // vertices behind the near plane are clamped in front of the near plane to avoid
  // culling such objects.
  output.position = (output.position.w < 0.0f) ? float4(clamp(output.position.xy,
    float2(-0.999f, -0.999f), float2(0.999f, 0.999f)), 0.0001f, 1.0f)
     : output.position;

  return output;
}

// pixel shader
[earlydepthstencil]
void main(VS_Output input)
{
  visBuffer[input.occludeeID] = 1;
}
```

Listing 1.2. Vertex and pixel shader for filling visibility buffer.

OBBs are rendered using a second instance buffer, where each instance matrix is pre-combined with a scale/ bias matrix that transforms a unit axis-aligned bounding box (AABB) into the mesh AABB before the actual instance transform is applied. Since rendering instanced meshes with a low triangle count used to be suboptimal [Bilodeau 2014], we tried to render all OBBs in a single draw call without instancing. At an overall bounding-box count of approximately 7000 it turned out that this approach is slightly slower than the instanced approach (tested on a NVIDIA Geforce GTX 970). Therefore, we decided to render bounding boxes with instancing.

As with conventional hardware occlusion queries, it is possible that when the camera is inside the bounding box of an occludee that the corresponding mesh occludes its own bounding box, leading to false occlusion (Figure 1.3). Therefore, bounding box vertices behind the camera near plane are clamped directly in front of the camera near plane, in order to ensure that such objects are always marked as visible.

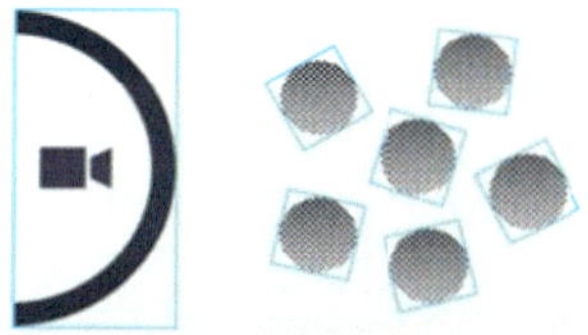

Figure 1.3. Since the object to the left occludes its own bounding box, the corresponding mesh is not rendered and is therefore missing in the updated depth buffer. Because the updated depth buffer doesn't contain this major occluder, almost all occluded objects to the right will be marked as visible and rendered later on.

Instead of using auto-computed bounding boxes, with the help of `ExecuteIndirect` it is also possible to optionally use artist-created meshes with a low triangle count to better approximate the shape of the meshes to be culled.

Generating indirect draw information. For each relevant mesh (at least one instance-passed frustum culling on the CPU), a compute shader thread group is dispatched. Each thread in the group checks the previously generated visibility buffer to see if the corresponding mesh instance is visible. Indices for all visible instances are written into the visible instance-index buffer, and for all occluded instances, into the occluded instance-index buffer. Additionally, if at least one instance of a mesh is found to be visible, a new indirect draw command is written into the indirect draw buffer. In order to support multiple mesh types (opaque, alpha-tested, tessellated, skinned, etc.), that require a different shader to efficiently fill the geometry buffers, indirect draw commands are written into the indirect draw buffer from a mesh type specific offset. The number of indirect draw commands for each mesh type is accumulated into separate entries at the beginning of the visible instance-index buffer, and the number of occluded instances is written into the `InstanceCount` member of the first indirect draw command. This is used later on to render all occluded bounding boxes indirectly at once, to test for false negatives. These buffer entries have to be cleared before the compute shader is dispatched that generates the indirect draw information (Listing 1.3).

```
#define THREAD_GROUP_SIZE 64

groupshared uint visibleInstanceIndexCounter;

[numthreads(THREAD_GROUP_SIZE, 1, 1)]
void main(uint3 groupID: SV_GroupID, uint groupIndex: SV_GroupIndex,
          uint3 dispatchThreadID : SV_DispatchThreadID)
{
  if(groupIndex == 0)
  {
    visibleInstanceIndexCounter = 0;
  }
  GroupMemoryBarrierWithGroupSync();


  MeshInfo meshInfo = meshInfoBuffer[groupID.x];
  for(uint i=0; i<meshInfo.numInstances; i+=THREAD_GROUP_SIZE)
  {
    uint elementIndex = groupIndex + i;
    if(elementIndex < meshInfo.numInstances)
    {
      uint instanceIndex = meshInfo.instanceOffset + elementIndex;
      if(visBuffer[instanceIndex] > 0)
      {
        uint index;
        InterlockedAdd(visibleInstanceIndexCounter, 1, index);
        visibleInstanceIndexBuffer[meshInfo.instanceOffset+index+NUM_FILL_PASS_TYPES] =
          instanceIndex;
      }
      else
      {
        // Occluded instances will be rendered as occludees to determine false
        // negatives.
        uint index;
        InterlockedAdd(drawIndirectBuffer[0].instanceCount, 1, index);
        occludedInstanceIndexBuffer[index] = instanceIndex;
      }
    }
  }
  GroupMemoryBarrierWithGroupSync();


  if(groupIndex == 0)
  {
    if(visibleInstanceIndexCounter > 0)
    {
      // Increment counter of visible meshes.
      uint cmdIndex;
      InterlockedAdd(visibleInstanceIndexBuffer[meshInfo.meshType], 1, cmdIndex);
      cmdIndex += meshInfo.meshTypeOffset + 1;

```

```
      // Visible instances will be rendered directly as meshes into GBuffers.
      DrawIndirectCmd cmd;
      cmd.instanceOffset = meshInfo.instanceOffset;
      cmd.materialID = meshInfo.materialID;
      cmd.indexCountPerInstance = meshInfo.numIndices;
      cmd.instanceCount = visibleInstanceIndexCounter;
      cmd.startIndexLocation = meshInfo.firstIndex;
      cmd.baseVertexLocation = 0;
      cmd.startInstanceLocation = 0;
      drawIndirectBuffer[cmdIndex] = cmd;
    }
  }
}
```

Listing 1.3. Compute shader for generating indirect draw information.

Render indirectly visible meshes. In this step, all visible mesh instances are rendered into the geometry buffers, used later on for material rendering and lighting. For each mesh type (opaque, alpha-tested, tessellated, skinned, etc.), a separate `ExecuteIndirect` command is issued, using the previously generated indirect draw buffer as source for indirect draw calls. For each `ExecuteIndirect` command, the corresponding mesh type specific offset from the previous step is used as an offset into the indirect draw buffer, and the corresponding entry at the beginning of the visible instance-index buffer is used to specify the number of indirect calls. With the help of the visible instance-index buffer for each mesh instance, the transformation matrix can be retrieved from the instance buffer. It is necessary that each vertex knows at which offset to start reading from the visible instance-index buffer. This information is provided by a root constant parameter, specified at the beginning of each indirect draw command. A second root constant parameter provides the material ID, which is required to be written into the geometry buffers for subsequent rendering. Listing 1.4 shows the vertex shader that is used for rendering.

```
VS_Output main(VS_Input input, uint instanceID: SV_InstanceID)
{
  VS_Output output;

  uint instanceIndex = instanceInfoCB.instanceOffset + instanceID;

  // first members of buffer are counters for visible indirect draw commands
  instanceIndex = visibleInstanceIndexBuffer[instanceIndex + NUM_MESH_TYPES];

  matrix transformMatrix = instanceBuffer[instanceIndex].transformMatrix;
  ...
}
```

Listing 1.4. Vertex shader for rendering indirectly visible meshes.

False negatives pass. Since, in the main pass, visibility culling is performed using the down-sampled, re-projected depth buffer from the last frame, false negatives can occur. The first obvious reason for this are errors introduced by re-projecting information obtained from the previous frame. The second reason is that, due to performance considerations, bounding boxes are rendered in the first occlusion pass at quarter resolution. Thus, it is possible that very small bounding boxes in screen space fail to be rasterized and, therefore, the corresponding objects will be marked as occluded (Figure 1.4).

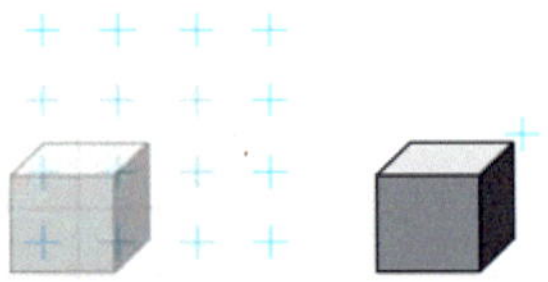

Figure 1.4. Very small bounding boxes in screen space can fail to be rasterized at quarter resolution.

To prevent such objects being incorrectly culled, potential false negatives have to be checked against a full resolution depth buffer. In theory, with conservative rasterization, the second occlusion pass could use a quarter resolution depth buffer too. However, we tested this approach and encountered multiple problems:

- The graphics card we used for testing (NVIDIA GeForce GTX 970, second generation Maxwell architecture) only supports tier 1 of conservative rasterization. Unfortunately, tier 1 culls very small triangles that get degenerated due to sub-pixel grid snapping, thus potentially culling visible objects. Moreover, tier 1 has a very large uncertainty region (half of the size of a pixel), leading to over-conservativeness and significantly lower culling efficiency. Though these problems are addressed by tier 2, at the time of writing, Intel's Skylake architecture was the only one supporting this tier.

- In our tests at 1920 × 1080 screen resolution, the time taken to down-sample the current depth buffer to quarter resolution was higher than the benefit obtained from using a quarter resolution depth buffer with conservative rasterization for the second occlusion pass. Therefore, the second occlusion pass uses the depth buffer from the current frame at full resolution, obtained after rendering the visible meshes in the first occlusion pass, to detect false negatives and can be subdivided into 4 distinct steps.

Clear visibility buffer. As was done in the main occlusion pass, the entries of the visibility buffer are cleared to zero.

Fill visibility buffer. Analog to the main occlusion pass, the OBBs of all occluded mesh instances are rendered in a single indexed instanced draw call. But this time, rendering is done indirectly using the first entry of the indirect draw buffer that was reserved for occluded objects. With the help of the occluded instance-index buffer, the transformation matrices can be retrieved from the instance buffer in order to transform the bounding boxes. As in the main occlusion pass, the pixel shader marks each instance as visible in the visibility buffer if at least one fragment passes the early depth-stencil test. As described above, the depth buffer of the current frame is used at full resolution for depth testing. It is not necessary to execute the clamping code for bounding-box vertices behind the camera near plane, since all problematic objects were rendered anyway in the first pass.

Generate indirect draw information. Indirect draw information is generated as in the main occlusion pass. However, this time only visible instance draw information is generated, as no further processing is required for occluded instances.

Render indirectly false negatives. This step doesn't differ from the corresponding step in the main occlusion pass and ensures that only occluded objects are culled by the proposed system.

1.3.2 Rendering

The rendering part of the system can be subdivided into 3 distinct steps (Figure 1.5).

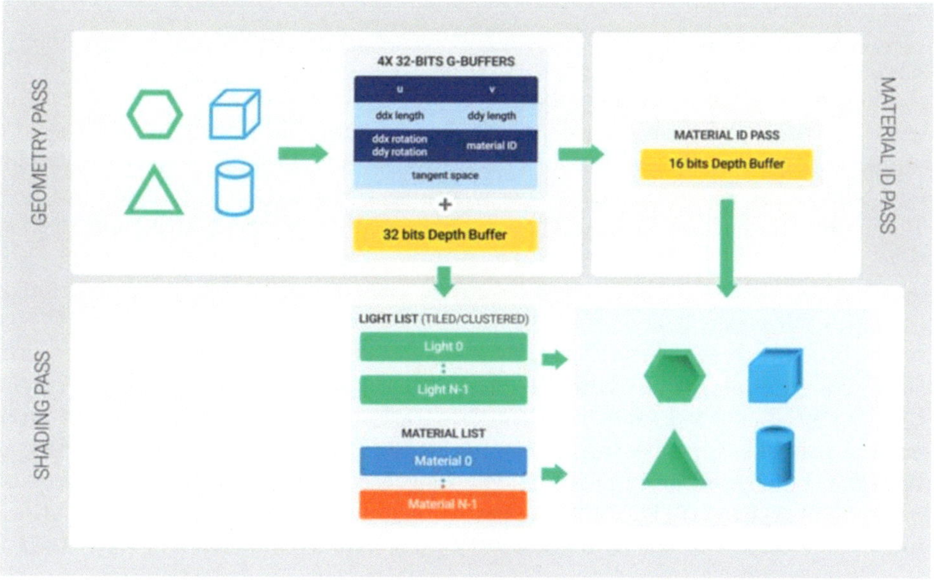

Figure 1.5. Overview of the steps involved in the rendering system.

Geometry pass. All mesh instances that pass the culling system are rendered indirectly into a set of compressed geometry buffers (4×32 bits per pixel). In contrast to traditional deferred rendering, no material specific code is executed or textures fetched except for some special cases, such as alpha testing with an alpha-mask texture or GPU hardware tessellation with displacement mapping that samples a height map. By outputting vertex attributes into the geometry buffers that are required for subsequent material rendering and lighting, it is possible to completely separate geometry processing from materials and lighting.

Geometry buffer layout. Since, in general, memory bandwidth of current consumer graphics hardware is much more limited than computational power, it is important to keep the size of the geometry buffers as low as possible. In the following section we explain how the required vertex attributes are compressed into the geometry buffers.

Texture coordinates. To avoid precision artifacts, texture coordinates need to be stored with at least 2×16 bits per pixel. As soon as texture coordinates are wrapped, i.e., exceed the $[0, 1]$ range, 16 bits per component is generally not enough anymore. Fortunately, there is an easy way to store wrapped texture coordinates with enough precision in 2×16 bits per pixel, by storing only their fractional part in the pixel shader after interpolation. Since the derivatives of the original texture coordinates are stored alongside, no seams will be visible later on. Texture coordinates are stored as `DXGI_FORMAT_R16G16_SNORM` in the first geometry buffer.

Texture coordinate derivatives. In theory, derivatives can be reconstructed in the shading pass by using the neighbor texture coordinates. However, in the case of geometry edges, where appropriate neighbor texture coordinates can't always be obtained, artifacts will be visible. This is especially noticeable under camera motion with dense alpha-tested foliage, where temporal artifacts can be observed. Therefore, we decided to store the texture coordinates along with their derivatives.

Texture coordinate derivatives require at least 4×16 bits per pixel for enough precision. However, it is possible to do an artifact-free compression from 64 bits to 48 bits by treating the derivatives in the X- and Y-direction as 2D vectors. By decoupling the vector length from the orientation, the vector length can be stored as 2×16 bits, and the orientation as 2×8 bits, which still gives enough precision for anisotropic texture filtering. Listing 1.5 shows how derivatives can be en/decoded in HLSL. The lengths of the derivatives are stored as `DXGI_FORMAT_R16G16_FLOAT` in the second geometry buffer, and the orientations in the red channel of the third geometry buffer (`DXGI_FORMAT_R16G16_UINT`).

```
void EncodeDerivatives(in float4 derivatives, out float2 derivativesLength, out uint
                       encodedDerivativesRot)
{
```

```
    derivativesLength = float2(length(derivatives.xy), length(derivatives.zw));
    float2 derivativesRot = float2(derivatives.x/derivativesLength.x,
                                   derivatives.z/derivativesLength.y) * 0.5f + 0.5f;
    uint signX = (derivatives.y < 0) ? 1 : 0;
    uint signY = (derivatives.w < 0) ? 1 : 0;
    encodedDerivativesRot = (signY << 15u) | (uint(derivativesRot.y * 127.0f) << 8u) |
                            (signX << 7u) | uint(derivativesRot.x*127.0f));
}

float4 DecodeDerivatives(in uint encodedDerivativesRot, in float2 derivativesLength)
{
    float2 derivativesRot;
    derivativesRot.x = float(encodedDerivativesRot.r & 0x7f) / 127.0f;
    derivativesRot.y = float((encodedDerivativesRot >> 8) & 0x7f) / 127.0f;
    derivativesRot = derivativesRot * 2.0f - 1.0f;
    float signX = (((encodedDerivativesRot.r >> 7u) & 0x1) == 0) ? 1.0f : -1.0f;
    float signY = (((encodedDerivativesRot.r >> 15u) & 0x1) == 0) ? 1.0f : -1.0f;
    float4 derivatives;
    derivatives.x = derivativesRot.x;
    derivatives.y = sqrt(1.0f - derivativesRot.x * derivativesRot.x)*signX;
    derivatives.z = derivativesRot.y;
    derivatives.w = sqrt(1.0f - derivativesRot.y * derivativesRot.y)*signY;
    derivatives.xy *= derivativesLength.x;
    derivatives.zw *= derivativesLength.y;
    return derivatives;
}
```

Listing 1.5. HLSL code for en/de-coding texture coordinate derivatives.

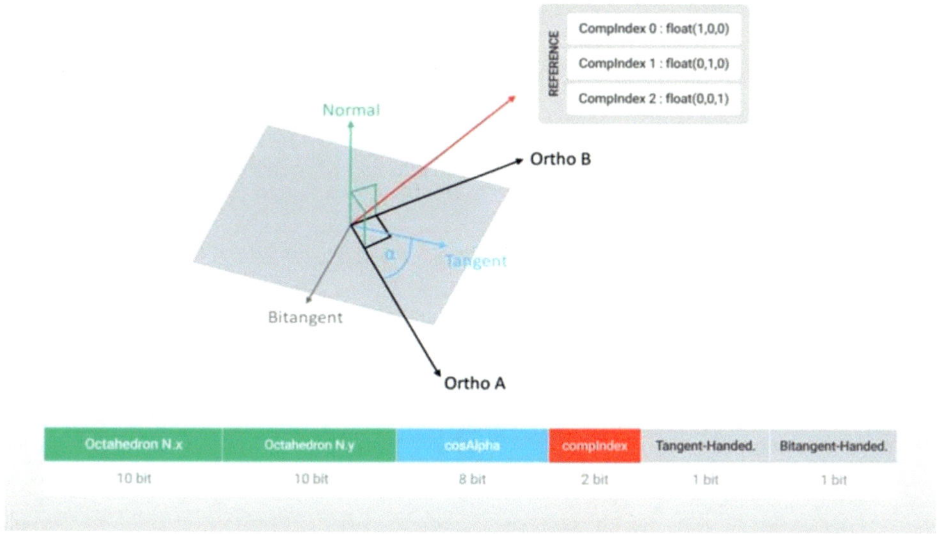

Figure 1.6. Relationship of the vectors involved in en/de-coding the tangent space and storage layout of the corresponding geometry buffer.

Tangent space. For normal mapping, parallax occlusion mapping, etc. it is required to store the tangent space, consisting of a tangent, bitangent and normal. We looked into storing the tangent space as a quaternion in 32 bits per pixel according to [McAuley 2015], but dismissed this approach due to visible faceting on smooth shiny surfaces. Instead, we store the tangent space as an axis-angle representation, where the normal is stored as an axis and the tangent as an angle. Normals are stored in 2×10 bits by using octahedron normal vector encoding [Meyer et al. 2010]. For tangents, first a vector has to be found that can be easily reconstructed for decoding and that is guaranteed to be orthonormal to the normal. Choosing an arbitrary orthonormal vector produces severe artifacts due to singularity issues and noise at different frequencies. To overcome these issues, we first select a reference vector by taking the largest component of the tangent and store this vector into two bits for decoding. With the help of this vector, we calculate an orthonormal vector and store the angle between this vector and the tangent into eight bits. The handedness of the tangent and bitangent are both stored in one bit. In this way, we can store the entire tangent space as `DXGI_FORMAT_R10G10B10A2_UINT` in the fourth geometry buffer (Figure 1.6, Listing 1.6). It should be noted that this method requires about half the instruction count to encode the tangent space into 32 bits as when converting a TBN matrix into a quaternion in a mathematically stable, precise manner and packing it into 32 bits.

```
uint4 EncodeTBN(in float3 normal, in float3 tangent, in uint bitangentHandedness)
{
  // octahedron normal vector encoding
  uint2 encodedNormal = uint2((EncodeNormal(normal) * 0.5f + 0.5f) * 1023.0f);

  // find largest component of tangent
  float3 tangentAbs = abs(tangent);
  float maxComp = max(max(tangentAbs.x, tangentAbs.y), tangentAbs.z);
  float3 refVector;
  uint compIndex;
  if(maxComp == tangentAbs.x)
  {
    refVector = float3(1.0f, 0.0f, 0.0f);
    compIndex = 0;

  else if(maxComp == tangentAbs.y)
  {
    refVector = float3(0.0f, 1.0f, 0.0f);
    compIndex = 1;
  }
  else
  {
    refVector = float3(0.0f, 0.0f, 1.0f);
    compIndex = 2;
  }

  // compute cosAngle and handedness of tangent
  float3 orthoA = normalize(cross(normal, refVector));
  float3 orthoB = cross(normal, orthoA);
  uint cosAngle = uint((dot(tangent, orthoA) * 0.5f + 0.5f) * 255.0f);
  uint tangentHandedness = (dot(tangent, orthoB) > 0.0001f) ? 2 : 0;

```

```
  return uint4(encodedNormal, (cosAngle<<2u) | compIndex, tangentHandedness |
               bitangentHandedness);
}

void DecodeTBN(in uint4 encodedTBN, out float3 normal, out float3 tangent, out float3
               bitangent)
{
  // octahedron normal vector decoding
  normal = DecodeNormal((encodedTBN.xy / 1023.0f) * 2.0f - 1.0f);

  // get reference vector
  float3 refVector;
  uint compIndex = (encodedTBN.z & 0x3);
  if(compIndex == 0)
  {
    refVector = float3(1.0f, 0.0f, 0.0f);
  }
  else if(compIndex == 1)
  {
    refVector = float3(0.0f, 1.0f, 0.0f);
  }
  else
  {
    refVector = float3(0.0f, 0.0f, 1.0f);
  }

  // decode tangent
  uint cosAngleUint = ((encodedTBN.z >> 2u) & 0xFF);
  float cosAngle = (cosAngleUint / 255.0f) * 2.0f - 1.0f;
  float sinAngle = sqrt(saturate(1.0f - (cosAngle * cosAngle)));
  sinAngle = ((encodedTBN.w & 0x2) == 0) ? -sinAngle : sinAngle;
  float3 orthoA = normalize(cross(normal, refVector));
  float3 orthoB = cross(normal, orthoA);
  tangent = (cosAngle * orthoA) + (sinAngle * orthoB);

  // decode bitangent
  bitangent = cross(normal, tangent);
  bitangent = ((encodedTBN.w & 0x1) == 0) ? bitangent : -bitangent;
}
```

Listing 1.6. HLSL code for en/de-coding the tangent space.

The quality that can be achieved with this compression method is nearly equivalent to storing tangent, bitangent and normal uncompressed in 3×30 bits per pixel (Figure 1.7).

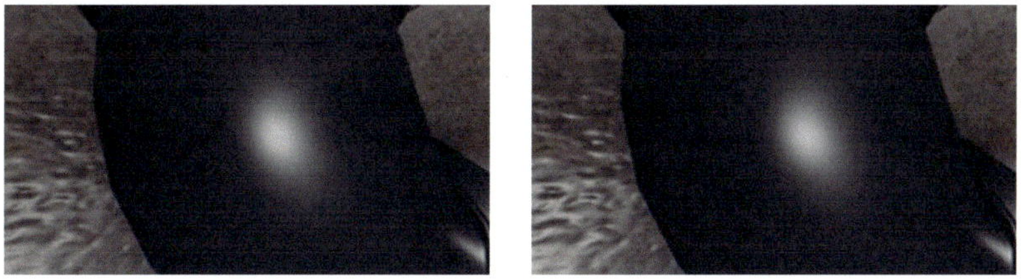

Figure 1.7. Both images show a smooth shiny surface illuminated by a spherical area light source with GGX as the specular lighting term. For the left image, tangent space was stored uncompressed in 3×30 bits per pixel and for the right image, tangent space was store with the proposed compression scheme in 32 bits per pixel.

Material ID To apply deferred materials, each material must store a unique ID. This material ID is stored in 16 bits as the green channel of the third geometry buffer (`DXGI_FORMAT_R16G16_UINT`), and supports up to 65,536 individual materials, which should be enough even for large-scale projects.

Additional vertex attributes. In practice, it can be possible that additional vertex attributes are required, such as multiple texture coordinate sets and vertex colors. As long as the texture coordinates that are stored in the geometry buffers are not wrapped (in [0,1] range), it should be possible to reconstruct additional texture coordinate sets per material that are just scaled and biased relative to the stored texture coordinates. Proper derivatives can then be obtained by scaling the stored derivatives.

For all other cases, such meshes can be treated for culling as separate mesh types, which allows them to write additional vertex attributes into further geometry buffers. In the shading pass, the corresponding materials are rendered separately as described later, which allows efficient fetching of additional geometry buffers. Obviously this is only a feasible solution as long as the number of additional vertex attributes is low or such materials are not used frequently.

Material ID pass. After filling the geometry buffers, the stored material ID is transferred into a 16-bit depth buffer in a simple full-screen pass. This is done by dividing the material ID with the maximum number of supported materials and outputting this value via `SV_Depth` in the pixel shader. For standard materials, that use the same shader and are rendered together in the shading pass, a special reserved depth value (e.g., 0) is output.

Shading pass. In this pass materials and lighting are applied. For all standard materials that use the same shader and resource binding layout, a single full-screen pass is executed and required textures are fetched by dynamically indexing into a common shader-resource descriptor table with the help of the material ID from the geometry buffers.

However, processing materials together that require different shader paths in an Übershader is a bad idea, since adjacent screen pixels can use completely different shader paths. This results in divergent dynamic branching with poor performance characteristics. Instead, for each non-standard material, a screen-space rectangle is rendered that encloses the boundaries of all visible meshes that use this material. The depth of the rectangle vertices is set to the same depth that was output for this material in the material ID pass. By setting depth comparison to equal, early depth-stencil testing will prevent pixels with a different material ID from being processed further. Since the same binary depth value is used as was output in the material ID pass, equal depth testing doesn't produce any precision issues and incorrect material classification is avoided. The same rejection technique is used for commonly rendered standard materials to prevent pixels with non-standard materials from being processed by using the same special, reserved depth value as was output in the material ID pass.

The calculation of the screen-space rectangle boundaries is done on the GPU. For this, the indices of all mesh instances that were frustum-culled on the CPU, are stored per material in a contiguous GPU buffer. A second GPU buffer stores, per material, the first and last index into the former buffer. Additionally, separate visibility buffers have to be used for the first and second occlusion pass, in order to be able to check each instance for visibility. A compute shader is dispatched that runs a thread group per material, where each thread processes one mesh instance. If a mesh instance is visible, its OBB is projected into screen space and a bounding rectangle is inflated in the shared thread group memory. Finally, each thread group outputs the inflated bounding rectangle, in a structured buffer, at a position specific for each material (Listing 1.7). Consequently, this structured buffer is manually fetched in a vertex shader with `SV_VertexID` to construct the corners of the bounding rectangle in clip space for each processed material.

```
#define GROUP_SIZE 1024

groupshared uint2 iBoundsMins, iBoundsMaxes;

[numthreads(GROUP_SIZE, 1, 1)]
void main(uint3 groupID: SV_GroupID, uint groupIndex: SV_GroupIndex)
{
  if(groupIndex == 0)
  {
    iBoundsMins = uint2(0xffffffff, 0xffffffff);
    iBoundsMaxes = uint2(0, 0);
  }
  GroupMemoryBarrierWithGroupSync();

  MaterialBoundsInfo materialBoundsInfo = materialBoundsInfoBuffer[groupID.x];
  for(uint i=materialBoundsInfo.startMaterialIndex;
      i<materialBoundsInfo.endMaterialIndex; i+=GROUP_SIZE)
  {
    uint materialIndex = groupIndex + i;
    if(materialIndex < materialBoundsInfo.endMaterialIndex)
    {
      uint instanceIndex = materialIndexBuffer[materialIndex];

      // check if mesh is visible in visibility buffer of main or false negatives pass
      if((visBuffer0[instanceIndex] > 0) || (visBuffer1[instanceIndex] > 0))
      {
        // calculate AABB in view space
        const matrix modelViewMatrix = mul(cameraCB.viewMatrix,
                                           instanceBuffer[instanceIndex]);

        float3 boxMins = float3(999999.0f, 999999.0f, 999999.0f);
        float3 boxMaxes = float3(-999999.0f, -999999.0f, -999999.0f);

        [unroll]
        for(uint j=0; j<8; j++)
        {
          // unit AABB position
          float3 position = float3(((j & 0x4) == 0) ? -1.0f : 1.0f,
                                   ((j & 0x2) == 0) ? -1.0f : 1.0f,
```

```
                                 ((j & 0x1) == 0) ? -1.0f : 1.0f);

          float3 positionVS = mul(modelViewMatrix, float4(position, 1.0f)).xyz;
          boxMins = min(boxMins, positionVS);
          boxMaxes = max(boxMaxes, positionVS);
        }


        // clip view space AABB against camera near plane and calculate screen space
        // bounding rectangle
        float2 mins = float2(1.0f, 1.0f);
        float2 maxes = float2(0.0f, 0.0f);

        [unroll]
        for(uint k=0; k<8; k++)
        {
          float3 positionVS = float3(((k & 0x4) == 0) ? boxMins.x : boxMaxes.x,
                                     ((k & 0x2) == 0) ? boxMins.y : boxMaxes.y,
                                     ((k & 0x1) == 0) ? boxMins.z : boxMaxes.z);
          positionVS.z = (positionVS.z > 0.0f) ? 0.0f : positionVS.z;

          float4 positionCS = mul(cameraCB.projMatrix, float4(positionVS, 1.0f));
          positionCS.xy /= positionCS.w;
          float2 positionSS = saturate(positionCS.xy * 0.5f + 0.5f);
          mins = min(mins, positionSS);
          maxes = max(maxes, positionSS);
        }

        // inflate bounding rectangle in screen space
        uint2 iMins = asuint(mins);
        uint2 iMaxes = asuint(maxes);
        InterlockedMin(iBoundsMins.x, iMins.x);
        InterlockedMin(iBoundsMins.y, iMins.y);
        InterlockedMax(iBoundsMaxes.x, iMaxes.x);
        InterlockedMax(iBoundsMaxes.y, iMaxes.y);
      }
    }
  }
  GroupMemoryBarrierWithGroupSync();

  // store bounding rectangle of material in clip space
  if(groupIndex == 0)
  {
    float4 bounds = (iBoundsMins.x == 0xffffffff) ?
                     float4(0.0f, 0.0f, 0.0f, 0.0f) :
                     (float4(asfloat(iBoundsMins), asfloat(iBoundsMaxes)) * 2.0f - 1.0f);
    materialBoundsBuffer[groupID.x] = bounds;
  }
}
```

Listing 1.7. Compute shader that generates boundaries for materials.

Though early depth-stencil testing rejects pixels with different materials, current consumer GPUs run in warps of 32 or 64 threads and use helper pixels to ensure that pixels are processed in 2×2 quads for derivative calculations. Thus, even when irrelevant pixels are rejected, there could be a large amount of processed helper pixels and inactive GPU threads. However, we also implemented a rendering prototype in OpenGL and measured the number of active (memory-outputting), helper and inactive GPU threads with the help of the OpenGL extension `GL_NV_shader_thread_group` (Listing 1.8).

```
uint activeThreadsMask = activeThreadsNV();
uint helperThreadMask = ballotThreadNV(gl_HelperThreadNV);
uint outputThread;
for(uint i=0; i<32; i++)
{
  uint bit = 1 << i;
  if(((activeThreadsMask & bit) != 0) && ((helperThreadMask & bit) == 0))
  {
    outputThread = i;
    break;
  }
}
if(gl_ThreadInWarpNV == outputThread)
{
  uint numActiveThreads = bitCount(activeThreadsMask);
  uint numInactiveThreads = 32 - numActiveThreads;
  atomicAdd(threadCounterBuffer.counters.numActiveThreads, numActiveThreads);
  atomicAdd(threadCounterBuffer.counters.numInactiveThreads, numInactiveThreads);
  uint numHelperThreads = bitCount(helperThreadMask);
  atomicAdd(threadCounterBuffer.counters.numHelperThreads, numHelperThreads);
}
```

Listing 1.8. GLSL pixel shader code to count number of active, inactive and helper GPU threads. Only active GPU threads output to memory.

It turned out that the number of helper and inactive GPU threads for material rendering and lighting was significantly lower in comparison to a forward renderer and drastically lower with the use of GPU hardware tessellation techniques. This was even true for situations where each material was processed in a separate pass and the amount of alpha-tested foliage was high.

The reason that GPU hardware tessellation performs much better with deferred+ is that, even with the use of adaptive tessellation techniques, the number of small triangles drastically increases. As the number of small triangles increases, so does the number of helper and inactive GPU threads for pixel shading. This makes per pixel operations inefficient. Since, with deferred+, most of the per-pixel operations are deferred from the geometry pass to subsequent screen passes with high warp utilization, the negative impact of small triangles is far less noticeable.

We also tried an alternative rendering strategy. After the initial geometry pass, with the help of atomic counters, the number of pixels with the same material ID is counted and corresponding chunks are reserved in a common GPU buffer. Each pixel's screen location is then recorded into the chunk with the corresponding material ID. After that, the number of thread groups necessary to process the pixels for each material is written into a GPU buffer by dividing the pixel count by the number of threads per group. Finally, for each material, an indirect dispatch command is issued, sourcing the number of thread groups from the aforementioned GPU buffer. In this step, materials and lighting are applied. Unfortunately, this system performed significantly slower than the early depth-stencil approach. On the one hand, there was an additional overhead for binning the screen pixels per material. On the other hand, shading the pixels was also slower than in the early depth-stencil approach. We thought the reason for this was that binned pixels did not have a spatial locality that matches the texture memory swizzling pattern of the fetched geometry buffer textures. Therefore, we also tried to bin pixels in screen tiles to achieve better texture cache efficiency, but couldn't achieve any notable performance improvement.

As mentioned previously, lighting can be done with a tiled [M. Billeter and Assarsson 2013] or clustered [Olsson et al. 2012] approach.

1.4 Comparison with Hierarchical Depth Buffer-based Culling

Similar GPU-based culling systems have already been proposed and used in games [Hill and Collin 2011, Haar and Aaltonen 2015]. However, these systems are based on a hierarchical depth buffer that is generated by conservative down-sampling. Occludee bounding boxes are manually projected into screen space and tested against the hierarchical depth buffer to determine visibility. This approach results in several problems that can be avoided with the proposed culling system:

- To determine visibility, occludee bounding boxes are projected in screen space into rectangular regions, which in some situations can significantly reduce culling efficiency (Figure 1.8).

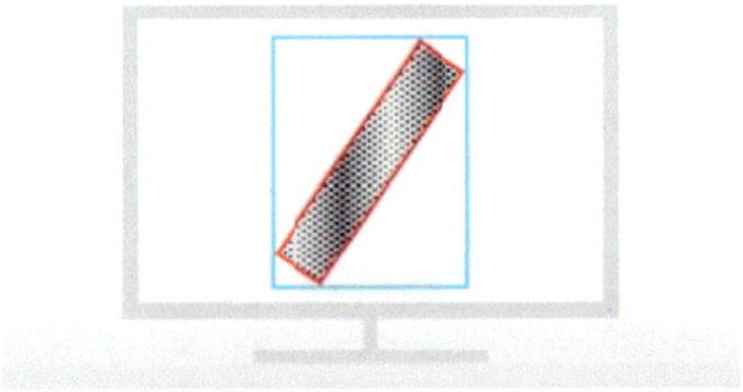

Figure 1.8. Viewport, showing an oblique object in screen space. With hierarchical depth buffer-based culling, the blue boundaries are used for visibility determination instead of the red boundaries that are used in our culling approach, resulting in lower culling efficiency.

- To determine visibility, a single conservative depth value is used for each occludee, which leads to false positives in some situations (Figure 1.9).
- In order to be able to test each projected bounding box against the hierarchical depth buffer with a fixed amount of texture samples, higher mip-map levels have to be used for larger occludees. The problem with this approach is that mip-maps were generated by conservative down-sampling, i.e., always taking the maximum of the depth values from the previous mip-map

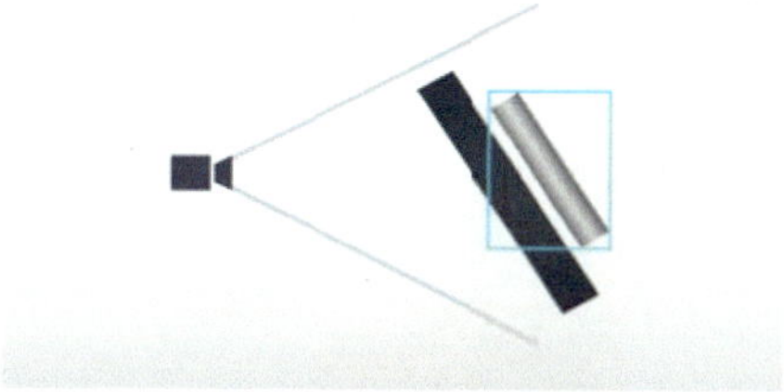

Figure 1.9. Top-down view of the camera frustum, where the object to the right is fully occluded, but since conservatively only one depth value is used, the object will still pass as visible.

levels. In consequence, large depth values (e.g., from the sky) propagate into higher mip-map levels thus making culling of larger objects in screen space inefficient (Figure 1.10).

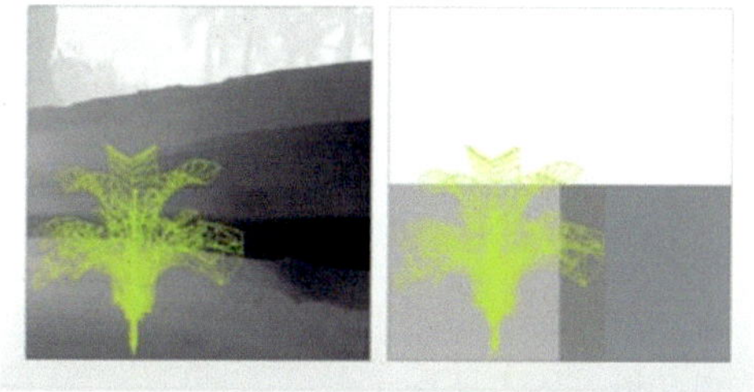

Figure 1.10. The object shown in wireframe is fully occluded but still passes as visible because a high mip-map level is used from the hierarchical depth buffer.

- If we would use a hierarchical depth buffer-based approach for the previously described two-pass culling system, first a hierarchical depth buffer would need to be constructed from the depth buffer of the last frame and then, after the main occlusion pass, reconstructed with the updated depth buffer of the current frame. On a PC, where Hi-Z tiles of the depth buffer can't be accessed, this has a high performance overhead compared to the remaining steps of the culling system.

The first three issues can be mitigated by subdividing mesh assets into small clusters [Haar and Aaltonen 2015]. However, in our case we wanted a culling system that does not rely on mesh clustering and is compatible with a traditional asset pipeline. Since scenes that were built with the current asset pipeline of the Dawn Engine consisted of relatively small modular blocks, with the proposed culling system we could avoid introducing a system for subdividing meshes into small clusters.

We compared how well the proposed culling system performs, in comparison to a hierarchical depth buffer-based culling approach, inside a natural jungle environment without using mesh clustering. On average we could achieve 2.3× higher culling rates and 1.6× faster frame times with the proposed culling system.

1.5 Pros and Cons

The following subsections give an overview of the pros and cons of the culling and rendering parts of the proposed system.

1.5.1 Culling

Pros

- Achieves the same pixel accuracy as conventional hardware occlusion queries while eliminating latency issues (popping).
- Highly dynamic, complex, alpha-tested occluders are supported without needing to author and render dedicated occluder geometry.
- High culling efficiency can be achieved without mesh clustering for modular composited scenes, thus maintaining full compatibility with standard mesh assets and asset pipelines.
- The system is compatible with CPU-based culling systems (such a frustum culling, portal culling, etc.) that can be considered as coarse pre-filtering.
- The culling system itself has a low performance overhead.
- The number of draw calls is massively reduced, which gives a performance benefit even with low-overhead graphics APIs such as DirectX 12 and Vulkan.

Cons

- Since the indirect draw buffer is generated in parallel in a compute shader, draw commands are no longer in a deterministic order. Thus, nearly coplanar surfaces are more likely to cause Z-fighting and should be avoided. Furthermore, depth sorting of draw calls is not given anymore, causing higher overdraw. However, since with deferred+ the geometry pass is light-weight and culling efficiency is high, this will have much less negative impact on performance than with traditional rendering systems.
- In situations where the camera changes drastically from one frame to the other (e.g., with teleportation), culling efficiency can significantly drop for a short amount of time.

1.5.2 Rendering

Pros

- Due to a light-weight geometry pass, a depth pre-pass, which can be expensive for meshes with high triangle counts, GPU hardware tessellation, alpha-testing or vertex-shader skinning, is no longer required,

- Warp utilization for applying materials and lighting is significantly better than with clustered forward shading [Olsson et al. 2012]. Thus small triangles are far less problematic, and GPU hardware tessellation performs much better.

- Deferred+ is a unified rendering system that, in contrast to deferred rendering, can handle a highly diverse range of materials efficiently.

- Geometry processing is completely decoupled from material rendering and lighting, resulting in fewer shader permutations and faster iteration times in game production.

- By decoupling geometry processing from shading, switching of GPU resources is significantly reduced.

- In contrast to a system where vertex attribute fetching is deferred [Burns and Hunt 2013], geometry information is only fetched once per frame in a cache-friendly, coherent manner.

- Compressed texture data does not need to be decompressed into GPU memory as with deferred rendering, thus texture memory bandwidth is significantly reduced.

- HDR textures are not a problem anymore as with deferred rendering.

- Modified geometry buffers contain useful information not available with deferred rendering:

    - Texture coordinate derivatives can be used to fix mip-mapping issues with deferred decals.

    - Vertex normals can be used to enhance screen-space ambient occlusion techniques.

    - Vertex tangents can be used for anisotropic lighting.

- The proposed rendering system does not depend on vendor-specific graphics features and is compatible with the entire range of DirectX 12-capable graphics hardware. When the supported range of dynamically indexed textures is too low, applications can still fall back to rendering common materials separately.

Cons

- Vertex attributes are much more limited in comparison to traditional rendering techniques.
- Transparent objects have to be handled separately.
- Antialiasing is still difficult to handle.

1.6 Results

To capture the results, we used two scenes from the game *Deus Ex: Mankind Divided* that we converted into a format we could load and render in an experimental framework that is based on DirectX 12. The first scene is illuminated by 1024, and the second by 256, moving spherical area lights using clustered lighting. To simulate dynamic objects for the first scene, the source of each area light is rendered as an emissive sphere. Each material uses a diffuse texture with an optional alpha mask, a normal texture, a specular texture, and a roughness texture. For diffuse lighting, a simple Lambert term is used, while specular lighting uses the GGX microfacet model; both terms were adapted for spherical area lights. Indirect lighting uses a simple constant ambient term. Frustum culling is performed on the CPU prior to GPU culling. The test machine used an NVIDIA GeForce GTX 970 graphics card and the screen resolution was set to 1920×1080.

For capturing the profiling results, the first scene was rendered from a point of view where 23,116 instances, distributed over 4073 meshes, 5,556,614 triangles, and 316 materials, are in the view frustum and processed (Figure 1.11). To be able to compare our rendering system with a reference clustered forward renderer while using GPU culling, all materials, except the emissive sphere material, use the same shading code. Tables 1.1 and 1.2 compare timings of deferred+ with a reference clustered forward renderer; Tables 1.3 and 1.4 show detailed GPU timings and efficiency of the culling system.

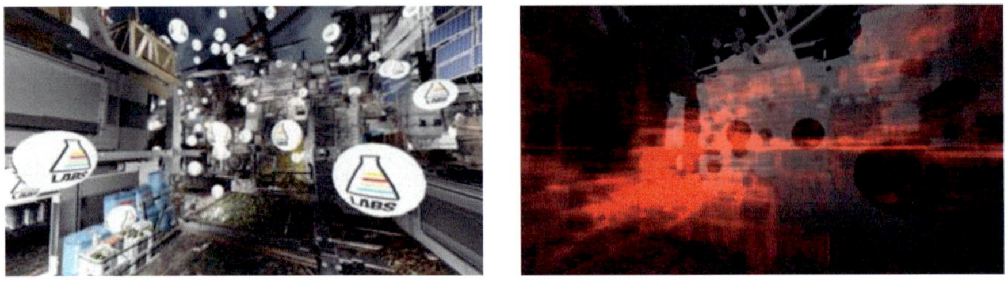

Figure 1.11. Scene from the game *Deus Ex: Mankind Divided*, culled and rendered with our system. The left image shows the final rendering result while the right image illustrates the boundaries of culled objects as red boxes.

	Deferred+ (single pass)		Deferred+ (multi-pass)		Clustered forward renderer	
	Culling on	Culling off	Culling on	Culling off	Culling on	Culling off
Frame time	5.86	6.92	6.50	8.29	9.33	12.47
Depth pre-pass	-	-	-	-	0.94	2.41
Light culling pass	0.34	0.34	0.34	0.34	0.34	0.34
Geometry pass	1.72	3.69	1.72	3.69	6.70	9.30
Material ID pass	0.13	0.13	0.13	0.13	-	-
Material bounds pass	0.02	0.03	0.13	0.51	-	-
Deferred pass	2.34	2.35	2.86	3.21	-	-

Table 1.1. Frame time and GPU times in ms for each rendering step. For deferred+ in single pass mode, all materials are rendered in a single fullscreen pass with the help of dynamically indexed textures. In multi pass mode, each material is rendered separately with the proposed depth-stencil reject method. The multi pass mode is only slightly slower than the single pass method.

	Deferred+ (single pass)		Deferred+ (multi-pass)		Clustered forward renderer	
	Culling on	Culling off	Culling on	Culling off	Culling on	Culling off
Frame time	10.00	21.43	10.77	22.78	17.96	36.15
Depth pre-pass	-	-	-	-	3.00	8.18
Light culling pass	0.34	0.34	0.34	0.34	0.34	0.34
Geometry pass	5.87	18.13	5.94	18.12	13.28	27.25
Material ID pass	0.13	0.13	0.13	0.13	-	-
Material bounds pass	0.02	0.03	0.13	0.51	-	-
Deferred pass	2.35	2.37	2.88	3.25	-	-

Table 1.2. Same as Table 1 with the exception that all mesh instances are rendered with adaptive GPU hardware tessellation, using a maximum tessellation factor of 5.

Culling overhead	0.90
Main pass	0.46
Downsample depth	0.0699
Clear visibility buffer	0.0050
Fill visibility buffer	0.3175
Generate draw list	0.0656
False negatives pass	0.44
Clear visibility buffer	0.0051
Fill visibility buffer	0.3774
Generate draw list	0.0531

Table 1.3. GPU times in ms for each step involved in the proposed culling system.

Main pass — number of visible instances	4163
Main pass — number of occluded instances	18953
False negatives pass — number of visible instances	275
Percentage of culled instances	80.80

Table 1.4. Culling statistics, acquired with the help of atomic GPU counters.

Figure 1.12 compares, in a second scene, the visual rendering results of deferred+ to that of a reference clustered forward rendering system. We used 8× anisotropic texture filtering to ensure that the compression of texture coordinate derivatives in deferred+ was working properly.

Figure 1.12. The image on the left was rendered with deferred+ and the image on the right with clustered forward shading. Quality-wise both rendering techniques are almost indistinguishable.

The captured results show that deferred+ runs faster than clustered forward shading, especially when GPU hardware tessellation is used, while producing almost equivalent results quality-wise. Under realistic game conditions with more complex materials (using more than 4 textures) and more complex lighting (different light types, shadow mapping), the performance benefit of deferred+ should be even more prominent.

1.7 Conclusion

We presented a comprehensive system for culling and rendering complex, highly dynamic scenes, which makes use of new graphics capabilities available with DirectX 12. The culling system provides high culling efficiency even for non-clustered, traditional mesh assets while having a low overhead. The rendering system outperforms a quality-wise comparable clustered forward rendering system, even more so when GPU hardware tessellation techniques are employed. It is fully compatible with conventional texture assets, doesn't depend on vendor-specific graphics features and can run on the entire range of DirectX 12 capable graphics hardware. By combining the proposed culling and rendering system it is possible to render an entire complex scene in just a few draw calls.

Acknowledgment

We would like to thank Francis Maheux for providing us with the assets for the prototype and Samuel Delmont and Uriel Doyon for their valuable input on the implementation itself.

Bibliography

BILODEAU, B. 2014. Vertex shader tricks. In *Game Developer Conference 2014 Talks.* URL: http://www.slideshare.net/DevCentralAMD/vertex-shader-tricks-bill-bilodeau.

BURNS, C. A., AND HUNT, W. A. 2013. The visibility buffer: A cache-friendly approach to deferred shading. *Journal of Computer Graphics Techniques 2*, 2, 55–69. URL: http://jcgt.org/published/0002/02/04/.

HAAR, U., AND AALTONEN, S. 2015. Gpu-driven rendering pipelines. In *Advances in Real-Time Rendering in Games, ACM SIGGRAPH Course*, ACM, New York. URL: http://advances.realtimerendering.com/s2015/index.html.

HILL, S., AND COLLIN, D. 2011. Practical dynamic visibility for games. In *GPU Pro 2*, W. Engel, Ed. A K Peters, Natick, MA, 329–347.

KUBISCH, C., AND TAVENRATH, M. 2014. OpenGL 4.4 scene rendering techniques. In *GPU Technology Conference 2014*. URL: http://on-demand.gputechconf.com/gtc/2014/presentations/S4379-opengl-44-scene-rendering-techniques.pdf.

M. BILLETER, O. O., AND ASSARSSON, U. 2013. Tiled forward shading. In *GPU Pro 4: Advanced Rendering Techniques*, W. Engel, Ed. A K Peters/CRC Press, Boca Raton, FL, 99–114.

MCAULEY, S., 2015. Rendering the world of Far Cry 4. URL: http://www.gdcvault.com/play/1022235/Rendering-the-World-of-Far.

MEYER, Q., SÜSSMUTH, J., SUSSNER, G., STAMMINGER, M., AND GREINER, G. 2010. On floating-point normal vectors. In *Proceedings of the 21st Eurographics Conference on Rendering*, Eurographics Association, Aire-la-Ville, Switzerland, EGSR'10, 1405–1409.

OLSSON, O., BILLETER, M., AND ASSARSSON, U. 2012. Clustered deferred and forward shading. In *Proceedings of the Fourth ACM SIGGRAPH / Eurographics Conference on High-Performance Graphics*, Eurographics Association, Aire-la-Ville, Switzerland, EGGH-HPG'12, 87–96.

REED, N., 2014. Deferred texturing. Blog post. URL: http://www.reedbeta.com/blog/2014/03/25/deferred-texturing.

III

2

Programmable Per-pixel Sample Placement with Conservative Rasterizer

Rahul P. Sathe

2.1 Overview

Rendering a scene with modern graphics hardware and APIs involves sampling pixel coverage at one or more locations, followed by shading (and blending for transparent objects). Using fewer, well-placed samples can produce an image with quality that is comparable to (or better than) one produced with more, naively placed, samples.

We propose a technique that generates sample locations programmatically in the pixel shader using the Conservative Rasterization feature in the Direct3D 12 API[1] or Direct3D 11.3 with Feature Level 12_1.[2] Our algorithm generates samples in parallel across the pixels on the GPU hardware. We also discuss how our technique can be combined with foveated rendering, which is becoming important for virtual reality (VR) rendering with commodity head mounted displays (HMDs).

2.2 Background

Multi-sample anti-aliasing (MSAA) [Akeley 1993] is a great way to increase image quality without significantly increasing shading costs (unlike supersampling). All modern graphics hardware supports MSAA; however, the locations at which coverage is sampled does not change from pixel to pixel. Jittering sample locations within the pixel bounds produces images with high-frequency (blue) noise. This noise tends to be less objectionable than aliasing and can be further reduced with filtering (Figure 2.1) [Pharr and Humphreys 2010].

Some hardware vendors provide a way to vary the sample locations from pixel to pixel through custom extensions, e.g., (`NV_Sample_locations`[3] and

[1] https://msdn.microsoft.com/en-us/library/windows/desktop/dn914594(v=vs.85).aspx
[2] https://msdn.microsoft.com/en-us/library/windows/desktop/ff476876(v=vs.85).aspx
[3] https://developer.nvidia.com/sites/default/files/akamai/opengl/specs/GL_NV_sample_

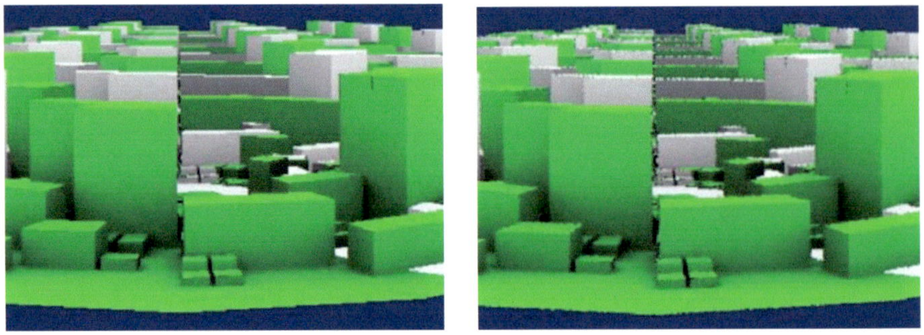

(a) (b)

Figure 2.1. (a) The image is generated with samples at the pixel centers;(b) the image is generated with samples jittered from the pixel centers to locations within the pixel bounds. As one can see, the aliasing has been replaced by high frequency noise.

`AMD_sample_positions`[4]), but these are somewhat limited and not fully programmable on the GPU. These extensions repeat the sample patterns and are only unique over a small screen-space region.

Unique per pixel sample locations are a desired feature of a lot of advanced lighting algorithms that use ray tracing and modern anti-aliasing techniques, like temporal supersampling [Karis 2014]). This type of programmable sample generation enables rich sample patterns like jittered sampling and low discrepancy sequences (e.g., $[0-2]$-sequence, Sobol sequence) [Pharr and Humphreys 2010]. Note that jittering the shading locations replaces not only geometric aliasing but also the shader and texture aliasing with high frequency noise.

2.3 Algorithm

Our algorithm is best described in terms of the specific shader stages it uses. We start at the top of the D3D12 pipeline and only describe the shader stages the algorithm requires. One can easily integrate these shaders in their existing asset pipeline to uniquely place the sample(s) within the pixel programmatically.

2.3.1 Geometry Shader (GS)

Our technique uses a geometry shader (GS) that calculates the coefficients of primitive-edge equations in screen space and passes those to the downstream pipeline. This GS invokes the rasterizer configured in the conservative rasterization mode. We also clip the triangle against the near plane for the reasons discussed in the section below on clipped triangles and blending.

---

locations.txt

[4]https://www.opengl.org/registry/specs/AMD/sample_positions.txt

2.3.2 Conservative Rasterizer (RS)

Conservative rasterization [Microsoft Developer Resources 2015a] works by rasterizing all the pixels that are partially covered by the primitive. This is invoked by creating and setting the rasterization state with the ConservativeRaster field set to D3D12_CONSERVATIVE_RASTERIZATION_MODE_ON.

2.3.3 Pixel Shader (PS)

When a pixel is partially covered by the primitive, the conservative rasterizer invokes the pixel shader (PS) that places the samples programmatically at the locations within the pixel bounds. We then use the triangle-edge equations that were passed down from the GS to decide whether the sample(s) are inside the primitive or not. If MSAA is enabled, we discard the pixel when all sample(s) lie outside the primitive. If some samples lie inside, we update the coverage mask to reflect the covered samples and use that in the rest of the shader.

We use pull-model interpolation to generate the attributes and depth values at the sample locations that are inside the primitive. Note that MSAA is not a requirement for this algorithm; per-pixel offsets can still be added to the pixel center when there is no MSAA.

Since we place the samples at locations that are not known before the pixel shader is launched, it would not make sense to do early depth-stencil testing. We use the discard operation in our pixel shader, which forces late depth-stencil testing.

For the depth-stencil test to make sense, our sample placement must be consistent within a given pixel for a given view (camera and viewport). If the samples are not placed at the exact same location, depth would be interpolated at different locations, and the depth-stencil test would not make sense. Samples may not be exactly one pixel apart from their neighboring pixels (in a non-MSAA case), because they are placed programmatically. As a result, the mip-map calculations done by the sampler hardware could be incorrect. This can be remedied by supplying the derivatives to the texture sampler.

This completes the basics of our algorithm for generating unique samples per pixel. The following code listings show the GS and PS. Note that edge-equation coefficients are marked with the interpolation modifier `nointerpolation` because it is constant for the primitive and needs no interpolation.

```
struct GSOutput
{
    float4 position  : SV_POSITION;
    float u          : TEXCOORD0;
    float v          : TEXCOORD1;
    float  z         : VIEW_Z;
    nointerpolation float3 edgeCoef[3] : EDGE_COEF;
    nointerpolation uint skipEdge[3] : SKIP_EDGE;

};

void UpdateClippedVertex(const float zNear,
                         inout float4 screenSpacePos[3],
                         in uint i, in uint j)
{
    float t = (zNear - screenSpacePos[i].w) / (screenSpacePos[j].w
```

```
                                               - screenSpacePos[i].w);
    screenSpacePos[i].xyzw = screenSpacePos[i].xyzw + t *
                             (screenSpacePos[j].xyzw - screenSpacePos[i].xyzw);
}


[maxvertexcount(3)]
void GSMain(triangle VSInput input[3], inout TriangleStream<GSOutput> TriStream)
{
    GSOutput output;
    float4 screenSpacePos[3];
    float3 edgeCoef[3];
    uint skipEdge[3] = { 0, 0, 0 };
    for (uint i = 0; i < 3; i++)
    {
       bool clipped[3] = { false, false, false };
       uint j = (i + 1) % 3;
       skipEdge[i] = 0;
       edgeCoef[i] = float3(0, 0, 0);

       screenSpacePos[i] = mul(float4(input[i].position, 1.0f), g_mWorldViewProj);
       screenSpacePos[j] = mul(float4(input[j].position, 1.0f), g_mWorldViewProj);

       clipped[i] = (screenSpacePos[i].w < 0);
       clipped[j] = (screenSpacePos[j].w < 0);

       // Clip the vertex with a negative w
       if (clipped[i] && !clipped[j]) {
           UpdateClippedVertex(g_zNearzFar.x, screenSpacePos, i, j);
       } else if (!clipped[i] && clipped[j]) {
           UpdateClippedVertex(g_zNearzFar.x, screenSpacePos, j, i);
       }   else if (clipped[i] && clipped[j]) {
           // Skip an edge if both vertices (and hence the edge) is behind the eye
           skipEdge[i] = 1;
       }

        if (skipEdge[i] == 0) {
            screenSpacePos[i].xyzw /= screenSpacePos[i].w;
            screenSpacePos[i].x = (screenSpacePos[i].x + 1.f) / 2.f * g_screenSize.x;
            screenSpacePos[i].y = (1.f - screenSpacePos[i].y) / 2.f * g_screenSize.y;

            screenSpacePos[j].xyzw /= screenSpacePos[j].w;
            screenSpacePos[j].x = (screenSpacePos[j].x + 1.f) / 2.f * g_screenSize.x;
            screenSpacePos[j].y = (1.f - screenSpacePos[j].y) / 2.f * g_screenSize.y;


            //
            // Edge tests source:
            // http://www.cs.unc.edu/~blloyd/comp770/Lecture08.pdf
            // a0*x + b0*y + c0 > 0 ==> Inside the edge 0
            //                  < 0 ==> Outside the edge 0
            //                  = 0 ==> On the edge 0.

            // Calculate the edge equations
            float a = (screenSpacePos[i].y - screenSpacePos[j].y);
            float b = (screenSpacePos[j].x - screenSpacePos[i].x);
            float c = screenSpacePos[i].x * screenSpacePos[j].y
                    - screenSpacePos[j].x * screenSpacePos[i].y;

            edgeCoef[i] = float3(a, b, c);
        }
    }


    [unroll]
```

```
    for (uint v = 0; v < 3; v++)
    {
        output.position = mul(float4(input[v].position, 1.0f), g_mWorldViewProj);
        output.u = input[v].uv.x;
        output.v = input[v].uv.y;
        output.z = mul(float4(input[v].position, 1.0f), g_mWorldView);

        OutputVertex.edgeCoef[0] = edgeCoef[0];
        OutputVertex.edgeCoef[1] = edgeCoef[1];
        OutputVertex.edgeCoef[2] = edgeCoef[2];
        OutputVertex.skipEdge[0] = skipEdge[0];
        OutputVertex.skipEdge[1] = skipEdge[1];
        OutputVertex.skipEdge[2] = skipEdge[2];
        TriStream.Append(output);
    }
    TriStream.RestartStrip();
}

struct PSOutput
{
    float4 color : SV_TARGET;
    float  depth : SV_DEPTH;
};
bool IsInside(in float3 edgeCoef[3], in uint skipEdge[3], in float2 p,
              bool isFrontFacing, inout bool isOnTheLine)
{
    bool result = true;
    [unroll]
    for (uint e = 0; e < 3; ++e)
    {
        if (skipEdge[e])
            continue;
        float a = edgeCoef[e].x;
        float b = edgeCoef[e].y;
        float c = edgeCoef[e].z;
        float halfSpace = (a * p.x + b * p.y + c);
        isOnTheLine = (halfSpace == 0);
        result = result && (isFrontFacing ? (halfSpace > 0) : (halfSpace < 0));
    }
    return result;
}
PSOutput PSMain(float4  position : SV_POSITION,
                float   u        : TEXCOORD0,
                float   v        : TEXCOORD1,
                float   z        : VIEW_Z,
                nointerpolation float3 edgeCoef[3]  : EDGE_COEF,
                nointerpolation uint skipEdge[3] : SKIP_EDGE;
                bool    isFrontFacing  : SV_IsFrontFace)
{
    PSOutput output;
    output.color = float4(0, 0, 1, 1);
    float2 pt = float2(0, 0);
    int2 offset = GenerateRandomOffsets(position.xy, pt);

    // Test if the new sample is inside or outside
    bool isOutSide = !IsInside(edgeCoef, skipEdge, position.xy + pt, isFrontFacing);
    if (isOutSide) {
        discard;
    }
    else {
        float2 pullModeUV;
        pullModeUV.x = EvaluateAttributeSnapped(u, offset);
        pullModeUV.y = EvaluateAttributeSnapped(v, offset);
        float pullModeZ = EvaluateAttributeSnapped(z, offset);

```

```
        // Un-project to get the actual Z
        output.depth = g_mProjection._33 + g_mProjection._43 / pullModeZ;
        output.color = g_txDiffuse.Sample(g_sampler, pullModeUV);
    }
    return output;
}
```

Listing 2.1. GS and PS demonstrating the basic algorithm. Note that view space Z is passed as an attribute in addition, because the pull-mode interpolation of the z-component of the attributes with the semantic SV_POSITION is not allowed by the HLSL compiler.

We now discuss some corner cases and possible solutions.

2.3.4 Clipped Triangles and Blending

Even though the GS passes the edge equations of the triangle, it can get clipped and new triangles can be introduced by the clipper. These newly generated triangles get rasterized and handled by the downstream pipeline. This is illustrated in Figure 2.2.

GS sets the edge equations for the triangle ABC. The clipper clips it and submits two triangles, AB_1C and CB_1B_2 to the downstream pipeline. As a result, the edge equations of the triangles actually being rasterized (AB_1C and CB_1B_2) do not match with the ones passed by the GS. If the PS uses the edge equations of the triangle ABC, the pixels along the shared internal edge B_1C (introduced by the clipper) will get shaded multiple times. This may differ from vendor to vendor, because the clipper guard bands can be different. Even worse—if the rasterization order of the clipper-generated triangles changes from one invocation to another, a given pixel along the edge B_1C will get processed in a different order each time introducing a flicker. Normal (non-conservative) rasterization rules [Microsoft Developer Resources 2015c] ensure that such pixels along the shared (internal or otherwise) edge get rasterized only once. Such a situation never arises along the shared edges of two separate triangles because we use the edge equations of the respective triangles to do the in-out test inside the PS.

One can avoid this interaction by avoiding the clipper invocation. One way to guarantee that the clipper will not be invoked is to clip the triangle inside the GS and send

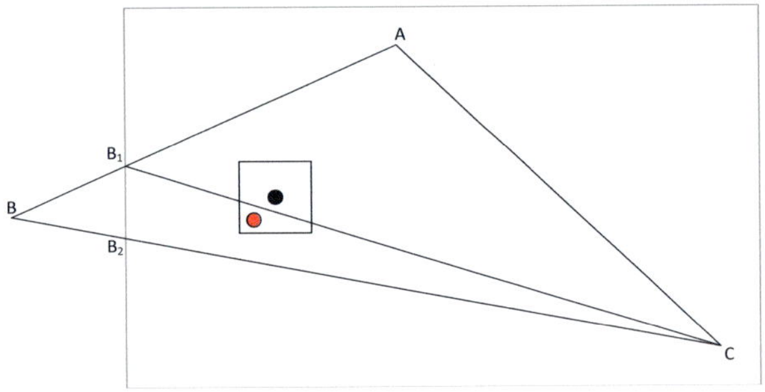

Figure 2.2. Triangle ABC gets clipped to generate two triangles AB_1C and CB_1B_2. Pixels along the edge B_1C are rasterized twice and PS will get invoked twice. One such pixel is shown with black pixel center and red sample location.

the clipped triangles' edge equations downstream along with those triangles. Clipping can generate a fixed number of triangles (with a small upper bound) and the GS could be written with this upper bound. The floating-point arithmetic is not associative, (i.e., `1.0f - (1.0f - t)` $\neq$ `t`); however, the fixed-point arithmetic is associative. To ensure that the new vertices being introduced by the clipper are consistent on either side of a shared edge, the fixed-point math must be used. Although conceptually simple, clipping inside the GS can result in serious performance degradation. If the application culls the triangles against the view frustum on the CPU, the clipper will never get invoked, and, in that case, one does not have to write the clipper in the GS.

Another detail to notice is the fact that we use edge equations of the parent triangle (ABC) only for doing in-out tests inside the PS. The pull-mode interpolation is done using the attribute values at the clipper-generated triangles. Figure 2.2 shows a pixel along the shared edge with the black pixel center and red programmatically-placed sample. While processing triangle AB_1C, `IsInside()` returns true because the sample location (red) is inside all three edges of the triangle ABC. However, the pull-mode interpolation uses the attribute values at the vertices A, B_1 and C and *extrapolates* the values at the sample location. This still produces correct results because triangle AB_1C and ABC are coplanar and AB_1C is contained within ABC. If the triangle CB_1B_2 gets rasterized before AB_1C, pull-mode interpolation *interpolates* the attribute values at vertices C, B_1 and B_2.

Another way to avoid the multiple PS invocations along an internal edge of the clipped triangle is to ensure that the pixels along those edges are processed only once. We generate a unique primitive ID in the GS by incrementing a UAV counter and pass down this primitive ID to the PS. Note that all the triangles that the clipper generates use the same primitive ID. We bind a rasterizer ordered view (ROV) [Microsoft Developer Resources 2015b] the size of the render target for storing these primitive IDs with an initial value of 0xFFFFFFFF. Using `InterlockedCompareStore`, we update the ROV with the primitive ID and process the pixel, but only if the contents of ROV at that pixel location are different from the primitive ID of that pixel. If the primitive has already processed a given pixel (by one of the clipper-generated triangles), we simply skip processing that pixel for that primitive. Use of ROV (instead of unordered access view (UAV)) ensures primitives process the pixels in the submission order. To understand the importance of using ROV, imagine another triangle $A'B'C'$ exactly at the same screen-space location but at a different Z. Assume $A'B'C'$ appeared after ABC in submission order. ROV (instead of UAV) ensures that $A'B'C'$ sees the same pixel after ABC is done processing that pixel.

Although the above mentioned technique takes care of triangles clipped against the side frusta and the far plane, near-plane clipping requires some extra treatment. Triangles that cross the eye plane generate external projections [Yeung 2012]. As a result, the edge equations for the edges containing these vertices are not useful in doing in-out tests. To avoid this, we clip the triangle edges against the near plane in the GS to produce correct edge equations. Note that we only need the edge equations. The vertices we generate in the neighboring triangles as a result of clipping in floating point can be different; as long as they are along the same line segment they produce the same edge equation. If both the vertices are behind the eye, we simply mark that edge as invalid and skip doing the in-out test for that edge in the PS.

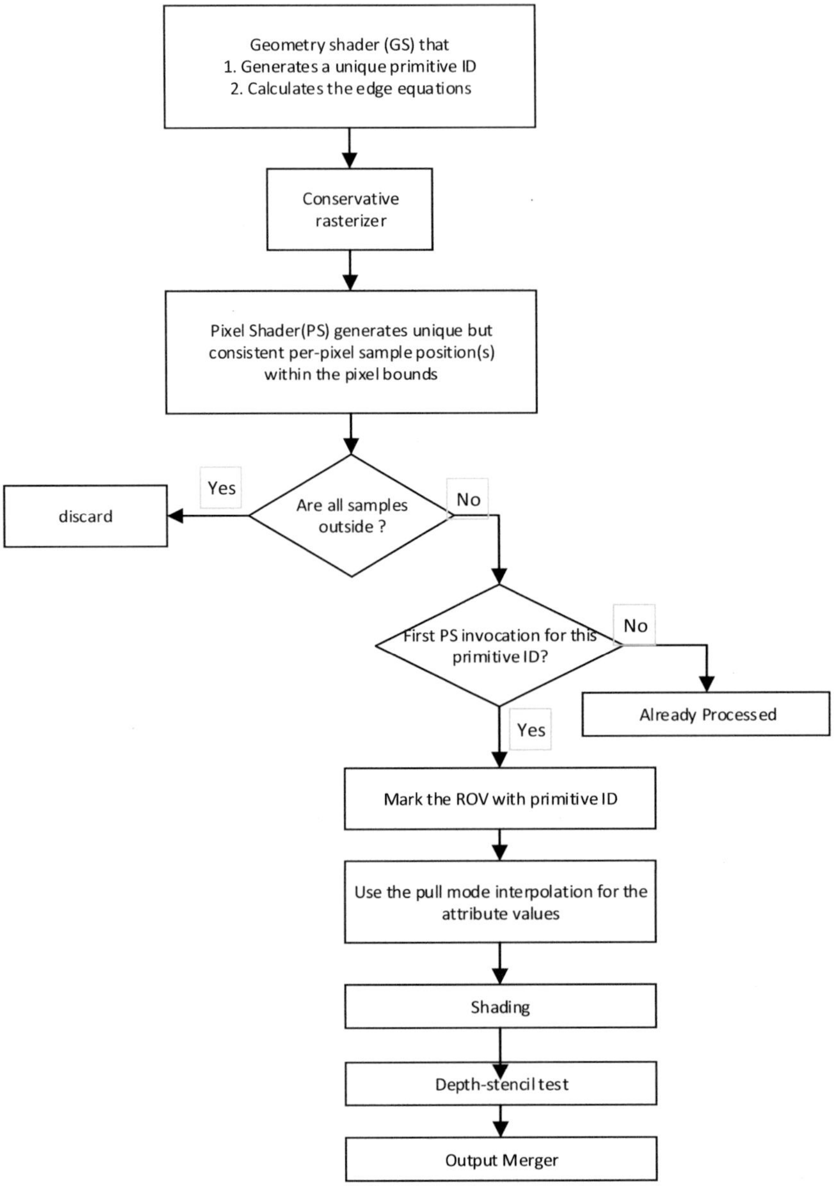

Figure 2.3. Algorithm to generate the programmable per pixel samples using conservative rasterization. Sample locations change from pixel to pixel, but is consistent for a given pixel and a view (camera and the viewport).

2.3.5 Foveated Rendering

Foveated rendering [Guenter et al. 2012] has become quite important with the recent advances in the commodity virtual reality head-mounted displays (HMD. In general, the term *foveated rendering* refers to improving the image quality in the center of the screen and progressively reducing the quality as one goes radially outwards (with the appropriate scaling for the aspect ratio). Adaptive supersampling can be used to adjust the image quality by shading at all sample locations for the pixels in the center region of the screen and shading fewer samples away from the center of the screen. However, by default, the sample locations within the pixel are not programmable. With the proposed algorithm (see Figure 2.3), one can move the sample locations in such a way that the sample density reduces as one goes away from the center of the screen. This is shown in Figure 2.4. In theory, one can dedicate as many samples per pixel as possible, but after a maximum number of MSAA samples supported by the API/hardware is reached, one must resort to doing the depth/stencil and alpha blending inside the shaders.

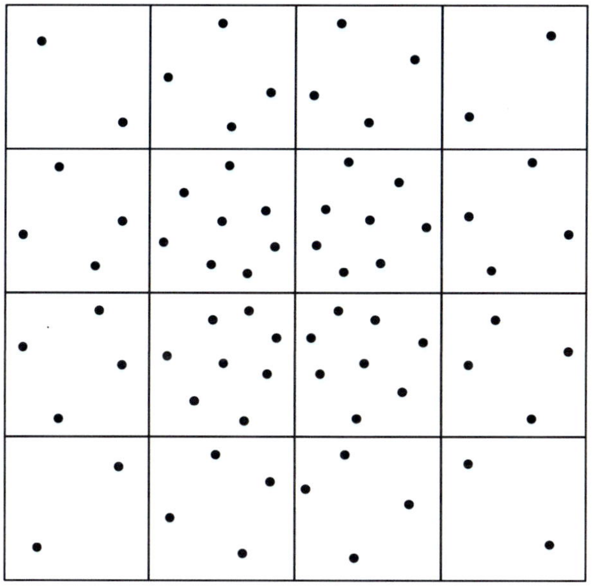

Figure 2.4. An example sample pattern for foveated rendering. Note that the density of samples reduces as one goes away from the center of the screen. Center four pixels have 8 samples per pixel (spp), the ones along the sides have 4 spp and the ones in the corners have 2 spp.

2.4 Demo

A real-time demo implemented using DirectX shader Model 5.1 is available.

Bibliography

AKELEY, K. 1993. Reality engine graphics. In *Proceedings of the 20th Annual Conference on Computer Graphics and Interactive Techniques*, ACM, New York, SIGGRAPH '93, 109–116.

GUENTER, B., FINCH, M., DRUCKER, S., TAN, D., AND SNYDER, J. 2012. Foveated 3d graphics. *ACM Trans. Graph. 31*, 6, 164:1–164:10.

KARIS, B. 2014. High quality temporal supersampling. In *Advances in Real-time Rendering in Games: SIGGRAPH Course*, ACM, New York. URL: http://advances.realtimerendering.com/s2014/#_HIGH-QUALITY_TEMPORAL_SUPERSAMPLING.

MICROSOFT DEVELOPER RESOURCES, 2015a. Conservative rasterization. https://msdn.microsoft.com/en-us/library/windows/desktop/dn914594(v=vs.85).aspx.

MICROSOFT DEVELOPER RESOURCES, 2015b. Rasterizer order views. https://msdn.microsoft.com/en-us/library/windows/desktop/dn914601(v=vs.85).aspx.

MICROSOFT DEVELOPER RESOURCES, 2015c. Rasterization rules. https://msdn.microsoft.com/en-us/library/windows/desktop/cc627092%28v=vs.85%29.aspx?f=255&MSPPError=-2147217396.

PHARR, M., AND HUMPHREYS, G. 2010. *Physically Based Rendering: From Theory to Implementation*, 2nd ed. Morgan Kaufmann Publishers Inc., San Francisco.

YEUNG, S., 2012. In depth: Software rasterizer and triangle clipping. http://www.gamasutra.com/view/news/168577/Indepth_Software_rasterizer_and_triangle_clipping.php.

III

3

Mobile Toon Shading

Felipe Lira, Felipe Chaves, Flávio Villalva, Jesus Sosa, Kléverson Paixão and Teófilo Dutra

3.1 Introduction

Photorealistic rendering is a common goal in the computer graphics industry. This rendering approach intends to produce high quality images through the realistic simulation of light interaction with the environment, and often places a high demand on computational resources. Sometimes, artistic direction or lack of computational resources will motivate developers to use other rendering techniques which are not based on physical illumination models or are not intended to be realistic. Non-photorealistic rendering (NPR) techniques have been widely adopted for giving a painting, drawing, or cartoonish artistic style to 3D rendering.

In this chapter, we describe a unique artistic style through a mobile-ready toon-shading technique. Toon shading is a recurrent NPR technique used in video games for giving a cartoonish aspect to the rendered scenes (Figure 3.1). In order to achieve this, it is necessary to make the 3D scene appear flat, often

Figure 3.1. NPR examples. Left: *The Legend of Zelda: The Wind Waker HD* [Nintendo 2013]; Right: *Guilty Gear Xrd* [Arc System Works 2014].

via nonrealistic illumination models with fewer shading colors and by drawing object outlines. Visual results can be enhanced further by using reprographic techniques such as halftone, which simulate continuous tone imagery through the use of varying sized or spaced geometries (usually dots) in a grid-like pattern.

The idea for the proposed shader arose from the desire to simulate a pop-art style using 3D in real time for games. Initially we tried to make the outline look like a newspaper clipping through the addition of a texture, with overlay blending to simulate the effect. We added particles to complement the outline and give a greater dynamic to the silhouette. For that technique to work nicely, we wanted each animation frame to resemble a paper cut; and then, it was necessary to synchronize each frame with the particle system. However, for animations at usual frame rates (up to 60 fps), the effect turned into a distraction and it was not visually pleasing. We tried to use non-interpolated animations in order to have a stepped animation that would enhance the poses and convey the idea of clipping paper to the screen. Nonetheless, the engine we use forces interpolation between frames by standard and did not allow us to achieve the desired effect. Since we were not able to synchronize the effect with the animation, we abandoned this idea.

Another graphical effect we tried was the use of offset values (exposed in the material), for each color channel of the diffuse texture, in order to simulate a kind of chromatic aberration. The technique works well if used carefully, but very large offsets make UV islands become visible. In the end, these experiments did not end up in the final shader.

In this chapter we describe the individual techniques that comprise our unique artistic style, including a flat shading (Section 3.3), soft light blending (Section 3.4), halftone-based shadows (Section 3.5) and threshold-based inverted hull outline (Section 3.6). We present our implementation of these techniques in Section 3.7 and end by drawing final conclusions in Section 3.8.

3.2 Technique Overview

To achieve a cartoonish artistic style, we used a combination of several different techniques. Toon shading is important in order for the 3D world to appear flat. The transition between light and dark areas has to be hard in order to mimic the shading found in cartoons (Figure 3.2 (left)). Another artistic feature, also observed in cartoons, is the presence of hard outlines (Figure 3.2 (left)). Finally, reproduction of printing patterns (also known as halftone patterns), observed in comics (Figure 3.2 (right)), were the final touch in our artistic style composition.

Our technique starts by pre-processing the model and storing both its normals per face (for flat shading) and normals per vertex (for outline generation). Then, at each iteration of the rendering loop, two passes are used to assemble the desired look. In the first pass, the threshold-based inverted hull outline is generated. Then, in the second pass, the softlight blending equation is used to blend the

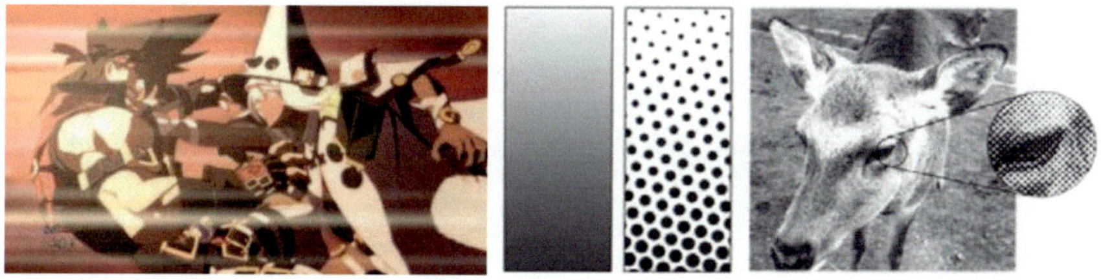

Figure 3.2. Left: rough transition between light and dark areas and hard outlines are features observed in cartoons [Arc System Works 2014]; Right: halftone pattern observed in comics [Scientific American 2012].

albedo with the halftone applied to the flat shading. An overview of the technique is shown in Figure 3.3, and the composition is demonstrated in Figure 3.4.

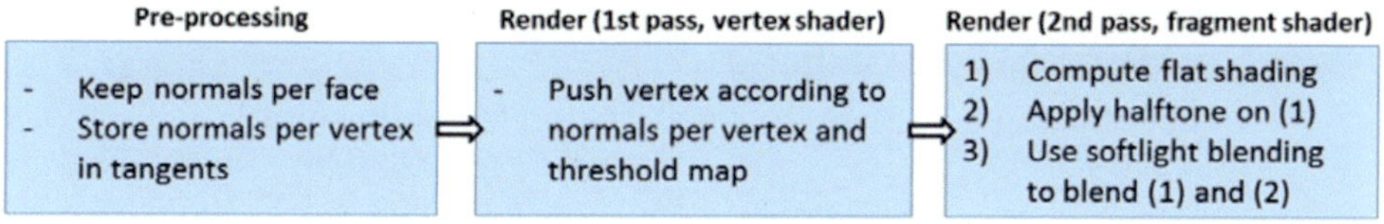

Figure 3.3. Technique overview.

3.3 Flat Shading

The flat shading is achieved through the use of a light-ramp texture in order to define the interaction between light and the surface of the model. The dot product of the surface normal and the light direction is used to sample the ramp texture. The ramp texture provides a hard transition, in our case in three steps, that will be useful for fading our halftone patterns later. Figure 3.4 (b) shows the flat shading obtained using the ramp in Figure 3.5.

3.4 Soft Light Blending

We then use the soft light equation for blending two layers of images. The effect consists of lightning or darkening a base layer according to a blend layer. If a pixel color component in the blend layer is lighter than 50% gray, the correspondent pixel in the base layer will be lighted; otherwise, the pixel is darkened. Mathematically, we have

$$\text{Softlight}(b, a) = \begin{cases} 2ab - a^2(1 - 2b) & \text{if } b \leq 0.5 \\ 2a(1 - b) + \sqrt{a}(2b - 1) & \text{if } b > 0.5 \end{cases}$$

(a) Albedo

(b) Ramp

(c) Softlight((b), (a))

(d) Halftone((b))

(e) Threshold-based outline

(f) Softlight((d), (a)) with outline

Figure 3.4. Technique composition.

Figure 3.5. Ramp texture.

where b is a color component that belongs to the blend layer and a belongs to the base layer. In Figure 3.4 (c), the soft light effect is applied using Figure 3.4 (a) as base layer and Figure 3.4 (b) as blend layer.

3.5 Halftone-based Shadows

We then apply a halftone pattern over the flat shading. In the halftone technique, images are printed using dots with different colors and sizes, and they can be spaced non-uniformly in order to simulate continuously filled areas via an

```
half HalfTone(half RepeatRate , half DotSize , half2 UV)
{
  half size = 1.0 / RepeatRate;
  half2 cellSize = half2(size, size);
  half2 cellCenter = cellSize * 0.5;

  // abs() to avoid negative values after rotation.
  half2 uvlocal = fmod(abs(UV), cellSize);
  half dist = length(uvlocal - cellCenter);
  half radius = cellCenter.x * DotSize;

  // Anti-Aliasing based on differentials
  half threshold = length(ddx(dist) - ddy(dist));

  return smoothstep(dist - threshold, dist + threshold, radius);
}
```

Listing 3.1. Halftone function.

optical illusion. To reproduce the halftone, we define a function based on three parameters: the repeat rate of the dots, the dot size, and a UV position. Our representation is screen-space–based, i.e., the UV passed to the halftone function is the normalized screen position. After the normalization, we are able to rotate the halftone pattern by rotating the UV. The function computes the diameter of the dot and its center position; then, we compute the distance of the UV with respect to the center, and, finally, we perform a smooth step considering that distance and the radius of the dot pattern. The function is shown in Listing 3.1.

The dot size is determined according to the dot product between the normal and light directions, and the result is scaled by a user-defined value. We also define a cutoff threshold for the pattern and a fade distance based on the camera distance. Figure 3.4 (d) shows the halftone pattern applied over the flat shading.

3.6 Threshold-based Inverted Hull Outline

Finally, we need to draw the model's outline. Usually, stencil buffers are used for drawing outlines [Learn OpenGL 2016]. However, since we wanted a mobile-friendly technique, we opted for using the inverted hull outline technique (also know as shell method [Akenine-Möller et al. 2008]) which has a lower computational cost.

The inverted hull outline technique uses an extra pass to render the outline. The outline generation consists of: 1) scaling up the model by pushing its vertices in the direction of their normals; 2) rendering the scaled model with a unique color, without lighting, while culling front faces and showing back faces (first pass); and, 3) rendering the original model (second pass).

This technique works fine if the normals at vertices are the average of the adjacent surface normals. The problem here is that our flat shading needs to use surface normals. The solution we found was pre-processing the model in order

Figure 3.6. Diffuse map (left) and threshold map (right).

to store the averaged normals at the tangents (since we are not using them). We also use a threshold map (Figure 3.6 (right)) to control the scale applied to each vertex. Figure 3.4 (e) shows the outline generated for our example model and Figure 3.4 (f) shows our final composition.

3.7 Implementation

The two passes used to compose the result can be seen in Listing 3.2. An emission map is used in the end of the second pass to highlight some parts of the diffuse map.

```
Pass {
  Name "Outline"
  Cull Front
  ZWrite Off
  ...
  CGPROGRAM
  ...

  VertexOutput vert(VertexInput v) {
    VertexOutput o = (VertexOutput)0;
    half thicknessOffset = tex2Dlod(_OutlineThicknessMap,
        half4(v.texcoord.xy, 0.0, 0.0)).r;
    half outlineWidth = clamp(thicknessOffset * _OutlineScale,
        _OutlineMinOffset, _OutlineMaxOffset);
    o.pos = mul(UNITY_MATRIX_MVP, half4(v.vertex.xyz +
        (v.normal * outlineWidth), 1.0));
    return o;
  }
  ... // frag shader is simple pass through.
  ENDCG
}
```

```
Pass {
  Name "Halftone"
  ...
  CGPROGRAM
  ... // vert shader is simple pass through.

  fixed4 frag(VertexOutput i) : COLOR {
    half2 screenUV = RotateUV(NormalizeScreenSpace(i.screenPos),
        _HtPatternAngle);
    half camDist = length(i.posWorld - _WorldSpaceCameraPos);
    half htAlphaFade = smoothstep(_MaxFade, _MinFade, camDist);

    // Apply Lambert Light term using a lightRamp
    half3 diffuseMap = tex2dLinear(_DiffuseMap,
        TRANSFORM_TEX(i.uv0, _DiffuseMap)).rgb;

    half NdL = saturate(dot(normalize(i.normalDir),
        normalize(_WorldSpaceLightPos0.xyz)));
    half lbtn = tex2dLinear(_LightRamp, half2(NdL, 0)).r * 0.5;
    half htCutoff = step(_HtCutoff, (1.0 - NdL) * _HtScale);
    half ht = HalfTone(_RepeatRate, (1.0 - NdL) * _HtScale,
        screenUV) * htCutoff * htAlphaFade;
    half3 htColor = lerp(half3(lbtn, lbtn, lbtn), _HtColor, ht);

    half4 emissionMap = tex2dLinear(_EmissionMap,
        TRANSFORM_TEX(i.uv0, _EmissionMap));
    half3 result = Softlight(htColor, diffuseMap) + diffuseMap *
        emissionMap.rgb * _EmissionIntensity;

    return gammaConvert(fixed4(result, 1));
  }
  ENDCG
}
```

Listing 3.2. Two passes used for composing the proposed artistic style.

3.8 Final Considerations

We presented a cartoonish shading composed of different NPR techniques. With this shading, we are able to reproduce the art style seen in comics or cartoons. Moreover, it is mobile-friendly and simple to implement. Despite the positive results achieved, there is still room for improvement. The halftone pattern, for example, is screen-space–based, and that can lead to unpleasant visual artifacts depending on the camera motion or the motion of characters in the scene. This is especially noticeable in VR where the user has more control over the camera. The outline can also present artifacts, such as spikes or holes, depending on the scale applied and the model shape (for example, concavities can lead to self-intersection).

Bibliography

Akenine-Möller, T., Haines, E., and Hoffman, N. 2008. Non-photorealistic rendering. In *Real-Time Rendering 3rd Edition*. A K Peters, Ltd., Natick, MA, USA, 1045.

Arc System Works, 2014. Guilty Gear Xrd. Available at: http://guiltygear.us/ggxrds/media.

Learn OpenGL, 2016. Object outlining. Available at: http://www.learnopengl.com/#!Advanced-OpenGL/Stencil-testing.

Nintendo, 2013. The Legend of Zelda: The Wind Waker HD. Available at: http://www.nintendo.com/games/detail/the-legend-of-zelda-the-wind-waker-hd-wii-u.

Scientific American, 2012. Dots, spots, and pixels: what's in a name? Available at: http://blogs.scientificamerican.com/symbiartic/dots-spots-and-pixels-whats-in-a-name/.

4

III

High Quality GPU-efficient Image Detail Manipulation

Kin-Ming Wong and Tien-Tsin Wong

GPU-powered image processing pipelines have become increasingly popular for real-time streaming and broadcast applications. It is quite common for small-scale image details to require manipulation in order to achieve a better visual experience, such as stylistic or cosmetic enhancement. Detail manipulation processes rely on edge-preserving filtering, which decomposes the original image into a base layer and one or more detail layers. Manipulations can then be applied onto the selected detail layer while keeping the base layer intact. Figure 4.1 shows an example of using our method to selectively suppress unwanted small-scale details.

We have designed a new edge-preserving filter called *sub-window variance filter* that powers our image detail manipulation process. This filter uses an intuitive and effective edge model which allows precise control of the filtering process. Accelerated by the *summed area table* technique [Crow 1984, Hensley

Figure 4.1. Original image (left) and the processed image (right).

et al. 2005], our filter makes the whole image manipulation pipeline highly GPU-efficient. We have included source code of a small GLSL compute shader-based image detail-manipulation application as supplementary material.

4.1 Image Detail Manipulation Pipeline

Figure 4.2 illustrates a typical image detail manipulation pipeline that enhances the contrast of small-scale details. The pipeline can be summarized as follows:

1. Decomposition by edge-preserving filtering:
   - Apply the edge-preserving filter $F()$ to the input image I to obtain the base layer B, i.e., $B = F(I)$.

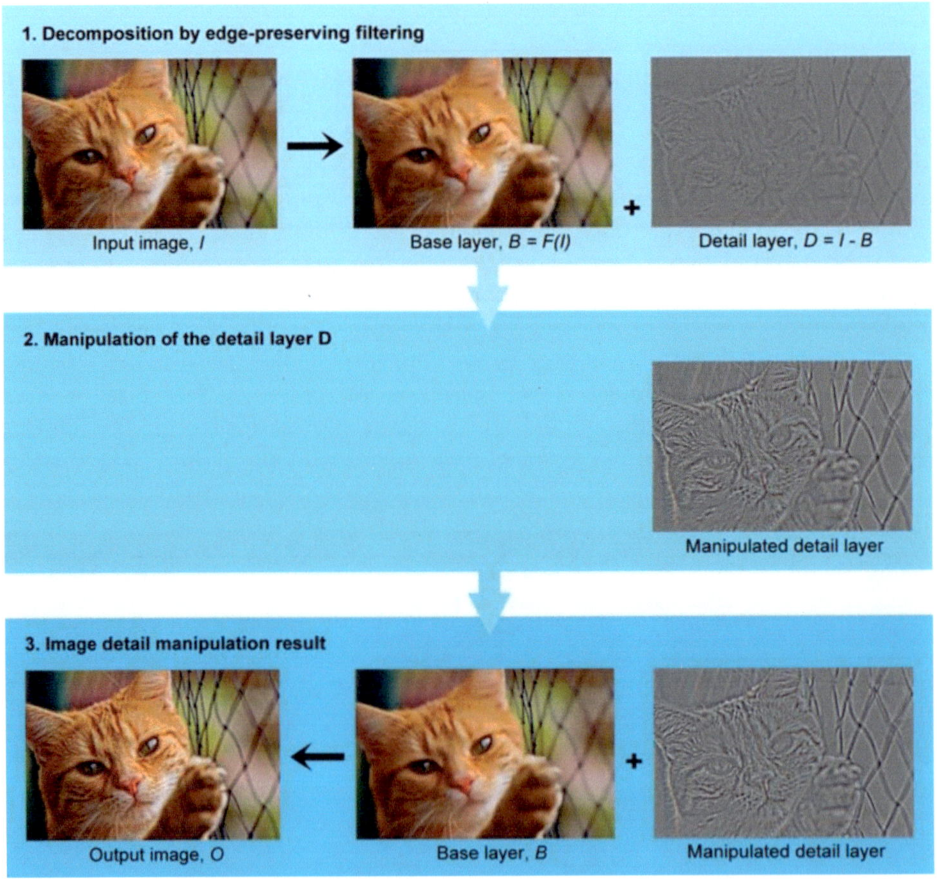

Figure 4.2. A typical image detail manipulation pipeline.

- Obtain the detail layer D by subtracting the computed base layer B from the input image I, i.e., $D = I - B$.

2. Manipulation on the detail layer D:

   - Apply a desired multiplication factor A to the detail layer D.

3. Image detail manipulation result:

   - Obtain the output image O by computing the sum of the base layer B and the manipulated detail layer $A \times D$, i.e., $O = B + A \times D$.

The pipeline illustrated in Figure 4.2 is known as single-scale image manipulation, where only a single detail layer is manipulated. It is possible to apply the edge-preserving filter to the base layer in order to obtain an additional detail layer and a new base layer. This type of iterative decomposition is the key to achieving a process called multi-scale image detail manipulation and our small example application demonstrates how a two-detail layer manipulation works.

Edge-preserving filtering is the instrumental process which makes image detail manipulation possible; it essentially smooths out image details while keeping the important image structure unchanged. For readers who are interested in the theoretical details and essential criteria of a good edge-preserving filter for the decomposition process, [Farbman et al. 2008] is a good article that covers the historical development and additional applications of multi-scale image decomposition. Processing Steps 2 and 3 in the above pipeline are seemingly parallel, and they map perfectly to GPU processing. In order to serve real-time applications, we need a GPU-efficient edge-preserving filter to power processing Step 1. We detail the design and intuition of our GPU-efficient edge-preserving filter in the following section.

Figure 4.3. Original image (left) and filtered image (right).

4.2 Decomposition by Sub-window Variance Filtering

A quality edge-preserving filter must separate the small-scale details defined by the user from a given input image. Figure 4.3 shows the filtered result using our sub-window variance filter.

4.2.1 Edge Awareness by Sub-window Variance

The filtered image in Figure 4.3 preserves important structures, such as the facial features and all high-contrast areas, while the small-scale features, such as the fur detail, are filtered. Our filter relies on an intuitive edge model to identify structural edges and this model is comprised of the following three conditions:

1. An edge is formed by two adjacent groups of pixels.

2. These two groups have contrasting intensities (overall high variance).

3. An edge is more distinct if pixels of at least one group share similar intensity (locally low variance in this subregion).

The intuition of this edge model is best illustrated by the two images as shown in Figure 4.4. Some edge-preserving filters, such as the guided filter [He et al. 2010], rely on measuring statistical variance of an image patch as indication of edges. A fuzzy edge as shown in Figure 4.4 (left), exhibits a high overall variance but it certainly does not represent a clear edge. This implies that by measuring only the overall statistical variance without any spatial information, we cannot ascertain the existence of an edge. A distinct edge as shown in Figure 4.4 (right), however, exhibits a sub-region of relatively low variance which serves as strong evidence of an edge.

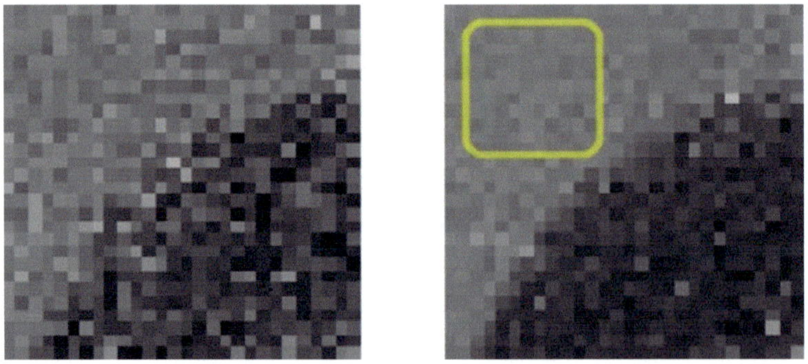

Figure 4.4. A Fuzzy edge (left) and a distinct edge (right).

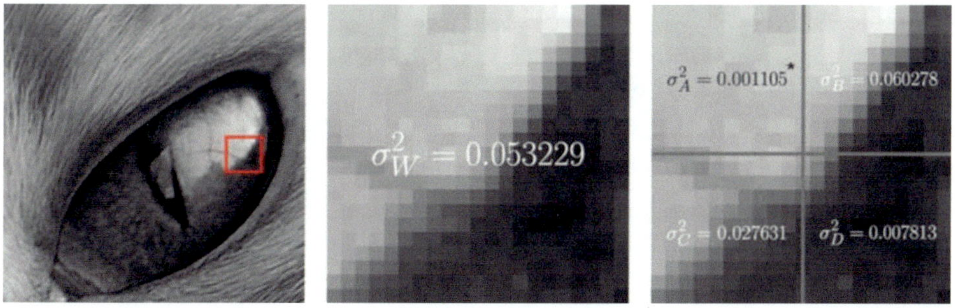

Figure 4.5. Local image patch highlighted (left), image patch variance value (middle) and sub-window variance values (right).

Based on this edge model, we demonstrate how we may use variance values of both the image patch and its sub-windows to quantify the potential existence of an edge. Our example (Figure 4.5) assumes pixel intensity values are encoded with floating-point numbers ranging from 0.0 to 1.0. We start by computing the variance value of the highlighted image patch, $\sigma_W^2 = 0.053229$. We then sub-divide the patch uniformly into four sub-windows A, B, C and D as shown in Figure 4.5 (right) with variance values $\sigma_A^2 = 0.001105^*, \sigma_B^2 = 0.060278, \sigma_C^2 = 0.027631$, and $\sigma_D^2 = 0.007813$, respectively.

We now introduce a factor A_k, which we call the per-patch preservation factor, with the following equation:

$$A_k = \min(1, \frac{\sigma_{\text{max}}^2}{\sigma_{\text{min}}^2 + \epsilon}), \tag{4.1}$$

where $\sigma_{\text{max}}^2 = \max(\{\sigma_W^2, \sigma_A^2, \sigma_B^2, \sigma_C^2, \sigma_D^2\})$, $\sigma_{\text{min}}^2 = \min(\sigma_A^2, \sigma_B^2, \sigma_C^2, \sigma_D^2)$, and ϵ is a positive-valued user parameter.

This per-patch preservation factor A_k reflects the potential existence of edge-like features and is valued from 0.0 to 1.0. A value of 0.0 indicates no edge found, and a value of 1.0 represents full preservation of a patch given the user parameter ϵ. The parameter ϵ has an intuitive physical meaning here; it defines the minimum variance value of a clear edge that one wants to preserve completely.

Assuming we want to preserve all clear edges with variance value above 0.05, i.e., we set $\epsilon = 0.05$ and by using Equation (4.1), the factor A_k for the image patch in Figure 4.5 is equal to $\min(1, 1.0416) = 1$ and implies this patch deserves full preservation. For any similar patch which has a higher value of σ_{min}^2 (i.e., less distinct edge), the value of A_k will be less than 1.

4.2.2 Sub-window Variance Filter

Based on the per-patch preservation factor introduced in Equation (4.1), we are able to develop a simple filter which delivers quality edge-preserving filtering.

Per-patch filtering. Given an image, a square image patch I_k centered on pixel k is defined by a chosen filter width W. The filtered version of I_k, namely I'_k, is defined as a linear blend of the original patch and its mean as follows:

$$I'_k = A_k I_k + B_k,$$

where A_k is the per-patch preservation factor (Equation (4.1)), $B_k = (1 - A_k)\mu_k$ and μ_k is the mean pixel intensity of patch I_k. This per-patch filtering process requires computation of five variance values for the per-patch preservation factor and the patch's mean. The mean μ_k and variance σ_k^2 of pixel intensity values of an image patch I_k are given by the following equations:

$$\mu_k = \frac{1}{|\omega|} \sum_{i \in \omega_k} p_i$$

$$\sigma_k^2 = \frac{1}{|\omega|} \sum_{i \in \omega_k} p_i^2 - \mu_k^2, \tag{4.2}$$

where p_i is the intensity value of pixel i on the patch, and ω_k defines the domain of the patch; hence, $|\omega|$ is the total number of pixels on the patch, i.e., $|\omega| = W^2$. By building summed-area tables [Crow 1984, Hensley et al. 2005] of p_i^2 and p_i of a given image, both the mean and variance values of any rectangular regions can be computed quickly.

Per-pixel filtering. In order to filter a whole image, we may densely evaluate per-patch preservation factors over the whole image. As every single pixel receives multiple preservation factor estimations from different image patches, the final filtered pixel output is given by

$$p'_i = \bar{A}_k p_i + \bar{B}_k,$$

where $\bar{A}_k = \frac{1}{|\Omega|} \sum_{k \in \Omega_i} A_k$, $\bar{B}_k = \frac{1}{|\Omega|} \sum_{k \in \Omega_i} B_k$, and Ω_i is the domain of all patches that offers estimation to pixel p_i (Ω_i is a square region of width W centered on pixel p_i.). The value $\bar{A}_k$ can be understood as a per-pixel preservation factor. Computation of both $\bar{A}_k$ and $\bar{B}_k$ can be accelerated by using summed-area tables of per-patch A_k and B_k.

In short, our sub-window variance filtering process can be summarized as a two-stage process as follows:

1. Evaluate densely, per-patch preservation factors based on the given filter width W and user threshold parameter ϵ.

2. Compute per-pixel filtered values using per-patch filtering results from Step 1.

4.3 GLSL Compute Shader-based Implementation

In order to illustrate the use of the sub-window variance filter for image detail manipulation, we have included the source code of a small OpenGL 4.3+–based application as supplemental material (compute shader support requires OpenGL 4.3+). A single-scale image detail manipulation cycle is summarized in Figure 4.6 and is comprised of five steps. Since summed-area table (SAT) computation is a rather mature GPU computation technique, we refer readers to [Crow 1984, Hensley et al. 2005] for a general introduction and to [Sellers et al. 2013] for a detailed implementation discussion, as our example application uses the same prefix-sum–based method for SAT computation.

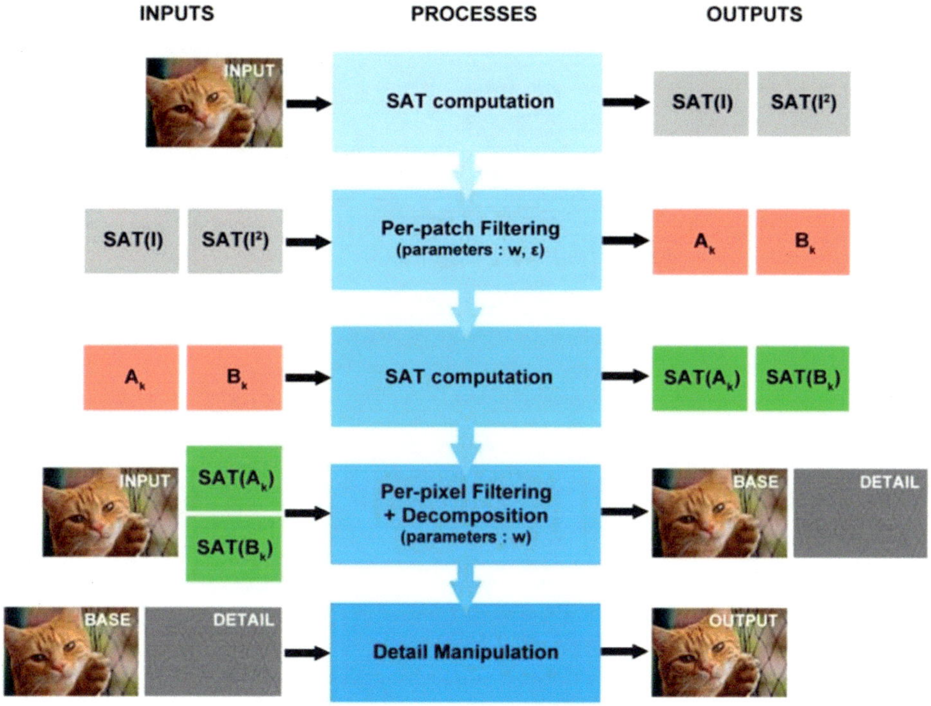

Figure 4.6. Detailed pipeline of an GLSL-based image-detail manipulation.

4.3.1 Per-patch Filtering Compute Shader, `perPatch.cs.glsl`

Listing 4.1 shows the variance computation function of the GLSL compute shader program named `perPatch.cs.glsl` in our example application. The function

```
#version 430 core

layout(local_size_x = 1024) in;

layout(binding = 0, rgba32f)  readonly uniform image2D sat_I2;
layout(binding = 1, rgba32f)  readonly uniform image2D sat_I;
layout(binding = 2, rgba32f) writeonly uniform image2D Ak;
layout(binding = 3, rgba32f) writeonly uniform image2D Bk;

uniform int r;
uniform float epsilon;

void compVar(in ivec2 coord, in int lx, in int ly,
             in int ux, in int uy, in float omega,
             out vec3 variance)
{

    ivec2 P0 = coord + ivec2(lx, ly);
    ivec2 P1 = coord + ivec2(lx, uy);
    ivec2 P2 = coord + ivec2(ux, ly);
    ivec2 P3 = coord + ivec2(ux, uy);

    vec3    a, b, c, d;

    a = imageLoad(sat_I2, P0).rgb;
    b = imageLoad(sat_I2, P1).rgb;
    c = imageLoad(sat_I2, P2).rgb;
    d = imageLoad(sat_I2, P3).rgb;
    vec3    u2 = vec3(omega) * (a - b - c + d);

    a = imageLoad(sat_I, P0).rgb;
    b = imageLoad(sat_I, P1).rgb;
    c = imageLoad(sat_I, P2).rgb;
    d = imageLoad(sat_I, P3).rgb;
    vec3    u = vec3(omega) * (a - b - c + d);

    variance = u2 - (u * u);

};
```

Listing 4.1. Per-patch filtering, `perPatch.cs.glsl`, Part 1.

`compVar()` looks up the input SATs with the given coordinates in order to compute a region's variance using Equation (4.2).

Listing 4.2 shows the first half of the `main()` function in the GLSL compute shader `perPatch.cs.glsl`, this part computes the whole window and sub-window variance values required by the sub-window variance filter computation. The second half of the `main()` function, as shown in Listing 4.3, computes the per-patch preservation factor using Equation (4.1). For processing of RGB images, we pick the maximum per-patch preservation factor A_k among three color channels as a unified preservation factor for downstream processing.

```
void main(void)
{
    ivec2   coord = ivec2(gl_LocalInvocationID.x,
```

```
                              gl_WorkGroupID.x);

    //  Whole-window mean:uG and variance:vG
    //
    float   blockSize = r + r + 1;
    float   omega = 1.0 / (blockSize * blockSize);

    int     lx = -r - 1;
    int     ux = r;
    int     ly = -r - 1;
    int     uy = r;

    vec3    a, b, c, d;

    a = imageLoad(sat_I, coord + ivec2( lx, ly )).rgb;
    b = imageLoad(sat_I, coord + ivec2( lx, uy )).rgb;
    c = imageLoad(sat_I, coord + ivec2( ux, ly )).rgb;
    d = imageLoad(sat_I, coord + ivec2( ux, uy )).rgb;

    vec3    uG = vec3(omega) * (a - b - c + d);
    vec3    vG;
    compVar(coord, lx, ly, ux, uy, omega, vG);

    //  Sub-window variances
    //
    vec3    vA, vB, vC, vD;
    blockSize = r + 1;
    omega = 1.0 / (blockSize * blockSize);

    //  sub-window A
    ux = 0;
    uy = 0;
    compVar(coord, lx, ly, ux, uy, omega, vA);

    //  sub-window B
    ly = -1;
    uy = r;
    compVar(coord, lx, ly, ux, uy, omega, vB);

    //  sub-window C
    //
    lx = -1;
    ux = r;
    ly = -r - 1;
    uy = 0;
    compVar(coord, lx, ly, ux, uy, omega, vC);

    //  sub-window D
    ly = -1;
    uy = r;
    compVar(coord, lx, ly, ux, uy, omega, vD);
    ...
```

Listing 4.2. Per-patch filtering, `perPatch.cs.glsl`, Part 2.

```
    ...

    //  Compute per-patch preservation
    //
    vec3    eps, vP, vMin, vMax;

    vMin = min( min(vA, vB), min(vC, vD) );
    vMax = max( vG, max(max(vA, vB), max(vC, vD)) );
```

```
    eps  = vec3(epsilon);

    vec3    ak;
    ak = vMax / (eps + vMin);
    ak = min(ak, vec3(1.0));

    //  Maximum ak among 3 channels
    //
    float akMax;
    akMax = max(ak.r, max(ak.g, ak.b));
    ak = vec3(akMax);

    //  Compute bk
    //
    vec3    bk  = uG * (vec3(1.0) - ak);

    imageStore( Ak, coord.xy, vec4(ak.rgb, 1.0) );
    imageStore( Bk, coord.xy, vec4(bk.rgb, 1.0) );

} //    end of main()
```

Listing 4.3. Per-patch filtering, `perPatch.cs.glsl`, Part 3.

4.3.2 Decomposition Compute Shader, `decomp.cs.glsl`

The decomposition compute shader `decomp.cs.glsl` integrates per-pixel filtering with the decomposition process. Per-pixel filtering, as shown in Listing 4.4, is fairly straightforward and relies on the SATs of per-patch preservation factors A_k and weighted means B_k as inputs. This compute shader outputs the base layer and a detail layer which can be used for downstream detail manipulation directly.

```
#version 430 core

layout(local_size_x = 1024) in;

layout(binding = 0, rgba32f) readonly uniform image2D input;
layout(binding = 1, rgba32f) readonly uniform image2D A_K;
layout(binding = 2, rgba32f) readonly uniform image2D B_K;

layout(binding = 3, rgba32f) writeonly uniform image2D base;
layout(binding = 4, rgba32f) writeonly uniform image2D detail;
uniform int r, lx, ly, ux, uy;

void main(void)
{
    ivec2   coord = ivec2(gl_LocalInvocationID.x,
                          gl_WorkGroupID.x);

    if ( coord.x < lx || coord.x > ux || coord.y < ly ||
         coord.y > uy ) {
        imageStore(   base, coord.xy, vec4(0.0) );
        imageStore( detail, coord.xy, vec4(0.0) );
        return;
    }

    //  Per-pixel filtering
    //
```

```
    float   blockSize = r + r + 1;
    float   omega = 1.0 / (blockSize * blockSize);

    vec3    a, b, c, d;
    int r1 = -r - 1;

    a = imageLoad(A_K, coord + ivec2( r1, r1 )).rgb;
    b = imageLoad(A_K, coord + ivec2( r1,  r )).rgb;
    c = imageLoad(A_K, coord + ivec2(  r, r1 )).rgb;
    d = imageLoad(A_K, coord + ivec2(  r,  r )).rgb;
    vec3 ai = vec3(omega) * (a - b - c + d);

    a = imageLoad(B_K, coord + ivec2( r1, r1 )).rgb;
    b = imageLoad(B_K, coord + ivec2( r1,  r )).rgb;
    c = imageLoad(B_K, coord + ivec2(  r, r1 )).rgb;
    d = imageLoad(B_K, coord + ivec2(  r,  r )).rgb;
    vec3 bi = vec3(omega) * (a - b - c + d);

    vec3 org = imageLoad(input, coord).rgb;
    vec3 res = ai * org + bi;

    //  Decomposition
    //
    imageStore(  base, coord.xy, vec4(res.rgb,1.0));
    imageStore(detail, coord.xy, vec4(org.rgb-res.rgb,1.0));
}
```

Listing 4.4. Per-pixel filtering and decompostion, `decomp.cs.glsl`.

4.4 Results

The most common forms of detail manipulation include suppression and contrast enhancement. Figure 4.7 shows a good example of enhancing the contrast of small details in order to emphasize the whole cat's face.

Figure 4.8 shows a multi-scale detail manipulation. The original image went through a two-scale decomposition, and the medium-scale detail layer is removed, with the fine detail layer reduced in a subtle way. This kind of manipulation maintains the natural fine details of skin and suppresses undesired blemishes.

4.5 Conclusion

Image detail manipulation often requires subjective input and control from the end user, which makes interactivity an important criterion of a good manipulation method. Our approach allows real-time manipulation, even on modest GPU hardware. The small two-scale manipulation example application included with this article runs interactively on a NVIDIA GTX 760 GPU and should run equally well on other GPU hardware supporting compute shaders and OpenGL 4.3 or higher. Although we demonstrate the algorithms using compute shaders, it should be equally simple to implement them using traditional fragment shaders on earlier OpenGL versions.

Figure 4.7. Original image (top) and the processed image (bottom) with image detail contrast doubled using filter radius = 5 and $\epsilon = 0.03$.

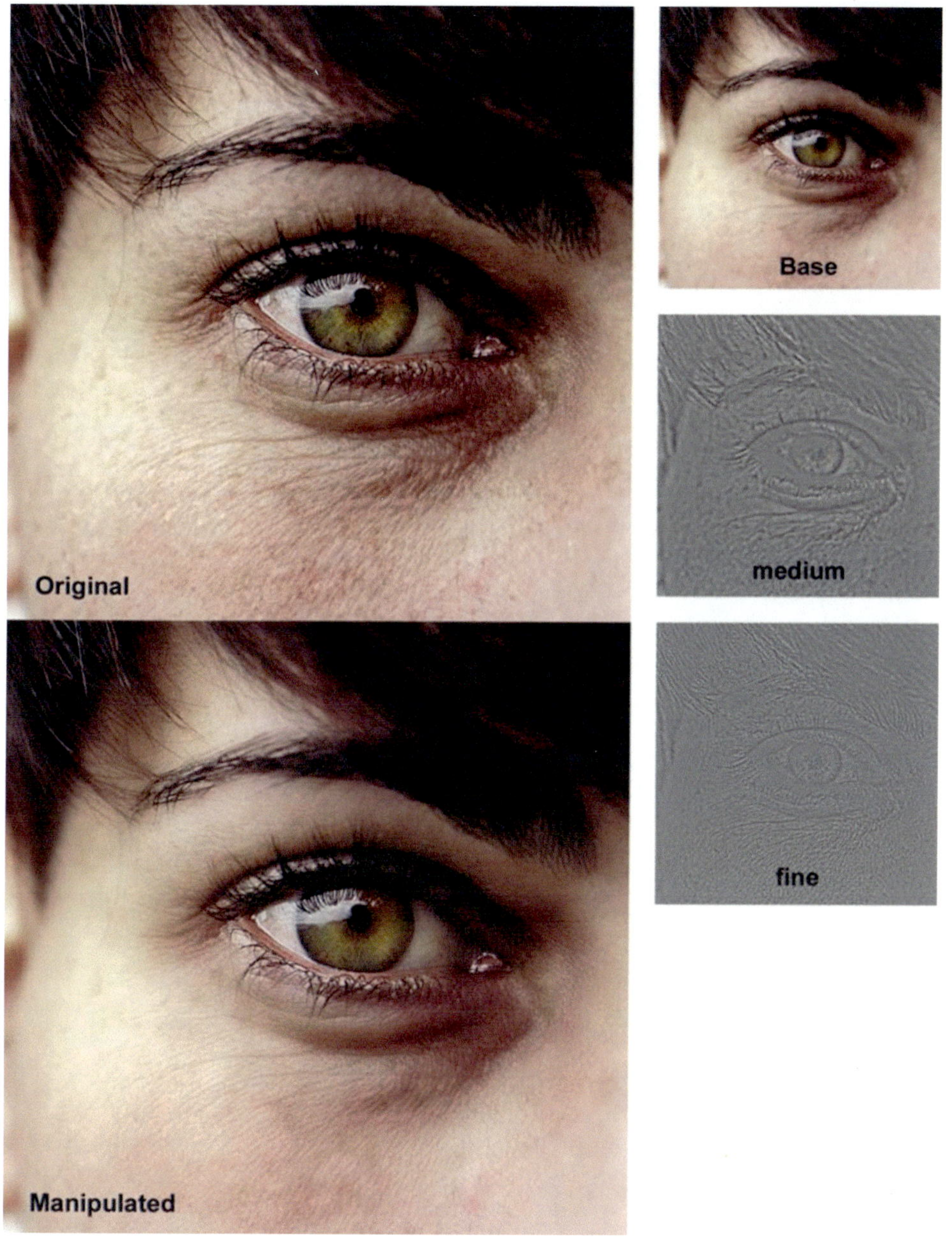

Figure 4.8. Original image (top) and the manipulated image (bottom) with the medium-detail layer removed and fine-detail layer lightly suppressed. Filter parameters—1st iteration: filter radius $= 5$ and $\epsilon = 0.023$, and 2nd iteration: filter radius $= 10$ and $\epsilon = 0.023$.

4.6 Acknowledgement

This project is supported by NSFC (Project No. 61272293) and Research Grants Council of the Hong Kong Special Administrative Region, under RGC General Research Fund (Project No. CUHK 14200915).

Bibliography

Crow, F. C. 1984. Summed-area tables for texture mapping. *SIGGRAPH Comput. Graph. 18*, 3, 207–212.

Farbman, Z., Fattal, R., Lischinski, D., and Szeliski, R. 2008. Edge-preserving decompositions for multi-scale tone and detail manipulation. *ACM Transactions on Graphics (TOG) 27*, 3, 67:1–67:10.

He, K., Sun, J., and Tang, X. 2010. Guided image filtering. In *Proceedings of the 11th European Conference on Computer Vision: Part I*, ECCV'10, Springer-Verlag, 1–14.

Hensley, J., Scheuermann, T., Coombe, G., Singh, M., and Lastra, A. 2005. Fast summed-area table generation and its applications. *Computer Graphics Forum 24*, 3, 547–555.

Sellers, G., Wright Jr, R. S., and Haemel, N. 2013. *OpenGL SuperBible: Comprehensive Tutorial and Reference*. Addison-Wesley, Reading, MA.

5

III

Linear-Light Shading with Linearly Transformed Cosines

Eric Heitz and Stephen Hill

5.1 Introduction

We recently introduced a new real-time area-light shading technique dedicated to lights with polygonal shapes [Heitz et al. 2016]. In this chapter, we extend this area-lighting framework to support *linear* (line-shaped) lights in addition to polygons. Linear lights are cheaper to shade than polygons and they provide a good approximation for thin emitting cylinders (fluorescent tubes, lightsabers, etc.), as shown in Figure 5.1.

Figure 5.1. We use linear lights to approximate thin cylindrical light shapes.

Our area-lighting framework is based on a spherical distribution called *linearly transformed cosines (LTCs)* introduced in our previous article [Heitz et al. 2016]. While not required, we encourage anyone interested in the mathematical details to consult it (or the associated slides) before reading this chapter.

The linear-light shading model. Linear lights share a limitation with point lights in that they cannot be found in the real world, since no real emitter is infinitely thin. However, in Section 5.2 we show that, in many scenarios, linear lights are a good approximation for cylindrical lights with a small but non-zero radius. We describe how to approximate these lights with linear lights that have similar power and shading, and discuss the validity of this approximation.

Note that in this chapter we use the classic definition of linear lights,[1] where they are modeled as cylinders with a diffuse emission profile and an infinitely small radius [Nishita et al. 1985, Bao and Peng 1993]. Since these linear lights only model the lengths of the cylinders, we discuss the addition of their emitting end caps in Section 5.5.

Finally, in Section 5.6, we briefly discuss an alternative definition of a linear light that models a rectangle with an infinitely small width instead of a cylinder with an infinitely small radius. The shading of these rectangle-like linear lights remains essentially the same as the cylinder-like linear lights: it is just modulated by the orientation of the rectangle's normal.

The material model. The key to real-time shading is the ability to integrate the product of the material (i.e., the BRDF) and the light. In the case of linear lights, we need to compute a line integral over the spherical distribution given by the BRDF. In the literature, the only spherical distributions with analytic line integrals are the diffuse distribution (we recall its derivation Section 5.3) and the Phong distribution for glossy materials [Nishita et al. 1985, Bao and Peng 1993]. However, the Phong distribution is an inaccurate approximation for recent physically-based shading models. Furthermore, the complexity of the line integral over a Phong distribution grows linearly with the exponent of the distribution. Hence, integrating almost specular materials over a linear light can be prohibitively costly for real-time shading.

These limitations were the same for polygonal lights, and we overcame them thanks to LTCs [Heitz et al. 2016]. LTC distributions yield good approximations for physically-based materials based on the GGX microfacet distribution [Walter et al. 2007] that are considered state of the art today in the video game industry [Hill et al. 2015] and can be analytically integrated over arbitrary polygons in

[1] An alternative definition of linear lights can be found in the literature [Poulin and Amanatides 1991, Picott 1992]. With this definition, the linear light is modeled as an infinite series of point lights instead of as a cylinder with an infinitely small radius. Hence, this model lacks the Jacobian that accounts for the light emission profile and its inclination, which yields incorrect shading behavior. Because of this, it cannot be used as an approximation for actual geometric shapes such as a cylinder.

constant time due to their polygon-integral invariance property. In Section 5.3, we recall the definition of LTCs and show that they have a similar line-integral invariance property. Again, thanks to this property, we can integrate them analytically over linear lights in constant time. Figure 5.2 shows the result obtained by shading materials based on the GGX distribution with linear lights.

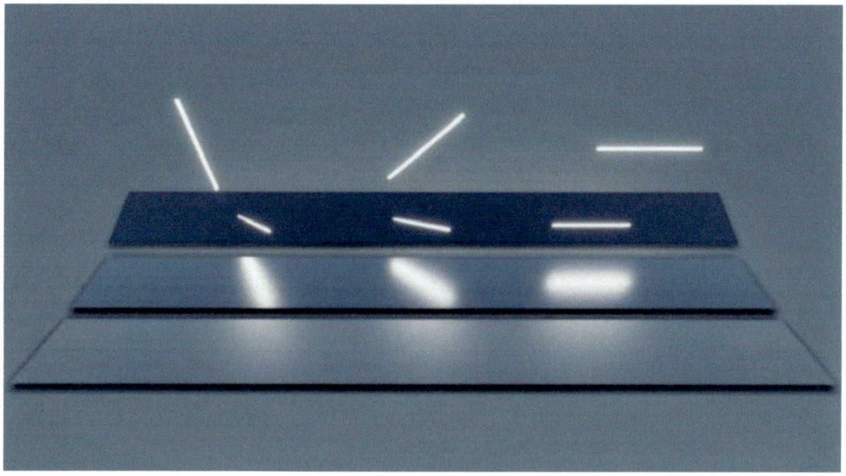

Figure 5.2. We shade linear lights with physically-based materials that use the GGX microfacet BRDF.

Associated demo. This book chapter is distributed with a WebGL demo that implements all the code snippets from the chapter (Figure 5.3). Note that the code provided in the chapter and the demo prioritizes readability over performance and is not meant to be shipped as-is to production.

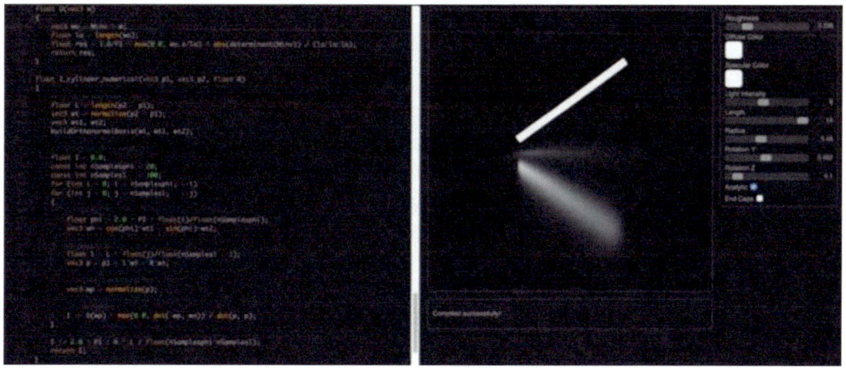

Figure 5.3. Our WebGL demo.

5.2 The Linear-Light Shading Model

In this section, we show that linear lights yield a good approximation to cylinder lights in many configurations. In order to validate the domain of validity of this approximation, we recall how the integrals of the BRDF over cylinders and lines are defined, and we implement numerical integration shaders to compute them. Thus, the goal of this section is to provide shader code for validating the approximation; the actual code one would use in practice is covered in the subsequent sections.

5.2.1 The Local Illumination Integral

Shading with area lights requires computing the illumination integral over the spherical domain Ω_L covered by the light:

$$I = \int_{\Omega_L} \rho(\boldsymbol{\omega}_v, \boldsymbol{\omega}_l) \cos\theta_l \, \mathrm{d}\boldsymbol{\omega}_l, \tag{5.1}$$

where $\boldsymbol{\omega}_v$ is the view direction, $\boldsymbol{\omega}_l$ is the light direction, and ρ the BRDF.

5.2.2 The Spherical Distribution

We use $D(\boldsymbol{\omega}_l) = \rho(\boldsymbol{\omega}_v, \boldsymbol{\omega}_l) \cos\theta_l$ to denote the cosine-weighted BRDF, and we show how to compute the integral of Equation (5.1) for cylindrical lights or lights composed of line segments.

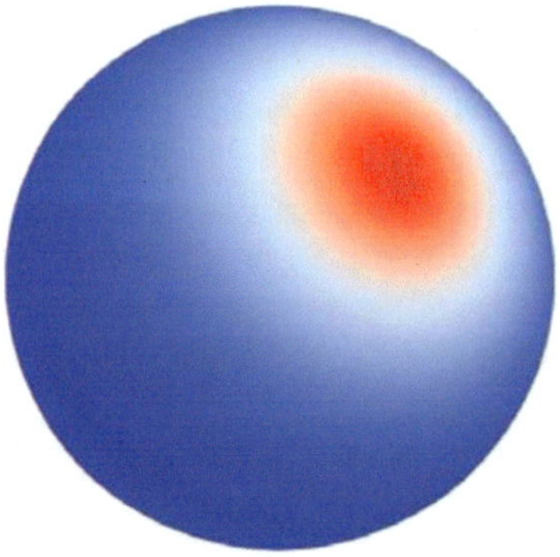

Figure 5.4. The spherical distribution D to be integrated.

```
float D(vec3 w)
{
    // .. brdf*cos
}
```

Listing 5.1. The distribution, D. This is typically a cosine-weighted BRDF, but the result of this section holds for any arbitrary spherical function D.

5.2.3 The Cylinder-Light Integral

Configuration. A cylinder is defined by two end points $\boldsymbol{p}_1$ and $\boldsymbol{p}_2$ and a radius R, as shown in Figure 5.5. We use $L = \|\boldsymbol{p}_2 - \boldsymbol{p}_1\|$ to denote the length of the cylinder, $\boldsymbol{\omega}_t = \frac{\boldsymbol{p}_2 - \boldsymbol{p}_1}{\|\boldsymbol{p}_2 - \boldsymbol{p}_1\|}$ the tangent direction of the cylinder, and $(\boldsymbol{\omega}_t^\perp, \boldsymbol{\omega}_t^\top)$ two orthonormal directions such that $(\boldsymbol{\omega}_t, \boldsymbol{\omega}_t^\perp, \boldsymbol{\omega}_t^\top)$ forms an orthonormal basis.

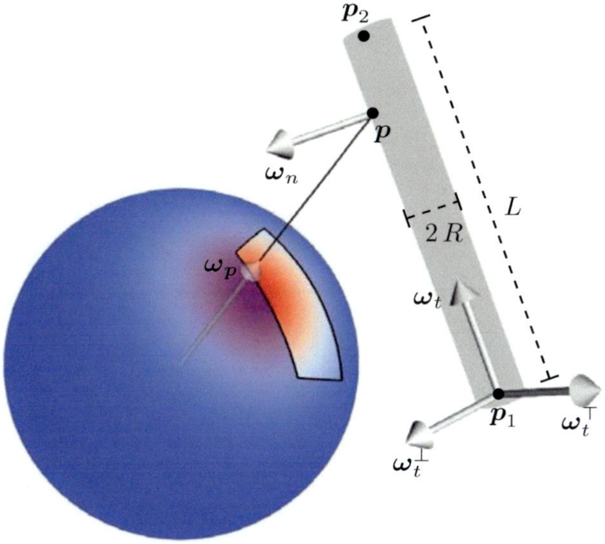

Figure 5.5. The cylinder-light integral.

Integral. We rewrite Equation (5.1) in the space of the light instead of the sphere. With a cylinder parameterization (ϕ, l) for the cylinder surface the integral is

$$I_{\text{cyl}} = \int_0^L \int_0^{2\pi} D\left(\boldsymbol{\omega}_{\boldsymbol{p}}\right) \frac{|-\boldsymbol{\omega}_{\boldsymbol{p}} \cdot \boldsymbol{\omega}_n|}{\|\boldsymbol{p}\|^2} R\, d\phi\, dl. \tag{5.2}$$

With this parametrization, a point (ϕ, l) on the cylinder surface has a normal

$$\boldsymbol{\omega}_n(\phi, l) = \cos\phi\, \boldsymbol{\omega}_t^\perp + \sin\phi\, \boldsymbol{\omega}_t^\top,$$

3D coordinates

$$\boldsymbol{p}(\phi, l) = \boldsymbol{p}_1 + l\, \boldsymbol{\omega}_t + R\, \boldsymbol{\omega}_n(\phi),$$

and the normalized direction towards this point is

$$\boldsymbol{\omega}_{\boldsymbol{p}}(\phi, l) = \frac{\boldsymbol{p}}{\|\boldsymbol{p}\|}.$$

Implementation. We provide the shader code for integrating the distribution over a cylinder in Listing 5.2.

```
float I_cylinder_numerical(vec3 p1, vec3 p2, float R)
{
    // init orthonormal basis
    float L = length(p2 - p1);
    vec3 wt = normalize(p2 - p1);
    vec3 wt1, wt2;
    buildOrthonormalBasis(wt, wt1, wt2);

    // integral discretization
    float I = 0.0;
    const int nSamplesphi = 20;
    const int nSamplesl   = 100;
    for (int i = 0; i < nSamplesphi; ++i)
    for (int j = 0; j < nSamplesl;   ++j)
    {
        // normal
        float phi = 2.0 * PI * float(i)/float(nSamplesphi);
        vec3 wn = cos(phi)*wt1 + sin(phi)*wt2;

        // position
        float l = L * float(j)/float(nSamplesl - 1);
        vec3 p = p1 + l*wt + R*wn;

        // normalized direction
        vec3 wp = normalize(p);

        // integrate
        I += D(wp) * max(0.0, dot(-wp, wn)) / dot(p, p);
    }

    I *= 2.0 * PI * R * L / float(nSamplesphi*nSamplesl);
    return I;
}
```

Listing 5.2. Numerical integration for the cylinder.

The helper function `buildOrthonormalBasis(in vec3 n, out vec3 b1, out vec3 b2)` takes a normalized direction as input and computes two orthonormal directions. We use the code snippet from [Frisvad 2012].

```
// code from [Frisvad2012]
void buildOrthonormalBasis(
in vec3 n, out vec3 b1, out vec3 b2)
{
    if (n.z < -0.9999999)
    {
        b1 = vec3( 0.0, -1.0, 0.0);
        b2 = vec3(-1.0,  0.0, 0.0);
        return;
    }
    float a = 1.0 / (1.0 + n.z);
    float b = -n.x*n.y*a;
    b1 = vec3(1.0 - n.x*n.x*a, b, -n.x);
    b2 = vec3(b, 1.0 - n.y*n.y*a, -n.y);
}
```

Listing 5.3. Code for building an orthonormal basis from a 3D unit vector.

5.2.4 The Linear-Light Integral.

Configuration. If the radius of the cylinder is zero ($R = 0$), we obtain a line segment defined by its end points $\boldsymbol{p}_1$ and $\boldsymbol{p}_2$, as shown in Figure 5.6. Here, $L = \|\boldsymbol{p}_2 - \boldsymbol{p}_1\|$ is the length of the line segment and $\boldsymbol{\omega}_t = \frac{\boldsymbol{p}_2 - \boldsymbol{p}_1}{\|\boldsymbol{p}_2 - \boldsymbol{p}_1\|}$ is the tangent direction of the line.

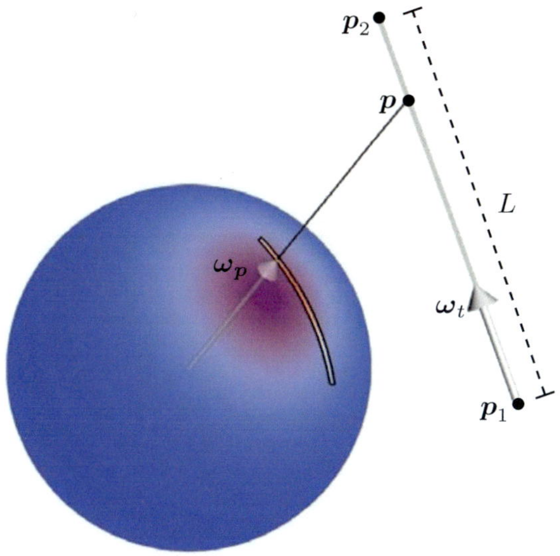

Figure 5.6. The linear-light integral.

Integral. We rewrite Equation (5.1) in the space of the light instead of the sphere. With a 1D parameterization of variable l for the line, the integral is

$$I_{\text{line}} = \int_0^L D(\boldsymbol{\omega_p}) \frac{2\,\|\boldsymbol{\omega_p} \times \boldsymbol{\omega}_t\|}{\|\boldsymbol{p}\|^2}\, dl. \tag{5.3}$$

We set the origin of the parameterization to $\boldsymbol{p}_1$, and it increases in the direction $\boldsymbol{\omega}_t$, such that at abscissa l on the line, the 3D coordinates of the point are

$$p(l) = \boldsymbol{p}_1 + l\,\boldsymbol{\omega}_t,$$

and the normalized direction towards this point is

$$\boldsymbol{\omega_p}(\phi, l) = \frac{\boldsymbol{p}}{\|\boldsymbol{p}\|}.$$

Implementation. We provide the shader code for integrating the distribution over a line segment in Listing 5.4.

```
float I_line_numerical(vec3 p1, vec3 p2)
{
    float L = length(p2 - p1);
    vec3 wt = normalize(p2 - p1);

    // integral discretization
    float I = 0.0;
    const int nSamples = 100;
    for (int i = 0; i < nSamples; ++i)
    {
        // position
        vec3 p = p1 + L * float(i)/float(nSamples - 1) * wt;

        // normalized direction
        vec3 wp = normalize(p);

        // integrate
        I += 2.0 * D(wp) * length(cross(wp, wt)) / dot(p, p);
    }

    I *= L / float(nSamples);
    return I;
}
```

Listing 5.4. Numerical integration for the line.

5.2.5 Approximating the Cylinder-Light Integral by the Linear-Light Integral

As illustrated in Figure 5.7, for any continuous distribution D and a cylinder of radius R, the integral over the cylinder of Equation (5.2) converges towards the line segment integral of Equation (5.3) as R goes to zero:

$$\lim_{R \to 0} \frac{I_{\text{cyl}}(R)}{R} = I_{\text{line}}.$$

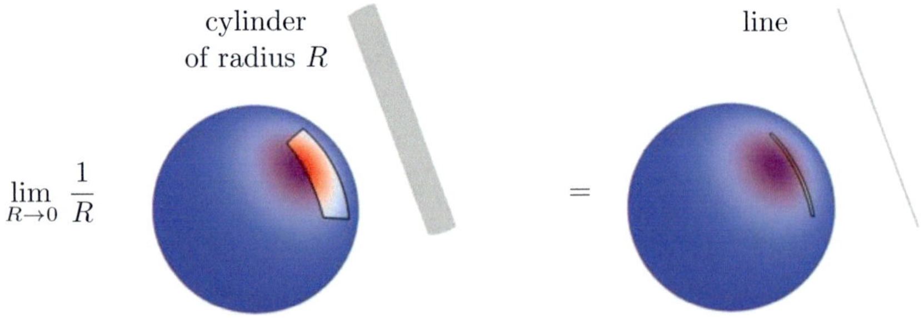

Figure 5.7. The linear-light integral is the limit of the cylinder-light integral when its radius tends towards zero.

Approximation. If the radius R is small enough, we can use the line integral as an accurate approximation for the cylinder integral:

$$I_{\text{cyl}}(R) \approx R\, I_{\text{line}}.$$

In cases where the radius is too large, the approximation can be inaccurate and produce overly high values (for instance if D is a specular material and if the linear light overlaps with the specular peak). In order to avoid this, we use the property that I_{cyl} cannot be greater than the integral of D over the sphere:

$$I_{\text{cyl}} \leq \int_{\Omega} D(\boldsymbol{\omega})\, \mathrm{d}\boldsymbol{\omega}.$$

This property is intuitive: I_{cyl} represents the integral of D over the spherical domain covered by the cylinder, so it can only be smaller than the integral of D over the entire sphere. Hence, we can prevent the approximation from overshooting by clamping it to $\int_{\Omega} D(\boldsymbol{\omega})\, \mathrm{d}\boldsymbol{\omega}$. In practice, we use distributions D that are normalized, so we clamp the approximation to 1.

Implementation. We provide the shader code for approximating the result of `I_cylinder` (from Listing 5.2) in Listing 5.5.

```
float I_cylinder_approx(vec3 p1, float p2, float R)
{
    return min(1.0, R * I_line(p1, p2));
}
```

Listing 5.5. Approximation of the cylinder-light integral by the linear-light integral.

Results of the approximation. In Figure 5.8, we compare the results obtained by the cylinder-light integral and the linear-light integral approximation with a GGX BRDF. We can see that the approximation is most accurate with:

- cylinders of small radius,
- cylinders far from the shading point, or
- low-frequency (large roughness parameter α) materials.

In summary, the approximation works well when the width of the solid angle covered by the cylinder is small compared to the variation of the distribution. However, the approximation typically cannot be used with specular materials and very large/close cylindrical light sources.

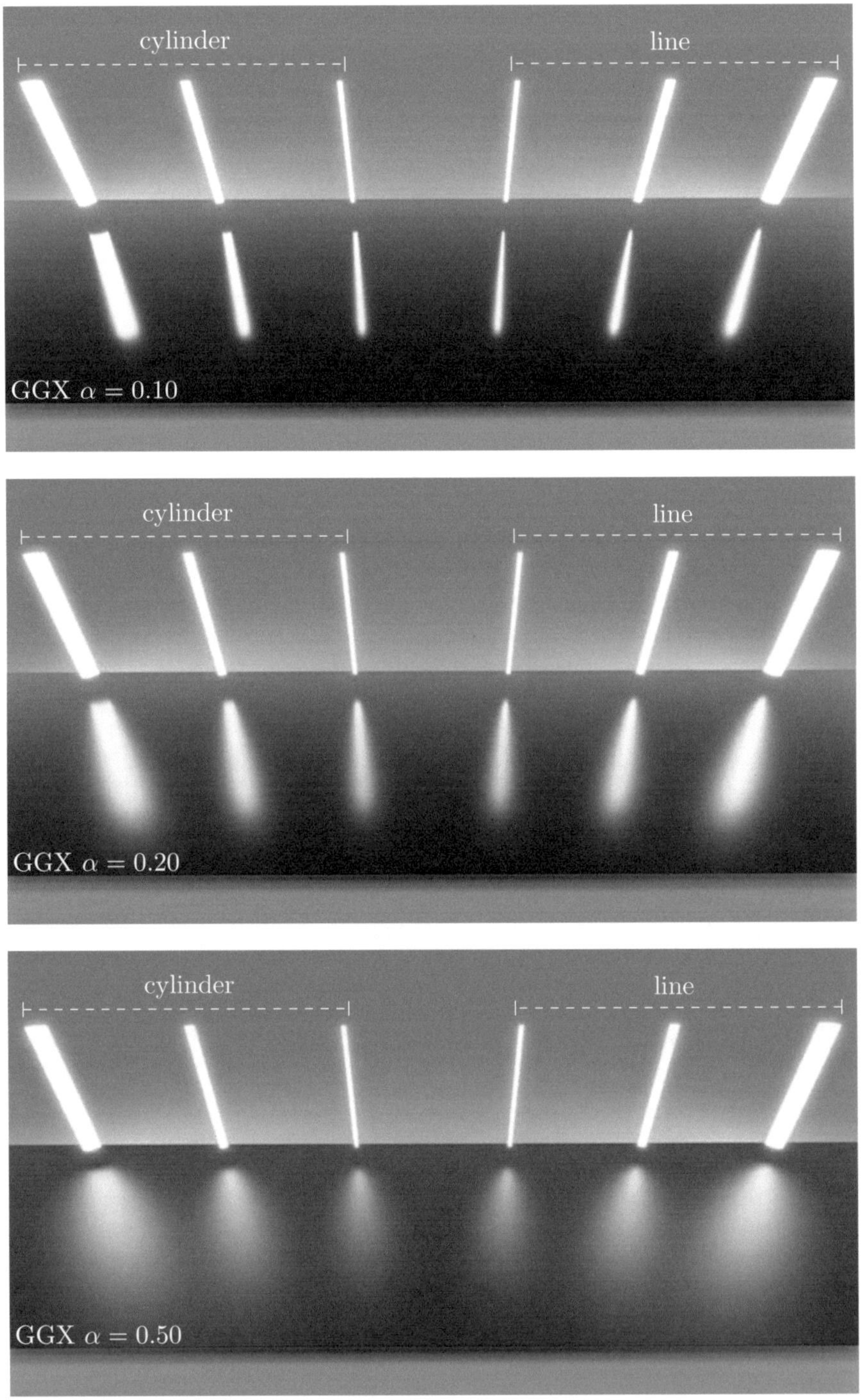

Figure 5.8. Results of the approximation with a GGX BRDF.

5.3 Line-integral of a Diffuse Material

In this section, we show how to integrate a line against a diffuse BRDF, i.e., with $D(\boldsymbol{\omega}) = \frac{1}{\pi} \max(0, \boldsymbol{\omega} \cdot \boldsymbol{z})$. In this case, the integral of Equation (5.3) is also called the *irradiance* $I_{\text{line}} = E[\boldsymbol{L}]$ of the line $\boldsymbol{L}$.

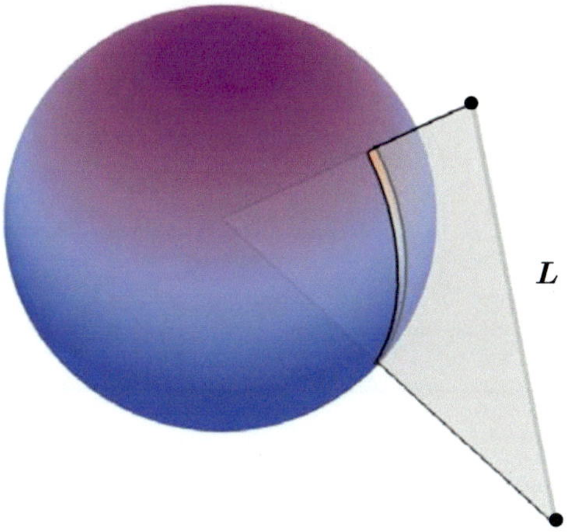

Figure 5.9. The diffuse-line integral (or the irradiance of the line).

Clamping the line below the horizon. The first step is to ensure that the parts of the light contributing to the diffuse integral are limited to the upper hemisphere ($z \geq 0$). To achieve this, we start by clamping the line to the upper part of the hemisphere. If one of the vertices is below the horizon—i.e., its z-component is less than zero—we replace it with the intersection of the line with the plane $z = 0$, as illustrated in Figure 5.10.

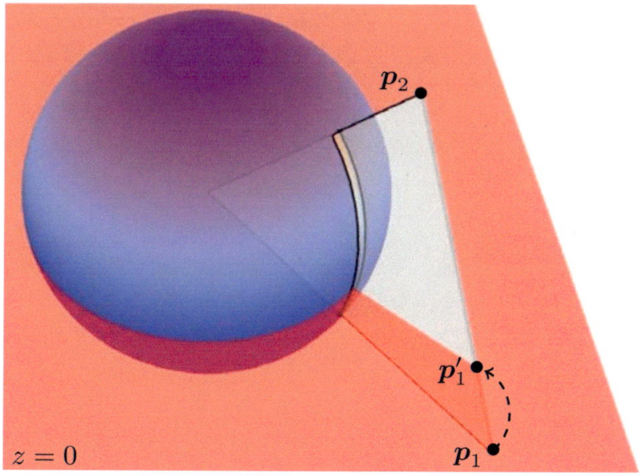

Figure 5.10. Clamping the linear light below the horizon.

Parameterization of the line. In order to compute the diffuse-line integral, we need a 1D parameterization for the linear light. Our parameterization is shown in Figure 5.11 and explained below.

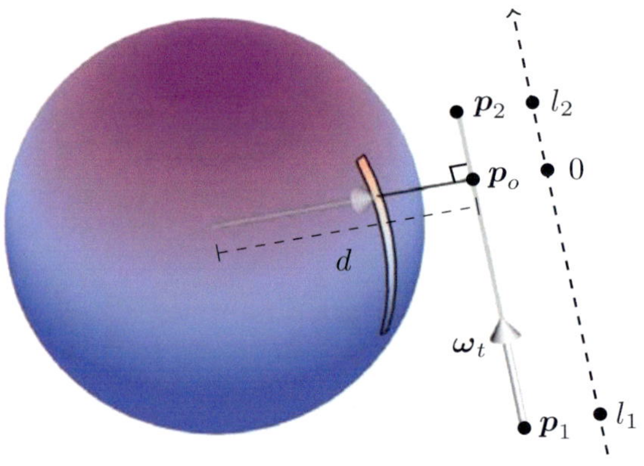

Figure 5.11. Line-integral parameterization.

The abscissas of the end points of the linear light are

$$l_1 = \boldsymbol{p}_1 \cdot \boldsymbol{\omega}_t,$$
$$l_2 = \boldsymbol{p}_2 \cdot \boldsymbol{\omega}_t.$$

The 0 abscissa is the orthonormal projection of the shading point onto the line, denoted $\boldsymbol{p}_o$. (It is not a problem if $\boldsymbol{p}_o$ is outside segment $[\boldsymbol{p}_1, \boldsymbol{p}_2]$.) The distance between the line and the shading point is the norm of this point:

$$\boldsymbol{p}_o = \boldsymbol{p}_1 - l_1\,\boldsymbol{\omega}_t,$$
$$d = \|\boldsymbol{p}_o\|.$$

To simplify the line integral, we parameterize the points on the line relative to $\boldsymbol{p}_o$, with an abscissa l

$$\boldsymbol{p}(l) = \boldsymbol{p}_o + l\,\boldsymbol{\omega}_t.$$

Integration of the line. We rewrite Equation (5.3) using the new parameterization. The terms in the integrand become

$$\|\boldsymbol{p}(l)\| = \sqrt{d^2 + l^2},$$
$$\|\boldsymbol{\omega}_{\boldsymbol{p}}(l) \times \boldsymbol{\omega}_t\| = \frac{d}{\sqrt{d^2 + l^2}},$$
$$D\left(\boldsymbol{\omega}_{\boldsymbol{p}}(l)\right) = \frac{1}{\pi}\,\frac{(\boldsymbol{p}_o + l\,\boldsymbol{\omega}_t)}{\sqrt{d^2 + l^2}} \cdot \boldsymbol{z},$$

and the integral becomes

$$I_{\text{line}} = \frac{2\,d}{\pi} \int_{l_1}^{l_2} \frac{(\boldsymbol{p}_o + l\,\boldsymbol{\omega}_t)\cdot \boldsymbol{z}}{(d^2+l^2)^2}\, dl,$$

which has the analytic closed form:

$$I_{\text{line}} = \frac{1}{\pi}\left\{\left[F_{\boldsymbol{p}_o}(l_2) - F_{\boldsymbol{p}_o}(l_1)\right]\boldsymbol{p}_o + \left[F_{\boldsymbol{\omega}_t}(l_2) - F_{\boldsymbol{\omega}_t}(l_1)\right]\boldsymbol{\omega}_t\right\}\cdot \boldsymbol{z},$$

with

$$F_{\boldsymbol{p}_o}(l) = \frac{l}{d(d^2+l^2)} + \frac{1}{d^2}\,\text{atan}\left(\frac{l}{d}\right),$$

$$F_{\boldsymbol{\omega}_t}(l) = \frac{l^2}{d(d^2+l^2)}.$$

Implementation. We provide the shader code for clamping, parameterizing, and integrating the linear light against the diffuse BRDF in Listing 5.6.

```
float Fpo(float d, float l)
{
    return l/(d*(d*d + l*l)) + atan(l/d)/(d*d);
}

float Fwt(float d, float l)
{
    return l*l/(d*(d*d + l*l));
}

float I_diffuse_line(vec3 p1, vec3 p2)
{
    // tangent
    vec3 wt = normalize(p2 - p1);

    // clamping
    if (p1.z <= 0.0 && p2.z <= 0.0) return 0.0;
    if (p1.z < 0.0) p1 = (+p1*p2.z - p2*p1.z) / (+p2.z - p1.z);
    if (p2.z < 0.0) p2 = (-p1*p2.z + p2*p1.z) / (-p2.z + p1.z);

    // shading point orthonormal projection on the line
    vec3 po = p1 - wt*dot(p1, wt);

    // distance to line
    float d = length(po);

    // parameterization
    float l1 = dot(p1 - po, wt);
    float l2 = dot(p2 - po, wt);

    // integral
    float I = (Fpo(d, l2) - Fpo(d, l1)) * po.z +
              (Fwt(d, l2) - Fwt(d, l1)) * wt.z;
    return I / PI;
}
```

Listing 5.6. Analytic line-diffuse integration.

5.4 Line-Integral of a Glossy Material with LTCs

5.4.1 Linearly Transformed Cosines (LTCs)

Linearly transformed cosines are the distributions obtained by applying a linear transformation, represented by a 3×3 matrix M, to the direction vectors associated with a clamped cosine distribution denoted D_o. Fig. 5.12 shows how the choice of M affects the properties of the distribution.

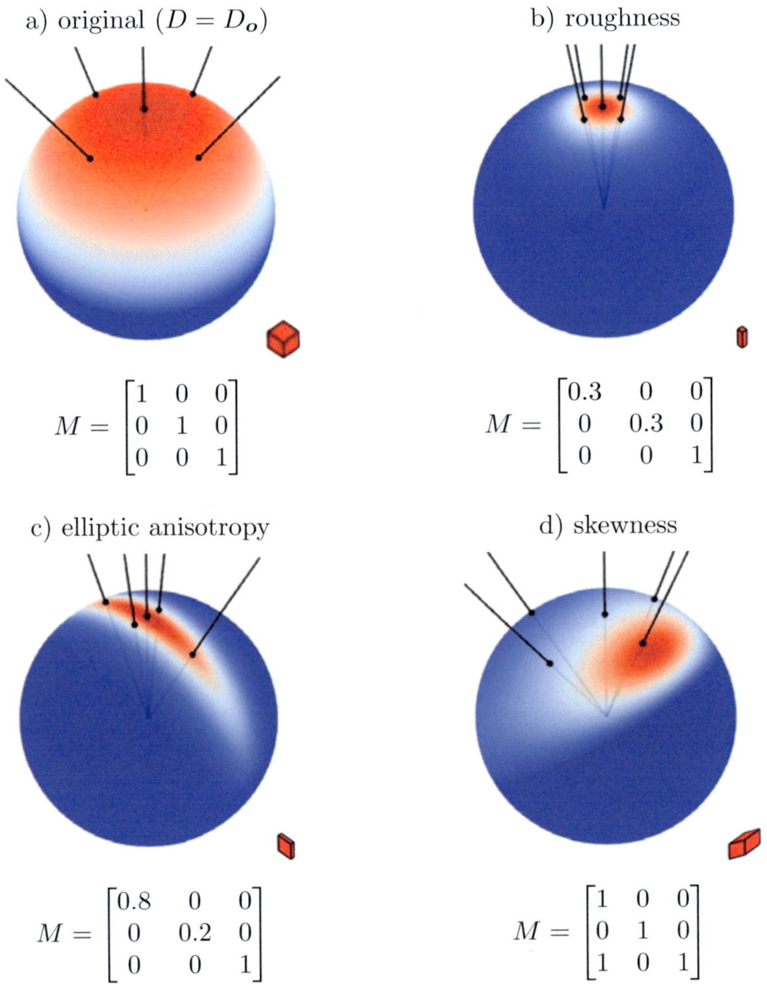

Figure 5.12. The parameterization of linearly transformed cosines (LTCs).

The matrix M provides control over roughness (b), anisotropy (c), and skewness (d) of the transformed distribution. The effect of the linear transformation can be seen on the lines and the red cube.

Closed-form expression. The magnitude of an LTC is the magnitude of the original distribution D_o in the original direction $\boldsymbol{\omega_o}$ multiplied by the change of solid angle measure due to the distortion of the spherical transformation. It has the closed-form expression:

$$D(\boldsymbol{\omega}) = D_{\boldsymbol{o}}\left(\frac{M^{-1}\boldsymbol{\omega}}{\|M^{-1}\boldsymbol{\omega}\|}\right)\frac{|M^{-1}|}{\|M^{-1}\boldsymbol{\omega}\|^3}. \tag{5.4}$$

Note that this closed form is never used at runtime in the shader. It is only used to fit physically-based materials with LTCs in an offline precomputation. In our shader, we approximate a GGX BRDF with LTCs whose parameters are stored in a look-up table that we access at runtime. The look-up table is the same as in [Heitz et al. 2016].

5.4.2 LTC-Polygon Integral Invariance

LTCs are invariant to linear transformations, i.e., if a linear transformation is applied to both the polygon and the distribution, the value of the integral remains the same:

$$\begin{aligned}\int_{\boldsymbol{P}} D\left(\boldsymbol{\omega_p}\right)\frac{|-\boldsymbol{\omega_p}\cdot\boldsymbol{\omega}_n|}{\|\boldsymbol{p}\|^2}\,d\boldsymbol{p} &= \int_{\boldsymbol{P_o}} D_{\boldsymbol{o}}\left(\boldsymbol{\omega_p}\right)\frac{|-\boldsymbol{\omega_p}\cdot\boldsymbol{\omega}_n|}{\|\boldsymbol{p}\|^2}\,d\boldsymbol{p}\\ &= E[\boldsymbol{P_o}].\end{aligned} \tag{5.5}$$

Thanks to this invariance, an LTC can be integrated over a polygon by multiplying the (vertices of the) polygon by the inverse linear transformation $\boldsymbol{P_o} = M^{-1}\,\boldsymbol{P}$ and computing the irradiance $E[\boldsymbol{P_o}]$ of this new polygon, as shown in Figure 5.13.

5.4.3 LTC-Line Integral Invariance

The invariance for linear lights is similar to the invariance for polygons given by Equation (5.5). If a linear transformation is applied to both the line segment and the distribution, then the value of the integral remains the same:

$$\begin{aligned}\int_{\boldsymbol{L}} D\left(\boldsymbol{\omega_p}\right)\frac{2\,\|\boldsymbol{\omega_p}\times\boldsymbol{\omega}_t\|}{\|\boldsymbol{p}\|^2}\,d\boldsymbol{p} &= \frac{1}{\|M^T\,\boldsymbol{\omega}_\perp\|}\int_{\boldsymbol{L_o}} D_{\boldsymbol{o}}\left(\boldsymbol{\omega_p}\right)\frac{2\,\|\boldsymbol{\omega_p}\times\boldsymbol{\omega}_t\|}{\|\boldsymbol{p}\|^2}\,d\boldsymbol{p}\\ &= \frac{1}{\|M^T\,\boldsymbol{\omega}_\perp\|}\,E[\boldsymbol{L_o}]\end{aligned} \tag{5.6}$$

except for the additional width factor $\frac{1}{\|M^T\,\boldsymbol{\omega}_\perp\|}$. Thanks to this invariance, an LTC can be integrated over a line segment by multiplying the (vertices of the) line segment by the inverse linear transformation $\boldsymbol{L_o} = M^{-1}\,\boldsymbol{L}$, computing the irradiance $E[\boldsymbol{L_o}]$ of this new line segment using the method presented in Section 5.3, and multiplying the result by the width factor.

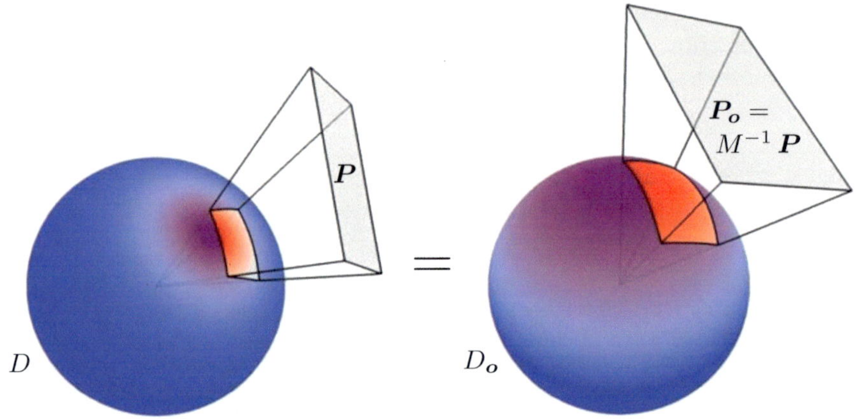

Figure 5.13. *Invariance of the polygonal integration.* The configuration on the right is the left configuration multiplied by matrix M^{-1}.

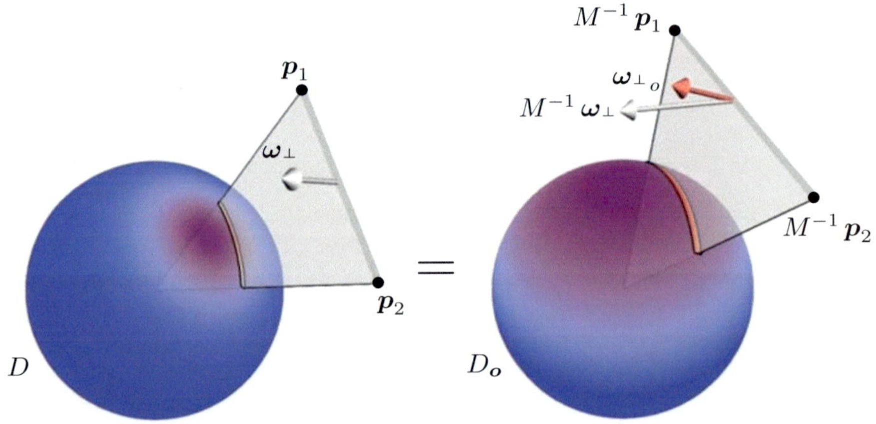

Figure 5.14. *Invariance of the linear integration.* The configuration on the right is the left configuration multiplied by matrix M^{-1}.

Proof of the line-integral invariance. We can see in Figure 5.14 that the infinitely small width of a linear light is defined by vector $\omega_\perp = \frac{p_1 \times p_2}{\|p_1 \times p_2\|}$. After the linear transformation, this vector can be scaled and/or no longer orthonormal. The actual orthonormal vector—illustrated in red in the figure—is defined by

$$\begin{aligned}
\boldsymbol{\omega}_{\perp_o} &= \frac{(M^{-1}(\boldsymbol{p}_1 - \boldsymbol{p}_2)) \times M^{-1}\boldsymbol{p}_1}{\|(M^{-1}(\boldsymbol{p}_1 - \boldsymbol{p}_2)) \times M^{-1}\boldsymbol{p}_1\|} \\
&= \frac{M^T[(\boldsymbol{p}_1 - \boldsymbol{p}_2) \times \boldsymbol{p}_1]}{\|M^T[(\boldsymbol{p}_1 - \boldsymbol{p}_2) \times \boldsymbol{p}_1]\|} \\
&= \frac{M^T\boldsymbol{\omega}_\perp}{\|M^T\boldsymbol{\omega}_\perp\|},
\end{aligned}$$

and is different from the transformed orthonormal vector $M^{-1}\boldsymbol{\omega}_\perp$. The transformation of this vector (its length and orientation) affects the evaluation of the linear light proportional to the width factor $\frac{1}{\|M^T\boldsymbol{\omega}_\perp\|}$. Indeed, the effective width after the transformation is the dot product between the transformed orthonormal vector and the actual orthonormal vector:

$$\begin{aligned}
\boldsymbol{\omega}_{\perp_o} \cdot (M^{-1}\boldsymbol{\omega}_\perp) &= \frac{1}{\|M^T\boldsymbol{\omega}_\perp\|}(M^T\boldsymbol{\omega}_\perp) \cdot (M^{-1}\boldsymbol{\omega}_\perp) \\
&= \frac{1}{\|M^T\boldsymbol{\omega}_\perp\|}(M^{-T}M^T\boldsymbol{\omega}_\perp) \cdot \boldsymbol{\omega}_\perp \\
&= \frac{1}{\|M^T\boldsymbol{\omega}_\perp\|},
\end{aligned}$$

which is the expression of the width factor in Equation (5.6).

Implementation. We provide the analytic LTC-line integral shader code in Listing 5.7. Note that, in practice, recovering the matrix M by inverting M^{-1} can be done in an optimized way, because the matrix is sparse (see demo and previous publication).

```
float I_ltc_line(vec3 p1, vec3 p2)
{
    // transform to diffuse configuration
    vec3 p1o = Minv * p1;
    vec3 p2o = Minv * p2;
    float I_diffuse = I_diffuse_line(p1o, p2o);

    // width factor
    vec3 ortho = normalize(cross(p1, p2));
    float w =  1.0 / length(inverse(transpose(Minv)) * ortho);

    return w * I_diffuse;
}
```

Listing 5.7. Analytic line-LTC integration.

5.5 Adding the End Caps

5.5.1 End Caps

So far, we have been using a line segment to approximate a cylindrical emitter. However, our line is only an approximation of the length of the cylinder, so it doesn't account for emission from the end caps of the cylinder. The shading with and without them is shown in Figure 5.15. We can see that a black spot shows up when the ends are not emitting.

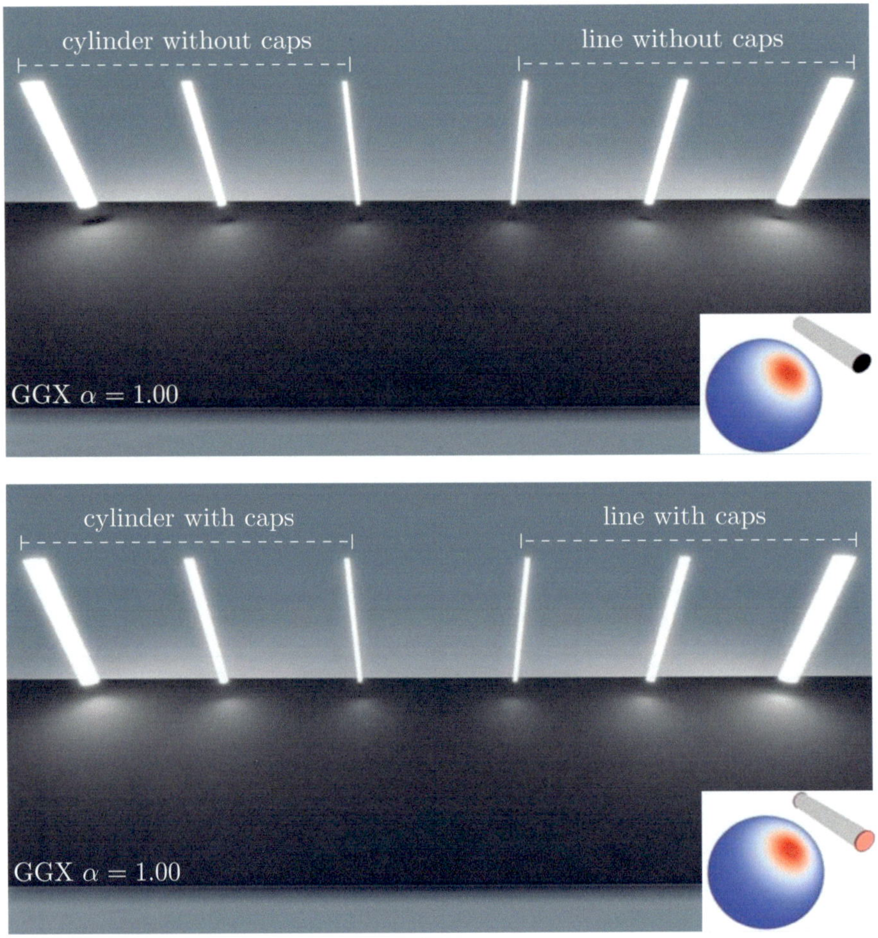

Figure 5.15. Test of the approximation with a GGX BRDF.

5.5.2 Integrating the End Caps

In order to remain consistent with the line-segment approximation of the cylinder's length, we approximate the two caps with infinitely small one-sided disks located at $\boldsymbol{p}_1$ and $\boldsymbol{p}_2$ and with normals $-\boldsymbol{\omega}_t$ and $\boldsymbol{\omega}_t$, respectively.

Numerical integration. The contribution of the disk located at $\boldsymbol{p}_1$ is

$$I_{\text{disk1}} = \int_0^R \int_0^{2\pi} D\left(\boldsymbol{\omega_p}\right) \frac{|\boldsymbol{\omega_p} \cdot \boldsymbol{\omega}_t|}{\|\boldsymbol{p}\|^2}\, r\, d\phi\, dr, \tag{5.7}$$

where we use a polar parameterization (ϕ, r) for the disk surface. With this parametrization, a point (ϕ, r) on the disk surface has 3D coordinates $\boldsymbol{p}$ and normalized direction $\boldsymbol{\omega_p}$

$$\begin{aligned} \boldsymbol{p}(\phi, r) &= \boldsymbol{p}_1 + r\, \cos\phi\, \boldsymbol{\omega}_t^{\perp} + r\, \sin\phi\, \boldsymbol{\omega}_t^{\top}, \\ \boldsymbol{\omega_p}(\phi, r) &= \frac{\boldsymbol{p}}{\|\boldsymbol{p}\|}. \end{aligned}$$

Implementation. In Listing 5.8, we provide the numerical integration shader code for Equation (5.7).

```
float I_disks_numerical(vec3 p1, vec3 p2, float R)
{
    // init orthonormal basis
    float L = length(p2 - p1);
    vec3 wt = normalize(p2 - p1);
    vec3 wt1, wt2;
    buildOrthonormalBasis(wt, wt1, wt2);

    // integration
    float Idisks = 0.0;
    const int nSamplesphi = 20;
    const int nSamplesr   = 200;
    for (int i = 0; i < nSamplesphi; ++i)
    for (int j = 0; j < nSamplesr;   ++j)
    {
        float phi = 2.0 * PI * float(i)/float(nSamplesphi);
        float r = R * float(j)/float(nSamplesr - 1);
        vec3 p, wp;

        p = p1 + r * (cos(phi)*wt1 + sin(phi)*wt2);
        wp = normalize(p);
        Idisks += r * D(wp) * max(0.0, dot(wp, +wt)) / dot(p, p);

        p = p2 + r * (cos(phi)*wt1 + sin(phi)*wt2);
        wp = normalize(p);
        Idisks += r * D(wp) * max(0.0, dot(wp, -wt)) / dot(p, p);
    }

    Idisks *= 2.0 * PI * R / float(nSamplesr*nSamplesphi);
    return Idisks;
}
```

Listing 5.8. Evaluating the end caps.

5.5.3 Approximating the End Caps with Point Lights

As the radius of the cylinder tends towards zero, the end caps converge towards disk-like point lights. The integral of Equation (5.7) converges towards

$$\lim_{R\to 0} \frac{I_{\text{disk1}}}{\pi\, R^2} = D(\boldsymbol{\omega}_{\boldsymbol{p}_1})\, \frac{\max(0, \boldsymbol{\omega}_{\boldsymbol{p}_1} \cdot \boldsymbol{\omega}_t)}{\|\boldsymbol{p}_1\|^2}.$$

Hence, if the radius is small enough, the integral can be approximated by

$$I_{\text{disk1}} \approx \pi\, R^2\, D(\boldsymbol{\omega}_{\boldsymbol{p}_1})\, \frac{\max(0, \boldsymbol{\omega}_{\boldsymbol{p}_1} \cdot \boldsymbol{\omega}_t)}{\|\boldsymbol{p}_1\|^2}. \tag{5.8}$$

Similarly, we approximate the integral of the second end by

$$I_{\text{disk2}} \approx \pi\, R^2\, D\left(\boldsymbol{\omega}_{\boldsymbol{p}_2}\right) \frac{\max(0, -\boldsymbol{\omega}_t \cdot \boldsymbol{\omega}_{\boldsymbol{p}_2})}{\|\boldsymbol{p}_2\|^2}. \tag{5.9}$$

Implementation. In Listing 5.9, we provide the analytic approximation of Equations (5.8) and (5.9).

```
float I_ltc_disks(vec3 p1, vec3 p2, float R)
{
    float A = PI * R * R;
    vec3 wt  = normalize(p2 - p1);
    vec3 wp1 = normalize(p1);
    vec3 wp2 = normalize(p2);
    float Idisks = A * (
    D(wp1) * max(0.0, dot(+wt, wp1)) / dot(p1, p1) +
    D(wp2) * max(0.0, dot(-wt, wp2)) / dot(p2, p2));
    return Idisks;
}
```

Listing 5.9. Evaluating the end disks.

For this we need the evaluation of D for an LTC, which is provided in Equation (5.4) and implemented in Listing 5.10.

```
mat3 Minv;
float D(vec3 w)
{
    vec3 wo = Minv * w;
    float lo = length(wo);
    float res = 1.0/PI * max(0.0, wo.z/lo) * abs(determinant(Minv)) / (lo*lo*lo);
    return res;
}
```

Listing 5.10. LTC Evaluation.

Summing the contributions. In order to account for the contribution of the caps, we simply add $I_{\text{disk1}} + I_{\text{disk2}}$ to I_{line} of Equation (5.3), and we clamp the sum to 1 as explained in Section 5.2.5.

5.5.4 Discussion

In practice, we found out that the caps approximation is less robust and useful than expected. Figure 5.16 shows that

- The approximation can result in visually disturbing artifacts: the reflection of the cylinder on the left exhibits a strange bulb at one end due to the cap approximation.

- Adding the caps is not always worth the cost, nor the risk of having artifacts. The two reflections in the middle (with and without caps) have similar reflection. In Figure 5.15, we can see that the absence of caps leaves black holes that are less visible with the line integral than with the cylinder integral anyway.

Hence, we recommend shading without the caps by default and adding them only for specific needs.

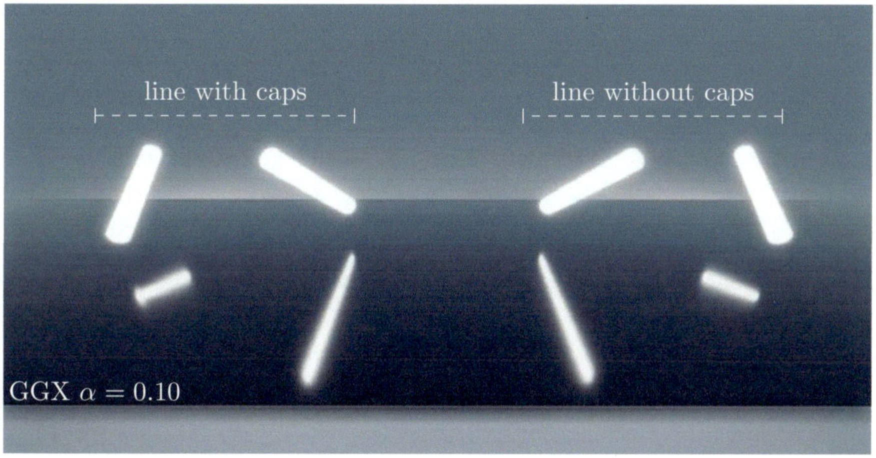

Figure 5.16. The caps approximation is not always worth it and can result in visually disturbing artifacts.

5.6 Rectangle-Like Linear Lights

Linear lights can also be used to model thin rectangular lights. In this case, the linear light parameters remain the same, with the addition of $\boldsymbol{\omega}_n$, the normal of the rectangle (Figure 5.17).

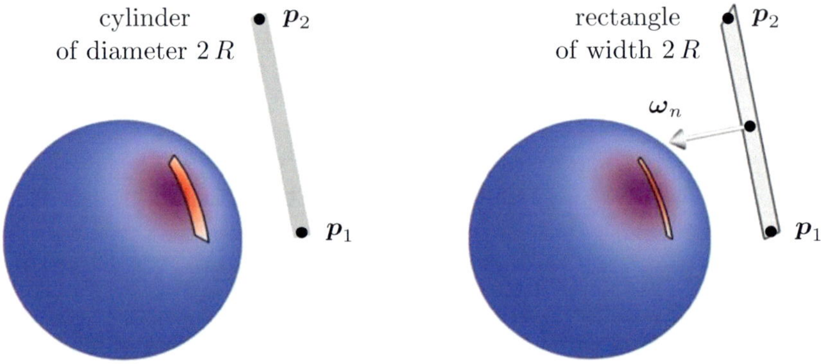

Figure 5.17. A linear light can also be used as an approximation for thin rectangular lights.

The line integral for the rectangle is the line integral for the cylinder of Equation (5.3) adjusted by the orientation of the line with respect to the shading point

$$I_{\text{lineRectangle}} = |\boldsymbol{\omega}_\perp \cdot \boldsymbol{\omega}_n|\, I_{\text{lineCylinder}},$$

where $\boldsymbol{\omega}_\perp = \frac{\boldsymbol{p}_1 \times \boldsymbol{p}_2}{\|\boldsymbol{p}_1 \times \boldsymbol{p}_2\|}$ is the orthonormal vector introduced in Figure 5.14.

Implementation. We provide the analytic LTC-line integral shader code for rectangular lines in Listing 5.11.

```
float I_ltc_line_rectangle(vec3 p1, vec3 p2, vec3 wn)
{
    vec3 wortho = normalize(cross(p1, p2));
    float I = abs(dot(wortho, wn)) * I_ltc_line(p1, p2);
    return I;
}
```

Listing 5.11. Analytic line-LTC integration for a rectangular line.

Test of the approximation. In Figure 5.18, we compare the results obtained by the rectangle-light integral and the linear-light integral approximation with a GGX BRDF. The approximation has the same properties as the cylinder light.

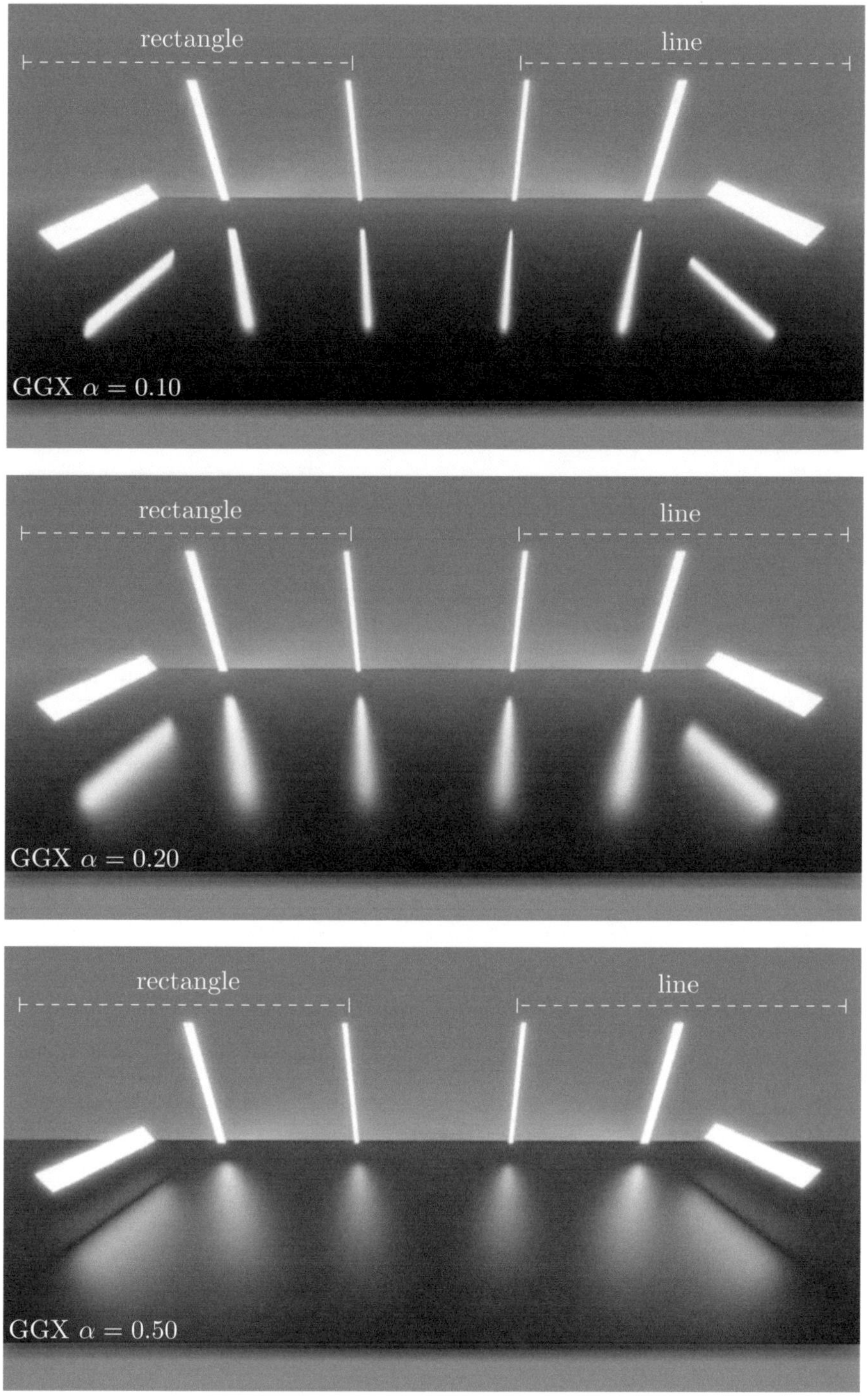

Figure 5.18. Test of the rectangle-light approximation with a GGX BRDF.

5.7 Performance

To assess the performance of our linear-light technique, we used the same Sponza scene (including viewpoint) as the original article. Although this is not a real production game environment, it is a suitable proxy in terms of pixel-shader workload and divergence, on account of the range of materials and surface orientations.

In our timings, using an NVIDIA Quadro M6000 GPU and a screen resolution of 1920×1080 pixels,[2] the primary lighting pass took 0.42 ms for a linear light without end caps, compared to 0.58 ms for a quadrilateral light. This demonstrates, as expected, that linear lights are cheaper to evaluate than their polygonal counterparts, since only a single line-integral is involved.

5.8 Conclusion

We have presented an extension to our existing area-lighting framework to support linear light sources, which can be used to model common real-world lights such as fluorescent bulbs. As we have shown, this approximation works well in many cases (with the exception of wide cylindrical lights or highly specular materials) and is cheaper than a full polygonal area light solution.

5.9 Acknowledgments

This work was supported by Unity Technologies (Eric Heitz) and Lucasfilm (Stephen Hill).

Bibliography

Bao, H., and Peng, Q. 1993. Shading models for linear and area light sources. *Computers & Graphics 17*, 2, 137–145.

Frisvad, J. R. 2012. Building an orthonormal basis from a 3D unit vector without normalization. *Journal of Graphics Tools 16*, 3, 151–159.

Heitz, E., Dupuy, J., Hill, S., and Neubelt, D. 2016. Real-time polygonal-light shading with linearly transformed cosines. *ACM Trans. Graph. 35*, 4, 41:1–41:8.

Hill, S., McAuley, S., Burley, B., Chan, D., Fascione, L., Iwanicki, M., Hoffman, N., Jakob, W., Neubelt, D., Pesce, A., and Pettineo, M. 2015. Physically based shading in theory and practice. In *ACM SIGGRAPH Courses 2015*, ACM, New York.

Nishita, T., Okamura, I., and Nakamae, E. 1985. Shading models for point and linear sources. *ACM Trans. Graph. 4*, 2, 124–146.

[2]We used an RGBA 8-bit render target and 1x MSAA to minimize bandwidth overhead and additional shading work.

PICOTT, K. P. 1992. Extensions of the linear and area lighting models. *IEEE Comput. Graph. Appl. 12*, 2, 31–38.

POULIN, P., AND AMANATIDES, J. 1991. Shading and shadowing with linear light sources. *Computers and Graphics 15*, 2, 259–265.

WALTER, B., MARSCHNER, S. R., LI, H., AND TORRANCE, K. E. 2007. Microfacet models for refraction through rough surfaces. In *Proceedings of the 18th Eurographics Conference on Rendering Techniques*, Eurographics Association, Aire-la-Ville, Switzerland, EGSR'07, 195–206.

6

III

Profiling and Optimizing WebGL Applications Using Google Chrome

Gareth Morgan

6.1 Overview

In recent years, the WebGL standard [Khronos 2014] has been adopted in a huge range of desktop and mobile web browsers. This is an exciting opportunity for graphics programmers to develop 3D applications that can be executed directly in the browser. The standard is supported on devices that range from high-end workstations to handheld mobile devices. However, programming GPUs via the WebGL architecture presents some unique challenges. In particular, optimizing WebGL-based 3D applications, so that their performance provides an interactive user experience, is challenging. This chapter will discuss these challenges and the profiling tools and language features available for the Google Chrome web browser that can overcome them.

6.1.1 History of WebGL

To understand how to produce efficient 3D applications with WebGL, a bit of history is required. WebGL has realized the promise of many attempts in the history of graphics to produce a standard that allows universal execution of 3D applications in the web browser. The idea of enabling 3D content in web browsers goes back to the early days of the internet. VRML (virtual reality mark-up language) was an attempt to describe virtual 3D worlds using the same kind of mark-up language utilized by the World Wide Web [Web3D Consortium 2006]. Later successors to VRML included technologies such as X3D and the browser plugin produced by Unity 3D [Unity 3D 2016].

All these technologies were held back by one fact: they required a native plugin compiled using the assembly code of the machine running the browser.

In order to view 3D content on websites using this technology, users had to install that plug-in. This plugin would actually communicate with the graphics processing uUnit (GPU) in their computer and render the 3D images. This was a huge barrier for adoption.

The key to the success of WebGL is integration with JavaScript [ECMA 2016]. JavaScript was developed as a means to add programmability to webpages. Its widespread adoption meant that every website could drive the CPU and execute algorithms, as if it were a native executable.

WebGL is based on the standard that remains the most widely used system for programming GPUs: OpenGL [OpenGL registry 2016]. Developed by Silicon Graphics in the 1990's, OpenGL is a simple application programmer interface (API). It allows programmers to produce three-dimensional images using a state-machine–based interface. WebGL implements the OpenGL specification in the JavaScript language. Just as with the adoption of JavaScript, the adoption of WebGL on all flavors of web browser, and on all kinds of devices, means any website can talk to the GPU to create interactive 3D worlds.

6.1.2 The WebGL Interface

The WebGL interface became universally adopted via the standards body, the Khronos Group. Khronos is the same standards body that produced the OpenGL standard. WebGL is based on the GLES standard, a cut-down version of OpenGL designed to run on embedded devices. In order to run on such a diverse community of web browsers, the WebGL 1.0 specification is based on an older version of OpenGLES, version 1.0. This version does not include some of the modern features to which graphics programmers are accustomed. Many features, howver, have been introduced via the Khronos extension mechanism and are now part of the newly supported WebGL 2.0 spec.

Despite its apparent similarity to OpenGL, in its implementation the WebGL interface differs drastically from the traditional 3D APIs, like OpenGL. A traditional 3D graphics API, such as OpenGL, is defined in terms of the interface between the application, compiled ahead of time to a native executable, and the 3D hardware. Even though it is using the same API, each operating system requires its own compiled version of the application. It is this compiled executable that is distributed to end users.

So, a Windows executable might be compiled from C++, using the Visual Studio toolchain. An IOS application, on the other hand, would be compiled from ObjectiveC using XCode even though it is fundamentally the same OpenGL code. Users then execute that application locally, directly sending instructions to the device driver on their machine. Though the user never sees it, a graphics driver builds those instructions into a command queue. This is a list of binary instructions in the proprietary language of the GPU. Those commands cause the GPU to render the 3D world that is displayed to the user. The purpose of the OpenGL standard is to ensure that different hardware, with different drivers, on

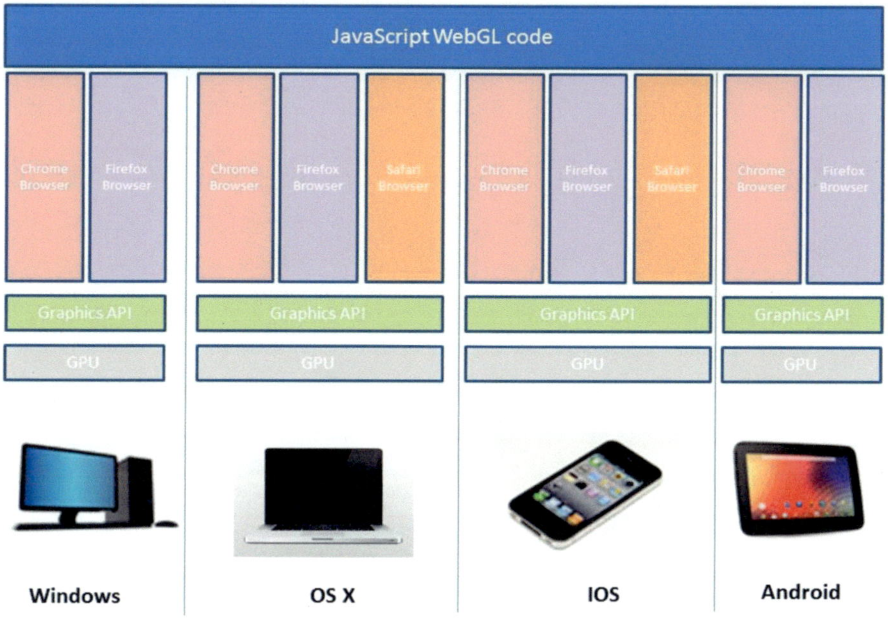

Figure 6.1. Cross platform 3D application using native code.

different operating systems, will produce approximately the same result when the same OpenGL commands are executed (see Figure 6.1).

WebGL works very differently. The JavaScript source code of a WebGL application is distributed in a webpage directly to users. A user accessing the webpage on a mobile phone will receive the same code as one accessing it on a desktop PC.

The web browsers native code interprets the JavaScript code and executes the WebGL commands within it. Within the web browser, a component is responsible for converting the WebGL in the websites HTML to native graphics commands that are sent to the GPU. The Khronos WebGL specification ensures that the same WebGL commands will produce the same results on any web browser, running on any device. But the specification does not stipulate how they will be implemented. Typically, the WebGL implementation in the browser will involve a second command queue, which queues up the commands to be executed on a separate thread. This thread then submits commands to the graphics driver. As it is part of the browser executable, this thread will run in user space, with the regular operating-system permissions any regular executable has. It cannot access the hardware directly. The WebGL specification does not

Figure 6.2. Cross platform 3D application using WebGL.

guarantee those commands will even be submitted using OpenGL; "under the hood" they could be executed on another API such as DirectX (see Figure 6.2).

The WebGL architecture is incredibly powerful, since it allows the same code to be executed on any browser on any device (including future devices and platforms), without recompiling your code. However, it adds an extra layer between the code and the GPU. This can make profiling and optimizing WebGL programs challenging. 3D application developers using WebGL do not directly control the interface to the GPU driver. That interface is part of the browser itself and varies between browsers on different devices. How, and when, WebGL commands will be translated to the commands that are sent to the GPU driver is not defined by the WebGL specification.

6.1.3 The Profiling and Optimization Process

The basic task of optimizing your application remains fundamentally the same, despite the differences discussed in the previous section between WebGL and native 3D application development. The process of profiling and optimization is a feedback loop. It is first necessary to profile the application and work out where time is being spent during its execution. Typically, the results will show that the majority of time during execution is spent in just a few sections of code. The bits of code that are taking the most time to execute are the focus of the optimization process. Hopefully, the result is that their performance improves to a satisfactory degree. The process then repeats. By profiling the newly optimized system again, having removed the "low-hanging fruit," the results will be different. Sections of code that did not appear significant in the previous profiling analysis will now become so, and the optimization process begins again.

The process is the same for any application. The complication in the 3D case is that the profiling process must take into account both the GPU and the CPU [Cok et al. 2000]. These two components execute asynchronously. Ideally, during execution both the GPU and CPU will be actively running application code at the same time. In many cases, profiling will reveal large periods where one component is idle, waiting for operations on the other to finish.

The same process should be followed for your WebGL applications. Failure to do so will likely result in spending time optimizing code that will have little effect on the overall performance of the application.

6.2 Browser Profiling Tools

Hardware vendors generally provide application profiling tools for applications that use their hardware and APIs. These tools are widely used and understood by native application developers. However, they cannot easily be used by WebGL developers, who are not using native APIs directly. Because WebGL code is run in the browser, tools incorporated into browsers must be used to profile it. All the commonly used web browsers provide browser profiling tools that can be used for this purpose. Web pages, and the code contained in them, can be profiled in the web browser, just as traditional applications are profiled using native vendor-

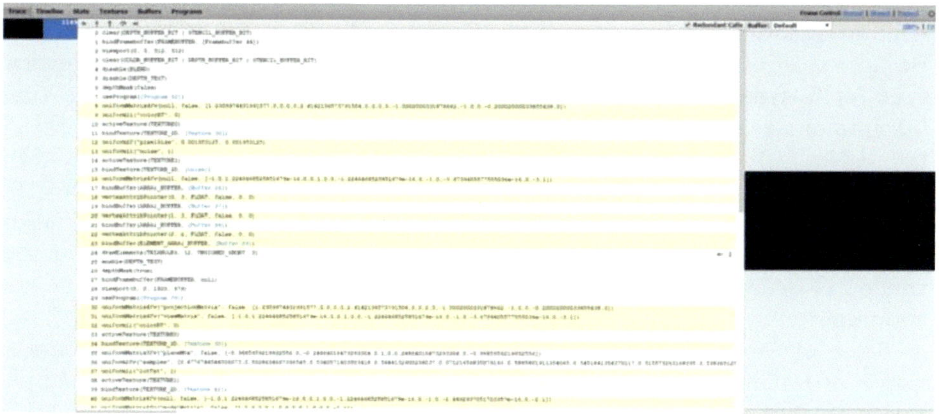

Figure 6.3. WebGL inspector plugin.

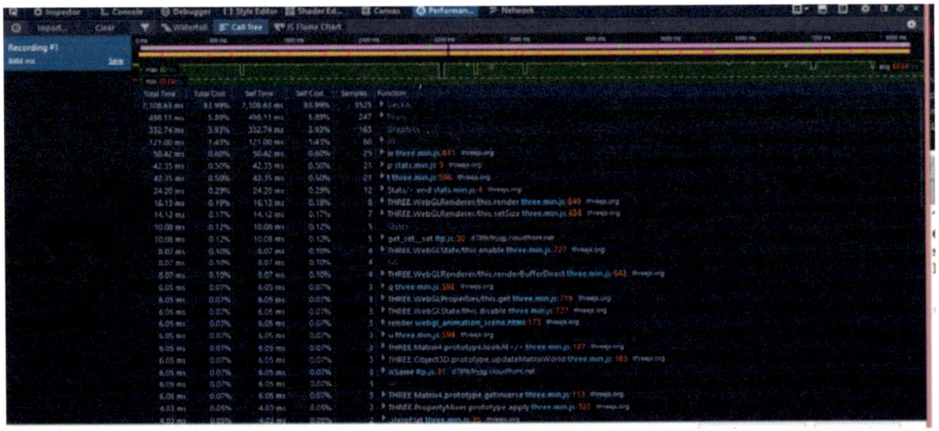

Figure 6.4. Firefox performance profilier.

supplied tools. Some of these tools are included in the web-browser application itself, whereas others are third-party plugins that must be installed separately (see Figures 6.3 and 6.4). This chapter will concentrate on the tools included in the Chrome web browser, but similar tools are available for other browsers.

6.2.1 Frame-rate Counters

The most fundamental profiling tool is the frame-rate counter. Frame rate is a measurement of the frequency that an application is rendering to the display, in frames per second (FPS). FPS is tied to the physical display hardware being used. It represents the number of times a second that an image is displayed on the device in order to create the illusion of movement. It is the inverse of the time between the start of one frame and the next. To achieve 60 frames-per-second, an application must spend no more than 16.666.. milliseconds rendering each frame. Because most display devices require frames to be displayed on the next vertical sync (or V-sync) signal, the frame rate does not simply depend on the time taken to render each frame. The V-sync signal is tied to the refresh frequency of the display hardware, measured in Hertz (hz). A frame may complete all of its rendering in 10 ms., but, the frame rate will still be measured as 60 FPS not 100 FPS, as the V-sync frequency is 60 hz. There is often a great deal of variation in timing between frames. So, the FPS displayed is typically an average over a window of many frames, not simply a measurement of the time between the last two frames.

Most 3D applications include a frame-rate counter, which is the coarsest means of profiling an application. The frame-rate counter reveals if an application is meeting its performance targets. Rather than rely on code within the application itself, WebGL applications can be profiled using the frame-rate counter included in the browser.

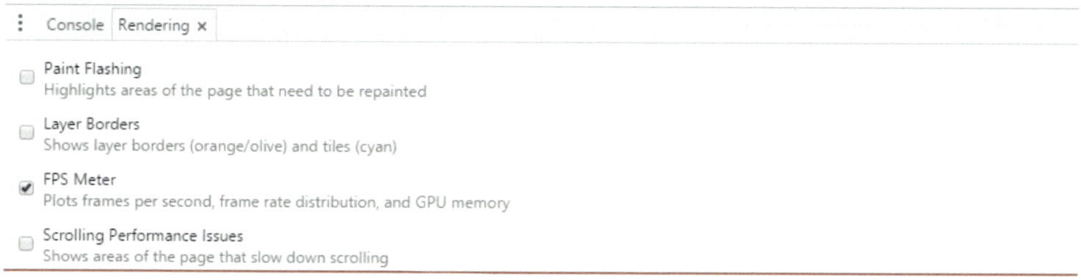

Figure 6.5. Chrome rendering options.

Chrome FPS meter. The Chrome FPS meter [Google Chrome 2016], for desktop Chrome, is enabled via the Rendering tab in the Chrome Developer Tools (see Figure 6.5).

This tab (Figure 6.6) will display a frame-rate window in the top right of the current tab. The window contains:

- the frame rate the current page;
- a graph of previous frames FPS;
- a histogram showing the range of FPS for recent frames;
- whether HTML rendering uses GPU rasterization;
- GPU memory statistics.

On mobile Android devices all the Chrome developer tools, including the FPS meter, must be accessed remotely. Chromes remote-debugging feature is used for this purpose. These tools are accessed from the developer tools window in Chrome on a desktop machine. The mobile device is connected via USB, having first enabled USB debugging (in the Android device settings). Use the Remote Devices pane within the developer tools window on the desktop machine to connect the device. Once the device is connected, bring up the inspector window and enable the FPS meter (Figure 6.7).

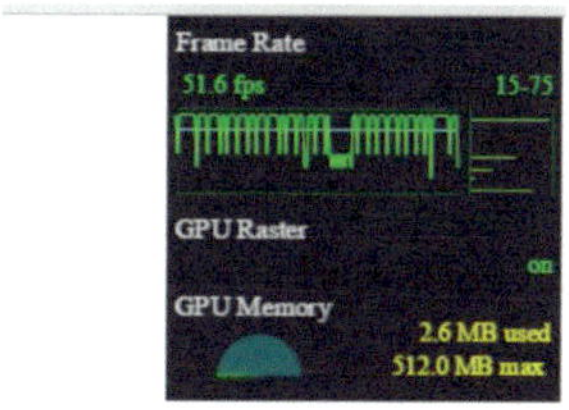

Figure 6.6. Chrome FPS meter.

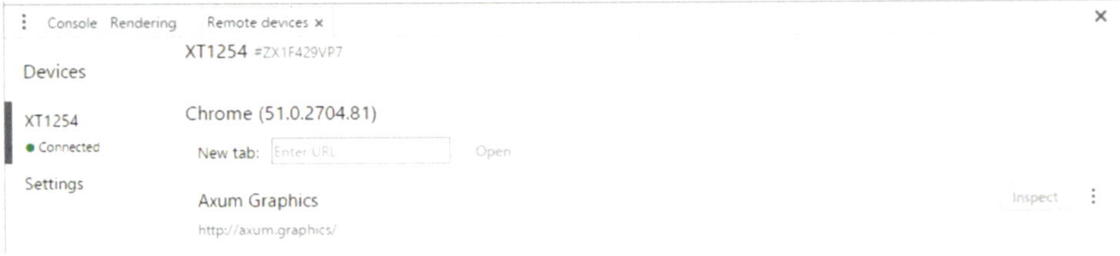

Figure 6.7. Chrome remote debugging.

6.2.2 WebGL Render Loop

Though the frame rate of a WebGL application seems straight forward, some understanding of the architecture of JavaScript applications is need to understand it. The render loop in a WebGL application looks different to a regular 3D application. Typically, at the heart of a 3D application there is a programming loop, the render loop, that looks something like this:

```
while(!done) {
  GetUserInput();
  UpdateApplicationState();
  RenderApplication();
}
```

A JavaScript application does not have a render loop in the traditional sense. JavaScript programs are embedded in HTML webpages, which is a technology designed to deliver static pages of multimedia content. HTML was never designed to incorporate dynamic animated content, let alone an application render loop. With the advent of JavaScript, there was an obvious need to support animated content. This type of content needed a mechanism for updating at a reliable frequency. Many techniques were used to implement animation using the existing JavaScript specification. However, none of these techniques were reliable on all browsers without stalling the user interface if the code being executed used too many resources.

So, in 2015, the `requestAnimationFrame` function was added to the Domain Object Model(DOM). The DOM is the formal specification of the browser interface that is used by JavaScript. This function takes a single argument, a callback function that is called by the browser at some point in the future. WebGL applications using this feature have a render loop that looks very different to a traditional application:

```
function RenderApplication() {
  RenderWorld();
  window.requestAnimationFrame(RenderApplication);
}
```

As an application developer, the upshot of this, is that the browser decides when to call the provided `requestAnimationFrame` function. It does this based on how busy it is and on the V-sync rate of the display. So the actual frame rate of the application is outside programmer control.

6.2.3 Event Tracing in Chrome

Once a WebGL application falls below an acceptable frame rate, it should be profiled using one of the more in-depth profiling tools available for web browsers. For Google Chrome, the most useful low-level profiling tool is the Chrome Event Tracing tool [The Chromium Projects 2016]. Entering `chrome://tracing/` in the URL bar of the Chrome web browser brings up the tracing user interface (on Android use chrome://inspect/?tracing having first enabled Chrome remote debugging). From there, a trace can be recorded using the record button. Different event categories can be chosen to record. The traces displayed in this chapter were produced with the following categories checked:

`Blink`	The renderer component within Chrome that generates the displayed webpage
`blink.console`	Events triggered from console commands in the webpage Javascript code
`v8`	The Chrome Javascript engine
`Ipc`	Inter-process communication between the Chrome processes
`devtools.timeline`	Useful human-readable timeline information

To profile a webpage once recording has started, move to the browser tab running the webpage being profiled, and perform the operation that requires profiling (that operation may just be letting the animation callback render a number of frames). When sufficient data has been recorded, return to the tracing tab and click stop. After processing the resulting data, the tracing tab will display everything that happened within the browser during the tracing period, as shown in Figure 6.8.

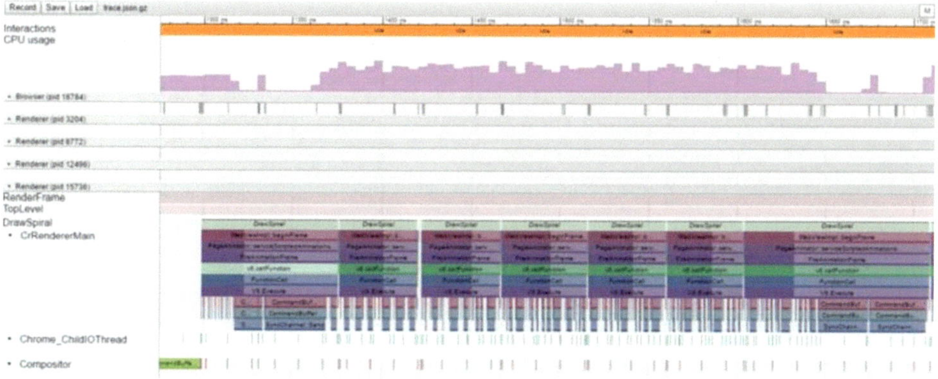

Figure 6.8. The Chrome event-tracing page.

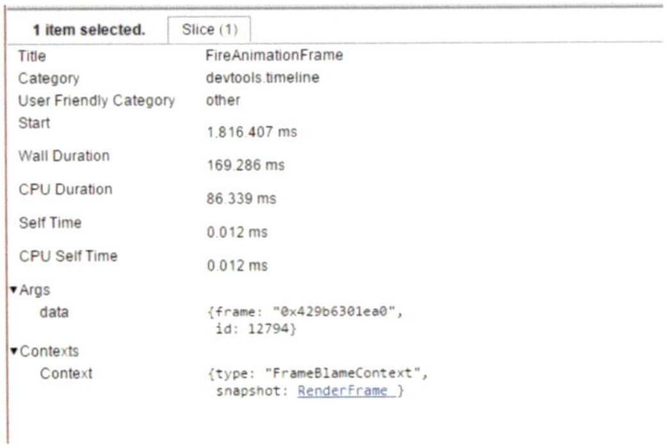

Figure 6.9. Event details.

This display is a color-coded visualization of what the browser was doing, over time, against a timeline at the top of the page. It can be navigated, zoomed, and panned, with the "first person shooter controls" (the keys W, S, A, and D). Each colored event bar represents a labeled event executing on one of the browser processes. Clicking on an event bar will show detailed information about that event (Figure 6.9).

The information shown includes:

- event title,
- tracing category,
- start time in milliseconds,
- Wall Duration: the absolute time spent executing the event,
- CPU Duration: time spent actually executing, rather than blocked,
- CPU Self Time: time spent in the event itself, rather than in functions further down the call-stack.

The ratio of Wall Duration to CPU Duration is extremely important when profiling WebGL applications (it is also shown visually as the dark- and light-colored section of each event bar). When one of the processes blocks waiting for the GPU to complete (or to wait on some other resource), this will appear as an event showing a much longer Wall Duration than CPU Duration.

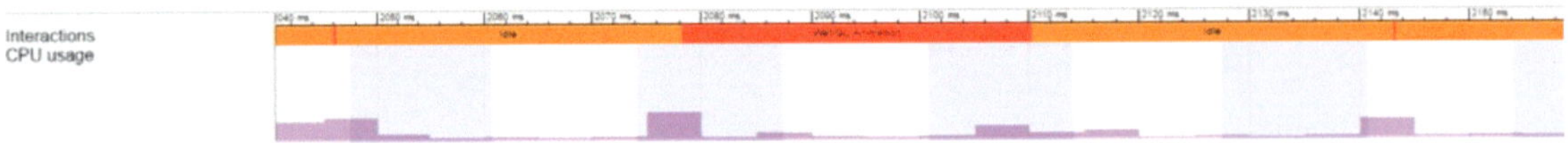

Figure 6.10. The timeline.

Below the timeline, a CPU counter will display the percentage the CPU is used by the browser as a whole, along with a bar showing the time spent interacting with the browser user interface (Figure 6.10).

Below this, the activity of each process is displayed, along with its process ID. Each Chrome tab is a separate operating-system process. The process is divided into two processes (Figure 6.11):

- The renderer: decomposes the HTML of the webpage (including the JavaScript) into commands to be rendered, under the `CrRendererMain` section (the label assigned to the main renderer thread).
- The compositor: displays different sections of the webpage onto the screen.

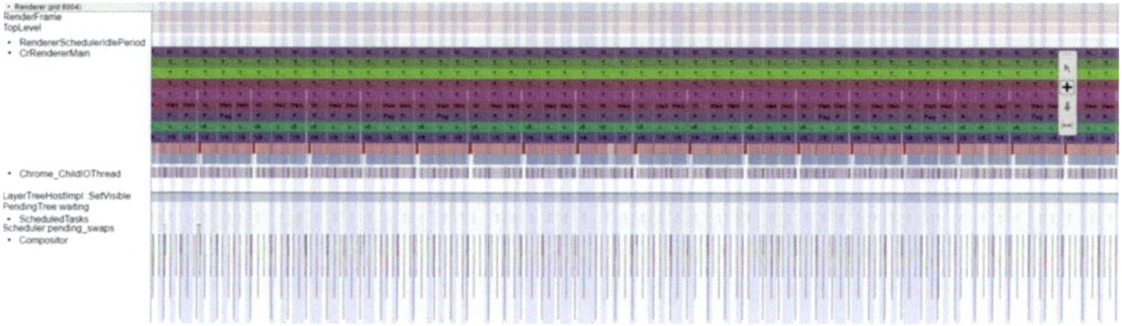

Figure 6.11. Process event tracing.

Sections of JavaScript of can be tagged using the functions `console.time()` and `console.timeEnd()`, as shown:

```
function  RenderApplication()
{
  console.time("Stuff");
  DoStuff();
  console.timeEnd("Stuff");
  window.requestAnimationFrame(RenderApplication);
}
```

As well as printing the time taken to execute that section to the console, the resulting label will appear in the tracing output, as shown below. It will appear in the section-headers column on the left of the page, and above the event bars representing the renderer trace (Figure 6.12).

All the commands being sent to the GPU, both WebGL commands and any internal browser GPU rendering, are done so from a single process. Tracing results for this process appear at the bottom of the tracing window (Figure 6.13). Analysis of this section is very important when profiling WebGL applications.

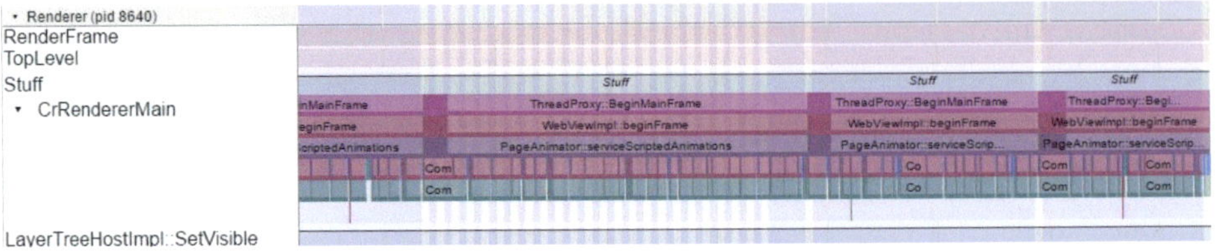

Figure 6.12. Labels in event-tracing view.

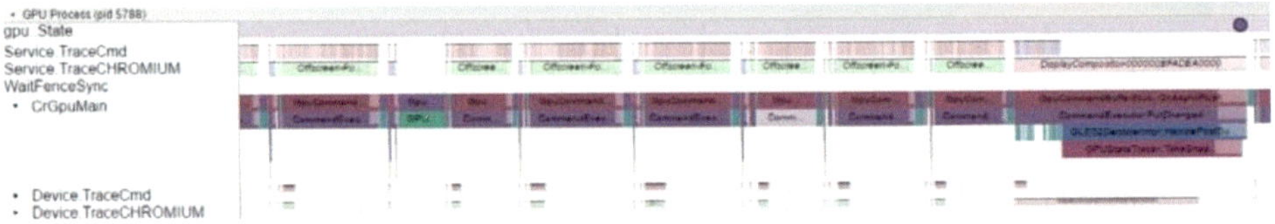

Figure 6.13. GPU process.

6.3 Case Studies

This chapter will discuss several case studies where simple WebGL applications are profiled and optimized. These studies will use the Chrome Event Tracing interface, though similar profiling tools are available for other browsers.

6.3.1 Case Study 1: Draw Call Bound

In this first case study, a spiral pattern is rendered using multiple cubes, as shown in Figure 6.14. This is done by creating the geometry for a single cube. Array buffers are created for the 24 position vertices representing the corners of

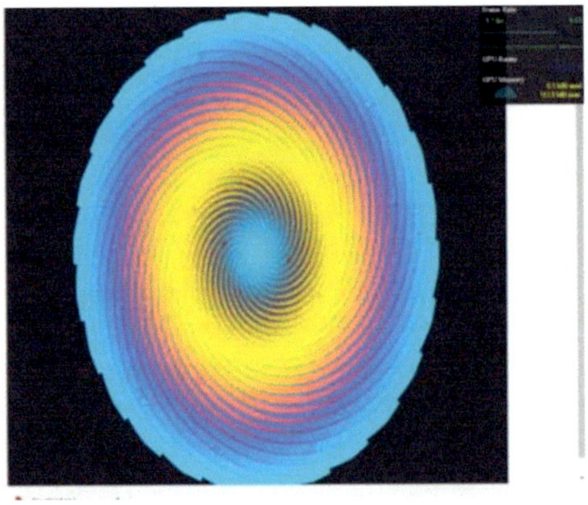

Figure 6.14. Simple WebGL application.

the cube and for the associated per-face vertex colors. Each face of the cube requires separate per-face varying data, so the result is 24 vertices rather than just eight. Next, an element array buffer for the 36 indices that produce the cube geometry is created.

In the render function, the cube is transformed with a 4×4 transform matrix multiple times to form the arms of the spiral. The transformation of each cube is implemented using a uniform variable set in the vertex shader and rendered each time using `drawElements`.

```
console.time("DrawSpiral");
var oIncr=1.0/(numObjects-1);
var aIncr=(2.0*Math.PI)/numArms;

for(var a=0;a<numArms;a++) {
   for(var o=0;o<numObjects;o++) {
      var modelMatrix=ComputeSpiralXformMatrix(o*oIncr,a*aIncr);
      mat4.multiply(modelViewMatrix,viewMatrix, modelMatrix);

      gl.uniformMatrix4fv(mvUniform, false, modelViewMatrix);
      gl.drawElements(gl.TRIANGLES, 36, gl.UNSIGNED_SHORT, 0);
   }
}
console.timeEnd("DrawSpiral");
```

The frame-rate counter shows that this application has far from ideal performance. Even on a powerful GPU increasing the number of cubes rendered causes the frame rate to drop drastically to under 10 fps. Running the event-tracing tool produces a trace like the one in Figure 6.15.

Examining the results, we can see that most of the CPU time is spent, as expected, within our animation frame callback function (`V8.Execute` within `FireAnimationFrame`). Each call of this function takes far longer than a render function should for an interactive application. In fact, several v-sync intervals take place during a single execution (shown by the vertical white and blue bars). For most of that time, the thread is blocked and not actually running (shown by the lighter color on right hand of bar). As shown in the zoomed view in Figure 6.16, most of the time is spent blocked in the function `CommandBufferProxyImpl::WaitForGetOffset`.

Figure 6.15. Case Study 1: Rendering process.

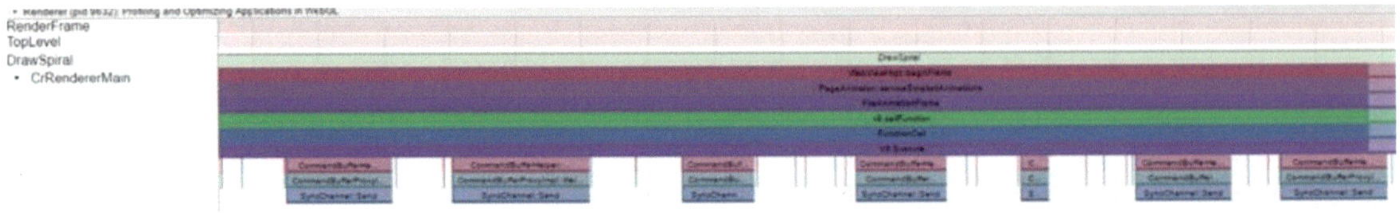

Figure 6.16. Case Study 1: Waiting for command queue.

This means the JavaScript thread is stalled. It is waiting for the GPU command queue to become free, so we can enqueue the render commands that correspond to our frame-render function.

Scrolling down to the tracing information for the GPU process reveals the problem (Figure 6.17).

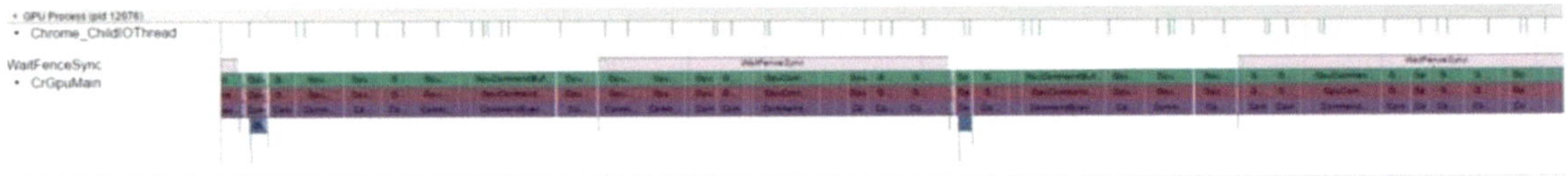

Figure 6.17. Case Study 1: GPU process.

The GPU thread is constantly busy in `CommandExecutor:PutChanged`, which is the function that actually executes the WebGL commands on the queue. The reason for this is the number of draw calls we are making in WebGL. Each cube has a tiny amount of geometry, so each WebGL `drawElements` function call only renders a small number of vertices. This is an extremely inefficient way to drive the GPU. The GPU itself is actually idle for most of the frame. The process feeding it is bogged down, setting up draw calls to send to the GPU.

6.3.2 Case Study 2: GPU Bound

In this simple test case, the solution is straightforward. The issue is that each cube is rendered with a single draw call. Instead, here, all the cubes that make up one arm of the spiral can be combined into a single set of array buffers and an element array buffer. Each arm can then be rendered with a single draw call.

```
for(var o=0;o<numObjects;o++) {
   var xformMatrix=computeXformMatrix(o*oIncr);
   for(var j=0;j<cubeVertexIndices.length;j++) {
      indexArray[indOffset]=cubeVertexIndices[j]+ind;
      indOffset++;
   }

   for(var j=0;j<vertices.length;j+=3)
   {
```

```
        var pos = vec3.fromValues(vertices[j+0], vertices[j+1], vertices[j+2]);
        var color = vec3.fromValues(vertexColors[j+0], vertexColors[j+1], vertexColors[j+2]);
        vec3.transformMat4(pos,pos,xformMatrix);
        posArray[ind*3+0]=pos[0];
        posArray[ind*3+1]=pos[1];
        posArray[ind*3+2]=pos[2];
        colorArray[ind*3+0]=color[0];
        colorArray[ind*3+1]=color[1];
        colorArray[ind*3+2]=color[2];

        ind++;
    }
}

gl.bindBuffer(gl.ARRAY_BUFFER, verticesBuffer);
gl.bufferData(gl.ARRAY_BUFFER, posArray, gl.STATIC_DRAW );
gl.bindBuffer(gl.ARRAY_BUFFER, vertexColorBuffer);
gl.bufferData(gl.ARRAY_BUFFER, colorArray, gl.STATIC_DRAW );
```

The render loop is now much simpler, with a single draw call for each arm of the spiral. This reduces the number of draw commands sent to the GPU process massively.

```
console.time("DrawSpiral");
for(var a=0;a<numArms;a++) {
    var armMatrix=ComputeSpiralArmXformMatrix(o*oIncr);
    mat4.fromZRotation(modelMatrix, armMatrix);
    mat4.multiply(modelViewMatrix,viewMatrix, modelMatrix);

    gl.uniformMatrix4fv(mvUniform, false, modelViewMatrix);

    gl.drawElements(gl.TRIANGLES, n*36, gl.UNSIGNED_SHORT, 0);
}
console.timeEnd("DrawSpiral");
```

The difference is stark compared to the previous case study. The frame rate remains high, even as the amount of geometry increases. Looking at the result

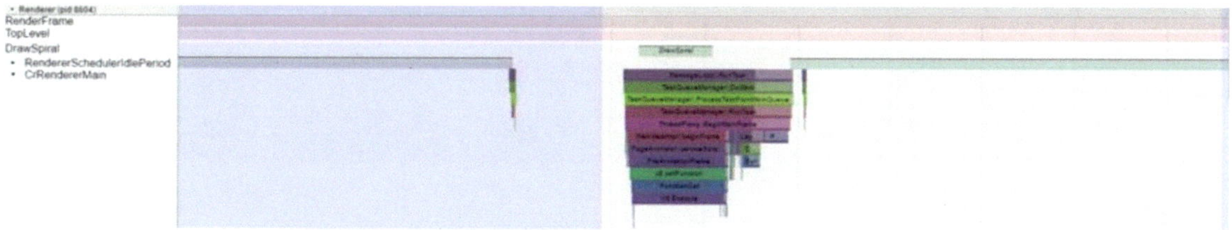

Figure 6.18. Case Study 2: Renderer process.

in the tracing view, `FireAnimationFrame` now just takes a fraction of a v-sync interval, and the process is idle for most of the frame. The WebGL commands have been submitted to the GPU process, and the Javscript code has finished executing without blocking. This is the ideal result of optimizing a WebGL application (Figure 6.18).

The GPU process is spent inside `GLES2DecoderImpl::HandlePostSubBuffer CHROMIUM`. This is the equivalent of functions such as `glSwapBuffers`. This function causes the internal front and back frame buffers (the back buffer being rendered to, and front buffer being displayed) to be swapped. A stall here means the process is waiting for the GPU to finish executing before it can swap to the next frame (Figure 6.19).

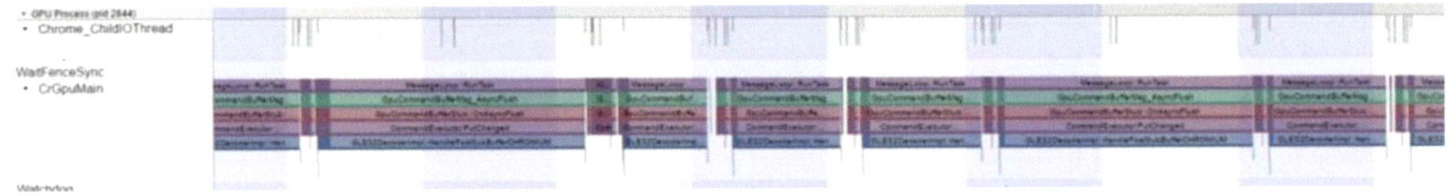

Figure 6.19. Case Study 2: GPU process.

6.3.3 Case Study 3: Sync Bound

A real-world application may be harder to optimize than this simple test case. In the previous case study, the geometry for the spiral arm can be pre-generated just once, outside the render loop. That geometry can then be rendered multiple times with a simple rotation transform to generate the spiral shape.

This is not always the case. Typically, the geometry being rendered changes from frame to frame and must be transferred to the GPU. If the previous case study is changed, so that every frame `bufferData` is called to upload new vertex data, the performance changes drastically.

Profiling using the tracing view reveals that `UpdateArm` function takes much longer than the `DrawSpiral` function. This shows that the `bufferData` call is taking far longer than the actual rendering commands to draw the spiral. This

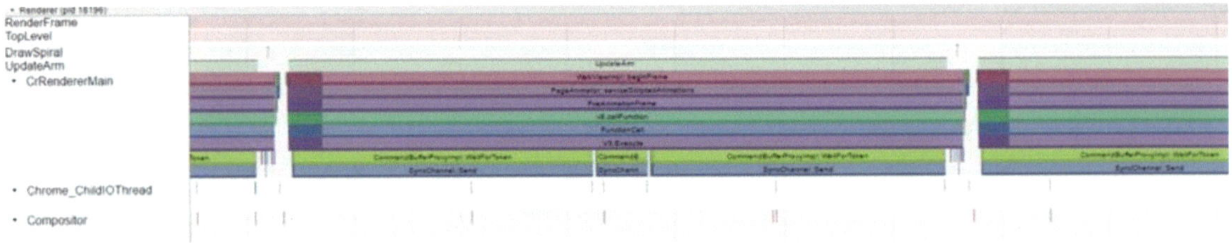

Figure 6.20. Case Study 3: Renderer process.

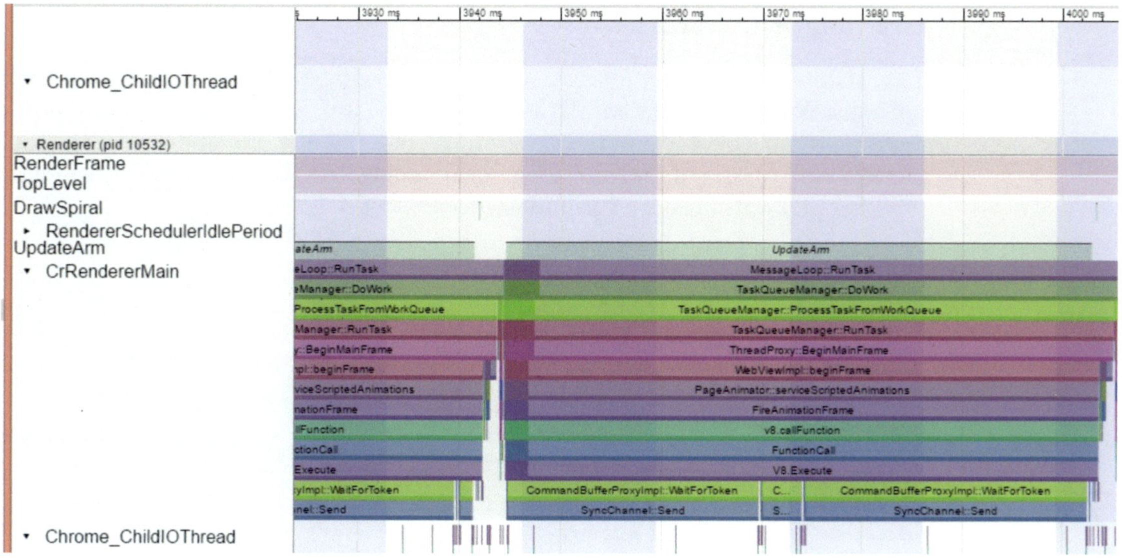

Figure 6.21. `WaitForToken` stall.

delay occurs because the application is now dependent on the transfer of the data between the CPU and GPU (Figure 6.20).

In the `UpdateArm` function, the thread is blocked waiting in `CommandBufferProxyImpl::WaitForToken`. This shows a dependency has been introduced between the CPU and GPU. The render function must stall and wait for the transfer of the vertex data to the GPU before continuing (Figure 6.21).

Minimizing the amount of data transferred from CPU to GPU within the render loop, and removing dependencies on those transfers, is critical for the efficient execution of a 3D application. Options for optimize this case include:

- is updating;
- performing the transform in the vertex shader, and transfering the transformation definitions as uniform data, rather than array buffers.

The recent WebGL extension `ANGLE_instanced_arrays`, allows geometry to be instanced without multiple draw calls. This could also be used to optimize this case (this extension is included in WebGL 2.0). Similarly, the WebGL 2.0 feature Transform Feedback buffer feature could allow complex geometry (such as the spiral arm in this example) to be rendered into a GPU buffer and reused in subsequent render calls.

6.4 Conclusion

This chapter was a brief discussion of the issues involved in profiling and optimizing a WebGL application. These simple case studies highlighted some of the main causes of slow GPU performance in WebGL. Real-world applications will be more complicated and may not be so easily analyzed. However, the fundamental profiling and optimization techniques used will be the same.

Bibliography

COK, K., CORRON, R., KUEHNE, B., , AND TRUE, T. 2000. Developing efficient graphics software: The yin and yang of graphics. In *SIGGRAPH Course Notes*, ACM, New York.

ECMA, 2016. ECMAScript 2016 language specification. http://www.ecma-international.org/publications/standards/Ecma-262.htm.

GOOGLE CHROME, 2016. Chrome developer settings. https://developer.chrome.com/devtools/docs/rendering-settings.

KHRONOS, 2014. WebGL specification. https://www.khronos.org/registry/webgl/specs/1.0/.

OPENGL REGISTRY, 2016. OpenGL 4.5 API specification. https://www.opengl.org/registry/doc/glspec45.core.pdf.

THE CHROMIUM PROJECTS, 2016. The trace event profiling tool. https://www.chromium.org/developers/how-tos/trace-event-profiling-tool.

UNITY 3D, 2016. Unity web player. https://unity3d.com/webplayer.

WEB3D CONSORTIUM, 2006. VRML97 functional specification and VRML97 external authoring interface (EAI). http://www.web3d.org/content/vrml97-functional-specification-and-vrml97-external-authoring-interface-eai,.

IV Screen Space

Welcome to the screen-space section of this new and exciting source of invaluable GPU programming wisdom. The selection of articles here reflects the industry's growing challenge of implementing high-quality, yet fast-executing screen-space processing effects. In particular, we focus on two of the most common but difficult effects: depth of field and screen-space ambient occlusion. Without further ado, here is a short introduction to each of the three articles you will find in this part.

First, Filip Strugar's article, "Scalable Adaptive SSAO," presents an implementation of a standard SSAO, tuned for scalability and flexibility with regard to trading-off quality versus performance; it is thus applicable to a wide range of hardware and usage scenarios, with uniform settings and visual consistency. Such flexibility and scalability is even more important with the requirements of VR applications.

Second, Wojciech Sterna presents the article, "Robust Screen-Space Ambient Occlusion in 1 ms in 1080p on PS4." This implementation was successfully used in two *Shadow Warrior* games. The implementation is fairly stable, gives plausible results, and depicts good performance characteristics, taking about 1 ms on PlayStation 4 in 1080p and 1 ms on Xbox One in 900p.

Finally, Wojciech Sterna's article, "Practical Gather-based Bokeh Depth of Field," describes a fast and easy-to-implement solution to the problem. This technique achieves a little over 1.5 ms in 1080p on GeForce 660 GTX by operating in quarter-resolution buffers and then finally compositing the results carefully using a special upsampling process. The result produces stable and convincing results at very good frame rates.

I hope you find this selection of articles inspiring and enlightening to your own work and investigation for the quest of pushing beautiful pixels at the fastest rates.

—Wessam Bahnassi

IV

1 Scalable Adaptive SSAO

Filip Strugar

1.1 Overview

Screen-space ambient occlusion has become a de-facto standard in real-time rendering for producing small-scale ambient and contact shadow effects. With ever expanding TDP (thermal design point) and, consequently, performance range in the GPU market, and the new at-runtime performance scaling needs for VR, this article presents a framework for implementing SSAO in a scalable way, in order to cover a wider range of hardware and use cases with the same implementation.

1.2 Problem Statement

The wide adoption of SSAO algorithms, high quality shadow maps, and global illumination in modern PC and console games often has an effect of completely replacing lower-cost solutions, such as lightmaps or various shadow-approximation effects (such as blob shadows under dynamic objects), without a suitable replacement for the low-end hardware. This is understandable, as it is difficult and costly to design, ensure consistency, and maintain multiple completely separate code and art paths for providing an effect at different quality/performance levels. However, the common outcome is that the lower quality presets in modern titles often do not have some of the effects that were previously standard on the graphics hardware with similar performance.

At the time of publication of this chapter, the most commonly used full resolution SSAO techniques only become applicable on GPUs of approximately 30W TDP and above, which practically excludes thin and light laptops, but also many VR scenarios on recommended or even minimum specs.

Using a below-full resolution SSAO (half $\times$ full or half $\times$ half) to cover lowest-end quality presets is often the only option, but this approach is limited by quality issues such as aliasing artifacts which then need to be addressed separately.

Adaptive SSAO aims at providing full resolution AO effect at a range of quality levels, for integrated graphics cards with TDP of 15W to discrete GPUs of 150W and above, as well as 90Hz VR rendering. The progressive sampling kernel is flexible enough to allow for incremental quality/performance tradeoff fine tuning, within the scaling range.

1.3 ASSAO—A High-level Overview

Adaptive screen space ambient occlusion is an implementation of a standard SSAO, tuned for scalability and flexibility with regard to trading off quality vs performance, and it is thus applicable to a wider range of hardware and usage scenarios, with uniform settings and visual consistency. AO implementation is based on a solid-angle occlusion model similar to horizon-based ambient occlusion [Bavoil et al. 2008] with a custom novel sampling kernel disk. The performance and scalability optimizations are based on depth buffer mip-map pre-filtering from scalable ambient obscurance [McGuire et al. 2012] and a 2×2 version of cache-friendly deinterleaved processing similar to [Bavoil 2014]. In addition, the progressive sampling kernel allows for easy tuning of individual preset performance, as well as an optional per-pixel dynamic-importance sampling approach for the highest-end implementation. The main passes of our approach at *high* preset (as shown in Figure 1.6) are:

1. Prepare depths
    - Convert input depth buffer into linear space and 2×2 deinterleave into four half $\times$ half viewspace.
    - Create MIPs for all four half $\times$ half depth textures.
2. Generate AO and edges and apply smart blur; loop four times for each of the four half $\times$ half deinterleaved slices.
    - Generate and output AO and edges into a R8G8 half $\times$ half texture, using the current depth slice generated in the previous step and input normals.
    - Apply edge-aware smart blur.
3. Interleave four outputs of the previous pass and apply final smart blur into the full resolution output render target.

Low preset will skip the depth mipmap and edge generation, while the *highest/adaptive* has an additional base AO pass and other changes as detailed in Section 1.7. When input normals are not available (for example, for forward renderers) a full resolution normal buffer is reconstructed from the input depths in Step 1 for use in Step 2. For a quick overview of performance numbers, please refer to Table 1.8.

Figure 1.1. Among other things, SSAO helps visually embed objects to scene.

1.4 SSAO—A Quick Refresh

Ambient occlusion refers to a computational model for producing small-scale shadows under certain conditions, mostly (but not exclusively) with regard to ambient lighting. Screen space refers to the calculation happening with only depth and (optional) normal buffers used as the inputs. This means that it is a post-process pass that has no knowledge of scene outside of the rendering frustum, as well as transparent or occluded geometry; this is its fundamental weakness.

However, in many scenarios SSAO is a good-enough approximation of global illumination, achievable at real-time on today's console and PC hardware, and it is thus used ubiquitously. It is an effective way of increasing visual fidelity and adding depth to a virtual world scene by approximating shadows between wall crevices, skin wrinkles, objects placed on/near other objects or surfaces, etc. Even with its limitations, it remains an effective and important tool in the real-time rendering toolbox (Figure 1.1).

As of recently, it is also used in conjunction with more advanced real-time global illumination techniques, which are usually calculated at a significantly lower spatial resolution due to performance constraints. There, SSAO can provide additional high-frequency AO to the smaller-scale scene details. It is also often extended to provide better lighting approximation (for example, SSDO [Ritschel et al. 2009]) or to export additional lighting information for use in the lighting pipeline (e.g., bent normals [Klehm et al. 2011]).

Although the idea of ambient occlusion has been around for a long time, it was only used in real-time since ca. 2007, with the first commercial implementation in Crysis [Mittring 2007] and was subsequently adopted by other game developers.

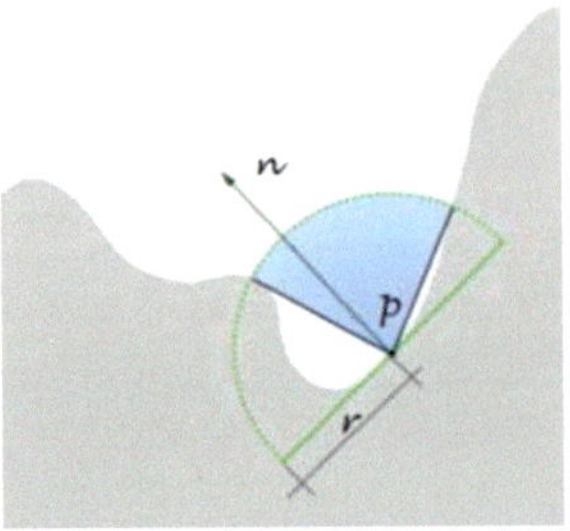

Figure 1.2. The hemisphere at a surface point p, normal n, and radius r, as seen from the side. The unoccluded part is shaded in blue.

It has been an active field of research since, with current cutting-edge solutions like HBAO+ appearing in many PC and console games.

In the simplest sense, ambient occlusion on a given surface point can be defined as the integral of the visibility function over the hemisphere defined by the surface normal (Figure 1.2). In practice, the visibility is determined only approximately and over a user-defined distance (radius) for performance reasons.

In the screen-space implementation, input data (depth buffer and optional normal map) provide the scene approximation used to evaluate the occlusion integral. Most AO approaches used in games rely on per-pixel occlusion approximation using a multi-tap depth-buffer sampling and processing kernel, although there are other implementations such as [Bunnell 2005] (which relies on disk proxies) or [Luft et al. 2006] (which relies on depth-buffer unsharp masking filters).

There are a large number of variations within the per-pixel occlusion approximation class of solutions, such as horizon-based ambient occlusion [Bavoil et al. 2008] and many others. For a more detailed overview of various SSAO methods, please refer to [Aalund 2012].

1.5 Scaling the SSAO

In this chapter, we present the individual steps taken to achieve the scalability goal. It should also be mentioned that, with the main focus on the framework that provides scaling, we have made it relatively easy to replace the AO logic if needed (SSAOTap() function in the main shader file) or to extend it with a more complex effect such as SSDO [Ritschel et al. 2009]. We will explore the framework around the AO core and the incremental kernel used for adaptive importance sampling implementation.

1.5.1 Step by Step Towards Scalable Performance

Budgeting. The industry standard for SSAO frame GPU budget is roughly below or around 10% of the frame time (3.3 ms at 30 FPS, 1.6 ms at 60 FPS) [Kaplanyan 2010, Donzallaz and Sousa 2011, McGuire et al. 2011]. Consequently, a budget in a VR scenario at 90 Hz would be at below 1 ms.

SSAO algorithms were used on Playstation 3 and Xbox 360-level hardware and above, although in order to stay within budget at 1280 × 720 resolution, they were often calculated at half resolution (e.g., 640 × 720). This trend was followed on PC games like *Battlefield: Bad Company 2* and *Battlefield 3*, etc. However, this simple lower-resolution approach causes visible aliasing and temporal artifacts (flickering) that require further attention, and we see the optimized full-resolution-only approaches like HBAO+ being more widely used currently.

We focus on a full-resolution approach as well, but aim at significantly expanded scaling range.

Starting point—a simplistic reference algorithm. To best understand the performance bottlenecks, we start with the basic SSAO implementation (Figure 1.3) using a full-resolution single-pass pixel shader that inputs depths and normals and outputs an ambient-occlusion term. It can provide final quality at impractical cost, but it is useful as a reference and as a starting point for performance optimizations.

In this form, the single pixel shader has a small amount of fixed (non-scalable) setup execution cost (loading center depth and normal, calculating radius and sampling pattern rotation, etc.), but the main work lies in iterating through depth samples and calculating occlusion. The more *taps* (sampling and AO math) there are, the higher the quality and execution cost (see Table 1.1 and Figure 1.4).

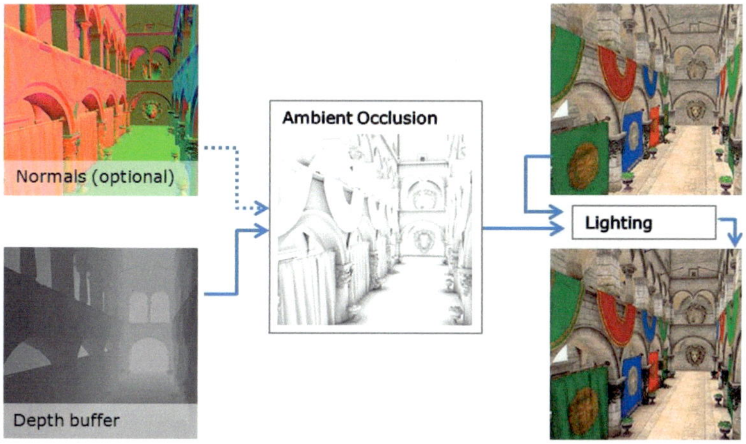

Figure 1.3. Basic SSAO.

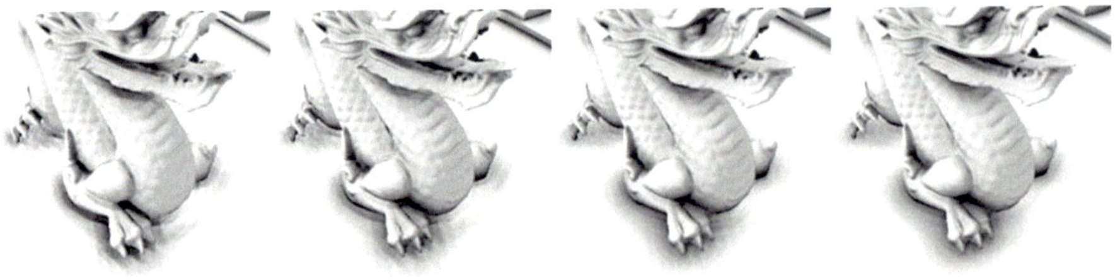

Figure 1.4. Basic SSAO, scaling quality with number of taps (8, 16, 32, 64).

Number of taps	1	8	16	32	64
GPU time in ms	0.2	0.77	1.53	2.96	5.81
GPU time per tap	0.2	0.096	0.096	0.093	0.091

Table 1.1. Performance scaling with number of taps, simplistic SSAO, GTX970, 1920 × 1080.

This is convenient as it allows us to easily increase quality with available performance: the execution cost increases linearly with the number of taps (although the perceived quality increase is not linear). However, at this stage there are two other variables that significantly affect the performance: resolution and depth sampling kernel on-screen size. When we measure the impact of increasing resolution, we see almost 2× increase in per-pixel cost (see Table 1.2).

Number of taps		800 x 600	1280 x 720	1920 x 1080	2560 x 1440	3840 x 2160
Megapixel count	MP	0.48	0.92	2.07	3.67	8.29
Simplistic	ms	0.42	0.98	2.57	5.07	13.43
SSAO	ms / MP	0.88	1.07	1.24	1.38	1.62

Table 1.2. Performance scaling with resolution, 32-tap, effect radius 0.5, GTX970.

The non-linear increase is purely due to loss of depth-texture–sampling cache efficiency. This assumption can be verified by modifying the algorithm to sample from a small subset of a source texture (e.g., by multiplying sampling texture coordinates by a small value such as 0.01) and noticing that the execution cost now scales linearly with the number of pixels.

The other effect of texture-sampling cache inefficiency is that varying the effect radius (which in turn varies the sampling kernel size) using our simple test SSAO shader can increase the cost by a factor of 3× (see Table 1.3).

Megapixel count	0.01	0.25	0.50	1.00	2.00
Simplistic SSAO, time in ms	1.34	2.02	2.58	2.95	3.06

Table 1.3. Performance scaling with effect radius, simplistic SSAO, 32-tap, GTX970, 1920× 1080.

The reason for this cost increase is the same—with bigger kernels there is less spatial coherence between samples, so the texture cache is used less efficiently. As the sampling kernel size depends on both the radius setting and viewspace distance, this means that the execution cost can also vary significantly based on scene contents and camera location.

This shows the inherent inefficiency in the simplistic algorithm version and points to the first scalability obstacle—better utilization of the texture cache hierarchy. Two separate approaches have been used to mitigate this problem in the past, and, unlike other SSAO techniques, ASSAO relies on using both in parallel.

Deinterleaved processing. Deinterleaved rendering was first mentioned in [Keller and Heidrich 2001] and used for SSAO in [Bavoil and Jansen 2013] and others.

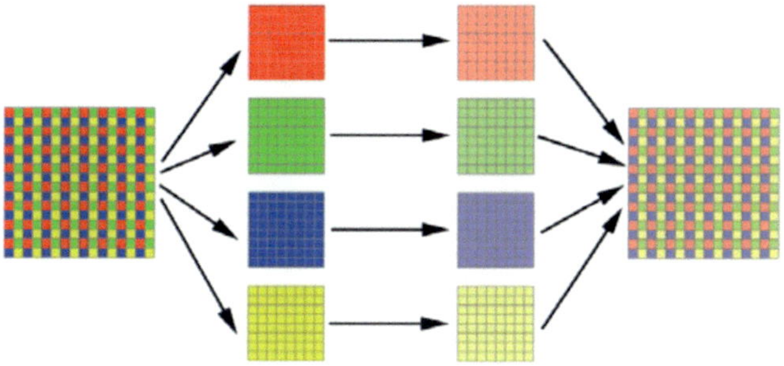

Figure 1.5. Deinterleaving, separate processing, reconstruction (interleaving).

In practice (Figure 1.5), we split our depth-sampling pattern into four separate ones, each constricted to one pixel from the 2×2 sub-quad. That lets us split the depth buffer, the main texture-sampling bottleneck, into four quarter-size buffers and then calculate the AO term independently for each, thus reducing per-pass memory domain by a factor of four. Then, we combine the results at the end (Figure 1.6).

Upgrading the simplistic SSAO to a simple 2×2 deinterleaved approach changes performance dramatically, as seen in Table 1.4.

Number of taps		800 x 600	1280 x 720	1920 x 1080	2560 x 1440	3840 x 2160
Megapixel count	MP	0.48	0.92	2.07	3.67	8.29
Simplistic	ms	0.42	0.98	2.57	5.07	13.43
SSAO	ms / MP	0.88	1.07	1.24	1.38	1.62
+ 2x2	ms	0.37	0.73	1.73	3.21	7.72
deinterleaved	ms / MP	0.77	0.79	0.84	0.87	0.93

Table 1.4. Performance scaling with resolution, 32-tap, effect radius 0.5, GTX970.

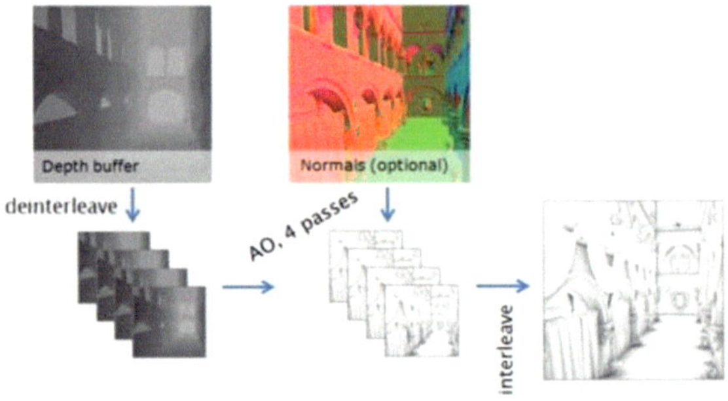

Figure 1.6. Deinterleaving, separate processing, reconstruction (interleaving).

By switching to 2×2 deinterleaved, we go from 85% increase in execution time per pixel between lower and highest resolutions, down to 21%. With the goal of completely eliminating the remaining 21% efficiency, we tried using a 4×4 deinterleaved approach; although it fully eliminates the cache coherency bottleneck, we find that the 4×4 approach also has some unwanted side-effects:

- While in the 2×2 version, the depth buffer deinterleaving adds fixed cost, this cost is amortized by performing depth values conversion into viewspace, needed later in the main AO pass. In the 4×4 version, this cost is not fully amortized, thus adding a fixed cost that reduces overall performance at low-end scaling range (in low/medium quality presets with fewer AO taps).
- Reconstruction (interleaving) is more complex for the 4×4 version, again adding fixed cost that reduces scaling at low-end.
- The 4×4 version is less flexible when used with different stochastic sampling kernels, reducing scaling flexibility with regards to quality.
- The 4×4 approach is not suitable for high-quality edge-aware smart blur on deinterleaved buffers, forcing us to interleave first and then apply it at the full resolution. However, in a 2×2 version, we can still apply a faster, more cache-friendly smart blur on individual deinterleaved slices.

For these reasons we opt for the 2×2 deinterleaved approach, but add another solution that lets us obtain optimal cache efficiency.

Depth mip-maps. A method introduced in [McGuire et al. 2012] is another way of extending cache efficiency. The idea is to pre-filter the depth buffer into MIP levels and use mip-mapping while sampling.

We first deinterleave the depth buffer into four and then create mip-maps on each deinterleaved depth-buffer slice. To downsample depth for mip levels, we use radius-based weighted averaging which effectively calculates the arithmetic

```
float closestD = min( min( depths.x, depths.y ),
                      min( depths.z, depths.w ) );
float4 weights = saturate( (depths - closestD.xxxx)
                 * weightCalcMul.xxxx + weightCalcAdd.xxxx );

float smartAvg = dot( weights, depths ) /
                 dot( weights, float4( 1.0, 1.0, 1.0, 1.0 ) );
```

Listing 1.1. Weighted average depth filter.

mean of samples within a radius of the closest one, resulting in a subjectively better looking and more temporally stable filter than the rotated grid subsample and other approaches tried in [McGuire et al. 2012]. The radius used is the same as the AO effect radius (Listing 1.1).

The variable `depths` is a float4 with four depths input; `weightCalcMul` and `weightCalcAdd` are pre-calculated constants used to calculate linear $[0, 1]$ weight based on the effect radius (used as well in AO sample weighing); `smartAvg` is the output.

For calculating the depth texture sample mip level for each tap, we use the following formula:

$$m = \log_2(ps) + sk + gk,$$

where

- ps is kernel screen size, in pixels, calculated in the AO shader at per-pixel frequency.
- sk is the per sample offset based on sample distance from the kernel center, stored in the sample kernel array. It is calculated offline as `log2(sampleLength)` + `random(-0.4, +0.4)`), stored in the sample coordinates array and loaded per-sample in the AO shader.
- gk is a global offset constant, set at the best tradeoff value between quality and performance.

Figure 1.7. Sampling kernel with depth mip sampling disabled (left) and enabled (right); colors indicate depth mip-level sampled: red = 0, green = 1, blue = 2, black = 3.

The constant gk corresponds to constant q' from [McGuire et al. 2012], where it is noted that "lower values caused multiple taps at adjacent pixels to map to the same texel at a low mip level, which amplified sample variance and manifested as temporal flicker. Higher values decreased performance because the working area no longer fit in cache."

This temporal flicker and loss in correctness is the main reason that we do not rely solely on the depth mip approach. However, when used in conjunction with 2×2 deinterleaving sampling, we can use a significantly higher gk value and avoid most temporal artifacts while still retaining optimum cache efficiency—offering the best of both worlds. Finally, we can see that with combined 2×2 deinterleaved rendering and the depth mip approaches, we have essentially removed the texture-sampling bottleneck in all scenarios (Table 1.5 and Figure 1.8):

Number of taps		800 x 600	1280 x 720	1920 x 1080	2560 x 1440	3840 x 2160
Megapixel count	MP	0.48	0.92	2.07	3.67	8.29
Simplistic	ms	0.42	0.98	2.57	5.07	13.43
SSAO	ms / MP	0.88	1.07	1.24	1.38	1.62
+ 2x2	ms	0.37	0.73	1.73	3.21	7.72
deinterleaved	ms / MP	0.77	0.79	0.84	0.87	0.93
+ 2x2 deinterleaved	ms	0.41	0.76	1.66	2.94	6.37
+depth MIPS	ms / MP	0.85	0.83	0.80	0.80	0.77

Table 1.5. Performance scaling with resolution, 32-tap, effect radius 0.5, GTX970.

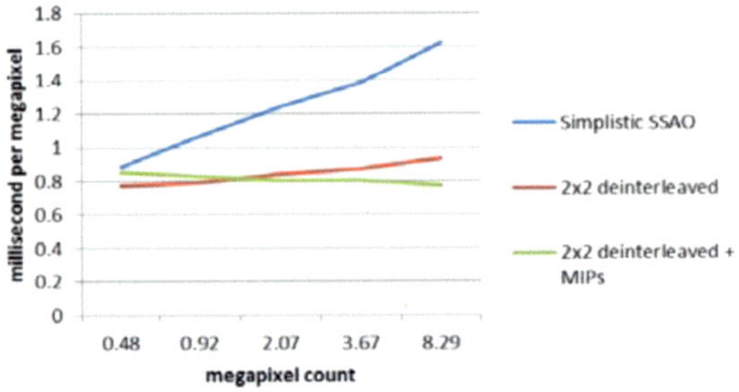

Figure 1.8. GPU time per megapixel scaling with resolution.

With varying AO effect radius, the cost remains stable as well (Table 1.6 and Figure 1.9).

An additional perk of using depth mips in combination with 2×2 deinterleaved rendering is that depth mipss can be easily switched off when not beneficial, for example, at lower resolutions and lower quality presets, where the fixed cost of mip-map pre-filtering and sample mip-level calculation is higher than the performance saved with more optimal cache access. This helps provide optimal performance between low and high quality presets, on various hardware and at various resolutions.

Radius (world space)	0.01	0.25	0.50	1.00	2.00
Simplistic SSAO	1.34	2.02	2.58	2.95	3.06
+ 2x2 deinterleaved	1.48	1.53	1.69	1.85	2.00
+ 2x2 deinterleaved + depth MIPs	1.58	1.59	1.59	1.59	1.59

Table 1.6. Performance scaling with effect radius, 32-tap, GTX970, 1920 × 1080.

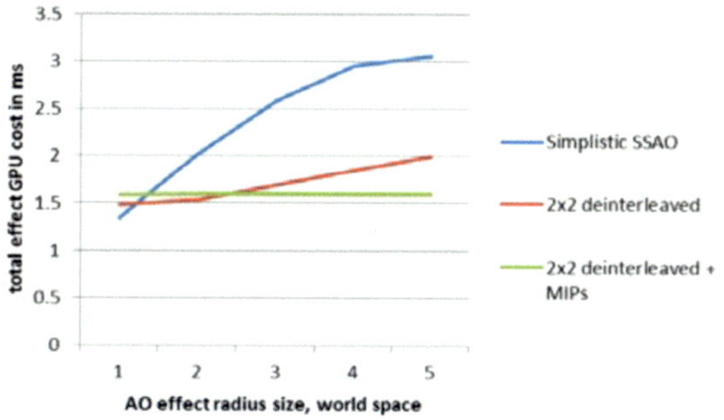

Figure 1.9. Performance scaling with effect radius, 32-tap, GTX970, 1920 × 1080.

Stochastic sampling and smart blur. For a good quality SSAO effect at reasonable performance, a stochastic rendering approach is needed. This allows sharing of the AO term between nearby pixels at the expense of some high frequency detail. We use a sampling disk rotation with scaling variation and apply a reconstruction blur pass to remove resulting noise (Figure 1.10).

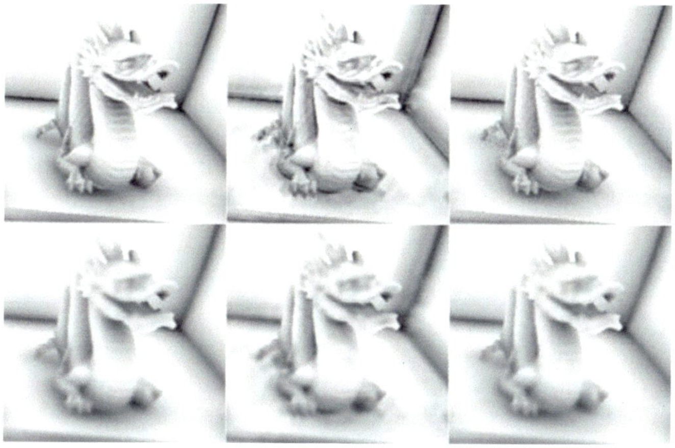

Figure 1.10. Left: reference 512 tap; center: basic 32 tap; right: 32 tap with stochastic sampling; bottom row left/center/right: added 4-pass smart blur.

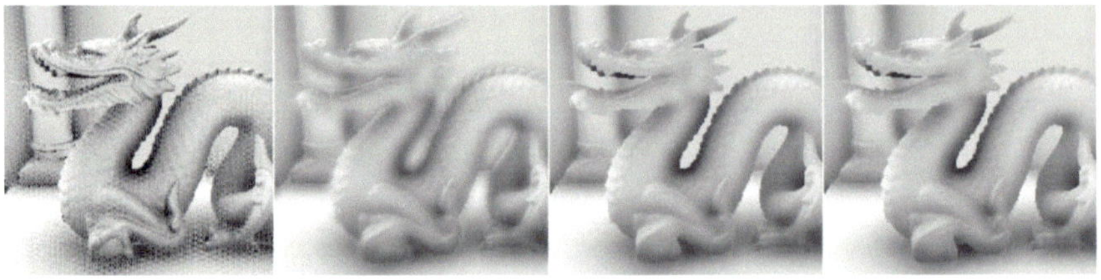

Figure 1.11. Left to right: no blur; simple blur; depth edge-aware blur; depth and normal edge-aware blur.

To prevent the effect from leaking between spatially separate surfaces during the reconstruction blur, we use depth-based (Listing 1.2) and (optional) normal-based edge detection (HLSL shader code in Listing 1.3) to inform the blur passes. Without this, the effect bleeds over to foreground/background objects which degrades sharpness and causes issues such as unwanted shadowing or haloing (see Figure 1.11).

```
// inputs are neighboring viewspace z-s from the current 2x2
// deinterleaved slice (cZ, leftZ, rightZ, topZ, bottomZ)
{
    // delta from center Z
    float4 edges = float4(leftZ, rightZ, topZ, bottomZ) - cZ;
    // slope-adjustment
    float4 edgesSA = edges.xyzw + edges.yxwz;
    edges = min( abs( edges ), abs( edgesSA ) );

    // 0 means edge, 1 means no edge (free to blur across)
    edgesLRTB = saturate( ( 1.3 - edges / (cZ * 0.04) ) );
}
```

Listing 1.2. Shader code for depth-based edge detection.

The edges (see Figure 1.12) are calculated between neighboring values in the 2×2 deinterleaved slice, which translates to a two-pixel offset in the full resolution depth to match the smart blur that operates in the per-slice domain as

Figure 1.12. Left: depth based edges; right: depth and normal based edges.

well. While this does not cause leaking over edges, it leaves a one pixel unblurred gap next to edges. This is mitigated in the last, full resolution reconstruction and blur pass that is edge-aware as well.

```
// inputs are neighboring normals s from the current 2x2
// deinterleaved slice (normC, normL, normR, normT, normB)
{
    const float t = 0.1; // dot threshold

    float4 normEdges;
    normEdges.x = saturate( ( dot( normC, normL ) + t ) * 2.0 );
    normEdges.y = saturate( ( dot( normC, normR ) + t ) * 2.0 );
    normEdges.z = saturate( ( dot( normC, normT ) + t ) * 2.0 );
    normEdges.w = saturate( ( dot( normC, normB ) + t ) * 2.0 );

    // apply to depth-based edges (0 means edge, 1 means no edge)
    edgesLRTB *= normEdges;
};
```

Listing 1.3. Weighted average depth filter.

It can be noted that the resulting edge values are not binary but in the $[0, 1]$ range—this fractional value is used to fade in or out the edge-aware blur in order to avoid sharp transitions and temporal artifacts as the camera or scene objects move. These edge values are calculated once in the main AO shader and stored in a compressed two-bit per edge format along with the occlusion term.

Blur sharpness can be fine-tuned using a global setting, as a tradeoff between reducing temporal aliasing and reducing AO bleeding/haloing effect.

The actual smart blur is performed in two separate places:

- In the multi-pass shader, smart blur is performed on each of the four deinterleaved AO buffers independently (see `PSSmartBlur` in the shader code).
- Once, in the final reconstruction/apply shader, at full resolution (see `PSApply` in the shader code).

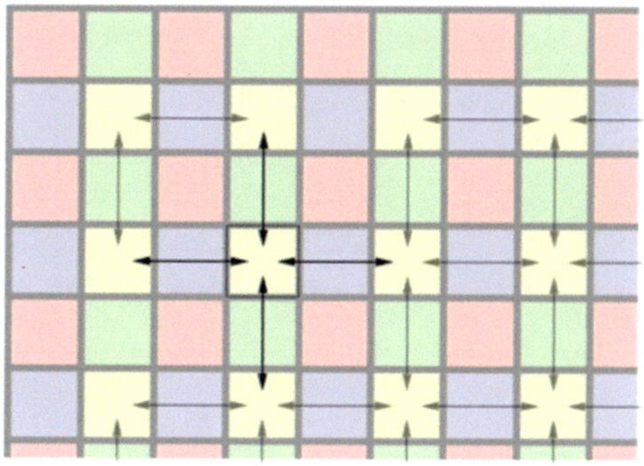

Figure 1.13. Single pass edge-aware blur on one (yellow) 2×2 deinterleaved (half $\times$ half resolution) slice; arrows represent edge-weighted occlusion term transfer directions.

As mentioned previously, edge detection and edge-aware blur are performed on four deinterleaved AO results independently, which leaves one-pixel processing gap between neighboring pixel horizontal and vertical lines. To fix this, the final full-resolution reconstruction pass includes additional edge-aware blur which bridges this gap. This also means that all but the last blur pass benefit from higher cache efficiency of working in the 2×2 deinterleaved domain. Only four texture samples (using bilinear filter) per pixel are actually needed for this pass (Figure 1.13). Finally, Figure 1.14 shows a simplified diagram with the steps involved.

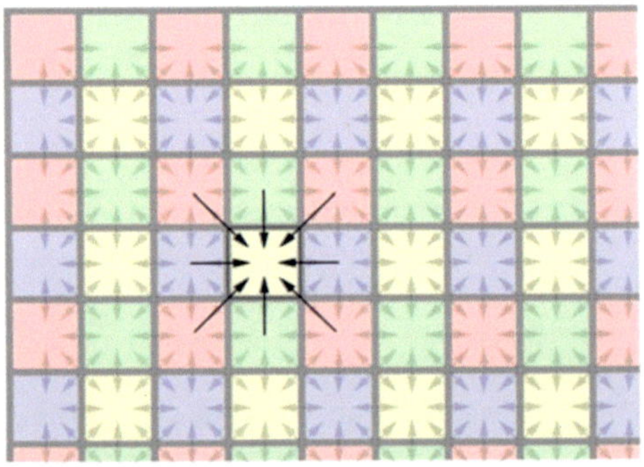

Figure 1.14. Final reconstruction pass combines all four slices into full resolution texture and applies last edge-aware blur pass.

The low-quality preset is an exception with regard to the edge-aware blur—for performance reasons, edges are not calculated and a simple blur is used.

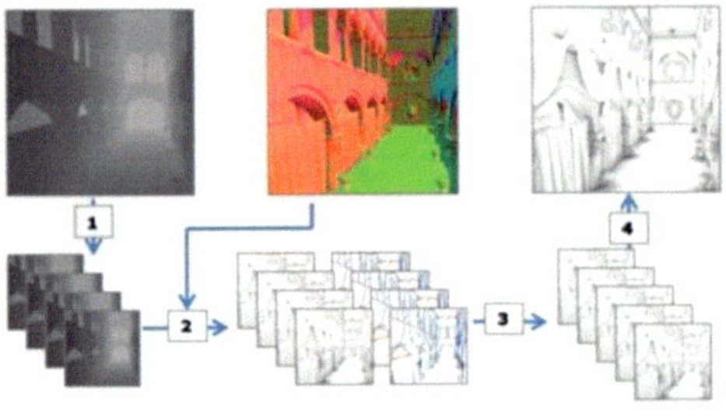

Figure 1.15. 1: Deinterleave into four depth $\frac{1}{2} \times \frac{1}{2}$ slices, convert to viewspace (and, optionally, create depth mips); 2: generate AO and edges; 3: apply edge-aware blur independently; 4: reconstruct and last pass blur.

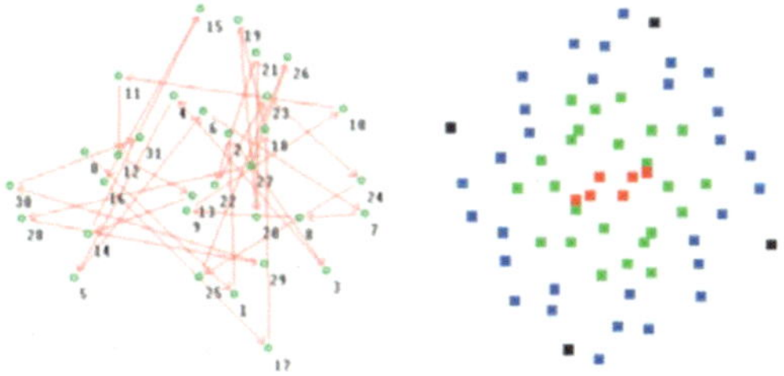

Figure 1.16. Left: sample disk with the sort order; right: resulting sampling points done by the shader (doubled by mirroring each point).

1.6 Sampling Kernel

The biggest difference between quality presets is in the number of taps used per pixel. In the version presented, low quality uses only six depth samples, medium uses 12, and high uses 24 depth samples.

Initially, we used a separate Poisson disk for each quality preset but this caused high visual difference between them, going against our goal of providing uniform settings and visual appearance between presets. It also meant that the algorithm couldnt easily adjust to a performance target between provided presets. For these reasons, we developed a sampling disk sorted so that each additional sample improves the quality without creating too much variation between the new and previous results (Figure 1.16). This progressive sampling disk lets us easily change the number of taps for any preset by simply changing a tap count for each preset, with the visual change being gradual. It also opens a possibility of changing the number of taps on a per-pixel basis, based on importance heuristics.

1.7 Adaptive SSAO

The idea of using importance heuristics to increase SSAO effect quality was presented in [Bavoil and Sainz 2009] where a lower resolution SSAO pass is used to inform the need for a following higher resolution pass. Instead of doing a low-resolution pass, we do a standard full-resolution AO base pass with a limited number of samples, calculate the importance map (Figure 1.17) based on variance in the base pass, and then proceed adding more samples where required.

This approach adds a significant amount of fixed cost, so it is only beneficial when extending the quality beyond the high preset. It also adds input-based execution cost variance, which we limit by calculating the total on-screen count of the additional samples by using an adaptive-limit constant to set an upper bound. The steps involved in the highest (adaptive) preset are (differences from high preset are in italic).

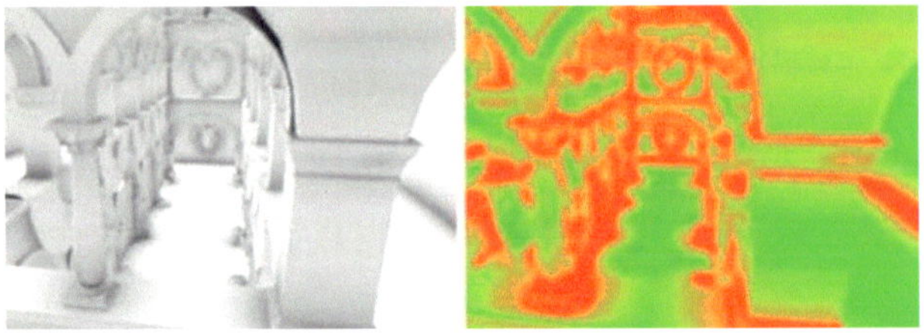

Figure 1.17. Highest (adaptive) AO preset and the associated importance map.

- Depth buffer de-interleaving and depth mipgeneration.
- *Low quality base AO pass using 14 samples per pixel.*
- *Importance-map calculation, based on the variance between neighboring pixel values from the previous pass.*
- *Blurring of the importance map and summation of the additional required total on-screen sample count (using* `InterlockedAdd`*).*
- *Adaptive quality AO pass, which builds upon results from the low quality base pass, using up to 50 additional samples per pixel based on the importance map, with the total additional on-screen sample count limited by the adaptive limit constant.*
- Smart blur passes.
- Final interleave and smart blur.

The adaptive preset thus has input-based variance but is guaranteed to stay below the preset limit that can be changed at runtime. To minimize temporal instability when varying per-pixel AO sample count, in addition to using the progressive sampling disk, we also always gradually blend in the last few samples.

To measure the effectiveness of the adaptive sampling approach, we compare it to the version that is using a fixed number of samples on identical inputs. We lower the adaptive limit on the adaptive preset until the total number of on-screen samples hits the limit—this way we know that the adaptive version is not going to get more costly depending on the inputs; performance-wise it is the worst case scenario for the adaptive approach. With the inputs used (Sponza atrium with AO radius of 1.2), we hit the limit at the value of 0.45.

Then, we measure the peak signal-to-noise ratio of 43.53 dB between adaptive (0.45 limit) and the 64 fixed sample AO used as a reference.

To find a comparable sample count for fixed preset, we measure PSNR at various sample counts using the same 64 sample reference. We find (Table 1.7) that a 52 fixed sample count version matches most closely the adaptive with 0.45 adaptive limit settings with PSNR of 43.17.

Fixed sample count	PSNR vs 64 sample reference, dB
24 (matches High preset)	37.82
32	40.61
40	42.97
48	43.17
52	43.46
56	44.18
60	47.21

Table 1.7. Error between various AO sample counts compared to the 64 sample reference.

We than measure the cost at the 4k (3840×2160) resolution, on GTX 1080, and get 5.46 ms for the fixed 52 sample AO, and 5.05 ms for the adaptive AO. In this worst-case scenario, the adaptive approach shows roughly 8% cost savings over the fixed sample-count version. If we rotate the camera to look mostly at the wall (with little AO), we get the approximate best-case scenario with the cost of 3.28 ms for the adaptive approach, which translates into 40% savings over the fixed 52 sample version.

Thus, we conclude that our adaptive approach is useful for extending the quality above the high preset, and especially in scenarios where not all parts of the scene (such as sky, water, or flat surfaces) are expected to produce AO or where the effect cost needs to be scaled at runtime (using the ‘adaptive limit).

1.8 Putting It All Together

Our final implementation has four quality/performance presets, starting from low with most features disabled with each further level increasing in quality but also cost by approximately 50%, with the third (high) being roughly similar in cost to HBAO+ (Table 1.8).

	Iris Pro 540	GTX 1080	
	$1600x \times 900$	1920×1080	3840×2160
Low	3.01	0.34	1.48
Medium	4.58	0.53	2.37
High	7.55	0.84	3.32
Highest (adaptive limit 0.45)	12.02	1.29	5.05

Table 1.8. Effect cost at various resolutions on different hardware.

Video-memory use at 1920×1080 is 22 Mb when using provided normals. Each preset can be further fine-tuned for required performance by varying the number of AO taps in the shader, with supported values from 3 to 32. See `g_numSamples` variable in the main shader file.

	2 × 2 deinterleaved	Depth mips	Edge-aware blur	Adaptive sampling
Low	yes	no	no	no
Medium	yes	no	yes	no
High	yes	yes	yes+	no
Highest (Adaptive)	yes	yes	yes+	yes

Table 1.9. Quality preset feature table.

1.9 Future Work

We plan to optimize the progressive sampling disk by using an automatic generator looking for the smallest error compared to the best-case reference.

With regard to temporal supersampling, our current implementation has provisional support by providing ability to easily vary the sampling disk rotation and scale, but it has not yet been tested in a TAA/TSS environment.

At the moment there is no support for MSAA in the provided code, but there are plans to add it in the future.

The current implementation supports rendering with enlarged frustum, which is used to avoid artifacts at screen corners. We avoid unnecessary computation outside of the provided scissor rectangle.

Bibliography

AALUND, F. P. 2012. A comparative study of screen-space ambient occlusion methods. Bachelor's thesis. http://frederikaalund.com/a-comparative-study-of-screen-space-ambient-occlusion-methods.

BAVOIL, L., AND JANSEN, J. 2013. Particle shadows & cache-efficient post-processing. In *Proceedings of GDC 2013*. https://developer.nvidia.com/sites/default/files/akamai/gamedev/docs/BAVOIL_ParticleShadowsAndCacheEfficientPost.pdf,.

BAVOIL, L., AND SAINZ, M. 2009. Multi-layer dual-resolution screen-space ambient occlusion. In *SIGGRAPH 2009: Talks*, ACM, New York, SIGGRAPH '09, 45:1–45:1.

BAVOIL, L., SAINZ, M., AND DIMITROV, R. 2008. Image-space horizon-based ambient occlusion. In *ACM SIGGRAPH 2008 Talks*, ACM, New York, SIGGRAPH '08, 22:1–22:1.

BAVOIL, L., 2014. Deinterleaved texturing for cache-efficient interleaved sampling. https://developer.nvidia.com/sites/default/files/akamai/gameworks/samples/DeinterleavedTexturing.pdf.

BUNNELL, M. 2005. Dynamic ambient occlusion and indirect lighting. In *GPU Gems 2*, M. Pharr, Ed. Addison-Wesley, 223–233.

DONZALLAZ, P., AND SOUSA, T., 2011. Lighting in crysis. http://www.gdcvault.com/play/1014915/Lighting-in-Crysis.

KAPLANYAN, A., 2010. CryENGINE 3: Reaching the speed of light. http://www.crytek.com/cryengine/presentations/CryENGINE3-reaching-the-speed-of-light. Crytek.

KELLER, A., AND HEIDRICH, W. 2001. Interleaved sampling. In *Proceedings of the 12th Eurographics Workshop on Rendering Techniques*, Springer-Verlag, London, 269–276.

KLEHM, O., RITSCHEL, T., EISEMANN, E., AND SEIDEL, H.-P. 2011. Bent Normals and Cones in Screen-space. In *Vision, Modeling, and Visualization (2011)*, The Eurographics Association, Aire-la-Ville, Switzerland, P. Eisert, J. Hornegger, and K. Polthier, Eds., 177–182.

LUFT, T., COLDITZ, C., AND DEUSSEN, O. 2006. Image enhancement by unsharp masking the depth buffer. *ACM Trans. Graph. 25*, 3, 1206–1213.

MCGUIRE, M., OSMAN, B., BUKOWSKI, M., AND HENNESSY, P. 2011. The alchemy screen-space ambient obscurance algorithm. In *Proceedings of the ACM SIGGRAPH Symposium on High Performance Graphics*, ACM, New York, HPG '11, 25–32.

MCGUIRE, M., MARA, M., AND LUEBKE, D. 2012. Scalable ambient obscurance. In *Proceedings of the Fourth ACM SIGGRAPH / Eurographics Conference on High-Performance Graphics*, Eurographics Association, Aire-la-Ville, Switzerland, EGGH-HPG'12, 97–103.

MITTRING, M. 2007. Finding next gen: Cryengine 2. In *ACM SIGGRAPH 2007 Courses*, ACM, New York, SIGGRAPH '07, 97–121.

RITSCHEL, T., GROSCH, T., AND SEIDEL, H.-P. 2009. Approximating dynamic global illumination in image space. In *Proceedings of the 2009 Symposium on Interactive 3D Graphics and Games*, ACM, New York, I3D '09, 75–82.

IV

2

Robust Screen Space Ambient Occlusion in 1 ms in 1080p on PS4

Wojciech Sterna

2.1 Introduction

Screen space ambient occlusion (SSAO) is a pretty well-known algorithm nowadays. It was first used in the game *Crysis* by Crytek as described by [Mittring 2007]. However, even though a massive amount of work has been invested by researchers to improve upon it and come up with neater implementations, still one can stumble upon AAA games that suffer from frames drops when SSAO is turned on or simply the quality can be questionable.

In this chapter, I present an implementation of an SSAO algorithm that is based on [McGuire et al. 2011] and [McGuire et al. 2012]. This implementation was used in *Shadow Warrior* by Flying Wild Hog in console ports of the game as well as the DX11 version (see Figures 2.1 and 2.2). The implementation is fairly stable, gives very nice results, and depicts good performance characteristics. It takes, depending on the scene of course as the SSAO radius varies based on underlying geometry, $\tilde{1}$ ms on PlayStation 4 in 1080p and $\tilde{1}$ ms on Xbox One in 900p which was one of the reasons the game looked and played nicely in 60 Hz on consoles—most of the time.

The implementation proved to be good enough that it appeared unchanged in a follow-up game *Shadow Warrior 2*.

2.2 Problem Formulation

Ambient occlusion is a simplified model for computing global illumination. The idea behind ambient occlusion is to "darken corners," which in a full global-illumination solution would receive less lighting than, say, a flat floor without

Figure 2.1. A shot from *Shadow Warrior*.

Figure 2.2. A shot from *Shadow Warrior*; SSAO buffer only.

any objects standing on it. The basic formula for ambient occlusion for point p and normal vector $\hat{n}$ is (after [Wikipedia 2016]) presented in Equation (2.1).

$$\mathrm{AO}_{p,\hat{n}} = \frac{1}{\pi}\int_{\Omega} \mathrm{V}_{p,\hat{\omega}}(\hat{n}\cdot\hat{\omega})\,\mathrm{d}\,\hat{\omega} \tag{2.1}$$

What this equation tells us is that to compute ambient occlusion for point p and normal $\hat{n}$ we need to cast a whole bunch of $\hat{\omega}$ vectors around the Ω hemisphere.

The ambient occlusion contribution consists of two parts. The first comes from the visibility function V, which returns 0 if point p is occluded in direction $\hat{\omega}$, and 1, otherwise. The second term is the well-known dot product which scales the importance—$\hat{\omega}$ oriented towards $\hat{n}$ is more important for occlusion.

The integral in Equation (2.1), even though formally correct, has one significant downside. The visibility function is binary. This is not a problem if we evaluated the equation with a large number of $\hat{\omega}$ directions (samples), which usually takes place in offline rendering. However, to fit the algorithm for real-time use, we have far less processing power available. Because of that, binary rejection or acceptance of a sample is a waste of information, namely distance to the occluder in this case. That is why ambient occlusion is often exchanged with ambient obscurance ([McGuire et al. 2011]), where the integral in Equation (2.1) remains unchanged, but the visibility function V is exchanged with a falloff function, that scales occlusion intensity based on the distance of the sample to the occluder. This will, overall, produce smoother results than pure ambient occlusion. Note that from here on we will use the term ambient occlusion to mean ambient obscurance.

To make ambient occlusion feasible for real time, it's not enough to use a small number of samples and a good falloff function. We also have to limit the domain of points that will contribute to occlusion of all points on the screen. In full-blown solutions, this domain is constituted by the entire scene's geometry. To make our algorithm fast, we cannot afford to store the entire scene in the GPU memory. That's why our domain will be composed only of the points that are visible on the screen (hence, the name screen space ambient occlusion). Motivation behind this idea is that the visible scene's geometry is already available when we are computing SSAO, namely in the form of the generated hardware depth buffer. The main downside of this approach is that sometimes the algorithm doesn't have all the necessary data to compute proper occlusion; since ambient occlusion is a low-frequency phenomenon, the artifacts that SSAO produces are usually not a problem.

2.3 Algorithm

The algorithm requires that the typical depth buffer is available (so we can reconstruct positions). Also, we will need a normal vector lying around. In our case, we have gbuffer filled with normal vectors so we will use that.

One of the reasons our implementation is so efficient is that SSAO buffer computation takes place in a quarter-resolution buffer (that is, $\frac{1}{2} \times \frac{1}{2}$ the frame-buffer size). This pass produces a quite raw and undersampled (partially due to quarter-resolution) image. The next step is to blur the SSAO output in two depth-aware (to not blur edges), separable horizontal and vertical passes. This also takes place in quater-resolution which allows us to have wide blur kernels without degrading performance significantly (actually, these two passes are very cheap). Finally, the quarter-resolution blurred SSAO image is upsampled with a bilateral filter.

Since output of the SSAO buffer is just a single monochromatic value, we will use RGBA8 buffer. It may seem excessive since only one of those channels is needed and, as such, R8 format would be enough. However, there is no discernible performance difference in using the two, and the remaining GBA channels can be used for some nice tricks (more on this in Section 2.5).

2.3.1 Downsample

In the very first pass of the algorithm we calculate the quarter-resolution version of the depth buffer. This downsampled depth buffer doesn't store the NDC (normalized device coordinates) depth value, as opposed to the original depth buffer, but stores depth in camera space. The good thing about camera-space depth is that it is linear, so the downsampled depth buffer's format can even be R16F. As compared to the original depth buffer, the downsampled one is eight times smaller and so will be the memory throughput during the computation pass. This is another reason why the algorithm is so efficient.

The downsampled depth buffer will be used to reconstruct camera-space positions of pixels in the computation pass.

2.3.2 Computation

Now comes the gist of the algorithm. This is a full-screen (in quarter-resolution) pass that samples the pixel's attributes (R16F depth which gets converted to camera-space position and the camera-space normal) and then iterates through 16 samples, integrating ambient occlusion.

We will now cover the integration function and how to generate well-distributed samples.

Integration. The formula for integrating ambient occlusion is taken from [McGuire et al. 2011] in modified form and is shown in Equation (2.2). This formula is used in the SSAO computation shader.

$$\mathrm{AO}_{p,\hat{n}} = \frac{1}{s}\sum_{i=1}^{s}\frac{\max(0, \vec{v_i}\cdot\hat{n} + p_{z_c}\beta)}{\vec{v_i}\cdot\vec{v_i}+\epsilon}, \qquad \vec{v_i} = p_i - p \tag{2.2}$$

In this equation, v_i is a vector from camera-space position p of the pixel we're shading to sample point p_i (We will cover how they are generated in a moment.). The variable s is the number of samples which, in our case, is 16. The sum is normalized by dividing by s.

Note that we're adding the $p_{z_c}\beta$ term to the numerator's dot product. More specifically, we're adding an offset which is equal to the scaled (by β) camera-space z-coordinate of the pixel p being shaded. This is needed to compensate for numerical errors, which arise from sampling a discrete depth buffer when finding

p and p_i. The value of β should vary depending on the buffer's resolution and its format. We found that for the demo application 0.002 works well for a R16F depth buffer in 720p resolution (for 1080p, a value of 0.001 is okay).

The factor ϵ in the denominator is there to prevent division by zero. However, since our implementation doesn't snap samples to pixels' centers, $\vec{v}$ will never be zero so ϵ here is redundant. We're using it for the sake of completeness.

Computing camera-space position from depth is a well-researched subject which can be found in [Sterna 2013].

Samples Generation. Developing a good ambient occlusion function like the one in Equation (2.2) is an art in itself, but generating a good set of samples is an even finer form of art.

A good set of samples should be characterized by a simple fact that when we rotate the samples by some angle, the new, rotated samples all end up at different points on the screen than the non-rotated samples. When we have this property, and apply semi-random rotation of these samples for each screen pixel, each local neighborhood of screen pixels will contain a decent number of different samples. When we later blur the result, all of those samples will eventually contribute to all the pixels in each neighborhood. [McGuire et al. 2012] covers this in more detail.

The demo application supports generation of two slightly different sets of samples, Vogel disk and (we call it like this here) Alchemy spiral, which both resemble some sort of a spiral (in 2D). Spiral-based samples are good because of the property mentioned previously. When we rotate a spiral, all of its points will map to a different set of points.

Equation (2.3) shows how to compute the ith (in $[0, s-1]$ range) Vogel disk sample u_i:

$$u_i = (r_i \cos\theta_i, r_i \sin\theta_i), \qquad r_i = \frac{\sqrt{i+0.5}}{\sqrt{s}}, \qquad \theta_i = 2.4\, i + \phi \tag{2.3}$$

In this equation, ϕ is an additional rotation angle which we will later fill with a per-screen pixel random number. The magic constant 2.4 is actually the rounded golden angle. See [Devert 2012] and [4rknova 2012] for more on Vogel disks.

Equation (2.4) shows how to compute the ith (in $[0, s-1]$ range) Alchemy spiral sample u_i:

$$u_i = (\cos\theta_i, \sin\theta_i), \qquad \theta_i = 2\pi\alpha_i\tau + \phi, \qquad \alpha_i = \frac{1}{s}(i+0.5) \tag{2.4}$$

In this equation, ϕ is an additional rotation angle which we will later fill with a per-screen pixel random number; τ is the number of spiral turns. For $s = 16$, this value should be 7. [McGuire et al. 2012] covers the generation of this spiral.

To make full use of the equations just presented, we need functions for generating random ϕ numbers. One of them is called interleaved gradient noise and is taken from [Jimenez 2014] where it was used for shadow filtering. The other one comes from [McGuire et al. 2012], and we will refer to it as Alchemy noise. The demo application supports both noise functions.

Equation (2.5) shows how to generate interleaved gradient noise, given screen pixel's w window coordinates (can be with or without the fractional part, like 134 or 134.5):

$$\begin{aligned} \phi &= \text{frac}(m_z \ \text{frac}(w_{xy} \cdot m_{xy})), \\ m &= (0.06711056, 0.0233486, 52.9829189) \end{aligned} \tag{2.5}$$

where frac is a function that returns the fractional part of the input number; and m is a magic constant. Actually, this constant differs from the one presented in [Jimenez 2014] in that the y-component is exactly four times larger. We found that this number behaves better under some circumstances.

Equation (2.6) shows how to generate Alchemy noise, given screen pixel's w integer window coordinates (that is, without fractional part due to xor used):

$$\phi = 30 \ w_x \wedge w_y + 10 \ w_x w_y \tag{2.6}$$

We found that interleaved gradient noise better fits to a Vogel disk and Alchemy noise better fits to an Alchemy spiral and these two pairs are what the demo application implements.

2.3.3 Blur

The output produced by the previous pass is raw SSAO buffer which has a lot of noise. To remedy this problem, we perform a bilateral depth-aware blur, still in quarter-resolution, which smooths the image but does preserve edges.

We perform two separable passes, one horizontal and then one vertical. Each of these passes takes seven samples (since this happens in quarter-resolution, after upsampling, this will equal 14 samples) of both the raw SSAO buffer and the R16F downsampled depth buffer. Based on the difference in depths between an off-center sample and the central sample, we determine the filter weight of the off-center sample. Additionally, the weight of each sample is multiplied by the Gaussian function for a smoother result (it's much better than equally-weighted box blur).

Using blur to cleanse a noisy image seems natural for us for the sake of aesthetics, but it has a more meaningful purpose, not only a purely artistic one. Consider computed raw SSAO values a and b of some pixels located at x and y, respectively, that are next to each other in screen space. Thanks to our well-defined sets of samples (either Vogel or Alchemy), a and b were probably computed using two different sets of samples. Since x and y are close in screen space (even assume they are "the same" for a moment) then why not incorporate the results of b into a and vice versa? We computed two SSAO values for two different sets of samples for the, more or less, same location on the screen. Combining (averaging) one with the other will give us the result of computing SSAO for 32, not only 16 samples. Of course x and y in the end are not the same but are close enough that this reasoning is justifiable.

It is worthwhile to keep in mind that bilateral filters (dependent on depths difference in this case) are not separable, so it is not formally correct to perform our depth-aware blur in two separable passes. However, the difference in produced images is most often negligible whereas performance gain is not. It's much cheaper to take $2 * 7$ than 49 samples.

2.3.4 Upsample

So far we have worked in quarter-resolution. To properly combine SSAO with the rest of the scene, we need to upsample the SSAO buffer.

The simplest way of upsampling would be to just use bilinear filtering when sampling the SSAO buffer. This is actually what we want with the exception that naive bilinear upsampling will also filter across the geometry edges which, as in case of SSAO blur, is not desirable. We can extend bilinear upsampling with depth-awareness, however. This will require us to implement custom bilinear filtering in the shader. The shader will take four samples from the quarter-resolution SSAO buffer (with one gather instruction), four samples from the R16F downsampled depth buffer (also one gather), and one sample from the full-resolution depth buffer. By comparing depth differences between the full-resolution buffer's sample and the four quarter-resolution samples, we will know what weights to apply to the four quarter-resolution SSAO samples, apart from weights coming from bilinear filtering.

2.4 Implementation

We shall now discuss some selected implementation details.

2.4.1 Downsample

The first pass downsamples the original hardware depth buffer to a R16F quarter-resolution depth buffer, but writing out camera-space depth rather than NDC (normalized device coordinates) depth.

For each quarter-resolution pixel, there are four input full-resolution pixels. The downsample function just takes the upper-left corner, ignoring the rest, as shown in Listing 2.1.

```
float2 texCoord = input.texCoord + float2(-0.25f, -0.25f)*pixelSize;

float depth_ndc = depthBufferTexture.Sample(pointClampSampler, texCoord).x;
float depth = DepthNDCToView(depth_ndc);

return depth;
```

Listing 2.1. Downsampling of the depth buffer.

pixelSize is the size of the pixel of the quarter-resolution buffer. The function DepthNDCToView converts NDC z-coordinate to camera-space z-coordinate as is shown in Listing 2.2.

```
float DepthNDCToView(float depth_ndc)
{
    return -projParams.y / (depth_ndc + projParams.x);
}
```

Listing 2.2. NDC depth to view-space depth conversion. projParams.x is the projection matrix $(3,3)$th entry, whereas projParams.y is the $(4,3)$th entry (row-major ordering).

The derivation of this equation is given by [Sterna 2013].

2.4.2 Computation

One important thing we did not cover in Section 2.3.2 is range of the effect. Samples generated by Vogel and Alchemy are defined on the unit circle and they need to be scaled down significantly (as they are added to texture coordinates which are in $[0,1] \times [0,1]$ range). Moreover, constant scale is not sufficient as that would result in range scale that is constant in screen space, whereas what we need is constant range in world (or view) space. In other words, pixels that are farther away from the camera should have smaller and smaller sample range (radius). Listing 2.3 shows how to compute screen-space radius based on world-space radius.

```
float2 radius_screen = radius_world / position.z;
radius_screen = min(radius_screen, maxRadius_screen);
radius_screen.y *= aspect;
```

Listing 2.3. Screen-space radius computation.

radius_world is a constant passed to the shader. To compute the screen-space radius, we divide the world-space radius by the camera-space z-coordinate of the pixel we are shading.

The next step is to enforce a maximum radius in screen space. If we moved the camera very close to a pixel, (position.z becomes very small) then the screen-space radius would become very large, possibly covering the entire screen. That's why we limit the screen-space radius to some constant maxRadius_screen to prevent texture cache trashing and performance degradation.

Finally, we multiply the y-coordinate of the radius by the screen's aspect ratio. Since we're using Vogel/Alchemy samples to alter texture coordinates, which are in $[0,1] \times [0,1]$ range, a unit sampling circle would become an ellipse on non-square monitor—hence, the aspect multiplication.

Code that performs integration is in Listing 2.4.

```
for (int i = 0; i < SAMPLES_COUNT; i++)
{
    float2 sampleOffset = VogelDiskOffset(i, TWO_PI*noise);
    float2 sampleTexCoord = input.texCoord + radius_screen*sampleOffset;

    float3 samplePosition = Position_View(sampleTexCoord);
    float3 v = samplePosition - position;

    ao += max(0.0f, dot(v, normal) + 0.002f*position.z) / (dot(v, v) + 0.001f);
}
```

Listing 2.4. Integration. `position` and `normal` are camera-space position and normal of the pixel being shaded.

This code implements Equation (2.2) directly. In this case, we're using a Vogel disk (whether Vogel or Alchemy produces better results is a matter of personal preference). Note that the second parameter to function `VogelDiskOffset` is the parameter ϕ, where we pass the value returned by the interleaved gradient noise function, multiplied by 2π. Interleaved gradient noise returns a value in the $[0, 1]$ range and so to travel the entire circle, we need to scale by 2π.

Once ambient occlusion `ao` has been computed, we're performing the final steps as shown in Listing 2.5.

```
ao = saturate(ao / SAMPLES_COUNT);
ao = 1.0f - ao;
ao = pow(ao, contrast);
```

Listing 2.5. Final steps.

First, we normalize the result and make sure it is in the $[0, 1]$ range. Next, we compute the inverse. Note that up to this point we're adding to `ao` occlusion, not visibility, so 1 means fully occluded and we want the reverse. Finally, contrast of the effect is altered using the application-provided `contrast` parameter.

2.4.3 Blur

The blur shader goes through seven samples in a loop, sampling the downsampled R16F depth buffer. The core of the loop is shown in Listing 2.6.

```
float depthsDiff = 0.1f * abs(depth - sampleDepth);
depthsDiff *= depthsDiff;
float weight = 1.0f / (depthsDiff + 0.001f);
weight *= gaussWeightsSigma3[3 + i];
```

Listing 2.6. Blur.

The depths difference is calculated and used in finding the sample's weight. Note that we're scaling the depth and squaring it. You might want to play with these parameters and come up with better constants for your scenario. Keep in mind that using only depths to determine geometry discontinuity is not much information; better results could be obtained by using normals as well. However, for low-frequency effects like SSAO, depths are usually enough. Weight is scaled by a Gaussian function, which is stored in 7-element array `gaussWeightsSigma3`. The value $\sigma = 3$ was used to generate this distribution, using [Mader 2014].

2.4.4 Upsample

The upsample pass shader starts by sampling all the necessary textures, as shown in Listing 2.7.

```
float2 texCoord00 = input.texCoord;
float2 texCoord10 = input.texCoord + float2(pixelSize.x, 0.0f);
float2 texCoord01 = input.texCoord + float2(0.0f, pixelSize.y);
float2 texCoord11 = input.texCoord + float2(pixelSize.x, pixelSize.y);

float depth = depthBufferTexture.Sample(pointClampSampler, input.texCoord).x;
depth = DepthNDCToView(depth);
float4 depths_x4 = depth16Texture_x4.GatherRed(pointClampSampler, texCoord00).wzxy;
float4 depthsDiffs = abs(depth.xxxx - depths_x4);

float4 ssaos_x4 = ssaoTexture_x4.GatherRed(pointClampSampler, texCoord00).wzxy;
```

Listing 2.7. Sampling textures.

`pixelSize` is the size of the pixel of the full-resolution buffer. As such, for each 2×2 full-resolution pixels quad, the lower-right pixel will generate four texture coordinates that all point to different texels in quarter-resolution buffers (R16F depth buffer and SSAO buffer). The upper-left pixel will point to the same four texels and upper-right and lower-left will point to two different texels. All variants exactly what we need for custom bilinear filtering. Note that we make use of the gather instruction. Always use it when an occasion arises as it can speed your shaders up measurably without any visual impact.

Next come bilinear weights in Listing 2.8. This is based on [Wikipedia 2016a].

```
float2 imageCoord = input.texCoord / pixelSize;
float2 fractional = frac(imageCoord);
float a = (1.0f - fractional.x) * (1.0f - fractional.y);
float b = fractional.x * (1.0f - fractional.y);
float c = (1.0f - fractional.x) * fractional.y;
float d = fractional.x * fractional.y;
```

Listing 2.8. Bilinear filtering weights.

Now that we have depth differences and bilinear weights we can apply it all to produce a final, full resolution SSAO buffer, as shown in Listing 2.9.

```
float4 ssao = 0.0f;
float weightsSum = 0.0f;

float weight00 = a / (depthsDiffs.x + 0.001f);
ssao += weight00 * ssaos_x4.x;
weightsSum += weight00;

float weight10 = b / (depthsDiffs.y + 0.001f);
ssao += weight10 * ssaos_x4.y;
weightsSum += weight10;

float weight01 = c / (depthsDiffs.z + 0.001f);
ssao += weight01 * ssaos_x4.z;
weightsSum += weight01;

float weight11 = d / (depthsDiffs.w + 0.001f);
ssao += weight11 * ssaos_x4.w;
weightsSum += weight11;

ssao /= weightsSum;
```

Listing 2.9. SSAO upsampled.

2.5 Possible Improvements

What we have covered so far is pretty much what was used for generating SSAO in *Shadow Warrior* and *Shadow Warrior 2*. However, this article wouldn't be complete without mentioning some potential improvements.

The algorithm requires a normal vector in the computation pass. We read it from the gbuffer but it might not always be available. In such cases, it is possible to reconstruct a geometrical normal using position differencing. Another reason for doing so is that normals in the gbuffer usually come from normal maps. Such high-frequency detail can produce unpleasant flickering in our quarter-resolution SSAO. In that case, reconstructing a geometrical normal may improve this, albeit at the same time we loose those high-frequency details. In the *Shadow Warrior* games, we used normals from the gbuffer, which was constructed using normal maps.

In the blur pass, we sample both the SSAO buffer and the R16F depth buffer, which sums up to 14 texture samples. Since the SSAO buffer has RGBA8 format and uses only one channel, there is the possibility to pack (as [McGuire et al. 2012] suggests), during the computation pass, depth to GBA channels and use only one sample for each offset, resulting in just seven samples. Not only the number of samples is smaller but memory traffic as well (we read four bytes per sample instead of six). I didn't implement that optimization because, in quarter-resolution, blur is already very cheap (less than 0.1 ms).

Increasing the radius of the effect produces a smoother and more stable result, but at the same time it degrades performance. The reason is that the bigger the radius, the more spread are the samples, and they do not fit in the GPU texture cache. Actually, [McGuire et al. 2012] addresses this problem by using a mipmap chain of the depth buffer. The further a sample is from the pixel, the smaller mip is used. This relatively simple approach allows us to have an arbitrary radius at constant cost. [Hoang and Low 2010] also addresses this problem but by computing SSAO directly at different depth-buffer resolutions and then combining the results.

The simplest way of improving quality of the effect is to perform all computations and blur in full resolution, as was done in *Assassin's Creed 4* (see [Wronski 2014]). One can then use a smaller number of samples and do not need to upsample. [Wronski 2014] reports that doing so costs 1.6 ms on consoles. One idea to improve on this is to compute SSAO in a half-resolution buffer ($\frac{1}{2} \times 1$ the framebuffer size) in a checkerboard pattern (for each 2×2 pixel quad we compute values only for the diagonal pixels). We once tested this pattern when generating sunlight shadows mask and it turned out to produce very stable results, very often indistinguishable from full resolution, most notably at oblique angles, which are most prone to instability and flickering in the quarter-resolution solution.

A pretty common solution for increasing quality, at the expense of a small performance hit (and harder implementation with occasional artifacts), is to make use of temporal supersampling, as in [Wronski 2014]. This can be paired with using a checkerboard pattern, where the pattern is alternated every second frame.

Finally, to improve performance for a larger radius (without using a depth buffer mip chain), we can deinterleave the SSAO computation pass. This is a more general technique that can help with speeding up not only SSAO but also other post-processing algorithms. Details can be found in [Bavoil and Jansen 2013].

2.6 Demo Application

There is an accompanying demo application to this chapter presenting the algorithm in action.

Configuration of the demo can be changed in the `config.txt` file located in the folder where the binary is located.

Key configuration:

- WSAD + mouse – camera movement,
- Shift – speeding up,
- Insert / Delete – increase/decrease world space radius,
- Home / End – increase/decrease max screen space radius,
- Page Up / Page Down – increase/decrease SSAO contrast,

Pass	Time
All	0.75 ms
Downsample	0.048 ms
Computation	0.353 ms
Blur X	0.089 ms
Blur Y	0.088 ms
Upsample	0.17 ms

Table 2.1. Exemplary performance on GeForce 660 GTX in 1080p.

- F1-F4 – diffuse + SSAO, diffuse, SSAO, raw SSAO,
- F5/F6 – Vogel/Alchemy; full computation,
- F7/F8 – Vogel/Alchemy; precomputed and read from array,
- ESC – exit.

There are four variants of sample generation implemented. Two of them (F5, F7) use Vogel disk, and two (F6, F8) use Alchemy spiral. Each pair additionally differs in that one variant in the pair uses the full Equation (2.3) or (2.4), whereas the other reads samples from a precomputed array and performs rotation. Which one is faster will be dependent on the GPU used.

In the folder where the binary is located, a file called `profiler.txt` will be generated upon exit, where average performance of each consecutive batch of 100 frames is dumped. Table 3.1 shows exemplary performance on GeForce 660 GTX in 1080p.

2.7 Conclusions

In this chapter an efficient SSAO implementation has been presented that was production-proved in two games —*Shadow Warrior* and *Shadow Warrior 2*. The algorithm's theory and implementation were covered in detail as well as possible modifications and improvements to make it even more suitable to a different set of requirements.

2.8 Acknowledgments

I would like to thank Krzysztof Narkowicz of Flying Wild Hog who was my supervisor when I was integrating SSAO into the Roadhog Engine. My thanks also go to Adam Cichocki from CD Projekt RED for introducing me to the Vogel disk. I also thank Wessam Bahnassi, the editor of this section, for a smooth cooperation and of course Wolfgang Engel, the editor of the entire book, for his editorial work from the early *ShaderX* books up to this one :).

Bibliography

4RKNOVA, 2012. Shadertoy: Vogel's distribution method. URL: https://www.shadertoy.com/view/XtXXDN.

BAVOIL, L., AND JANSEN, J. 2013. Particle shadows & cache-efficient post-processing. In *Proceedings of GDC 2013*. https://developer.nvidia.com/sites/default/files/akamai/gamedev/docs/BAVOIL_ParticleShadowsAndCacheEfficientPost.pdf,.

DEVERT, A., 2012. Spreading points on a disc and on a sphere. Marmakoide's Blog. URL: http://blog.marmakoide.org/?p=1.

HOANG, T.-D., AND LOW, K.-L. 2010. Multi-resolution screen-space ambient occlusion. In *Proceedings of the 17th ACM Symposium on Virtual Reality Software and Technology*, ACM, New York, VRST '10, 101–102. URL: https://www.comp.nus.edu.sg/~lowkl/publications/mssao_cgi2011.pdf.

JIMENEZ, J. 2014. Next generation post processing in *Call of Duty: Advanced Warfare*. In *Advances in Real-Time Rendering in Games, SIGGRAPH 2104 course*, ACM, NY. URL: http://www.slideshare.net/guerrillagames/killzone-shadow-fall-demo-postmortem.

MADER, T., 2014. Gaussian kernel calculator. The Devil in the Details Blog. URL: http://dev.theomader.com/gaussian-kernel-calculator/.

MCGUIRE, M., OSMAN, B., BUKOWSKI, M., AND HENNESSY, P. 2011. The alchemy screen-space ambient obscurance algorithm. In *Proceedings of the ACM SIGGRAPH Symposium on High Performance Graphics*, ACM, New York, HPG '11, 25–32. URL: http://graphics.cs.williams.edu/papers/AlchemyHPG11/.

MCGUIRE, M., MARA, M., AND LUEBKE, D. 2012. Scalable ambient obscurance. In *Proceedings of the Fourth ACM SIGGRAPH / Eurographics Conference on High-Performance Graphics*, Eurographics Association, Aire-la-Ville, Switzerland, EGGH-HPG'12, 97–103. URL: http://graphics.cs.williams.edu/papers/SAOHPG12/.

MITTRING, M. 2007. Finding next gen: Cryengine 2. In *ACM SIGGRAPH 2007 Courses*, ACM, New York, SIGGRAPH '07, 97–121.

STERNA, W., 2013. Reconstructing camera space position from depth. URL: http://wojtsterna.blogspot.com/2013/11/recovering-camera-position-from-depth.html.

WIKIPEDIA, 2016. Ambient occlusion. URL: https://en.wikipedia.org/wiki/Ambient_occlusion.

WIKIPEDIA, 2016a. Bilinear filtering. URL: https://en.wikipedia.org/wiki/Bilinear_filtering.

WRONSKI, B., 2014. Temporal supersampling pt. 2 ssao demonstration. URL: https://bartwronski.com/2014/04/27/temporal-supersampling-pt-2-ssao-demonstration/.

IV

3

Practical Gather-based Bokeh Depth of Field

Wojciech Sterna

3.1 Introduction

Depth of field is one of the most common post-process algorithms used in today's games. As it turns out, it might often end up being one of the most expensive as was the case of the initial implementation in *Killzone: Shadow Fall* [Valient 2013]. Some implementations rely on easy-to-implement, good-looking, but costly, scatter-based approaches, as in [Pettineo 2011]. In this chapter, we describe a fast (a little over 1.5 ms in 1080p on GeForce 660 GTX which is our test hardware of choice) and easy to implement gather-based solution, strongly inspired by [Sousa 2013]. Figure 3.1 shows the results. Note that the ornaments to the left and in the center are in focus.

3.2 Problem Formulation

The idea behind implementing fast real-time depth-of-field effects is rather simple. We need to blur the out-of-focus areas of the image. The area that is in focus remains sharp. The area in between the out-of-focus and in-focus areas should be blended between the two to achieve a smooth effect.

There are two out-of-focus areas. One is right in front of the camera and the other is the background. The former we will refer to as the near field and the latter is called the far field. There is also a focal plane perpendicular to the frustum's near plane, whose distance to the plane is the distance at which the image is completely sharp. Usually, depth-of-field effects allow pixels to be sharp only on the focal plane. In our implementation, we allow the size of the sharp area to be customized (see Figure 3.2).

How much a pixel is to be blurred depends on its circle-of-confusion (CoC) value. This value is computed based on the pixel's distance from the camera, or actually, to be more precise, on nb, ne, fb, and fe values. Pixels between nb and

Figure 3.1. Depth-of-field implementation.

ne as well as fb and fe can be blended linearly or in any other fashion we want. In the demo accompanying this chapter, we use linear blend although [Sousa 2013] suggests using different blending functions. It is worth noting that we are using an empirical CoC compuation model; [Sousa 2013] explains how to use a physical one.

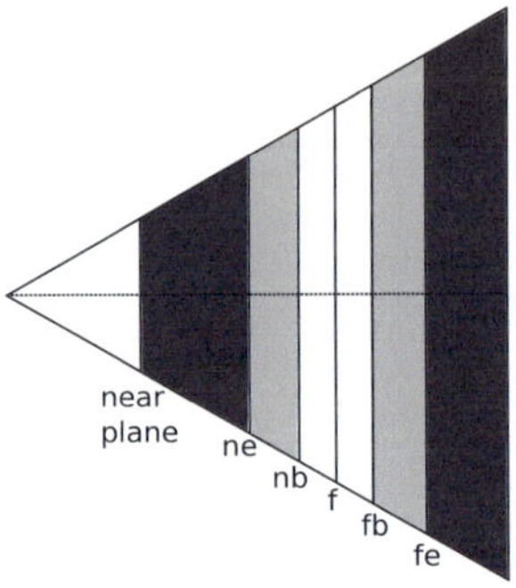

Figure 3.2. The dark grey areas represent full out-of-focus areas called the near and far fields. The light gray represents the areas where blending of out-of-focus areas towards sharp areas occur. The white areas in the middle are completely sharp. The value f is the distance from the camera to the focal plane; nb (near-blend begin) and ne (near-blend end) describe the distances at which in-focus and near field out-of-focus regions blend. Similarly, fb (far-blend begin) and fe (far-blend end) describe the distances at which in-focus and far field out-of-focus regions blend.

Figure 3.3. The gun in the center of the screen should bleed onto the sharp background but instead the blur is limited to the object's screen boundaries. This might make an impression that the object uses a low-res texture rather than that it is out-of-focus (i.e., blurred).

3.2.1 Fundamental Problem of Near Field

As you already know or will see later in this chapter, generating the far field and blending it with the in-focus area is much easier than doing this for the near field. One of the first well-known implementations of real-time depth-of-field is [Scheuermann and Tatarchuk 2003]. A similar implementation can be found in the *Shadow Warrior* game. It handles far field nicely but struggles with making near field look believable as is shown in Figure 3.3.

The proper solution is to make the near-field pixels bleed onto the sharp in-focus background (an effect called occlusion). However, in real life, this effect also makes an out-of-focus foreground object become more semi-transparent, as can be seen in Figure 3.4.

This problem cannot be solved properly in our case because we don't have pixels that are behind. One obvious solution would be to store layers of pixels (this way also solving, to some extent, the general transparency problem), but that solution would be too expensive for real-time rendering purposes.

There are ways to handle this situation without layering. One approach is simply to not allow any semi-transparency on a foreground near-field object. This might, however, create an impression that the near-field object is a little bigger (caused by pixels that bleed onto the background) when it is in an out-of-focus near-field foreground area. Also, we might end up with blur that has effectively twice as small a radius than required (see Figure 3.5 (a)).

Figure 3.4. The greenish ball is on the near field (in the foreground). It is not only blurred but also transparent on the edges. This indicates strong out-of-focus effect.

A handful of practical solutions is presented in [Jimenez 2014], where they "extend" the background to create a sort of a second layer so that the out-of-focus foreground can become transparent.

The solution proposed in this chapter is to blur the out-of-focus near field along with the sharp background, dragging in background pixels outside of an

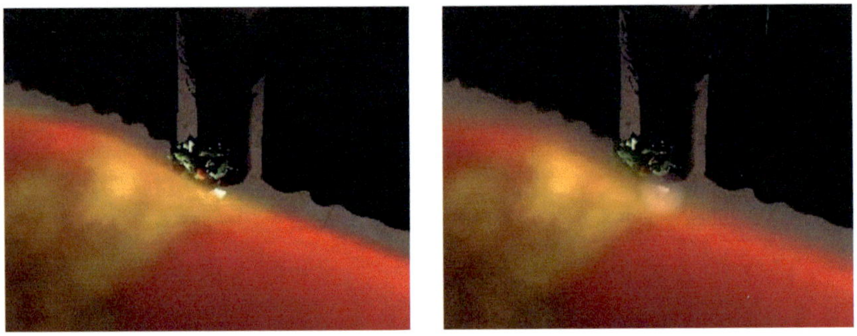

(a) (b)

Figure 3.5. (a) pixels only bleed out onto the background and prevent any background-to-foreground bleeding. As a result the blur is less pronounced than it is in (b), which shows the solution proposed in this article. Note, however, how the pad of the ornament in the background renders partially blurred (the pad corner's circle in the middle of image (b)).

object's silhouette onto the foreground region of the image. This will create an inaccurate effect that the sharp background is actually blurred near the silhouettes of near-field objects. However, this artifact is not really that distracting, and the solution itself is very easy to implement (see Figure 3.5 (b)).

3.3 Algorithm

We assume that the input color buffer that we will be using is in R11G11B10F (float) format, which is one of the most popular formats used in today's games for storing color values that go into post process.

One of the basic ideas allowing fast depth-of-field implementation is to render to a lower-resolution render target, as is done with many other post-process effects. Here we render the near and far fields, separately, into quarter-resolution buffers and then up-sample the results, blending them with the original input color buffer.

Figure 3.6 outlines the algorithm with passes specified along with various buffers that are used.

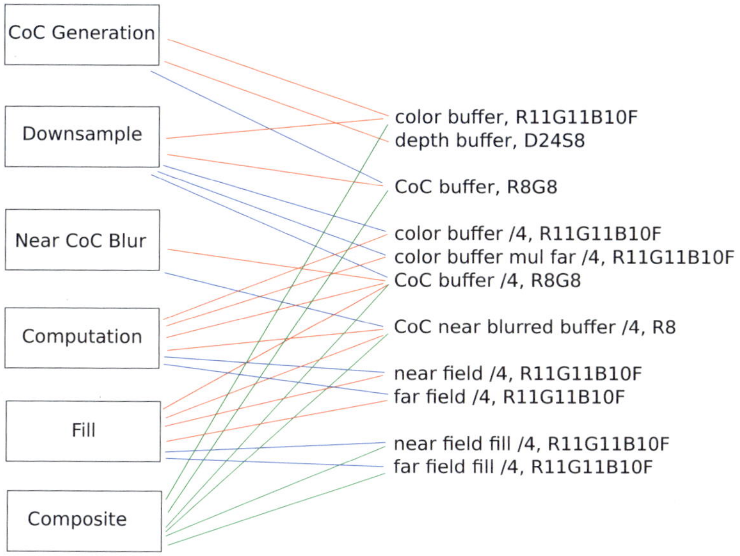

Figure 3.6. Consecutive passes of the algorithm on the left and input/output buffers on the right. A red line indicates that a buffer is an input to a pass. A blue line indicates that a buffer is generated in a pass. Green lines indicate input buffers to the composite pass specifically (to avoid confusion). The term "/4" indicates that a buffer is of quarter resolution. At the end of the description of each buffer is its format.

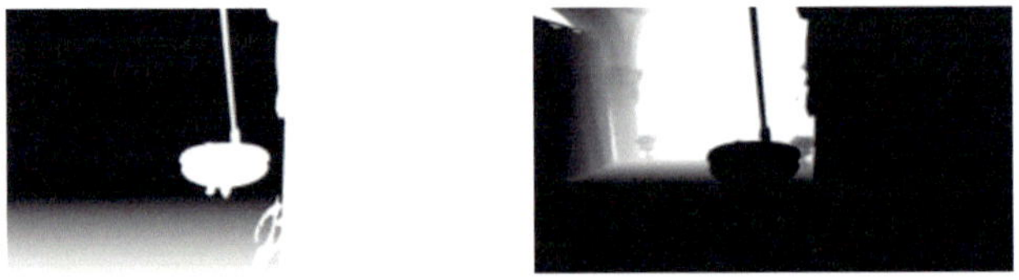

Figure 3.7. Near (left image) and far (right image) circle of confusion values.

3.3.1 Circle of Confusion Generation

In the first pass we calculate the circle of confusion and render it to a full-screen R8G8 (two single-byte components) buffer. The R component holds the CoC value for the near field whereas the G component holds the CoC value for the far field. Those values are calculated based on variables introduced in Section 3.2. However, in the demo application we don't actually expose these to the user to control. Instead, we expose the focal plane distance and range in which the interpolation between the in-focus and out-of-focus near and far fields occur. These values are converted to nb, ne, fb, and fe and fed to the shader. Figure 3.7 shows near and far CoC values.

3.3.2 Downsample

The next step is to downsample two buffers—the input color and the CoC buffer.

There are two reasons we need a downsampled CoC buffer. The first reason is to have a lower bandwidth in the actual depth-of-field calculation pass. The other reason is to be able to perform edge-aware upsampling of the quarter-resolution far field in the final composite pass. The CoC buffer is downsampled simply by using point filtering, taking a pixel from the upper-left corner in each 2×2 input CoC texture quad.

The color buffer can be downsampled in various ways—with point, linear, or some other kind of filtering. Point filtering (that is, taking only one out of four pixels) causes aliasing, which manifests as unpleasant flickering in the final effect. Linear filtering, on the other hand, eliminates flickering at the expense of introducing occasional haloing (between sharp in-focus foreground and blurred out-of-focus background). A good middle-ground is to use edge-aware bilateral downsampling; i.e., performing linear interpolation of all pixels in each 2×2 quad that have depth-buffer values close to, say, the upper-left pixel in the quad. That solves the problem of flickering and eliminates haloing (which is caused by color bleeding). This is exactly what the algorithm does with one exception; it is not the depth buffer that is used to compare samples but rather the far CoC values. The reason for this is that flickering only appears on the far field and it would be a waste of bandwidth to sample the depth buffer given that CoC values are already available.

Figure 3.8. Color buffer multiplied by far circle of confusion. Note that there is no color bleeding on the edges of the "black objects."

To sum up, the downsampled color buffer is output twice, once in unaltered form and the second time multiplied by the downsampled far CoC value. Why this is done will be clear later.

Please note here that this pass renders to three render targets: two downsampled color buffers (one multiplied by far CoC, as depicted in Figure 3.8) and to the downsampled CoC buffer.

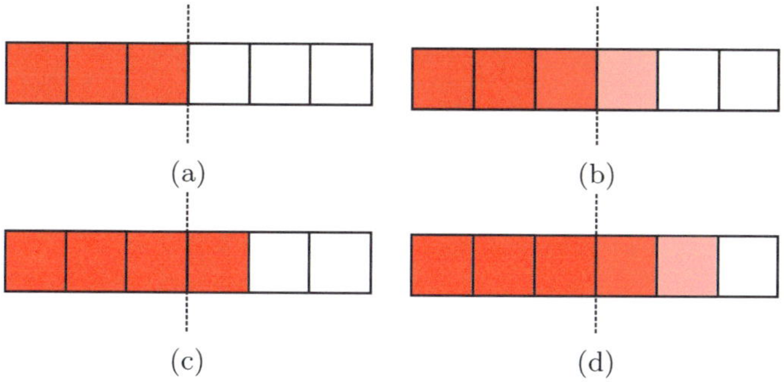

Figure 3.9. Image (a) is the input image; (b) shows the result of applying a three-pixel-wide blur filter to (a). In (c), a three-pixel-wide max filter is applied to (a). Finally, in (d), blur is applied to (c). Performing an n-width max filter followed by an n-width blur will have the effect of blurring outwards. For blurring inwards, min filter should be used.

Figure 3.10. Near circle of confusion buffer (left) and its outwardly blurred variant (right).

3.3.3 Near CoC Blur

To bleed the near field onto the background, we are going to need a blurred version of the near CoC buffer. However, our blur needs to go outwards only (why this is the case will be clear later). To compute an outward blur we need to first apply a max filter to the image and then perform blur (see Figure 3.9).

Figure 3.10 shows the original near CoC buffer as well as the blurred variant of the near CoC buffer. Note that the blur indeed goes outwards.

Max (and min) filters are separable, so we can find a block's max value using two separable (horizontal and vertical) passes. Also, we perform blurring using two separable passes. All in all near CoC blur computation requires four passes.

3.3.4 Computation

The crucial part of the algorithm is the actual depth of field computation. In this pass we compute both the near field and far field and output them to two separate render targets. Both fields are computed by taking a bunch of samples in a circular pattern and computing their average.

The circular pattern used is shown in Figure 3.11. We take 49 samples using three circles. The distance between two consecutive circles (the red line)

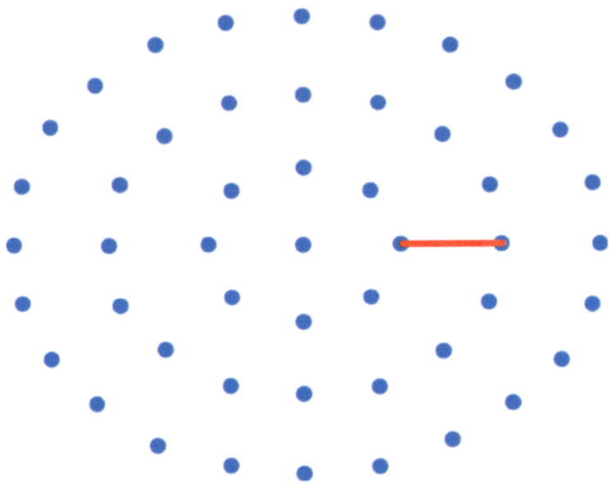

Figure 3.11. Circular sampling pattern for bokeh depth of field effect.

Figure 3.12. (a) Without and (b) with filling. (*Courtesy of* [Sousa 2013].)

is actually two pixels, not one. This way, the radius of the filter is larger at the cost of undersampling, as shown in Figure 3.12(a) (how to fix this will be covered in the next section). We can achieve different bokeh effects by generating other than circular sets of samples, for instance hexagonal. [Sousa 2013] presents formulas for computing various n-gons.

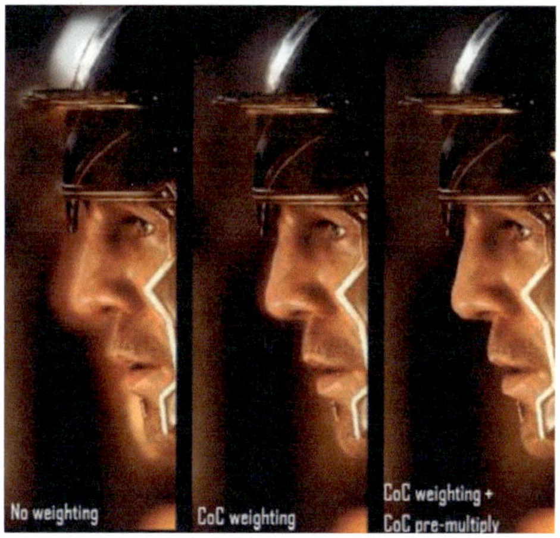

Figure 3.13. The left figure does not perform any far CoC weighting; thus, the in-focus sharp pixels bleed onto the out-of-focus background. In the middle figure, each bilinearly sampled color buffer's sample is weighted by a bilinearly sampled far CoC. By premultiplying the bilaterally filtered color buffer with the far CoC in the downsample pass all bleeding is gone in the right figure. (*Courtesy of* [Sousa 2013].)

When generating the far field each sample is weighted additionally by the far CoC value. This weighting could either be done in the shader that is computing the depth-of-field effect (using the original color and CoC buffers), or we can use the color buffer that is already premultiplied by the far CoC value. We choose the latter option. The reason that this is better is that we want to make use of bilinear filtering when sampling the color buffer, but we also want to avoid color bleeding. That is why we downsampled the color buffer in the downsample pass using bilinear filtering weighted by far CoC values. Figure 3.13 shows different variants.

In our algorithm, since we don't care that the near field will also blur the sharp background (as shown in Figure 3.5), we don't weight by the near CoC. We simply perform vanilla blurring of pixels (in circular pattern).

3.3.5 Fill

As was shown in Figure 3.12, the kernel we use leaves holes in the bokeh pattern. There are a few options to fill them. We could perform an additional 3×3 blur on both the near and far fields once they have been processed in the computation pass. However, [Sousa 2013] proposes to use the max filter instead (also 3×3 kernel). This makes the image violate energy conservation but produces a more appealing bokeh effect.

Taking 49 samples and undersampling in the calculation pass and filling thereafter with nine samples to compensate for this undersampling is much faster (almost three times) than doing only the computation pass, without undersampling, as this requires 144 samples to have the same kernel width.

Computation together with fill passes generate, in our case, a bokeh effect with a circular pattern of 13 pixels in diameter—three circles on each side, separated by two pixels that sum to six pixels on the side. This is in quarter-resolution, so eventually we end up with 12 pixels on the side in full resolution.

3.3.6 Composite

Finally, once we have generated the CoC buffers, near field, and far field and filled the latter two, it's time to composite these with the scene.

First, we sample the input color buffer without depth-of-field effect. Then, we blend the far field on top of it. Note that the far field is in quarter resolution, whereas the input color buffer is in full resolution. As such, blending the far field is a bit tricky because we have to avoid bleeding— that means that vanilla bilinear upsampling will not suffice. Bilateral filtering comes to the rescue, in a similar fashion as in Section 3.3.2, with the exception that there we used bilateral filtering to downsample and now we are upsampling. We could use the depth buffer to compare pixels' depths, but since we have the full-resolution far CoC value around and quarter-resolution buffer far CoC values we can use them. By comparing the full-resolution CoC value with each quarter-resolution CoC, we know which ones to use in the upsampling process. We then use the full-resolution far CoC value to blend between the color buffer and the upsampled far field.

Contrary to the far field, the near field can bleed as much as possible. We upsample the near field bilinearly and blend it with the color buffer (already blended with the far field) using the blurred near CoC buffer (from Section 3.3.3).

3.4 Implementation Details

We now discuss some selected implementation details.

3.4.1 Circle of Confusion Generation

The circle of confusion pass, based on the depth buffer, generates a R8G8 buffer with near and far CoCs. The depth buffer stores depth values in NDC (normalized device coordinates)in the $[0,1]$ interval in Direct3D and $[-1,1]$ interval in OpenGL. We convert this value from NDC coordinates back to view space and from this we compute CoC values. Listing 3.1 shows how to do the conversion (a derivation can be found in [Sterna 2013]).

```
float DepthNDCToView(float depth_ndc)
{
    return -projParams.y / (depth_ndc + projParams.x);
}
```

Listing 3.1. NDC-depth to view-space depth conversion; `projParams.x` is the projection matrix's $(3,3)$th entry, whereas `projParams.y` is the $(4,3)$th entry (row-major ordering).

In the demo application, a right-handed coordinate system is used; thus, the view-space depth value that is returned by `DepthNDCToView` is negative (because `projParams` values passed to the shader are based on a right-handed perspective matrix). We negate it to obtain a positive number. The CoC is then computed using linear interpolation.

3.4.2 Downsample

In this pass we downsample a couple of buffers from their full resolution, outputting to quarter-resolution buffers. For each output pixel, there are four input pixels in a 2×2 quad (see Figure 3.14). We compute their coordinates as in Listing 3.2.

Downsampling of the color buffer and CoC buffer is shown in Listing 3.3. The color buffer is downsampled using bilinear filtering. We can do so because this buffer will be used for the near field blurring, whose bleeding is desirable for us. The CoC buffer, on the other hand, is sampled using the top-left sample

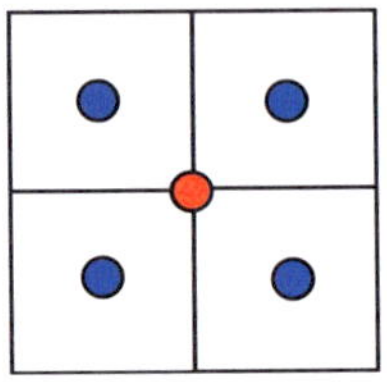

Figure 3.14. The red dot is the middle of the quarter-resolution buffer's pixel. The blue dots are centers of corresponding full-resolution buffer's pixels. If we want to sample full-resolution pixels, given the quarter-resolution pixel's coordinates), we need to shift by half of the full-resolution pixel's size in each UV axis. Or, equivalently, by 0.25 of the quarter-resolution pixel's size.

```
float2 texCoord00 = input.texCoord + float2(-0.25f, -0.25f)*pixelSize;
float2 texCoord10 = input.texCoord + float2( 0.25f, -0.25f)*pixelSize;
float2 texCoord01 = input.texCoord + float2(-0.25f,  0.25f)*pixelSize;
float2 texCoord11 = input.texCoord + float2( 0.25f,  0.25f)*pixelSize;
```

Listing 3.2. Since `input.texCoord` points in the middle of the quarter resolution buffer's pixel, we need to offset that by half the size of the full resolution pixel size, which is 0.25 of quarter resolution pixel's size. `pixelSize` is the size of the quarter resolution buffer's pixel. Figure 3.14 shows more details.

of the full-resolution buffer. In this case, we can't bilinearly filter because of the nature of the CoC data. This data is "edge sensitive" so we will need accurate data, not in-between values, to perform upsampling later on.

```
float4 color = colorTexture.SampleLevel(linearClampSampler, input.texCoord, 0);
float4 coc = cocTexture.SampleLevel(pointClampSampler, texCoord00, 0);
```

Listing 3.3. Downsampling of color and CoC buffers.

Downsampling of the color buffer for the far field requires more attention. To prevent flickering we need a bilinear filter. On the other hand, to prevent haloing (Figure 3.13) we can't do this recklessly. We can bilinearly filter, but only values that are close enough to each other. This closeness can be defined, for instance, in terms of differences in depths in the depth buffer, but since we have far CoC values lying around, which are based on the depth buffer, we can use those (see Listing 3.4).

```
float cocFar00 = cocTexture.SampleLevel(pointClampSampler, texCoord00, 0).y;
float cocFar10 = cocTexture.SampleLevel(pointClampSampler, texCoord10, 0).y;
float cocFar01 = cocTexture.SampleLevel(pointClampSampler, texCoord01, 0).y;
float cocFar11 = cocTexture.SampleLevel(pointClampSampler, texCoord11, 0).y;

float weight00 = 1000.0f;
```

```
float4 colorMulCOCFar = weight00 * colorTexture.SampleLevel(pointClampSampler, texCoord00, 0);
float weightsSum = weight00;

float weight10 = 1.0f / (abs(cocFar00 - cocFar10) + 0.001f);
colorMulCOCFar += weight10 * colorTexture.SampleLevel(pointClampSampler, texCoord10, 0);
weightsSum += weight10;

float weight01 = 1.0f / (abs(cocFar00 - cocFar01) + 0.001f);
colorMulCOCFar += weight01 * colorTexture.SampleLevel(pointClampSampler, texCoord01, 0);
weightsSum += weight01;

float weight11 = 1.0f / (abs(cocFar00 - cocFar11) + 0.001f);
colorMulCOCFar += weight11 * colorTexture.SampleLevel(pointClampSampler, texCoord11, 0);
weightsSum += weight11;

colorMulCOCFar /= weightsSum;
colorMulCOCFar *= coc.y;
```

Listing 3.4. Downsampling of the color buffer for far field.

We take all four full-resolution buffer color samples and their CoC values. We assume the top-left sample is sort of a reference, and we will use that always. For the remaining three samples, we compute a weight factor based on the difference of their far CoC values and the reference sample. The closer the samples are to each other, the larger their contribution. Finally, the computed value is normalized (divided by `weightsSum`) and multiplied by the far CoC.

3.4.3 Near CoC Blur

Near CoC blur (the quarter-resolution, downsampled one) is required so that we can blend the blurred near field with the rest of the scene. We know from Section 3.3.4 that our effective maximum kernel radius is six pixels. This means that it would be optimal to blur, outwardly, by six pixels to each side. Technically, we are not obliged to use exactly six-pixels-wide blur. We have the background, we have the blurred near field, we can blend them the way that meets our expectations. We chose to use 12-pixels-wide blur, because the near field looks smooth enough and the artifacts from Figure 3.5 are not yet that objectionable.

To perform the (outward) blur, we first need to apply the max filter. We do this in two passes, first horizontally and then vertically, for performance reasons. The filter's width is 13 (six pixels to each side). Once we've maxed the near-CoC buffer, we blur it using a box filter (We've tried Gauss but found the difference is meaningless). Here again a 13-pixels-wide kernel is used. As a result we end up with a 12-pixels-wide (to the side) outward blur.

This part of the algorithm requires four passes—two for max and two for blur. All those passes sample only the x-component of the input buffer. On tested hardware, this is cheaper than sampling all four channels (by calling shader sample functions and not specifying which components we want to sample), even though the remaining three channels lie next to the x-channel in memory (or actually the remaining one channel because our CoC buffer has two channels).

3.4.4 Computation

To blur the near and far fields we use a circular samples pattern. The generated samples can be found in the depth-of-field computation shader `dof.hlsl`.

Blur of the (downsampled) color buffer to generate the near field is nothing fancy. We just take all samples in the circular pattern and compute the average.

Generating the far field is a bit trickier. Here we don't sample the unaltered, downsampled color buffer, but it is multiplied by the far CoC version. Code is shown in Listing 3.5.

```
float4 Far(float2 texCoord)
{
    float4 result = colorMulCOCFarTexture.SampleLevel(pointClampSampler, texCoord, 0);
    float weightsSum = cocTexture.SampleLevel(pointClampSampler, texCoord, 0).y;

    for (int i = 0; i < 48; i++)
    {
        float2 offset = kernelScale * offsets[i] * pixelSize;

        float cocSample = cocTexture.SampleLevel(linearClampSampler, texCoord + offset, 0).y;
        float4 sample = colorMulCOCFarTexture.SampleLevel(linearClampSampler, texCoord + offset, 0);

        result += sample; // the texture is pre-multiplied so don't need to multiply here by weight
        weightsSum += cocSample;
    }

    return result / weightsSum;
}
```

Listing 3.5. Computation of the far field.

Since the texture is already multiplied by the far CoC, the result will get darker as we move away from fully blurred areas, as shown in Figure 3.8. Combining that with the full resolution color buffer in the composite pass would result in unpleasant dark haloes around objects. A much better solution is to renormalize brightness while still in the computation pass. That's what we're doing here by dividing by `weightsSum`.

An insightful reader will quickly notice that `weightsSum` can actually be zero. This will happen for pixels that, along with their surroundings, are black. However, this is not going to be a problem as `Far` function is only called for pixels that have a far CoC larger than 0. This also, or actually most importantly, acts as a significant early-out optimization, which in this case makes great use of coherence (near field's pixels lie next to each other as well as the far field's do)—see Listing 3.6.

```
PS_OUTPUT PSMain(PS_INPUT input)
{
    PS_OUTPUT output;

    float cocNearBlurred = cocNearBlurredTexture.SampleLevel(pointClampSampler, input.
      texCoord, 0).x;
    float cocFar = cocTexture.SampleLevel(pointClampSampler, input.texCoord, 0).y;
    float4 color = colorTexture.SampleLevel(pointClampSampler, input.texCoord, 0);

    if (cocNearBlurred > 0.0f)
        output.near = Near(input.texCoord);
    else
        output.near = color;

    if (cocFar > 0.0f)
        output.far = Far(input.texCoord);
    else
        output.far = 0.0f;

    return output;
}
```

Listing 3.6. Main function of the computation pass.

We see in the listing that the early-out is applied not only to the far field but also to the near field. In the case of the far field, when depth-of-field is not computed, we output black color. We need to do this to prevent bleeding of non-far-field pixels onto the far field, which would happen in the next pass of the algorithm—fill—if this care was not taken.

In the case of the near field, to the contrary, we like bleeding and we need to output the color buffer's value. Otherwise, due to bilinear filtering, a slight black halo would appear (if we output black color) when blending the near field with the full-resolution color buffer.

As can be seen, the computation pass writes to two output buffers, near field to the first one and the far field to the other.

Since the input color buffer is a HDR floating-point buffer, it might contain large values. Usually this is not a problem unless those large values come from undersampled data, like high frequency specular. This will result in flickering bright pixels (called fireflies) in the depth-of-field effect when this effect is computed before tone mapping. This problem can be alleviated for instance by applying a Karis average, as explained in [Karis 2013]. After increasing the scene's contrast by producing larger lighting values, we found that using this trick indeed resulted in a more appealing rendered image, although a darker one.

3.4.5 Fill

In order to compensate for undersampling introduced in the computation pass, we use max filter to spread bigger values onto smaller values. The effect can be seen in Figure 3.12. We do this for both the near and far fields.

```
if (cocNearBlurred > 0.0f)
{
    for (int i = -1; i <= 1; i++)
    {
        for (int j = -1; j <= 1; j++)
        {
            float2 sampleTexCoord = input.texCoord + float2(i, j)*pixelSize;
            float4 sample = dofNearTexture.SampleLevel(pointClampSampler,
   sampleTexCoord, 0);
            output.nearFill = max(output.nearFill, sample);
        }
    }
}
```

Listing 3.7. Fill of the near field.

The kernel we need to use is barely 3×3, so this pass is very fast. This kernel is sufficient as the holes that are present in our bokeh pattern are one-pixel-width. Code for performing this operation for the near field is given in Listing 3.7. It is analogous for the far field.

Here we're just iterating through all samples in the 3×3 kernel and outputting the max value found. Also, to speed-up that process, we make use of early-out.

3.4.6 Composite

Finally, once we have generated the near and the far fields, we can blend them with the color buffer. First, the far field has to be blended in, and, once we have done that, we can blend in the near field. This order has to be maintained.

The shader starts by sampling the color buffer as in Listing 3.8 and stores that result in a temporary variable `result`.

```
float4 result = colorTexture.SampleLevel(pointClampSampler, input.texCoord, 0);
```

Listing 3.8. Color buffer sample.

Later on, we will want to blend the far field with the color buffer, but first we have to upsample it to full resolution. Listing 3.9 shows part of this process which is sampling all necessary textures.

First, we compute texture coordinates that will be used to sample the quarter-resolution far field. Note here that `pixelSize` used is the full-resolution pixel size. It means that when sampling the quarter resolution far field with those texture coordinates, one of the four pixels in each 2×2 quad will sample the same pixel in the quarter-resolution far field, two of the four will sample two different pixels, and only one will sample four pixels. This is desired since, for some full-resolution pixels, we want to have values exactly from the quarter-resolution far field and every second column and row a blend of two or four quarter-resolution far-field pixels.

```
float2 texCoord00 = input.texCoord;
float2 texCoord10 = input.texCoord + float2(pixelSize.x, 0.0f);
float2 texCoord01 = input.texCoord + float2(0.0f, pixelSize.y);
float2 texCoord11 = input.texCoord + float2(pixelSize.x, pixelSize.y);

float cocFar = cocTexture.SampleLevel(pointClampSampler, input.texCoord, 0).y;
float4 cocsFar_x4 = cocTexture_x4.GatherGreen(pointClampSampler, texCoord00).wzxy;
float4 cocsFarDiffs = abs(cocFar.xxxx - cocsFar_x4);

float4 dofFar00 = dofFarTexture_x4.SampleLevel(pointClampSampler, texCoord00, 0);
float4 dofFar10 = dofFarTexture_x4.SampleLevel(pointClampSampler, texCoord10, 0);
float4 dofFar01 = dofFarTexture_x4.SampleLevel(pointClampSampler, texCoord01, 0);
float4 dofFar11 = dofFarTexture_x4.SampleLevel(pointClampSampler, texCoord11, 0);
```

Listing 3.9. Sampling of textures needed for far field upsampling.

Later in the listing we sample the full-resolution CoC, quarter-resolution CoCs, and compute their differences which we will use as bilateral upsample weights. We use a gather instruction to sample all four CoCs at once, and this decreased the speed of the whole composite pass by 10%. Finally, we sample the far field in four different coordinates.

We have the far field sampled in correct coordinates and `cocsFarDiffs` that will act as weights for upsampling. We will now calculate vanilla bilinear filtering weights that will be used to blend all four far-field samples. Code for this is presented in Listing 3.10 and is based on [Wikipedia 2017].

```
float2 imageCoord = input.texCoord / pixelSize;
float2 fractional = frac(imageCoord);
float a = (1.0f - fractional.x) * (1.0f - fractional.y);
float b = fractional.x * (1.0f - fractional.y);
float c = (1.0f - fractional.x) * fractional.y;
float d = fractional.x * fractional.y;
```

Listing 3.10. Bilinear filtering weights.

We now have weights for bilinear filtering. From previous code, we have CoC-aware weights. We can now combine the two to compute the upsampled bilateral far-CoC value, as shown in Listing 3.11.

```
float4 dofFar = 0.0f;
float weightsSum = 0.0f;

float weight00 = a / (cocsFarDiffs.x + 0.001f);
dofFar += weight00 * dofFar00;
weightsSum += weight00;

float weight10 = b / (cocsFarDiffs.y + 0.001f);
dofFar += weight10 * dofFar10;
weightsSum += weight10;

float weight01 = c / (cocsFarDiffs.z + 0.001f);
dofFar += weight01 * dofFar01;
weightsSum += weight01;

```

```
float weight11 = d / (cocsFarDiffs.w + 0.001f);
dofFar += weight11 * dofFar11;
weightsSum += weight11;

dofFar /= weightsSum;

result = lerp(result, dofFar, blend * cocFar);
```

Listing 3.11. Far field upsampled value computed.

The final `dofFar` value is composed of the four samples using the same formula we saw during downsampling so there is really nothing new here. At the end of the code, we blend (lerp) the color buffer (stored in `result`) with `dofFar` using the full-resolution far CoC, multiplied by `blend` which is a user-specified constant passed to the shader from the application.

The hard part of composition, the far field, is done. Blending in the near field is way easier, as shown in Listing 3.12.

```
float cocNear = cocBlurredTexture_x4.SampleLevel(linearClampSampler, input.texCoord,
    0).x;
float4 dofNear = dofNearTexture_x4.SampleLevel(linearClampSampler, input.texCoord, 0);

result = lerp(result, dofNear, blend * cocNear);
```

Listing 3.12. Blending in the near field.

We just upsample the near field and blend it with the current result (color buffer blended with the far field), using plain hardware bilinear filtering. It is advisable [Sousa 2013] to use custom bicubic filtering here for better quality. The `blend` parameter will be explained in the next subsection.

3.4.7 Application

Up till now, we have described mostly what takes place on the shader side of the effect. However, the discussion would not be complete without mentioning some subtleties that take place on the application side.

The header of the function that performs the whole effect is shown in Listing 3.13.

```
void DOF(float focalPlaneDistance, float focusTransitionRange, float strength, const
    Matrix& projTransform)
```

Listing 3.13. Header of the DoF function in the application.

The function takes the description of the focal plane. Those values are used to compute variables from Section 3.2 which are later passed to the CoC generation shader.

The value projTransform, which is passed as the last argument, is just the perspective projection transform. It is used to properly convert NDC depth values to view space values.

The parameter strength says how strong the DoF effect should be. Actually, even though it may not seem so at first, it's not that obvious how that should work. We will discuss that now.

At the beginning of the DOF function there are two variables—kernelScale and compositeBlend. The variable kernelScale is used to scale the circular kernel used in the computation pass. We can use it to control the radius of the effect; compositeBlend, on the other hand, is used to multiply the CoCs in the composite pass (but only during blending with the color buffer). While it is obvious what the former does, the latter usage might be a bit vague. The kernel scale is useful if we want the application to fade-in or fade-out of the DoF effect. The problem is, however, that if we set it to 0 (or, in general, some small value) the quarter-resolution nature of the fields will become apparent. When the kernel scale is 0, we would like to completely fade out the fields, displaying the original color buffer. This can be achieved with compositeBlend. We choose that, if the DoF's strength falls below 0.25, the kernel scale is clamped to 0.25 and the composite blend is changed so that it fades from 1 to 0 (leaving only the original color buffer). Code that does just that is shown in Listing 3.14. Also, code that uses compositeBlend is in the last lines of Listings 3.11 and 3.12.

```
float kernelScale = 1.0;
float compositeBlend = 1.0;

if (strength >= 0.25f)
{
    kernelScale = strength;
    compositeBlend = 1.0f;
}
else
{
    kernelScale = 0.25f;
    compositeBlend = 4.0f * strength;
}
```

Listing 3.14. Calculation of kernel scale and composite blend based on DoF strength.

3.5 Per-pixel Kernel Scale

You might have noticed that in the DoF computation pass we don't scale the filter kernel by the pixel's CoC value. That would actually be more natural, and some depth-of-field implementations do that. We went on to implement that modification and found that even though it produces a slightly more realistic DoF, it also produces a kind of undesirable near field, related to the core problem of our algorithm depicted in Figure 3.5. The far field does not have that problem, and it might be visually beneficial to apply per-pixel kernel scaling for it.

To change the current implementation to accommodate for per-pixel kernel scale, you need to add multiplication by pixel's CoC in the sample texture coordinates offset calculation. Also, the filling pass has to be changed slightly. In that pass, we didn't care about depth discontinuities as they were not problematic for us. When per-pixel CoC kernel scaling is applied, we must not use neighboring samples whose CoC is much different than that of the pixel that is being processed.

Once these changes have been applied, we can alter blending factors in the composition pass. To better show off the effect of scaling, we could output the far field without blending with the sharp color buffer for a broader specturm of far CoC values. One just has to remember that the far field is actually of quarter resolution, and once the kernel scaling goes down, this fact will be revealed more.

All in all, given the problems related to per-pixel kernel scaling we decided to not use it at all in the demo application.

3.6 Demo Application

There is an accompanying demo application to this chapter presenting the algorithm in action.

Configuration of the demo can be changed in `config.txt` file located in the folder where the binary is located. The key configuration is

- WSAD + mouse—camera movement,
- Shift— speeding up,
- Insert / Delete—shift focal plane,
- Home / End—increase/decrease in-focus region,
- Page Up / Page Down—increase/decrease DoF effect,
- ESC—exit.

Pass	**Time**
All	1.506 ms
CoC generation	0.13 ms
Downsample	0.145 ms
Near CoC Max X	0.08 ms
Near CoC Max Y	0.08 ms
Near CoC Blur X	0.08 ms
Near CoC Blur Y	0.08 ms
Computation	0.455 ms
Fill	0.122 ms
Composite	0.334 ms

Table 3.1. Performance on GeForce 660 GTX in 1080p.

In the folder where the binary is located, a file called `profiler.txt` will be generated upon exit, where average performance of each consecutive batch of 100 frames is dumped. Table 3.1 shows performance on a GeForce 660 GTX in 1080p.

3.7 Conclusions

In this chapter we presented an efficient, production-quality algorithm for generating depth-of-field effect. It produces stable, convincing results at very good frame rates.

3.8 Acknowledgments

I would like to thank Krzysztof Narkowicz of Flying Wild Hog for taking the time to read the chapter and to provide feedback. I also thank Wessam Bessam, the editor of this section, for smooth cooperation and, of course, Wolfgang Engel, the editor of the entire book, for his editorial work starting with the early *ShaderX* books up to this one :).

Bibliography

Jimenez, J., 2014. Next generation post processing in *Call of Duty: Advanced Warfare.* URL: http://www.slideshare.net/guerrillagames/killzone-shadow-fall-demo-postmortem.

Karis, B., 2013. Tone mapping. URL: http://graphicrants.blogspot.com/2013/12/tone-mapping.html.

Pettineo, M., 2011. How to fake bokeh. URL: https://mynameismjp.wordpress.com/2011/02/28/bokeh/.

Scheuermann, T., and Tatarchuk, N. 2003. Improved depth of field rendering. In *ShaderX3: Advanced Rendering with DirectX and OpenGL.* Charles River Media, Boston, MA, pages 363–377.

Sousa, T. 2013. CryEngine 3 graphics gems. In *Advances in Real-Time Rendering SIGGRAPH 2013 course*, ACM, New York, pages 22–44. URL: http://www.crytek.com/download/Sousa_Graphics_Gems_CryENGINE3.pdf.

Sterna, W., 2013. Reconstructing camera space position from depth. URL: http://wojtsterna.blogspot.com/2013/11/recovering-camera-position-from-depth.html.

Valient, M., 2013. Killzone Shadow Fall postmortem. pages 77-83. URL: http://www.slideshare.net/guerrillagames/killzone-shadow-fall-demo-postmortem.

Wikipedia, 2017. Bilinear filtering. URL: https://en.wikipedia.org/wiki/Bilinear_filtering.

V

Virtual Reality

Virtual reality (VR) has become the hottest new graphics technology, again. While the basic idea has been explored for many years, the recent availability and variety of inexpensive electronic components has brought this field to the fore. Just as GPUs themselves suddenly became affordable for consumers two decades ago, high-quality VR rigs are now mass-market products.

In this section, we present two chapters by experts in the field. Over the years the vast preponderance of articles about the GPU have been focused on how to efficiently code various rendering effects. For VR, the absolutely critical principle to a good user experience is to minimize lag whenever possible. Accordingly, both articles focus on how to render the frames as a whole in ways to get the proper result to the viewer at the right time.

The first chapter, "Efficient Stereo and VR Rendering," by Íñigo Quílez, focuses on a variety of ways that computations and data can be shared in order to more rapidly generate two or more separate views of the same scene. The article discusses high-level decisions about the rendering engine's architecture, along with various low-level optimizations possible on different systems.

The second chapter, "Understanding, Measuring, and Analyzing VR Graphics Performance," by James Hughes, Reza Nourai, and Ed Hutchins, is really two articles in one. The first part discusses sources of lag and various strategies, including timewarp, to combat these. The second section takes a deep dive into event tracing, specifically ETW (Event Tracing for Windows). This tool gives a view into where time is being spent in an application, but it takes some skill to run and interpret the results. The authors also provide concrete examples where this tool has identified problems and helped them improve performance.

VR equipment will improve in quality, drop in price, and evolve over time. However, the principles of efficient frame rendering and bottleneck detection presented in these articles will almost assuredly apply to future designs and so is worth learning well. We hope this section will help you develop these skills.

—Eric Haines

V 1

Efficient Stereo and VR Rendering

Íñigo Quílez

1.1 Introduction

With the recent advent of consumer virtual reality (VR) through inexpensive head-mounted displays, real-time rendering for VR is a topic of great interest to academia, hobbyists, and businesses. From hardware to software developers, from presentation to rendering to content makers, all disciplines involved in visualizing content are rethinking their methods.

From a purely rendering standpoint, VR brings huge challenges, because current content needs to be rendered at high resolution (often twice the amount of pixels of HD), high frame-rate (usually 90 fps), and unusual levels of supersampling or antialiasing, making the amount of pixel computations required easily six times that of a conventional HD game running at 30 fps. This difference between the requirements of traditional 3D rendering and VR will only increase as the display resolutions for VR are expected to grow over the next decade. This disparity requires graphics programmers to change some of the established practices and optimize their engines differently. In this article we'll go through some of the basic ideas and methodologies recommended for efficient rendering in VR.

The first half of the article will focus on high-level architectural design, and the second half will discuss some of the lower-level optimizations available by using modern OpenGL 4.5.

1.2 Engine Design

1.2.1 The Point

Traditional engine design involves performing the posing and rendering of the whole content in a loop. Posing includes animating the characters in a film or cinematic moment and also more complex tasks, such as evaluating physics and simulations in a game. Rendering usually takes the whole pose and projects it into the screen in a single conceptual step, then proceeds to the next frame or iteration of the "pose and render" loop.

This works great for single monoscopic display systems such as a TV or a computer monitor. On the other hand, displays systems for VR are sophisticated and include several displays with stereoscopic images in each. Current VR headsets will typically have one virtual display that is stereoscopic. However, a CAVE VR system consists of five projection walls at 90 degree angles with stereo images. A fancy imaginary, but plausible, head-mounted device might one day contain one central display with stereo and two peripheral mono lower-resolution displays at 45 degree angles. So VR rendering is potentially done with multiple configurations of displays, where a display can be conceptually mapped to a planar projection with a monoscopic or stereoscopic frame buffer.

All these scenarios mean that rendering the whole pose of the game or film in a single step assuming a single pinhole camera doesn't work anymore. The renderer could treat each display and each left/right eye in each display as an individual render task, but that would make for a poorly performing renderer, since there are missed opportunities for reusing data which is neither eye nor display dependent.

1.2.2 Identifying Contexts

In order to exploit this optimization opportunity we need to identify the context in which data exists uniquely:

- *Frame context.* This is the context in which things that are constant across the frame exist and need to be processed. These include posing the worlds animated characters and performing sound simulations or global LOD computations, but also some rendering of global elements such as global shadow maps, reflection maps, cloud animated textures, water caustic maps, etc. Basically, anything that needs to be rendered and is view-orientation independent belongs in the frame context.

  The main subjects of the frame context are the viewer position (or player or camera) and perhaps the frustum that is the union of all the display frustums.

- *Display context.* This is the context where we want to do display-specific work, such as rendering a shadow map for the frustum of the display which can be shared across both stereo eyes on the display, or rendering distant geometry which won't benefit from stereo disparity and therefore can be rasterized once and shared between both eye projections. It is also in this context where we compile our command buffers or `glMultiDrawIndirect` buffers that will contain all the rendering work needed for the left and right eyes belonging to this display.

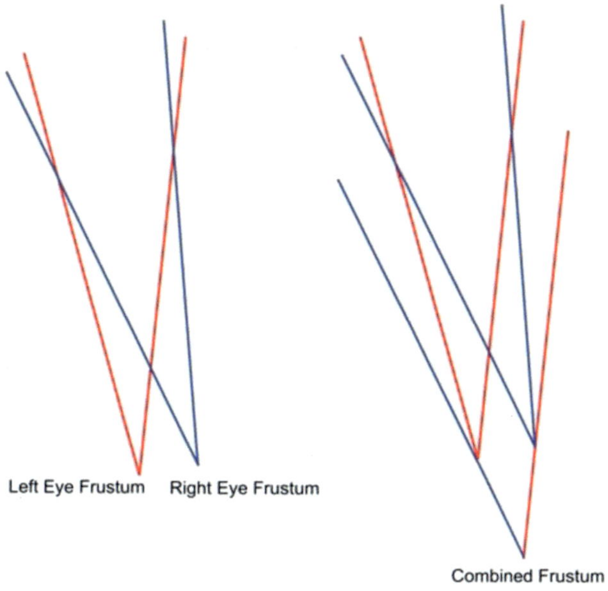

Figure 1.1. Viewer position, display frustum, and eye frustums and positions.

The subject of the display context is the frustum that is the union of the left and right eye projections for this display. Note that the apex of this frustum does not correspond to the viewer's position nor the midpoint location of both eyes. Usually the apex of the display frustum will be behind the viewer's head position and potentially skewed to one side as well if the displays are not parallel to the line connecting the eyes, such as in a CAVE, a tilted HMD, or peripheral display of an HMD (see Figure 1.1.

- *Eye context.* In this context belong the elements that are absolutely eye dependent and cannot be reused across left and right eyes, such as close-by objects which do need stereo disparity. When talking of shading, the eye context also includes the data necessary for correct specular computations.

  The subject of the eye context is the actual projection of the scene for this eye and its frustum (although it's not worth doing culling on this frustum). The center of projection (or apex of the frustum) is located at the position of the viewer's corresponding eye's eyeball in the world.

Given these three contexts, Listing 1.1 shows how a VR-ready engine could organize its rendering.

```
ComputeFrame( k )
{
    DoProcessFrame( k );                  // Compute animation, sound,
                                          //  LOD computation, simulations
    DoRenderFrame( k );                   // Render reflection maps,
                                          // clouds layers, global shadow maps

    for( int j=0; j<numDisplays; j++ )    // numDisplays = 5 for a CAVE, 1 for a HMD
    {
        DoProcessDisplay( k, j );         // Do frustum culling, compile draw
                                          // indirect buffers

        DoRenderDisplay( k, j );          // Render eye-shared shadow maps,
                                          // and distant geometry

        for( int i=0; i<2; i++ )          // stereo
        {
            DoRenderEye( k, j, i );       // Render regular geometry with parallax
                                          // and postpro
        }
    }
}
```

Listing 1.1. Organizing rendering in a VR-ready engine.

1.2.3 Culling and Contexts

Depending on your VR setup, frustum culling might need to happen at different stages. Most typically, for a single display stereoscopic system, the frame and display contexts can be considered the same, and we do the frustum culling in either. All that matters is that culling is not done per eye since both eyes' projections overlap considerably.

However, for a three-display system (a central and two peripheral displays), it might be a good idea to do a rough frustum-culling pass in the frame context and then do three frustum-culling passes at the display context on the results of the previous step. Depending on the nature of the content, skipping the cull at frame level might be an option.

Beware that this analysis is implementation agnostic. Even in the case of modern multi-projection enabled GPUs (such as NVidia's Pascal-powered hardware) where the vertex shader (or geometry or tessellation shader) can project the geometry into multiple viewports with different projection matrices and viewport transforms (hence, NDC locations) in a single non-instanced geometry pass, there's still the potential benefit of performing per-display (viewport) culling in the shaders themselves.

It might also happen that in such a multi-projection-enabled GPU, the limited amount of available viewport/projections is already in use for other purposes, such as stereoscopic lens-matched shading (which consumes eight viewports), so we might need to still iterate and render to the displays one at a time.

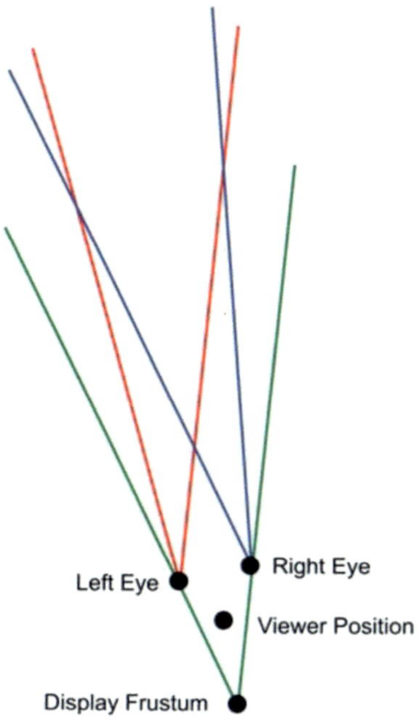

Figure 1.2. Combining left and right eyes frustums to create the Display frustum.

When it comes to combining display frustums to create a frame frustum, picking the correct clipping planes of each frustum gives a good solution.

When combining left- and right-eye projection frustums in order to generate a display frustum, a more elaborate technique is required. Something that works well is constructing a new frustum like this: the right plane of the new frustum will be constructed by taking the left eye's right-frustum plane and choosing a parallel plane that passes through the right eye's position. The left plane is constructed similarly, and the top and bottom planes can be picked from either eye, as shown in Figure 1.2.

Note that the combined frustum does not have its apex at or even near the average position of the eyes frustum's apices. Also, the near clipping plane of this frustum will need to be pushed forward to match the near clipping plane position of either eyes' frustum in order to perform efficient display-frustum culling.

1.2.4 Shader Uniforms per Context

At render time, the different shading stages will need to access data from the different contexts. For example, a tessellation shader might need to access the viewer position in order to choose the level of detail of a given mesh, which should not be computed based on an individual eyes position (as you would normally do). Conversely, the specular response of a material's surface should be computed based on the eye position for which we are rasterizing and not based on the viewer's (or camera's) position, as we would usually in a regular 3D engine (see Listing 1.2).

```
layout (row_major, binding=0) uniform FrameContext
{
    mat4x4      mLocation;
    mat4x4      mLocationInverse;
    vec3        mViewerPos;
    vec3        mViewerDir;
    float       mTime;
}frame;

layout (row_major, binding=1) uniform DisplayContext
{
    mat4x4      mLocation; // think modelview
    mat4x4      mLocationInverse;
    mat4x4      mProjection;
    mat4x4      mProjectionInverse;
    vec3        mPosition; // apex of the frustum
    vec2        mResolution;
}display;

layout (row_major, binding=2) uniform EyeContext
{
    mat4x4      mLocation; // think modelview
    mat4x4      mLocationInverse;
    mat4x4      mProjection;
    mat4x4      mProjectionInverse;
    vec3        mPosition; // apex of the frustum
}eye;
```

Listing 1.2. Shader uniforms grouped for virtual reality.

Please note again how the display and eye uniform blocks have both location and projection matrices which are different.

This data breakup works great conceptually. Conveniently, these three pieces of data can be updated at different time granularities (once per frame, per display, and per rendered eye).

However, for performance reasons, we'll shortly see that rendering the left and right eyes of a stereoscopic display is possible and recommended, so it makes sense to group the display and the two instances of the eye context together in practice to minimize the number of state changes in the renderer (see Listing 1.3).

```
layout (row_major, binding=0) uniform FrameContext
{
    mat4x4      mLocation;
    mat4x4      mLocationInverse;
    vec3        mViewerPos;
    vec3        mViewerDir;
    float       mTime;
}frame;

layout (row_major, binding=1) uniform DisplayContext
```

```
{
    mat4x4      mLocation; // think modelview
    mat4x4      mLocationInverse;
    mat4x4      mProjection;
    mat4x4      mProjectionInverse;
    struct
    {
        mat4x4      mLocation; // think modelview
        mat4x4      mLocationInverse;
        mat4x4      mProjection;
        mat4x4      mProjectionInverse;
        vec3        mPosition; // apex of the frustum
    }mEye[2];
    vec3        mPosition; // apex of the frustum
    vec2        mResolution;
}display;
```

Listing 1.3. Rendering-efficient shader uniform contexts.

1.2.5 Other Considerations

Before diving into efficient stereo rendering, we'd love to make the note that a VR-ready engine should respect a real physical scale for the scenes and objects in it. Make sure modellers are modelling and lighters are lighting your world using real units, otherwise the VR experience will be wrong. Hacking scene scales or eye-separation units will lead you and your team to an ugly, messy situation very quickly. For the same reason that ad-hoc shading models have been replaced by physically based shading and materials in many pipelines, you want your VR to be physically based, not random-scale-factors-based. When done properly, the size of objects in VR are unambiguously perceived as the correct size. If you currently don't, don't compensate with scale factors—go and fix your math or the assets.

1.3 Stereo Rendering

Within a given display, rendering in stereo is normally sped up by sharing the left- and right-eye rendering work to some degree. Different techniques achieve a greater or lesser degree of sharing when trying to render both eyes simultaneously, but in general they are all faster than rendering each eye separately.

At the most basic level, instead of rendering all the objects for the left eye and then all the objects for the right eye, one can iterate all the objects and render them twice sequentially, first for the left and then for the right eye. This reduces the number of state changes (texture, shader, and uniform bindings) to half, which is always good. In this case the rendering architecture is as given in Listing 1.4.

This requires allocating frame-buffer space for both left and right eyes, which can be expensive in some cases. For example, it is recommended to use 8X MSAA buffers for rendering in VR. Under these conditions, the cost of duplicating the depth and color buffers, or G-Buffer if in a deferred engine, can be too high.

```
ComputeFrame( k )
{
    DoProcessFrame( k );                   // Compute animation, sound,
                                           // LOD computation, simulations
    DoRenderFrame( k );                    // Render reflection maps, clouds layers,
                                           // global shadow maps

    for( int j=0; j<numDisplays; j++ )     // numDisplays = 5 for a CAVE, 1 for HMD
    {
        DoProcessDisplay( k, j );          // Do frustum culling, compile draw
                                           // indirect buffers

        DoRenderDisplay( k, j );           // Render eye-shared shadow maps,
                                           // and distant geometry

        DoRenderLeftAndRightEye( k, j );   // Stereo render regular geometry
                                           // with parallax and postpro
    }
}
```

Listing 1.4. Rendering architecture.

However, the efficiency gained by rendering left and right eyes at the same time is well worth the trouble if possible.

An even greater speed-up can be achieved by reducing the amount of draw calls as well. These days the standard way to do so is to use instancing in combination with multiple viewports or layered textures.

Using multiple viewports involves setting up a large texture that will hold both the left- and right-eye rendered content, with twice the size of the individual framebuffers, by calling `glTextureStorage2D` as usual for the color and depth (or G-buffer). Then the two viewports are prepared by using `glViewportIndexedf`, making each viewport occupy half the space reserved in the texture.

Another way to set up the framebuffers that is somewhat easier is by using layered textures. It involves creating only a single texture of the original resolution with two layers, one for each eye, by calling `glTextureStorage3D`.

Once the framebuffer is ready and multiple viewports have been set in the case of the non-layered framebuffer approach, the rendering happens by using the instancing-flavored version of the usual render commands, such as `glDrawElementsInstanced`. The point is to have the draw function called only once but set the invocation count to two, so that the graphics pipeline will be invoked twice for the whole piece of geometry. This alleviates the stress on the graphics driver, which no longer has to process the render call twice.

Then, in the shaders, the geometry must be routed to the left or right viewport or layer (depending on the choice made) for each one of the two instancing invocations. This can be done by using `gl_ViewportIndex` and `gl_Layer`, respectively, in the vertex, geometry or tessellation shader. Note that though this is primitive routing, which usually is done in the geometry or tessellation evaluator, it can still be done at vertex level in the vertex-shader stage as well, provided the extension GL_ARB_shader_viewport_layer_array is present in the system. The viewport or layer to which a triangle will be routed depends on the index set by the provoking vertex of the triangle, which is GL_LAST_VERTEX_CONVENTION by default.

This mechanism of using vertex shader-level routing and indexed viewports or using layered rendering has two benefits. First, the impact in the code is minimal, since there's no need to add geometry shaders to the system to do the routing. Second, we avoid using geometry shaders, which are not recommended because of their poor performance. Furthermore, since we are using viewport arrays or texture layers, we also do not need to set up custom clipping planes to prevent leaking pixels across eyes. Basically, the technique is very non-intrusive and trivial to implement without any serious modifications to the engine.

Since we already set up our uniform blocks to have all the display- and eye-context information ready, the only changes needed to make a regular shader work in stereo is the following:

```
// regular 3D rendering vertex shader:

vec3 worldPos = ;

gl_Position = display.mProjection *
              display.mLocation *
              vec4( worldPos, 1.0 );


// instanced stereo rendering vertex shader:

vec3 worldPos = ;

gl_ViewportIndex = gl_InstanceID;
gl_Position = display.mEye[gl_InstanceID].mProjection *
              display.mEye[gl_InstanceID].mLocation *
              vec4( worldPos, 1.0 );
```

Listing 1.5. Regular and stereo view vertex shader code.

Note again the lack of gl_ClipDistance[0] or any other hacks to deal with a single viewport and how minimal the change is. The geometry is still sent twice down the input assembler and vertex shader, but both state changes and render calls have been reduced to half.

If hardware instancing was already in use for fast rendering of object instances, then the number of instances to be submitted should be twice the original. In the shaders, dividing gl_InstanceID by two can be used to index into the correct instance data, such as object to world matrix and material information, and the last bit of the same built-in variable can be used to index into the correct viewport (Listing 1.6).

A similar option, which makes use of multiple viewports but does not require instancing, is to use viewport multicast, which is available through the NV_stereo_view_rendering and NV_viewport_array2 extensions. This method

```
// instanced stereo rendering of instanced objects, vertex shader:

int eyeID = gl_InstanceID & 1;
int insID = gl_InstanceID >> 1;

vec3 worldPos =  ; // use insID to index object to world matrix

gl_ViewportIndex = eyeID;
gl_Position = display.mEye[eyeID].mProjection *
              display.mEye[eyeID].mLocation *
              vec4( worldPos, 1.0 );
```

Listing 1.6. Eye selection using the instance ID.

processes the geometry only once, which makes it potentially faster than stereo instancing. By simply performing both left- and right-eye transformation in the vertex shader (or geometry or tessellation), one can avoid submitting the geometry twice. The left eye's clip-space coordinates are typically output to `gl_Position` as usual, and the right's eye coordinates to `gl_SecondaryPosition`. At the same time, `gl_ViewportMask[0]` and `gl_SecondaryViewportMask[]` must be used to route each polygon to the correct viewport (Listing 1.7).

```
// regular 3D rendering vertex shader:

vec3 worldPos =  ;

gl_Position = display.mProjection *
              display.mLocation *
              vec4( worldPos, 1.0 );


// stereo rendering vertex shader:

vec3 worldPos =  ;

gl_ViewportMask[0] = 1;
gl_Position = display.mEye[0].mProjection *
              display.mEye[0].mLocation *
              vec4( worldPos, 1.0 );

gl_SecondaryViewportMask[0] = 2;
gl_SecondaryPosition = display.mEye[1].mProjection *
                       display.mEye[1].mLocation *
                       vec4( worldPos, 1.0 );
```

Listing 1.7. Viewport multicasting.

1.4 Conclusion

Architecting a rendering engine to work in VR is not difficult, but needs some care from developers who are accustomed to traditional single-display monoscopic rendering. There no longer exists a single frame of reference or "context" that combines viewer position, display, and eye spaces. These three concepts are different and play different roles at different moments along the rendering process.

Rendering stereo can be done at less than twice the cost of a mono rendering if instancing and other techniques are used which can reduce the renderer's state changes, the number of draw calls, and the amount of geometry flowing down the shading pipeline.

V

2

Understanding, Measuring, and Analyzing VR Graphics Performance

James Hughes, Reza Nourai, and Ed Hutchins

Given the meteoric growth of virtual reality (VR), augmented reality (AR), and mixed reality (MR) applications, it is important for us as graphics programmers to understand the performance characteristics of these apps. Specifically, we want to understand how output is generated and displayed and how frames are timed. With those goals in mind, we can then understand how to better optimize our applications. This chapter aims to do just that, providing not only an explanation of how things work, but also how to measure and analyze VR application performance.

Given our backgrounds, we focus on freely available Windows tools. We sometimes describe these in the context of the Oculus Rift consumer VR device. However, the concepts and approaches are broadly applicable.

2.1 VR Graphics Overview

Let's start by defining a few terms used throughout this discussion.

- An application is a software client on the system. These are typically what we as developers write.
- A system service is a component that is running externally to our application. Normally a service is part of the OS or software runtimes we have installed. For example, the audio mixer on Windows is a system service that is part of the OS.
- A compositor service is any specific system service that arbitrates the display between the applications running on the system, potentially mixing their outputs into a single output to send to the display. An example is the

Desktop Window Manager (DWM) on Windows. In all cases of interest for this discussion, either the operating system or the VR runtime environment we are targeting provides this compositor service. This is not a component we typically write, but it's important to understand its function at a basic level.

- An HMD is a head-mounted display, the hardware that presents a stereo-pair of images to the user's eyes.
- The position sensor is comprised of one or more hardware components responsible for establishing the position of the user's HMD in the real world.
- A pose is the position and orientation of the HMD measured from the position sensors and possibly extrapolated to some future point in time.
- A frame is a single iteration of the application in order to update its output. Typically, each time a frame is run, the output of the application is updated. This is often in the form of an image containing the rendered results.
- VSync refers to the interval of time during which the display can select a new frame to output. In the original electron-beam based displays (cathode ray tubes or CRTs), this interval was used to return the electron beam to the start point of the display to begin scanning out the next frame's scanlines.
- Frame start is the time that the application starts processing a frame based on the latest pose. The synchronization of frame start may be optimized for the application by the compositor service.
- The display interval is the time that a particular frame's pixels are illuminated for viewing.
- Latency, in the context of this discussion, is the delay between drawing a frame and displaying it to the user. Unless otherwise clarified, this will be specifically the time from application frame start to the time when the pixels become visible to the user.

2.1.1 Background

In VR applications, too much latency can lead to user discomfort and break the immersive experience. Minimizing latency, and therefore increasing user comfort, is a major goal of most VR systems. The way frames are timed and produced in these systems is optimized around minimizing latency, which is somewhat different than how traditional graphics applications are tuned.

In a non-VR application, frames are produced at some frequency and displayed on a two-dimensional screen. On most modern operating systems, the frame produced is not displayed directly, but buffered to a system-wide compositor service such as the Desktop Window Manager (DWM) on Windows or SurfaceFlinger on Android. The compositor service then prepares a final frame for sending to the output display device, combining the output of one or more running applications. Typically, the compositor service produces frames for output at a frequency that matches the display's refresh rate. It is often a requirement that the frequency of display in the compositor is coupled only to the display refresh, not to the frequency at which multiple applications may be producing frames.

Let's look at the typical breakdown of a frame for traditional applications targeting a two-dimensional display, such as a monitor. First, the application starts executing logic on the CPU, and then eventually starts calling a graphics API such as DirectX or OpenGL. Once the application has either completed its calls to the graphics API or exceeded the buffering limit for driver commands, the workload is submitted to the OS kernel or graphics driver. This work eventually gets submitted to the GPU hardware, where it begins execution. The GPU processes these commands asynchronously to the CPU. While this is happening, the CPU is often able to continue on and start doing the work for the next frame.

Once the GPU work for the frame is complete, the system-wide compositing service is notified. On the next composition iteration, the updated output of this app is composed into the final frame buffer and submitted to the display controller for scanout. Some display systems have additional latency while output is transmitted over a physical link before it can be displayed to the user. This all adds up to substantial latency between the frame start and the time the

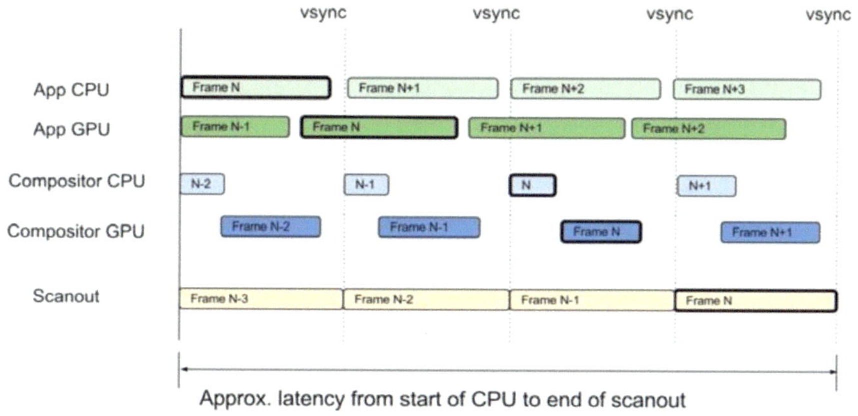

Figure 2.1. Example of traditional frame timing.

photons generated by that frame reach the user's eye (see Figure 2.1). Note the highlighted sequence that shows how Frame N gets from the CPU all the way to being scanned out.

In fact, applications often buffer multiple frames to the compositor service in order to smooth animation across variable workloads or OS interruptions. This adds additional latency. Some games incur additional latency even beyond that, if they decouple their simulation and rendering threads and let the simulation thread run ahead of the render thread. For example, both Unity and Unreal Engine do this.

What does all of this latency mean for VR? In a naive implementation (for example, a simple port of an existing 3D app), the position and orientation of the user's head is read at the frame start and an image is rendered based on that pose. That image is going to be sorely out of date by the time the user actually sees the pixels. Their actual head pose could have changed dramatically in that amount of time. This leads to swimmy, or laggy, visuals that can often make the user feel sick (https://en.wikipedia.org/wiki/Virtual_reality_sickness).

2.1.2 Pose Prediction

Virtually all VR libraries available today include the ability to predict the head pose at some specified point in the future. This increases comfort, because if you get an accurate prediction of where the user's head will be at the time you expect the pixel to illuminate, then you can render an image appropriate for that pose. However, since the head can change direction a lot in a relatively short period of time, prediction accuracy drops significantly as the time interval over which you are predicting increases. Predictions are generally pretty accurate for small intervals, on the order of five to ten milliseconds into the future. But the average error in the prediction, particularly in rotation, grows exponentially with interval length beyond that.

If the predicted pose matches the actual head pose when those pixels are displayed to the user, then the user does not perceive any latency. It does not mean the latency isn't there—it is. It still took some number of milliseconds between when the rendering occurred and the pixels were illuminated for the user. For a great VR experience, it is therefore critical to reduce the perceived latency as much as possible. This necessitates having great prediction algorithms and reducing the prediction intervals to improve accuracy.

For more information about prediction, please see the following blog post: http://ocul.us/2awPpcy.

2.1.3 The Modern VR Frame

One of the simplest improvements over typical frame timing for VR is to bypass the default operating system compositor service, and this is exactly what many of the current VR rendering systems on the market do. Technically, they still go

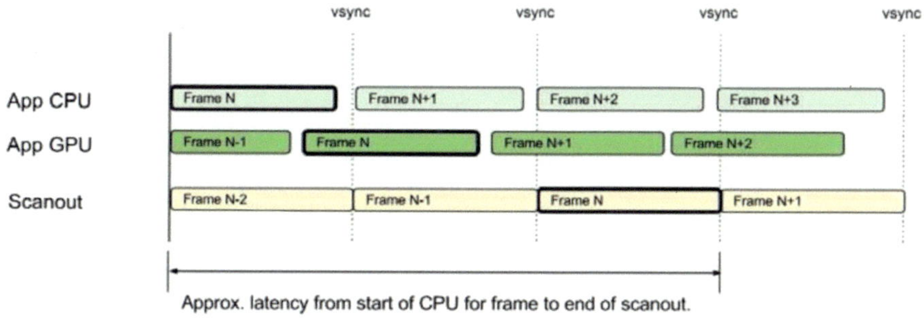

Figure 2.2. Removing the OS compositor.

through a separate composition pass, but it's their own highly tuned replacement for the OS default one. See Figure 2.2, which is a large improvement!

Looking closer at the diagram, we see that the total amount of time for both the app's CPU and GPU usage is greater than a single frame. This is quite common, and it is what allows applications to fully utilize the hardware available. However, for some trivial titles, it may be possible to fit both the CPU and GPU work into a single frame. This would allow you to complete the GPU work in the same frame as you started the CPU work, and scanout immediately on the next frame, reducing latency by another full frame. This is certainly possible, but does limit the utilization of the CPU and GPU resources, which is quite restricting to the application. Instead of making that scenario a special case, a couple of other techniques have been developed to help minimize the perceived latency.

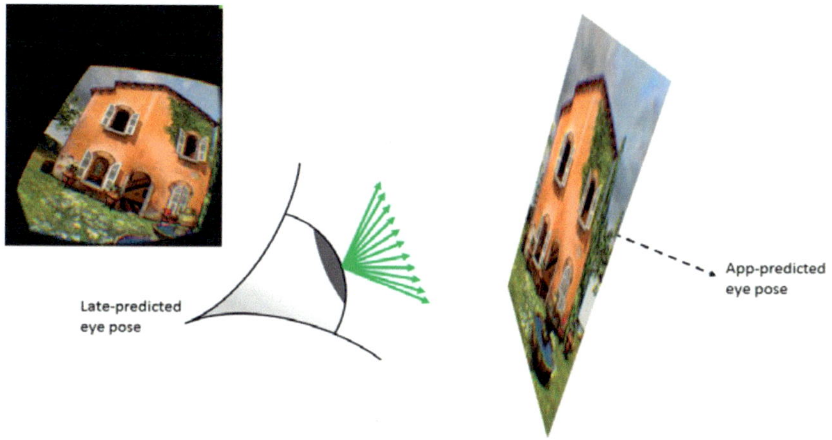

Figure 2.3. Actual vs predicted pose.

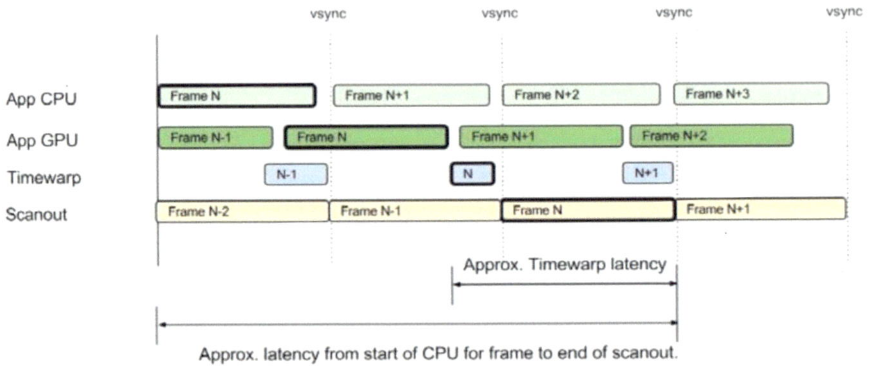

Figure 2.4. Timewarp.

The first of these is a reprojection technique called timewarp. Timewarp is a post-processing step that runs after the app's GPU work has completed. A new head-pose prediction is made for the same point in time for which the original was intended. Since this is happening much later, the accuracy of that prediction is much better than the original one. The difference of the two head-pose predictions is calculated and used to reproject or "warp" the original output from the application to a more accurate location so that it matches the user's head orientation more closely.

Figure 2.3 shows a particularly large change in actual versus predicted pose; in the typical case the change is small and there is a sufficient excess border around the rendered frame to hide the effect of the warping. Timewarp reduces perceived latency dramatically (see Figure 2.4).

For more information about Timewarp and how it can operate asynchronously, please see the following post on the Oculus developer blog: http://ocul.us/1TGXXtY.

Another technique for reducing latency is to delay the start of the CPU frame if the full time is not needed. Even if the full time is needed, the application can delay requesting the predicted pose until as late as possible. This can be done by the application or by the VR library being used. For example, the Oculus Rift PC SDK already manages and optimizes frame start times for the application, so no additional work is required. In the illustration in Figure 2.5, frame start is delayed by the SDK to allow a more accurate pose estimation based on the performance of prior frames:

This optimization of frame start times can work both ways. For example, it is not uncommon for the application to complete its CPU work while the GPU is still busy rendering the results. In this case the VR runtime can increase inter-frame parallelism by starting the CPU work for the next frame early, before the current frame has been displayed. Whether it is starting the work earlier, or

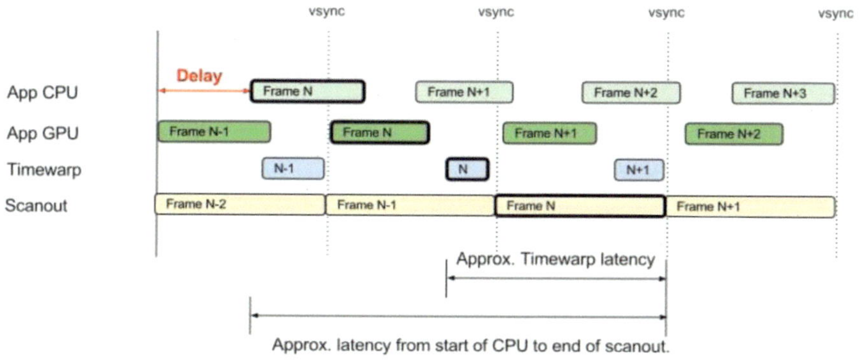

Figure 2.5. Delayed frame start.

later, carefully optimized frame starts are a key to reducing overall latency and improving prediction accuracy.

2.1.4 Optimizing Stereo Rendering

Current VR libraries expect the application to render two views, one for each eye. A naive implementation would just run the rendering code in the game or application twice, but this is the theoretical worst case for performance due to bandwidth duplication and poor cache utilization. These two views have many similarities that can be exploited, and many techniques and GPU features have been developed to help reduce the duplication of work. See Íñigo Quílez's article (Chapter 1 in this section) for a discussion of major methods. There are many other good resources available online for further reading.

2.2 Trace Collection

Understanding where an application's performance can potentially be improved requires the collection and analysis of data from typical use cases. In the past, rolling your own instrumentation or using any of the vendor-specific analysis tools worked well enough for 3D applications where the metric to be tuned was frame throughput. For VR applications, a whole-system approach is required due to the multi-process nature of frame composition and the increased emphasis on reducing latency.

High-end desktop VR is currently primarily a Microsoft Windows ecosystem phenomenon. Therefore, we will focus on Event Tracing for Windows (ETW), the primary system-level tracing mechanism for Windows. If you come from a Linux or Apple background, ETW is the rough equivalent of ptrace or dtrace. In addition, we will focus on the practical use of ETW as it relates to VR application analysis. We refer you to the literature (http://tinyurl.com/j9fohk3) for in-depth discussion of ETW itself. Finally, due to the authors' familiarity with the Oculus SDK, we will also focus on that particular vendor's support for ETW.

2.2.1 A Brief Description of ETW

ETW is a high-performance thread-safe structured logging mechanism that permits both kernel-level and per-process recording of events in an efficient binary (as opposed to textual) format. Events have a common header that identifies the event type, process and thread Id, timestamp, optional call stacks, and other common information. The optional payload can contain fixed or variable-sized binary-format primitives described using an XML-format manifest file that is also used to decode the collected trace data.

When tracing is disabled, the tracing code is skipped with an inline conditional, making the inclusion of instrumentation in released code practical. Traces can be written to a file or processed in real time, but be aware that the current implementation uses a fixed-size circular buffer and can drop events when the system is under heavy load. The trace will indicate dropped data if this occurs. In practice, ETW has proven to be quite robust when analyzing VR applications.

Instrumented code is identified as one or more ETW "providers" and has an associated globally unique name and GUID. Since ETW is a system-level tracing mechanism, external tooling typically is used to enable trace collection. In Microsoft's nomenclature, these apps are called "controllers," examples of which include LogMan, wevtutil, TraceLog and XPerf. These tools manage tracing sessions, which can remain active across multiple process invocations.

Finally, ETW analysis applications are referred to as "consumers," some examples of which include PerfView, Windows Performance Analyzer, and GPUView. We will focus on GPUView in this chapter since it provides the best view of the internal workings of GPUs and the graphics software stack.

2.2.2 Collecting ETW Traces

The Windows tool XPerf has a wrapper script called `log.cmd` that can be used to collect ETW traces suited for use with GPUView (https://msdn.microsoft.com/en-us/library/windows/desktop/jj585574.aspx). The Oculus SDK provides an enhanced version of this script named `ovrlog.cmd` under the `OculusSDK\Tools\ETW` directory of the Oculus SDK. In addition, there is an `ovrlog_win10.cmd` for Win10 users, and an `install.cmd` for installing Oculus-specific ETW manifests. Installation of the manifests is required in order to enable ETW consumers to parse the binary-format event payloads. Installed manifests will persist in the system once installed until explicitly removed or updated with newer versions.

Assuming you've installed the Oculus SDK, open an Administrator shell and change directory to the SDK's `Tools\ETW` directory. In this directory you should see the following:

```
EventsForStackTrace.txt
LibOVREvents.man
OVRUSBVidEvents.man
install.cmd
ovrlog.cmd
ovrlog_win10.cmd
```

The `EventsForStackTrace.txt` file is used by XPerf to annotate certain ETW events with full stack traces. The `.man` files are the ETW manifests that describe the providers and custom payloads for the Oculus SDK. The `install.cmd` script will install these manifests into the system so that Oculus providers can be properly enumerated and so that recorded SDK events will be parsed correctly by tools such as GPUView. Run the `install.cmd` script from an Administrator console and verify that it has installed the manifests correctly. Note that one failure mode that is difficult to diagnose is having a mismatch between runtime and installed manifests; when in doubt re-run `install.cmd`.

You should now be able to run the appropriate `ovrlog.cmd` or `ovrlog_win10.cmd` to start collecting an ETW trace. After running the application or applications to be traced and performing whatever actions you are interested in analyzing, run the same command with the argument "stop" to stop tracing. Note that running the command again with no arguments from the same command prompt will also stop tracing, much like the original Microsoft `log.cmd`. However, this method is more failure-prone due to its reliance on environment variable settings.

2.2.3 GPUView

While there are a number of tools that consume ETW traces and provide graphing and event-search features, the most useful of these tools for VR purposes is Microsoft's GPUView.

GPUView provides an interactive graphical view of an ETW trace, with an emphasis on GPU and CPU utilization. It displays per-packet and per-thread details for these key resources along with per-process breakdowns. These views allow you to visually trace the impact of a process' actions on the system as a whole. Arbitrary events can be filtered for and displayed as time markers on the utilization graphs, allowing accurate measurement of time deltas between events.

An in-depth introduction to using GPUView is beyond the scope of this article (see https://graphics.stanford.edu/~mdfisher/GPUView.html). However, we will show how to identify an HMD's VSync, which can be somewhat tricky. This example will assume you've captured a trace of an active VR application and loaded it into GPUView.

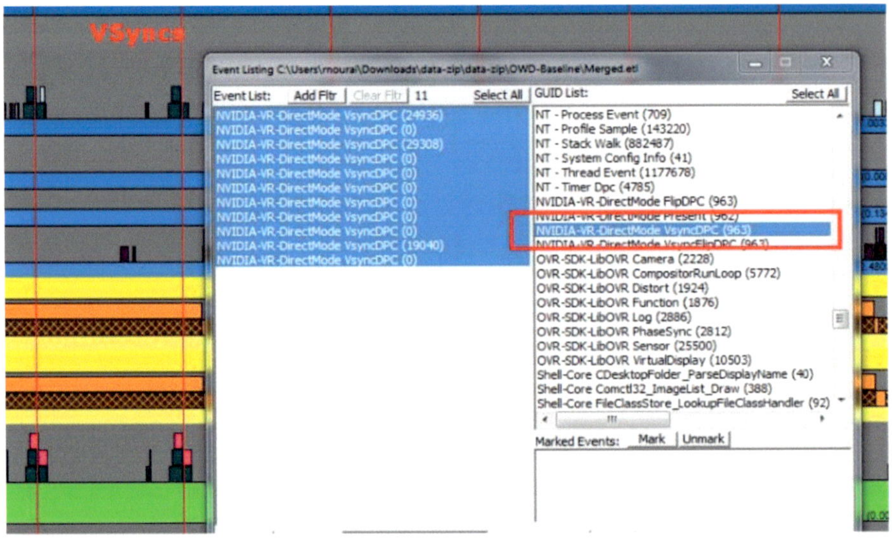

Figure 2.6. VSync event list.

Identifying VSync. GPUView has built-in support for displaying vertical sync information when the Windows OS is aware of the display. As of the time this chapter was written, HMD support is implemented by the GPU vendors in a way that hides their display from the OS in order to prevent the OS from using the HMD as part of the desktop. This means that traces gathered on these systems won't have VSync information available. As Windows improves native support for HMDs, this limitation will disappear and the standard GPUView VSync display information should work.

The good news is that, in the meantime, GPU vendors have instrumented the HMD's vertical sync to enable performance analysis. To view the information, you'll need an ETW manifest from the GPU vendor. AMD deploys the manifest as part of their typical driver install. NVIDIA provides theirs only with their GameWorks VR SDK.

Once installed, both GPU vendors provide VSync events in the event list. Figure 2.6 shows an example using an NVIDIA GPU.

2.2.4 Adding Custom Tracing Events

In some cases, additional visibility into the internal workings of your application would be very helpful when combined with the rest of the ETW data being collected. The Oculus SDK provides `ovr_TraceMessage()`, which can be used to trace string messages as ETW events. In cases where structured events are desired it is also possible to add your own custom provider to your application.

While ETW is powerful, it unfortunately suffers from a cumbersome API that makes adding ETW tracing support to your application fairly difficult (https://mollyrocket.com/casey/stream_0029.html). We'll briefly sketch what needs to be done in order to accomplish this.

The first step is to create a manifest. Look for `ecmangen.exe` under `Windows\Kits` and launch it. Try loading the `LibOVREvents.man` file and examine how the different categories are utilized. Hitting F1 to open the help page is a good idea at this point. Create a new manifest and try adding the application tasks you wish to trace (e.g., loading, rendering, AI, etc.) and templates for any custom data structures. Then try adding events corresponding to specific points in your code you wish to trace.

Once you save the manifest, you'll need to compile it using the message compiler `mc.exe` found under the top-level `Windows\Kits` directory. For a detailed description and example C++ code see https://blogs.msdn.microsoft.com/seealso/2011/06/08/use-this-not-this-logging-event-tracing/. Once successfully compiled, you will have a generated C++ header file that you can include in your application's source, as well as resources to add to your project.

Once your source is instrumented and compiled, you will need to install the manifest you've created. See the Oculus SDK's `install.cmd` as an example of how to do this. After installation, the command "wevtutil ep" should show your provider as available in your system. Add your provider's GUID and appropriate start and stop commands to a local copy of `ovrlog.cmd`, then start tracing, run your application, and stop tracing. If all has gone well, at this point you should be able to see your custom events in GPUView's event viewer.

2.3 Analyzing Traces

Now that we've seen how to capture and look at traces, it's time for deeper investigation. We will cover examples demonstrating the lifecycle of a VR frame to better understand the effects of CPU and GPU constraints. Analyzing the behavior of a number of different applications will allow us to decode the interaction between the application and runtime and identify potential problems. We'll conclude by discussing common pitfalls and possible tradeoffs.

2.3.1 Let's Baseline

Let's work towards understanding a frame in VR. Ideally, an application exploits the asynchronous nature of the GPU by beginning the next frame on the CPU before the prior frame finishes. Nowadays this staggering of the CPU work relative to the GPU work is optimized by the SDK's frame start API. We'll assume this is happening for this example. Let's begin by taking a look at a well-behaved VR frame's lifetime.

We start by selecting a VSync and working backwards through the lifecycle of a frame. Once the VSync is selected, we determine what application GPU

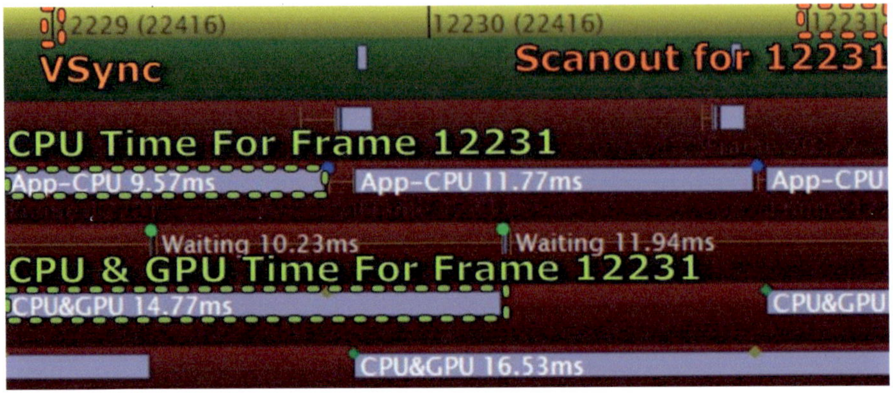

Figure 2.7. Conceptual view.

work was scanned out at the VSync and when that GPU work was scheduled. In Figure 2.7, the topmost diagram depicts the high-level concept of a real-world frame—the conceptual view. You'll see an actual GPUView trace of the application in Figure 2.8. In both diagrams, application-specific annotations are green while VR runtime or system specific annotations are orange.

In these two figure, we've chosen the VSync at which frame 12231 started scanning out. Both the conceptual view and GPUView traces in this section follow the lifecycle of this frame, but you could just as easily follow along in GPUView using some of your own data.

We'll begin with the high level conceptual view of the frame we intend to cover. In the conceptual view, finding the CPU work for our frame is straightforward: "CPU Time For Frame 12231" (App-CPU) and "CPU & GPU Time For Frame 12231" (CPU & GPU). "CPU Time" represents only the time spent by the application on the CPU, while "CPU & GPU Time" represents the time from the beginning of CPU work to when the application's GPU work finished. These conceptual regions align directly with the GPUView trace below.

In the GPUView trace in Figure 2.8, you'll notice the beginning of application CPU work denoted by "App CPU Begin" and the end of GPU work specified by "App GPU End." The VSyncs are clearly marked in both figures.

Using GPUView we want to deduce what CPU work interval led to the frame that was scanned out. Since we have already chosen a VSync in GPUView, look at the "LibOVR-Log - App EndFrame" event directly before this VSync. This event is denoted by "End Frame Timing." Figure 2.9 is a screenshot of the events dialog in GPUView showing the "End frame app timing" event selected. Find the "FrameIndex" data within this event since that contains which application frame index was scanned out at our target VSync. In this case "FrameIndex" contains 12231. This tells us the frame index we want to look for in the events that tell us the bounds of our CPU work.

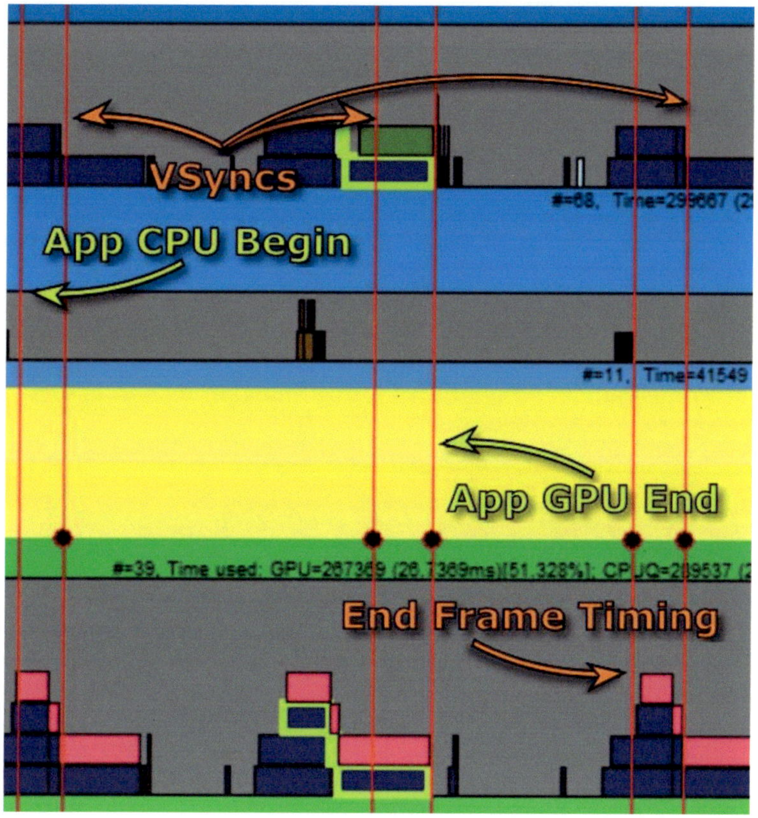

Figure 2.8. GPUView trace.

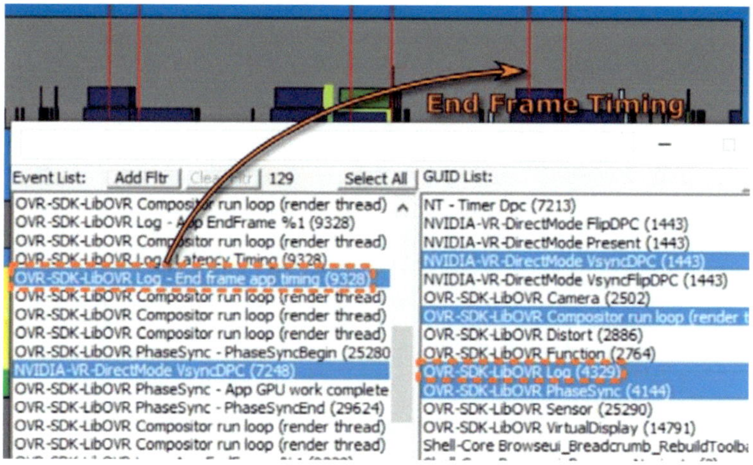

Figure 2.9. Events dialog in GPUView.

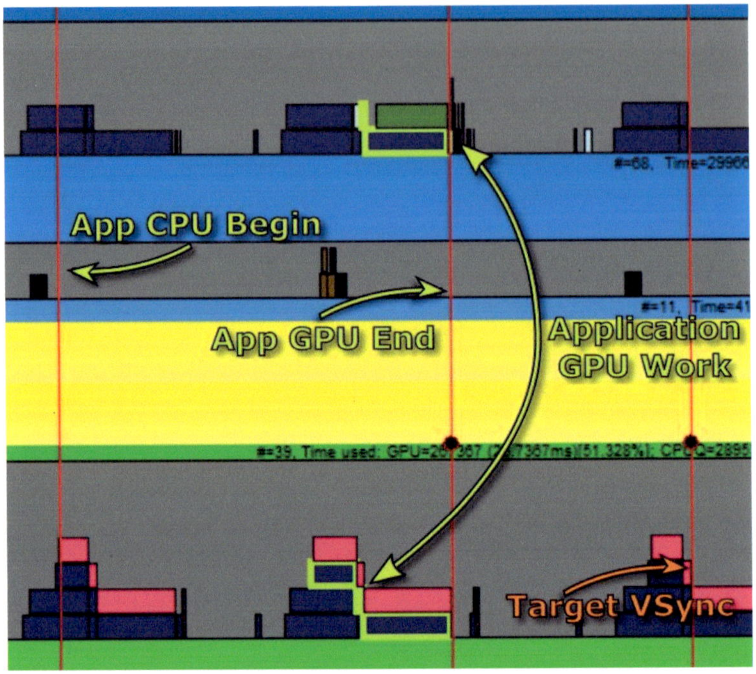

Figure 2.10. Example for frame 12231.

Find the "LibOVR-Phasesync – PhaseSyncEnd" event and match our frame index with the "FrameIndex" event data as before. It should occur within one VSync interval before our target VSync; an example for frame 12231 is given in Figure 2.10.

Now that we know the appropriate PhaseSyncEnd event we can easily identify when the CPU work began for the application: look for the corresponding

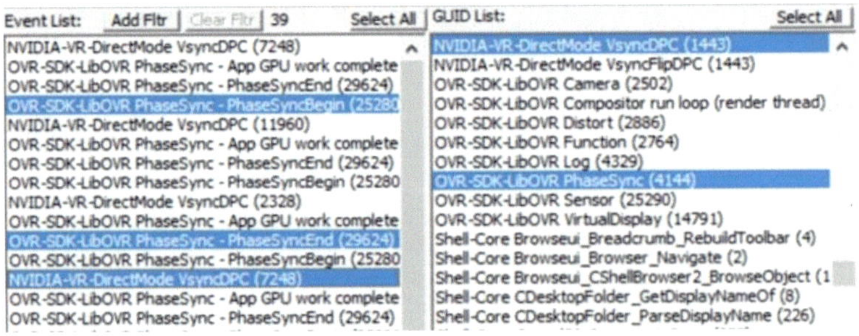

Figure 2.11. The events bounding the application's CPU work.

PhaseSyncBegin event. These two events bound the application's CPU work as depicted in Figure 2.11

Though these two events bound the application's CPU work, the PhaseSyncEnd event represents when the application GPU work ended, not when its CPU work finished. The PhaseSyncBegin event, on the other hand, truly demarcates when the application began CPU work.

Note the "Application GPU Work" in Figure 2.10. The selected regions depict the execution of the application's GPU work on hardware and the device context queue. Application GPU work will always finish directly before the PhaseSyncEnd event. This figure closely matches the intervals in the conceptual view of frame 12231. The time between the "App CPU Begin" and "App GPU End" markers are representative of the "CPU & GPU Time For Frame 12231" interval in the conceptual view.

Knowing the PhaseSync events, the end-frame timing event, and a target VSync, you will be able to follow the lifecycle of any VR frame as outlined above. If you run into performance issues, this is a good place to start diagnosing the problem.

You can find the compositor GPU distortion work for the frame presented at the VSync. The conceptual view (Figure 2.12) shows this work in the green "Compositor GPU" section directly below the VSync markers. In GPUView (Figure 2.13), look for GPU packets directly before VSync that correspond to the process of the compositor (`OVRServer.exe` in the case of Oculus' runtime). Click on one of the packets in the hardware queue, and you'll be able to locate the corresponding process and CPU thread responsible for generating the GPU work. It is helpful to collapse all other processes' graphs and explicitly open only the CPU graphs for your application and `OVRServer.exe` to make this more obvious.

Once you've identified these major parts of a frame's anatomy you're well on the way to diagnosing the different possible failure modes of a misbehaving VR application!

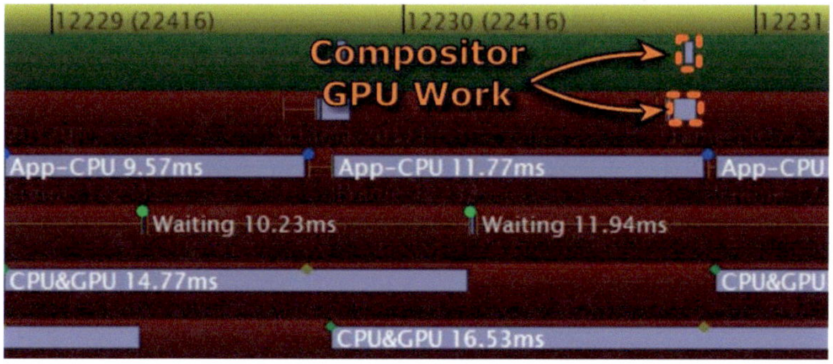

Figure 2.12. Conceptual view.

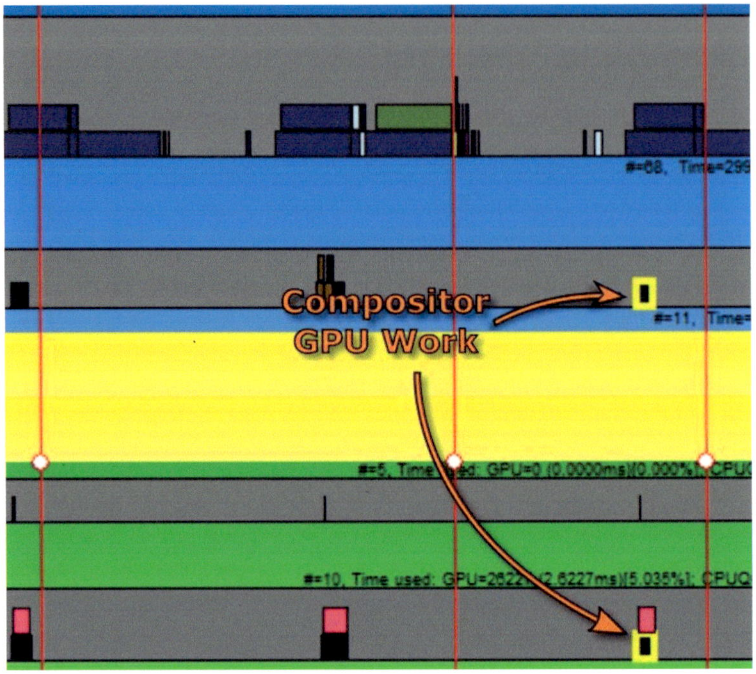

Figure 2.13. GPUView.

2.3.2 Lost App Frames

Now that we understand the lifecycle of a VR frame, let's look at problematic applications for additional perspective. In Figure 2.14, you'll see the lifecycle of frame 3744 where the application is under high GPU (and CPU) load.

Each pair of yellow boxes on the conceptual diagram (top) means the compositor flagged the application as missing a frame. In this case, frame 3743 was scanned out twice before the application was able to submit the next frame to the VR runtime. The runtime compensates for the missed frame by re-timewarping frame 3743 to correctly display it with the most recently available HMD pose.

In both the conceptual and GPUView diagrams (bottom), the "App CPU Begin" to "App GPU End" exceeds two VSync intervals, indicating the application has missed a frame. The application's CPU alone takes 16 milliseconds to complete, which means we can't meet the 11 millisecond (90Hz) refresh rate of the HMD. If we inspect the GPU work for the application, we also note that the total GPU work is roughly 20 milliseconds. So, while we take a combined time of 27 milliseconds to generate two frames in VR, more than twice the refresh rate of the device, we still only miss one frame every other VSync. This is due to starting the next frame before the GPU work for the prior frame completes.

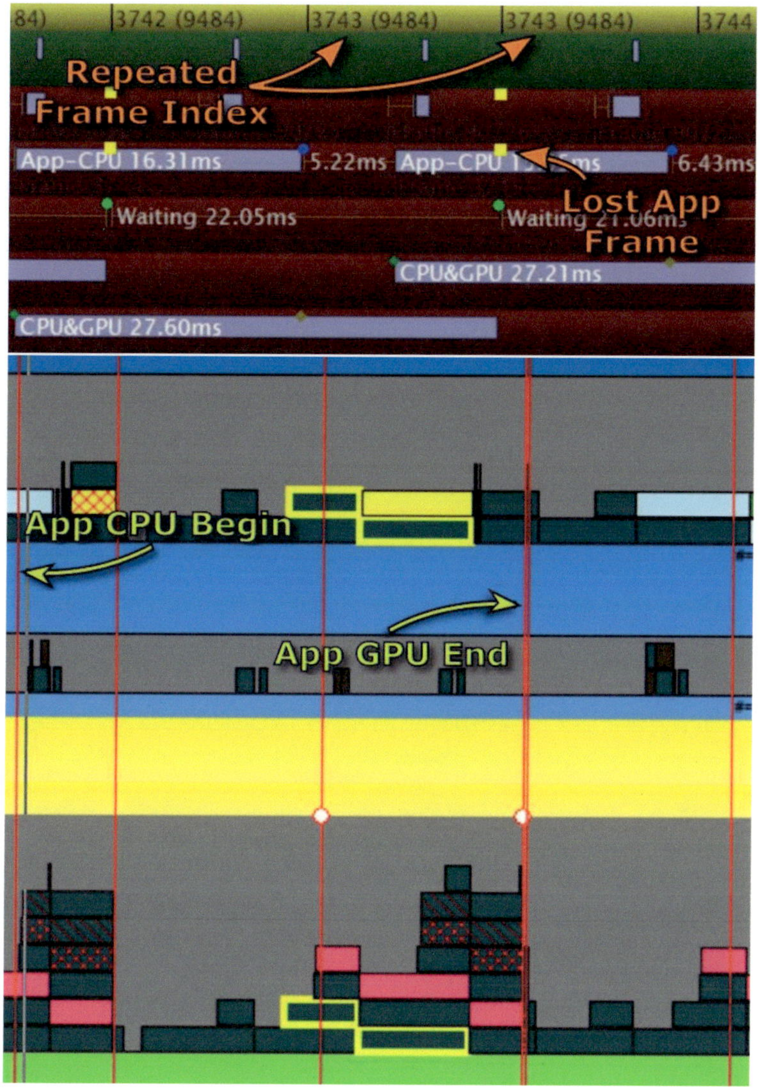

Figure 2.14. Lifecycle of frame 3744.

This staggering of frames 3744 and 3745 is easier to see in the conceptual view. In this case, the second frame begins work six milliseconds before the GPU work of the last frame completes, saving us from dropping two application frames in a row. In GPUView you can see this overlap between disjoint pairs of "PhaseSync Begin" and "PhaseSync End" events.

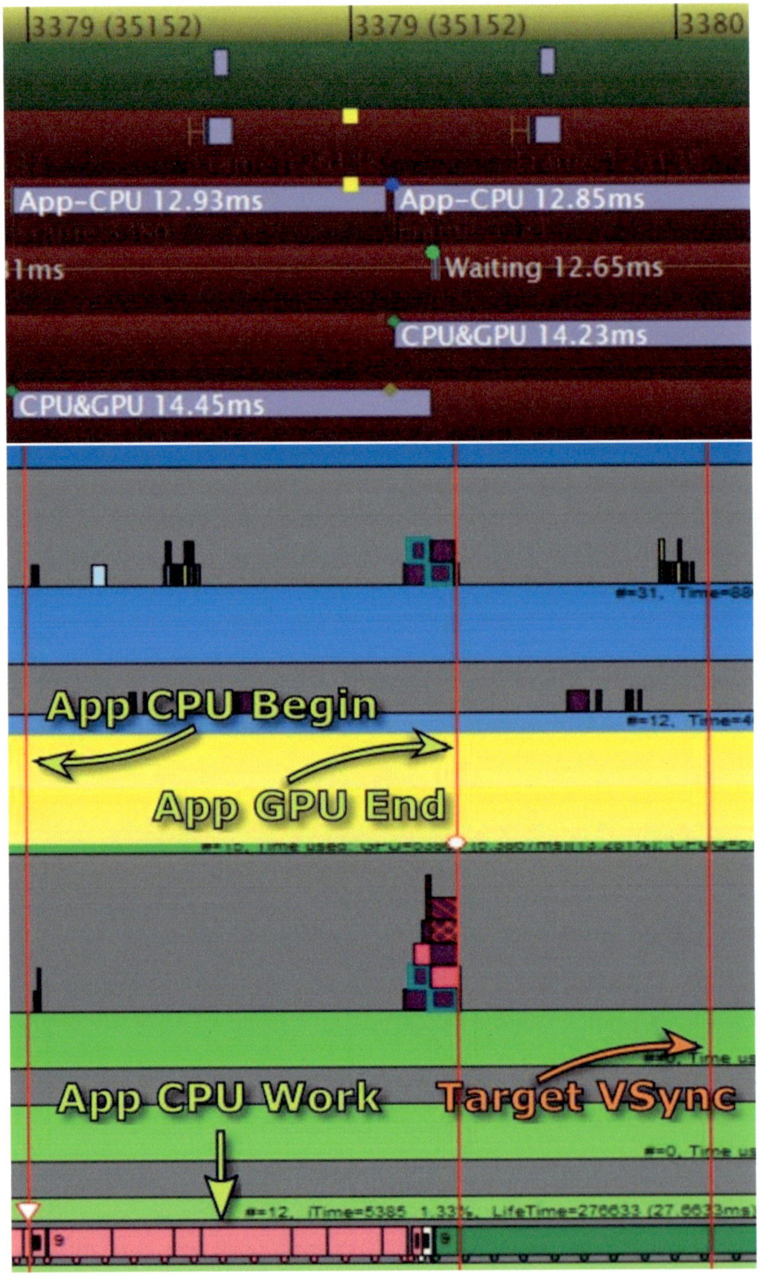

Figure 2.15. High CPU load.

2.3.3 High CPU Load

Moving on to a purely CPU-bound application, we'll find that there's not much the runtime can do to help with parallelism.

This application's CPU load (see Figure 2.15) is high relative to the amount of GPU work it performs. This is easy to see in GPUView (bottom image), as the hardware queue remains empty for nearly the entire frame. Worse yet, the frame CPU time of 12.85 milliseconds is longer than a frame interval. As such, the runtime is unable to compensate, and we see an application lost frame in the form of a re-timewarp of frame 3379. These sorts of failures are a strong indication that attempting to exploit further CPU parallelism and advancing the start of GPU work will benefit your application.

One Sundance Film Festival virtual reality experience utilized high-priority multi-threaded CPU video decoding. The total CPU load was sufficient to starve the VR compositor, causing lost frames. Switching to a different GPU-based decoding library and reducing the CPU thread priorities resulted in a flawless VR experience.

2.3.4 Lost Compositor Frames

In some cases the VR compositor may be the source of a missed frame. These cases are particularly bad since they result in judder perceived by the user. There's not much an application developer can do to prevent compositor lost frames, but it is useful to understand what these traces look like (see Figure 2.16).

In this case the distortion GPU-work for frame 21729 took too long to complete. As a result, the compositor missed VSync and was unable to present a frame on the device. In the conceptual view (top of figure), you see this manifest as no compositor GPU work following the missed VSync. In GPUView (bottom of figure), the GPU work that was unable to finish in time is highlighted and its work ends right against VSync, yielding no time to present the results. If this failure mode occurs frequently with your application or certain hardware configurations, consider reaching out to your VR SDK vendor.

In our experience, these sorts of reports have sometimes uncovered edge cases in the VR compositor. For example, one constructive solid geometry ray-tracing application was generating primitives that proved difficult to preempt, requiring collaboration with GPU hardware vendors to improve their preemption performance.

2.3.5 GPU Resource Contention

Since the GPU normally works on tasks asynchronously after the CPU is done submitting, there arise scenarios where the CPU would like to access the resource again but the GPU is not done with it. In these cases, contention often leads

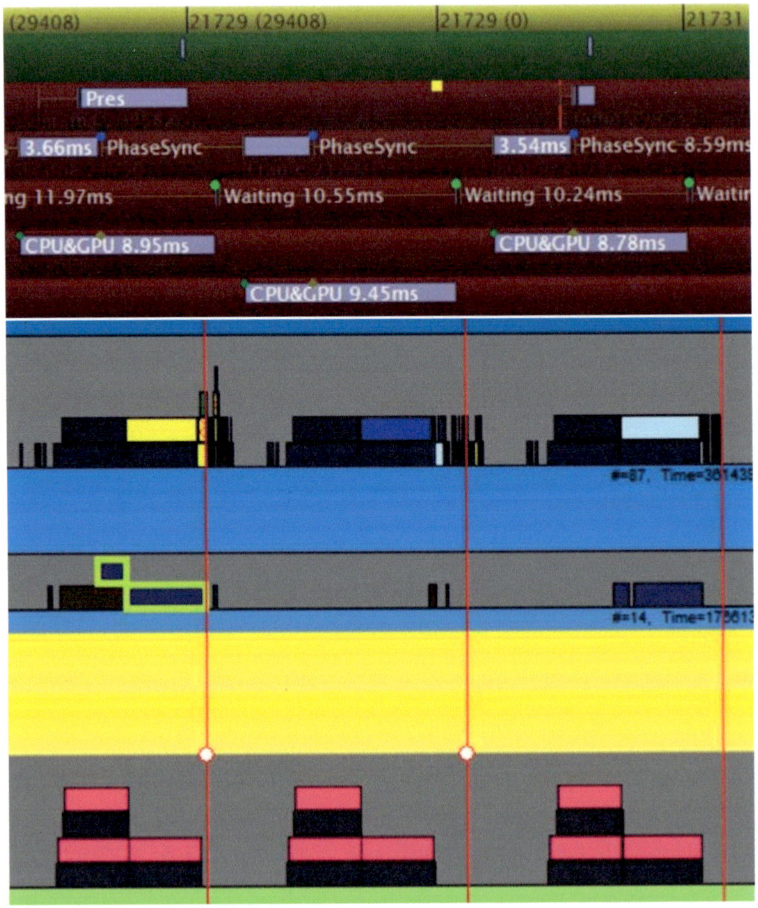

Figure 2.16. Lost compositor frames.

to the CPU stalling until the GPU work completes and no longer requires the resource. Some common examples of this are explored in the following sections.

Driver resource renaming. Prior to D3D12 and Vulkan, older graphics APIs normally did a bunch of work in the driver to assist applications with common use cases. One of the most common use cases is something called driver resource renaming. When an application wants to update a resource with new data from the CPU, it requires either gaining access to a pointer to the resource, or providing an application pointer to be copied to that resource. However, the GPU may still have work pending that depends on the existing data in the resource. In that case, the driver often creates a new copy of the resource (or, more practically, keeps a circular buffer of copies of that resource) and provides that new pointer to the application. In this way, the application updates this new instance, while the GPU is still referencing the old reference. Using the same constant buffer to feed world transforms to all draw calls might trigger this case, for example.

Once the GPU has completed using the previous copy, it is released back to the driver and reclaimed, to be used again. This trick is called "resource renaming." Drivers have limits on how much memory they set aside for renaming. When this limit is reached, the driver blocks in the call until the GPU has released and reclaimed some of the existing instances. This stall can cause dropped frames and jumps in the frame rate.

In VR applications, it can be tempting to reuse the same buffers between left and right eyes when doing stereo rendering. Be aware that this will generate twice as many updates to the resource in a single frame and can push you into the resource-renaming failure mode twice as soon as a typical application. In general, reuse of non-trivial buffers multiple times in a frame should be avoided to help prevent running into resource-renaming limits. For VR, in particular, it is good practice to use unique buffers for the left and right eye if sufficient memory is available.

As a concrete example, let's walk through a case where the application has a single constant buffer used to transfer constants (or uniforms) to the GPU for several different draw calls. Since the CPU work for the render thread is often ahead of the GPU work, when the app maps the constant buffer a second time to put in new values, it will trigger resource renaming.

With each additional mapping of that buffer to write new values, new copies are being created in the driver. Finally, when the GPU catches up a frame or two later (depending on how deep the rendering queue is) and those values are read from the older copies of the resource, the memory is again made available. Since rendering left and right eyes can double the draw calls in a naive implementation, you now have twice as many renames of the same buffer and, hence, are more likely to stall the CPU.

We ran into a particularly nasty example of this in a popular game engine right before a major trade show. A small dynamically-updated vertex buffer was causing many demos to drop a frame approximately once per second. Upon debugging with GPUView, we found that resource renaming was the culprit. Some heroic last-minute hex-editing of the binaries to enlarge the buffer swept the issue under the rug and saved our bacon at that show.

The new low-level graphics APIs such as Vulkan or D3D12 have eliminated driver renaming, making the tradeoff between buffer duplication and explicit synchronization visible to your application. One simple trick to avoid this particular pitfall on low level APIs is to avoid reusing the same constant buffer multiple times in a frame. Instead, create a unique buffer for each use. Leverage this to create your own circular buffer of resources to avoid stomping over in-use resources or causing stalls.

Mapping an in-use resource. Mapping a resource for CPU access can cause stalls in other scenarios as well. Consider the case where there are pending GPU writes to a buffer and the CPU would like to read from that resource by mapping a pointer to it. In this case, the CPU would not be able to read the latest data unless the GPU has completed the writes, which requires waiting for the GPU work to complete. Similarly, a stall can occur if the CPU attempts to map a surface for writing but the GPU is still reading from it. In these cases, advanced techniques such mapping the region no overwrite (which is an implicit promise from the app to the driver that it will take care not to write to portions being access by the GPU) may allow the driver to skip synchronization.

GPU preemption. In cases where the VR compositor is the cause of missed frames, one thing to consider is the possibility that the final GPU work is difficult to preempt. You can spot this in GPUView as a GPU packet spanning the period where the VR compositor should be running. This can arise when large full-screen quads are being rendered at the end of the scene for deferred rendering or post-processing steps. If you suspect this might be the case, experiment with dicing these large primitives into tiles to see if that improves compositor performance. Note that larger triangles may improve performance of your app itself, but if that is producing a workload that is difficult for your GPU to preempt, it can have detrimental effects on the overall VR experience.

2.4 The Big Picture

If there are only four things you remember after reading this chapter, they should be the following:

- Keep your CPU and GPU work per frame each under a single frame interval. Neither the CPU nor GPU work can individually exceed the frame interval;
- Keep the total time from the start of the CPU to the end of the GPU work under two frame intervals in total;
- Look for and avoid common resource contention cases that can cause stalls in the pipeline;
- Ensure no single draw call from the application is too expensive. For example, consider tiling full-screen passes if they appear to be causing problems with the performance of the compositor. Be sure to test your assumptions on hardware from all of the vendors your customers are likely to be using.

We hope that this introduction to VR performance analysis has given you a solid foundation on which to build a deeper understanding of the VR pipeline. Taking the time to learn the tools and examine collected traces will yield more comfortable and compelling VR experiences.

VI Compute

Exposing the compute capabilities of modern GPUs through APIs allows us to rethink techniques that use data sets tailored to GPUs.

The first chapter "Optimizing the Graphics Pipeline with Compute" by Graham Wihlidal outlines the basic principles on how to architect next-generation engines. It describes how to cull triangle clusters and how to filter single triangles to offload these tasks from the GPU.

Tests in combination with a visibility-buffer–based rendering system showed impressive performance improvements due to the GPU not having to deal with invisible or too small triangles.

The second chapter "Real Time Markov Decision Processes for Crowd Simulation" by Sergio Ruiz and Benjamin Hernandez covers a crowd-simulation algorithm running on the GPU for procedurally generated levels, and / or dynamically changing levels. Generating the simulation data happens over the time span of several frames. Currently the system only supports planes. Additional floors are not covered but might be added by layering data.

—Wolfgang Engel

VI

1

Optimizing the Graphics Pipeline with Compute

Graham Wihlidal

1.1 Overview

Modern graphics cards have a large amount of generic and flexible computational power. However, regular rasterization-based rendering pipelines still require the usage of fixed function hardware in order to be efficient enough for real time. Due to the design constraints of fixed function hardware, numerous bottlenecks and limitations are present which hurt throughput. Often, when the fixed function units are active, there are inactive compute resources sitting idle. By scheduling compute units in parallel alongside the graphics units, we can optimize the overall pipeline, and ensure we are utilizing all the available hardware resources at any given time.

The initial version of this technology was aimed at current consoles and high end AMD PCs. As such, the optimizations and algorithms discussed are specific to AMD Graphics Core Next hardware (Figure 1.1) [Mah 2013].

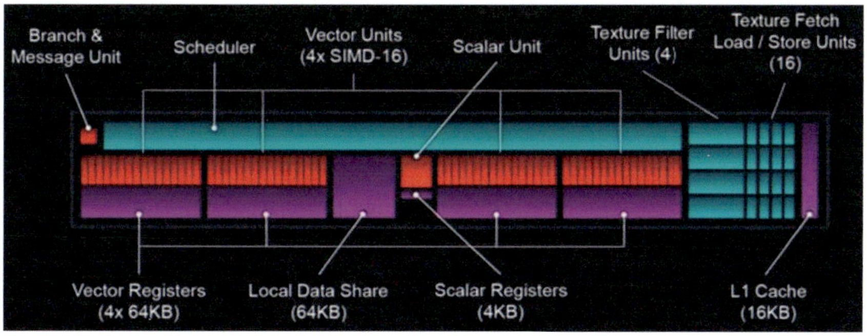

Figure 1.1. Diagram of an AMD GCN Compute Unit.

VGT	Vertex Grouper Tessellator
PA	Primitive Assembly
CP	Command Processor
IA	Input Assembly
SE	Shader Engine
CU	Compute Unit
LDS	Local Data Share
HTILE	Hierarchical Z with Compression
GCN	Graphics Core Next
SGPR	Scalar General-Purpose Register
VGPR	Vector General-Purpose Register
ALU	Arithmetic Logic Unit
SPI	Shader Processor Interpolator

Table 1.1. AMD Graphics Core Next acronyms.

The definitions in Table 1.1 map to GCN hardware concepts, and are used throughout this chapter.

1.2 Introduction

While optimizing *Dragon Age*™: *Inquisition* (Figure 1.2), it was clear that displacement mapping was performing poorly on AMD hardware. Despite small improvements to the shaders to reduce LDS usage, it was obvious that performance was at the mercy of various bottlenecks. Experiments were done to offload

Figure 1.2. Screenshot of *Dragon Age*™: *Inquisition*.

Figure 1.3. Early triangle and patch-culling prototype.

the hull-shader adaptive tessellation factor calculations to a compute shader, and read the results back within the hull shader. This prototype was quite successful, and included interesting approaches like HTILE sourced Hi-Z culling of the triangle patches.

This then led to building a new prototype for regular triangle and patch culling, as a spiritual successor to LibEdge on PlayStation® 3 (shown in Figure 1.3). This prototype was interesting; some scenes would be a win, and some would be a complete loss. By toying around with various GCN instructions, memory optimizations, and asynchronous compute, scenes were found which showed a significant win using compute-based triangle culling. These results motivated further extensive research and development into using the compute resources to supplement and optimize the fixed-function graphics pipeline and the integration of the technology into the cutting-edge Frostbite™engine.

Engines typically use various methods for coarse culling on the CPU, prior to GPU submission. Due to latency between the CPU and GPU, many optimizations are inappropriate, or it would mean tight lock stepping. The CPU is a limited resource on consoles, and this is not a great use of a CPU core. On a PC, you have to get the data over the PCIE bus which would be prohibitive. Because of this limitation, it is ideal to have the culling happen on the GPU's timeline, so the solution is to do GPGPU submission.

Depth-aware culling can be performed, such as tightening shadow bounds or sample distribution shadow maps [Lauritzen et al. 2010]. Additionally, shadow casters without contribution, or hidden objects in the color pass, can be removed.

VR late-latch culling can also be performed by having the CPU submit a conservative frustum and having the GPU handle refinement. The idea of performing triangle and cluster culling on the GPU is covered in detail in this chapter.

Compute-shader mesh processing opens up additional opportunities for more efficiently supporting a variety of high-fidelity features and improvements, such as:

- offload tessellation hull-shader work;
- offload entire tessellation pipeline [Brainerd 2014];
- procedural vertex animation (wind, cloth, etc.);
- reusing results between multiple passes and frames;
- bounding volume generation;
- pre-skinning;
- generating GPU work from the GPU;
- scene and visibility determination.

Better yet, by reusing post-shader results between multiple passes, and doing less draw setup work on the CPU, there is increased optimization potential. The GPU performs primitive assembly after the execution of multiple shader stages, so useless primitives will waste a lot of shader processing power. Reusing post-cull results between multiple passes will provide the GPU with the minimum amount of vertex data, resulting in performance amplification.

The mantra is to treat all draws as regular data. The data can be pre-built, cached and reused, and generated on the GPU. This approach offers increased flexibility, including the ability to work around various fixed function bottlenecks.

1.3 Motivation

Both Xbox One and the standard—as well as the PlayStation 4 Pro—have four shader engines, so a total of four triangles per clock.

By multiplying the number of compute units (CUs) by the number of VALUs per CU, and multiplying that value by two floating-point operations (FLOPS)—since one CU can execute 64 FMA in one cycle—we get the number of FLOPS that can be executed per cycle. There is a technical caveat to mention with this math. There are actually 4× as many waves running, but each VALU takes four clocks, so those two factors of four cancel out (see Table 1.2).

By taking the number of FLOPS that can be executed per cycle, and dividing that by the number of available shader engines, the result is the number of FLOPS that can be executed per triangle, shown in Table 1.3.

Finally, by dividing the number of FLOPS per triangle by the number of FLOPS per ALU, the result (shown in Table 1.4) is the final instruction upper-limit that is available for compute triangle culling, which still beats the fixed-function primitive setup and scan converter. Because of latency hiding, this is

Xbox One	12 CU * 64 ALU * 2 FLOPs **1,536** FLOPS / cy
PS4 Std	18 CU * 64 ALU * 2 FLOPs **2,304** FLOPS / cy
PS4 Pro	36 CU * 64 ALU * 2 FLOPs **4,608** FLOPS / cy
Fury X	64 CU * 64 ALU * 2 FLOPs **8,192** FLOPS / cy

Table 1.2. Number of FLOPs executed per cycle.

Xbox One	1,536 FLOPS / 2 shader engines **768** ALU ops per triangle
PS4 Std	2,304 FLOPS / 2 shader engines **1,152** FLOPS per triangle
PS4 Pro	4,608 FLOPs / 4 shader engines **1,152** FLOPS per triangle
Fury X	8,192 FLOPS / 4 shader engines **2,048** FLOPS per triangle

Table 1.3. Number of FLOPS executed per triangle.

not the actual duration, but rather, the VALU activity. It is also interesting to note that even though the PlayStation 4 Pro has 2× more compute units than the standard PlayStation 4, the addition of extra shader-engines results in the same instruction limit between both PlayStation 4 variants, as the ALU to geometry ratio is maintained.

Developers now have DirectX® 12 and Vulkan™, which promised thousands of draws, with very low overhead. The new API has given great CPU performance advancements through low overhead and places the power in the hands of experienced developers. However, the GPU still chokes on tiny draws; it is quite common to see the second half of the base pass barely utilizing the GPU. Typically, there are lots of tiny details or distant objects, of which most are Hi-Z culled. The efficiency loss comes from the GPU still having to run mostly empty

Xbox One	768 FLOPS / 2 FLOPS per ALU = **384 instruction limit**
PS4 Std	1,152 FLOPS / 2 FLOPS per ALU = **508 instruction limit**
PS4 Pro	1,152 FLOPS / 2 FLOPS per ALU = **508 instruction limit**
Fury X	2,048 FLOPS / 2 FLOPS per ALU = **1024 instruction limit**

Table 1.4. Compute culling instruction upper limit.

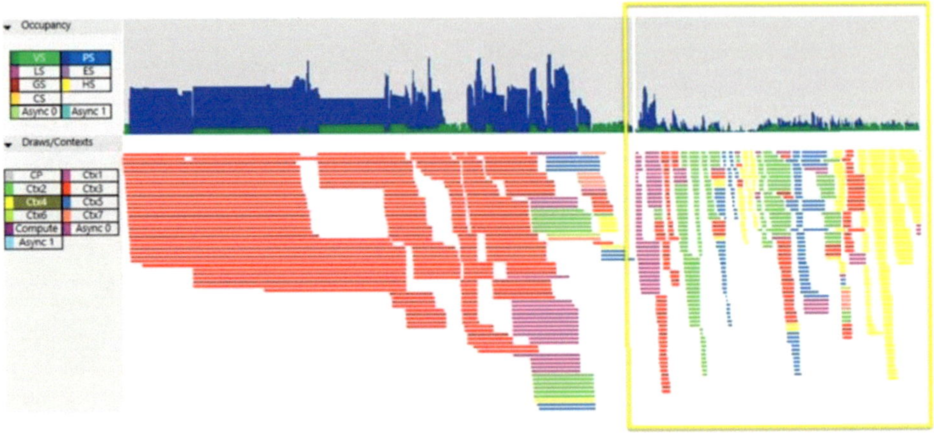

Figure 1.4. GPU spinning on empty vertex shader wavefronts.

vertex wavefronts. More draws are not necessarily a good thing. Figure 1.4 shows a GPU capture, where the left side starts out efficiently, but very quickly on the right, the GPU ends up spinning on vertex-shader wavefronts that that do not result in any pixels.

At a cursory glance, it seems quite easy to beat the peak primitive rate. However, the GPU has a lot more going on, so it is still important to profile and optimize the culling aggressively, especially bandwidth usage. A saving grace is that it is wildly optimistic to expect two triangles per clock cycle on consoles, as the rasterizer is subjected to other pipeline bottlenecks; on Xbox One, an actual rate of 0.9 triangles per clock was measured with regular rendering, which is really quite healthy, as primitive rate is not where you want to be bound.

In practice, if you are actually submitting geometry this fast, and doing any useful rendering, then you will be bound elsewhere in the pipeline, at least during some intervals. Also, you need good balance and lucky scheduling between the two VGTs and PAs to get max rate on each. For instance, the same vertex in two different waves might have to be shaded twice, because the waves alternate between PAs, and the PAs operate independently.

Due to the depth of the FIFO between VGT and PA, you need to get the positions of a vertex shader back in less than 4096 cycles, counting from the moment the vertex goes into the FIFO. This leaves you with slightly fewer cycles than that to compute your positions. If your vertex shader takes longer, primitive rate goes down linearly. Some games hit very close to peak perf (in the 95+% range) in shadow passes; there are usually some slower regions due to large triangles. The coarse rasterizer only does one super-tile per clock, so triangles with a bounding rectangle larger than 32×32 will need to multi-cycle on the coarse rasterizer, reducing primitive rate.

Benchmarks that get very close to two primitives per clock (around 1.97) have these characteristics:

- Vertex shader reads nothing;
- Vertex shader writes only `SV_Position`;
- Vertex shader always outputs 0.0 for position
  - so every primitive is trivially culled;
- Index buffer is all 0
  - so every vertex is a cache hit;
  - cache hits do not count as vertices for purposes of peak vertex rate;
  - that is the only way to get near two primitives per clock without hitting two vertices per clock first;
- Every instance is a multiple of 64 vertices;
  - unfilled vertex shader waves are less likely;
- No pixel shader bound;
  - no parameter cache usage;
- The peak primitive rate also requires that nothing after the vertex shader causes a stall;
  - parameter size$<=$ $4\times$ position size;
  - pixels drain faster than they are generated;
  - no scissoring occurs.

Apart from that, the PA can receive work faster than the vertex shader can possibly generate it. It is common to see tessellation achieve peak vertex-shader primitive throughput—for one shader engine at a time.

1.4 Draw Association

We review some terms in order to reduce ambiguity and confusion. A *scene* consists of a collection of meshes, displayed from a specific view (shown in Figure 1.5(a)).

A *batch* is a configurable subset of meshes in a scene (shown in Figure 1.5(b)). Except on Xbox One, all meshes in a batch are required to share the same shader; also all meshes share the same vertex and index strides. These requirements are due to the way that GPU-driven rendering works currently, at least on a PC.

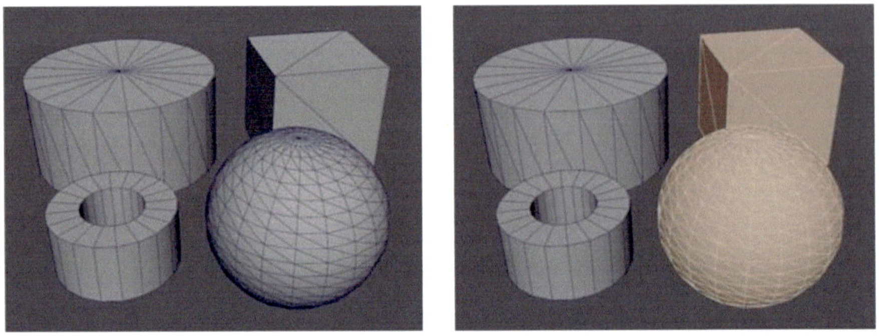

(a) (b)

Figure 1.5. (a) A scene is a collection of meshes displayed from a particular view; (b) a batch is a configurable subset of meshes in a scene.

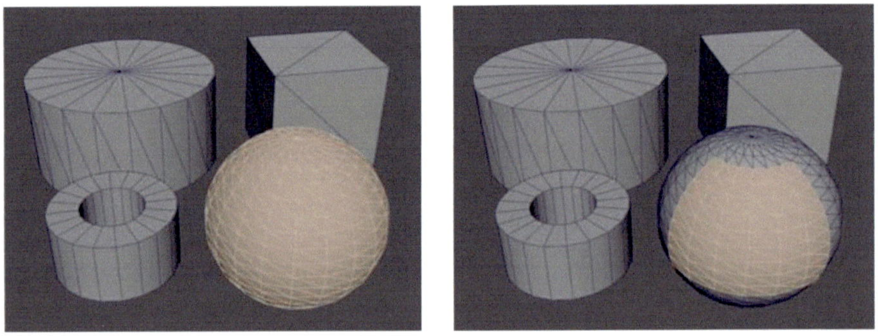

(a) (b)

Figure 1.6. (a) A mesh section represents an indexed draw call; (b) a work item represents a subset of triangles in a batch.

A batch here can be thought of as a near 1 : 1 with DirectX® 12's Pipeline State Object concept (PSO).

A *mesh section* represents an indexed draw call. A mesh section has its own vertex buffers, index buffer, primitive count, and other properties (shown in Figure 1.6(a)).

Finally, there is a *work item* (shown in Figure 1.6(b)), which represents a subset of triangles in a batch that will be processed by the culling compute shader. The number of triangles has been chosen based on the underlying hardware and characteristics of the algorithm. AMD GCN has 64 threads per wavefront (which includes both consoles), each culling thread processes one triangle, and each work item processes 256 triangles.

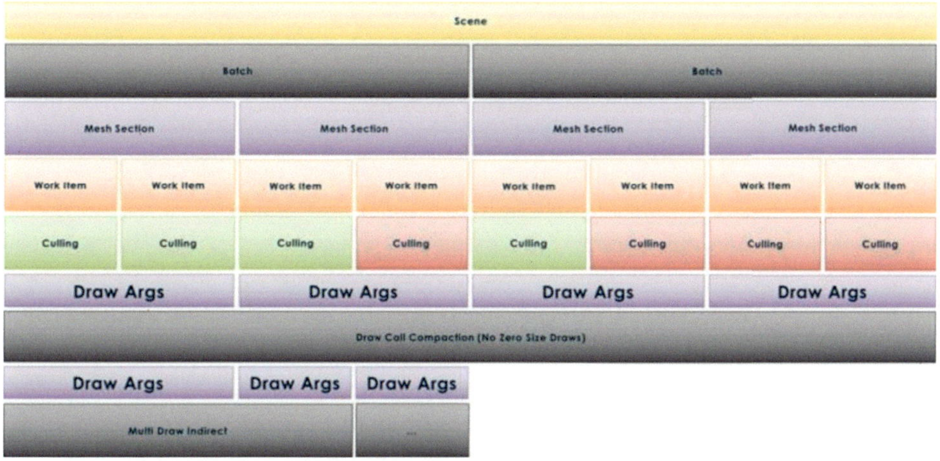

Figure 1.7. Overview of scene processed by culling system.

Figure 1.7 describes a high level overview of how a scene breaks down into work items that first undergo coarse view-culling, and then surviving clusters undergo triangle culling, with a variety of tests. A quick compaction pass is performed that ensures there are no zero-size draws if a mesh section is entirely culled (as in the case of occlusion or frustum culling).

At the end of the pipeline, there is a group of indexed draw arguments that can be kicked from the GPU with `ExecuteIndirect` on DirectX® 12, the `VK_AMD_draw_indirect_count` extension on Vulkan™, or via the `AMD_multi_draw_indirect` extension on OpenGL. On Xbox One, `ExecuteIndirect` has some incredible extensions where PSOs can be switched by indirect arguments, meaning a single `ExecuteIndirect` can be issued for the entire scene, regardless of state or resource changes.

Constructing each draw argument block is fairly straightforward, as it is mostly a matter of determining what starting index and count each block is responsible for during rendering. However, things get complicated when you try to load constants or other resource data from a regular vertex or pixel shader, unaware that this culling pass has occurred. In order to avoid state changes, there is an instancing buffer that contains the transforms, colors, etc. per instance, but in this case it is no longer 1 : 1 with a draw call. Essentially, a custom 32-bit word needs to be added to the argument buffer that tracks what original draw index it is associated with. A DirectX® 12 trick is to create a custom command signature. Doing so allows for parsing a custom indirect-arguments buffer format, where a custom id can be packed alongside the other hardcoded draw indexed argument values.

On a PC, drivers use compute-shader patching, where the id is loaded into a register for a shader to reference per invocation. On OpenGL, you can use

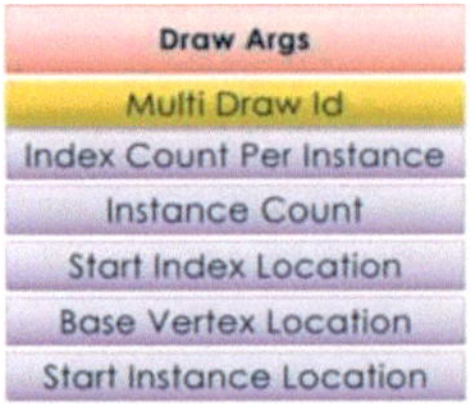

Figure 1.8. Multi-draw indirect structure layout.

gl_DrawId for this purpose. The command processor microcode on Xbox One handles indirect draws without intermediate steps or patching, which is the most optimal approach. An alternative would be to bind a buffer with a per-instance step rate of one, which maps from instance id to draw id. Depending on the driver implementation, this might be faster than the root-constant approach for the time being while drivers mature.

Listing 1.1 shows the appropriate command signature description to configure the dispatch to load the draw id into a register. Argument 0 defines the 32-bit mesh section id, including the parameter index into the root signature. Argument 1 then follows, which is the fixed list of five arguments that make up a draw indexed packet (format shown in Figure 1.8).

```
D3D12_INDIRECT_ARGUMENT_DESC args[2];
args[0].Type = D3D12_INDIRECT_ARGUMENT_TYPE_CONSTANT;
args[0].Constant.RootParameterIndex = 9; // Multi Draw Id Constant
args[0].Constant.DestOffsetIn32BitValues = 0;
args[0].Constant.Num32BitValuesToSet = 1;
args[1].Type = D3D12_INDIRECT_ARGUMENT_TYPE_DRAW_INDEXED;

D3D12_COMMAND_SIGNATURE_DESC desc;
desc.NumArgumentDescs = 2;
desc.pArgumentDescs = args;
desc.ByteStride = sizeof(MultiDrawIndexedIndirectArgs);
desc.NodeMask = 1;
```

Listing 1.1. Example DirectX® 12 command signature for multi-draw id.

This mapping will cause the 0th word of your argument block to be loaded into an SGPR register for use by the shader (shown in Listing 1.2). On a PC, having a command signature with complex commands will cause ExecuteIndirect processing to go through a compute shader. However, having a single extra word to represent the draw id, processing will remain on a fast path—similar to AGS MultiDrawIndirect or gl_DrawId.

```
cbuffer MultiDrawData : register(b3)
{
    uint g_multiDrawId;
}
```

Listing 1.2. HLSL syntax for accessing multi-draw id.

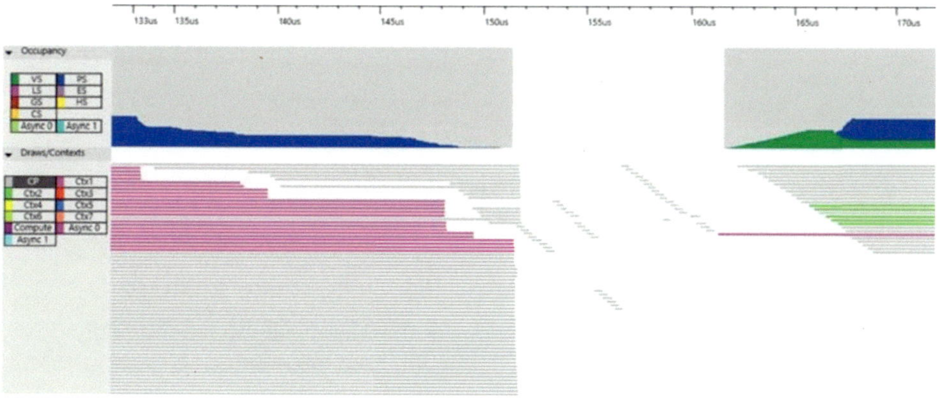

Figure 1.9. GPU zero-size draw inefficiency.

1.5 Draw Compaction

With cluster and triangle culling of draws on the GPU, it is extremely important to remove zero-sized draws from submission. The grey draws in the GPU capture shown in Figure 1.9 are empty indirect draws. At first, the command-processor (CP) cost is hidden by in-flight draws. Around 133 μs, the efficiency drops as the GPU hits a string of empty draws. At 151 μs, the GPU suffers around 10 μs of idle time. However, the total impact is worse than 10 μs, since the GPU does not instantly resume 100% efficiency, since it takes time to fill the CUs with waves. Clusters of culled draws can easily overwhelm the command processor, which is potentially 1.5 ms in a 60 Hz frame (seen in actual shipped games with real content).

While the savings from GPU culling still exceeds this cost, it is very important that zero-size draws are compacted in order to get the biggest gain. Even with 0 primitives, fetching indirect arguments is not free; there is a memory latency of approximately 300ns. The CP can hide a few of these fetches in a row, but they add up. Additionally, the CP is consuming command buffer packets, and state changes are not free.

The CPU will issue the worst-case number of draws, so zero-size draws will cause the GPU to process indirect arguments even if they have zero surviving primitives. The GPU needs control over the draw count and state changes. The `ExecuteIndirect` API in DirectX® 12 has an optional count buffer and offset, which the GPU will use to clamp the upper bound of draws that the command processor will unroll (Listing 1.3). Some independent hardware vendors (IHVs) currently patch this value with a compute shader, or run other sub-optimal paths. However, the feature is new, and widespread use will encourage IHVs to improve the drivers in this area.

```
Count = min(MaxCommandCount, pCountBuffer)

void ExecuteIndirect(
  [in]            ID3D12CommandSignature *pCommandSignature,
  [in]            UINT                    MaxCommandCount,
  [in]            ID3D12Resource         *pArgumentBuffer,
  [in]            UINT64                  ArgumentBufferOffset,
  [in, optional] ID3D12Resource         *pCountBuffer,
  [in]            UINT64                  CountBufferOffset
);
```

Listing 1.3. Function prototype of DirectX® 12 `ExecuteIndirect`.

In order to optimize for empty draws, compaction is needed so that only draws with surviving triangles reach the GPU command processor. A cross-platform approach to draw compaction is to do a parallel reduction with atomics in group shared memory (shown in Listing 1.4); each thread loads the indirect arguments for a draw and determines if the draw is worth keeping. A barrier allows all threads to complete and then the first thread in a group allocates output space for the surviving draw arguments. Another barrier is performed so each thread gets the output location, and then the surviving draw arguments are written to the destination buffer.

In this example, `batchData` is the `ExecuteIndirect` count buffer, and the offset is the location of `drawCountCompacted`.

```
groupshared uint localValidDraws;

[numthreads(256, 1, 1)]
void main(uint3 globalId : SV_DispatchThreadID,
          uint3 threadId : SV_GroupThreadID)
{
    if (threadId.x == 0)
        localValidDraws = 0;

    GroupMemoryBarrierWithGroupSync();

    MultiDrawIndirectArgs drawArgs;
    const uint drawArgId = globalId.x;

    if (drawArgId < batchData[g_batchIndex].drawCount)
        loadIndirectDrawArgs(drawArgId, drawArgs);

    uint localSlot;
    if (drawArgs.indexCount > 0)
        InterlockedAdd(localValidDraws, 1, localSlot);

    GroupMemoryBarrierWithGroupSync();

    uint globalSlot;
    if (threadId.x == 0)
        InterlockedAdd(batchData[batchIndex].drawCountCompacted,
                       localValidDraws, globalSlot);

    GroupMemoryBarrierWithGroupSync();

    if (drawArgId < drawArgCount && thisLaneActive)
        storeIndirectDrawArgs(globalSlot + localSlot, drawArgs);
}
```

Listing 1.4. Cross-platform compaction compute shader.

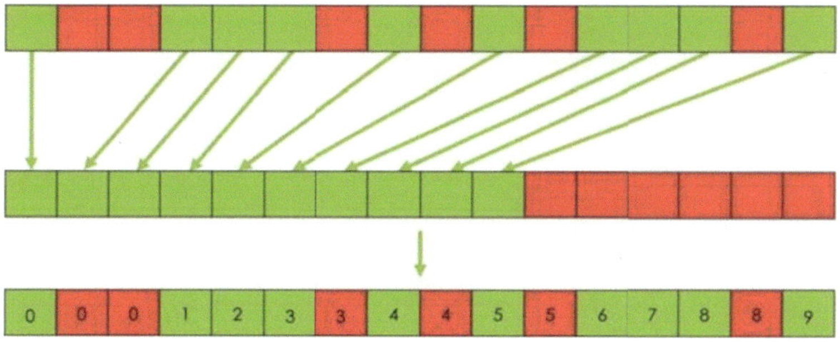

Figure 1.10. Expected result of index compaction.

With GCN intrinsics, and a thread group size of 64, we can do better! The issue with optimizing the compaction is that each thread needs to write in a contiguous range, so using the thread id as the index would not be correct, and it is ideal to avoid global synchronization like the previous compaction algorithm.

This is where parallel prefix sum comes to the rescue! In Figure 1.10, you can see the indices we want computed per thread in order for each active thread to write into the correct contiguous slot.

The first thing to mention is a compiler-intrinsic known as *ballot*. A ballot can be used to construct a 64-bit map, where each bit is an evaluated predicate per wavefront thread. For inactive threads, based on the execution mask, the bit will be 0.

Figure 1.11 shows the results of `__XB_Ballot64(threadId & 1)`, which is a predicate that sets 0 for even threads, and 1 for odd threads.

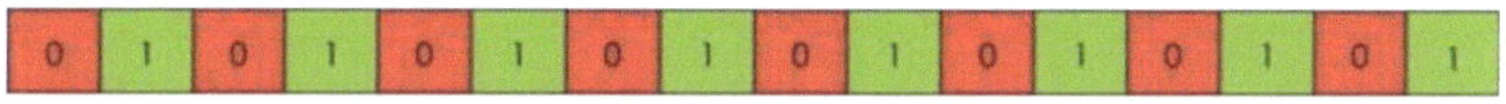

Figure 1.11. Result of simple ballot predicate.

Taking `ballot` further, Figure 1.12 is an example showing the results of a predicate running on thread 5. Before thread 5, there are three other threads that are valid, so the goal is to calculate the value three for thread 5's output slot.

By using `ballot` to generate a bit mask of surviving draw calls, the resultant mask can be & against a thread-execution mask where all bits are 0 except for threads lower than the current thread.

In this example, the execution mask for thread 5 is shown, with only bits 0 to 4 set. Looking at the resultant bit range, one can see that a population count of the 1s will produce our expected output slot.

GCN has two instructions that can be paired with `ballot` to produce the correct compaction results. `V_MBCNT_LO` will produce a masked bit count of the lower 32 threads (0–31), and `V_MBCNT_HI` will produce a masked bit count of the

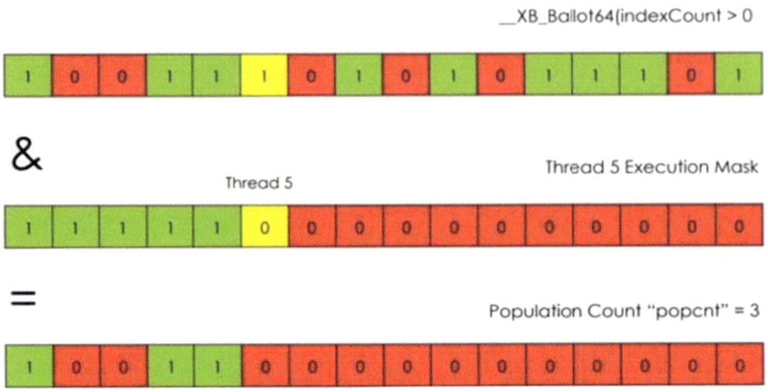

Figure 1.12. GPU population count example.

upper 32 threads (32–63). Chaining these instructions together will, for each thread, count the number of active threads which come before it, similar to the reference implementation in Listing 1.5.

```
uint2 mask;
mask.x = laneId >= 32 ? ~0 : ((1 <<  laneId)  1);
mask.y = laneId  < 32 ?  0 : ((1 << (laneId  32))  1);
uint compactIndex = countbits(ballot.x & mask.x) +
                    countbits(ballot.y & mask.y);
```

Listing 1.5. Reference implementation of masked bit count.

The reference implementation can be completely replaced by the following:

`uint compactIndex = __XB_MBCNT64(ballot.xy);`

Combining `ballot` and masked-bit count will compact the surviving draw-call stream within a wavefront without the need for any synchronization or group shared memory (shown in Figure 1.13).

The GCN-optimized compaction shader is shown in Listing 1.6; there are no longer any barriers. In order to compact across multiple wavefronts, there is a single atomic operation per wavefront that reserves the output space for all the surviving draw calls across each wavefront. Instead of using a barrier so that all threads get `globalSlot` calculated correctly, the value of `globalSlot` can be read directly from the lane that computed it.

```
[numthreads(64, 1, 1)]
void main(uint3 globalId : SV_DispatchThreadID,
          uint3 threadId : SV_GroupThreadID)
{
    const uint laneId = threadId.x;

    const uint drawArgId = globalId.x;
    const uint drawArgCount = batchData[g_batchIndex].drawCount;

```

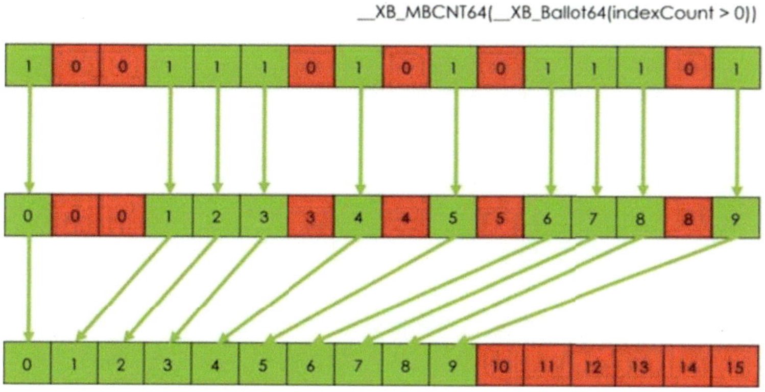

Figure 1.13. Masked bit count compaction.

```
    MultiDrawIndirectArgs drawArgs;
    if (drawArgId < drawArgCount)
        loadIndirectDrawArgs(drawArgId, drawArgs);

    const bool thisLaneActive = (drawArgs.indexCount > 0);
    uint2 clusterValidBallot = __XB_Ballot64(thisLaneActive);

    uint outputArgCount = __XB_S_BCNT1_U64(clusterValidBallot);

    uint localSlot = __XB_MBCNT64(clusterValidBallot);

    uint globalSlot;
    if (laneId == 0)
    {
        InterlockedAdd(batchData[g_batchIndex].drawCountCompacted,
                       outputArgCount, globalSlot);
    }

    globalSlot = __XB_ReadLane(globalSlot, 0);

    if (drawArgId < drawArgCount && thisLaneActive)
        storeIndirectDrawArgs(globalSlot + localSlot, drawArgs);
}
```

Listing 1.6. GCN-optimized compaction compute shader.

1.6 Cluster Culling

In order to make efficient use of the GPU, a coarse GPU culling pass is first performed on the mesh data [Haar and Aaltone 2015]. An offline process partitions meshes into 256 triangle clusters using a greedy spatially- and cache-coherent bucketing algorithm. For each cluster, we generate an optimal bounding cone [Barequet and Elber 2005]. The general idea is to project each triangle normal on to the unit sphere, and take this 256 projected-normal collection and calculate a minimum enclosing circle against the phi and theta pairs (shown

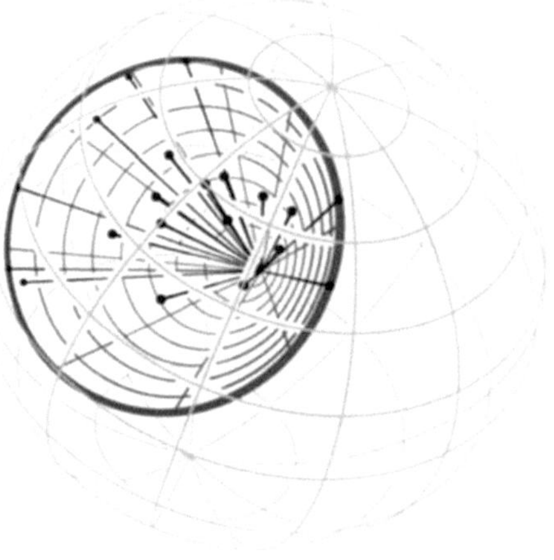

Figure 1.14. Minimum enclosing circle of unit sphere coordinates.

in Figure 1.14). Since the algorithm is operating on a difference of angles, we can use the circle diameter as the cone angle, and project the center back to Cartesian for the cone normal.

The four-component 8-bit SNORM has enough precision to store this cone, which can be culled on the GPU by taking the dot product of the cone normal and a conservative cluster-centroid view vector and comparing it to the negative sine cone angle. The obvious optimization is to store the cone angle with the negative sine calculated in to the value.

```
dot(cone.Normal, -view) < -sin(cone.angle)
```

You will want to make an allowance for rounding, like slightly enlarging the cone angle to avoid false rejection. The cone normal will quantize as well. Any of the typical g-buffer encodings to improve normal accuracy would be applicable here, as long as they are not the ones that bias depth precision towards viewer facing.

Various configurations were profiled in order to determine the ideal cluster size. Using a cluster size of 64 is convenient on consoles, as doing so opens up intrinsic optimizations. However, this was found to be sub-optimal, since the CP bottlenecks on too many draws, and the culling was never bound by LDS atomics. Based on profiling, a cluster size of 256 seems to be ideal. The 2 VGTs flip back and forth every 256 triangles, and vertex re-use does not survive the flip, making a cluster size of 256 a wise choice.

This approach allows us to coarse-reject entire clusters of triangles prior to the per-triangle culling pass. Additional per-cluster tests include bounding sphere vs frustum, and testing the bounding sphere's screen-space bounding box against a

Figure 1.15. Spheres become ellipsoids under projection.

Hi-Z depth pyramid. Be careful to account for perspective distortion, as spheres become ellipsoids under projection [Mara and McGuire 2013], shown in Figure 1.15.

1.7 Triangle Culling

There are a number of filters applied to the mesh during the triangle-culling phase. Each thread in a wavefront processes one triangle. Various culling operations are applied, and the surviving triangles across a wavefront need to be balloted and counted to determine the compaction index, or, the location in the resultant index buffer where the surviving indices will be written. This step is important for maintaining vertex reuse across a wavefront. Each wavefront then writes out the block of surviving indices to its output location (Figure 1.16).

If ordering across all wavefronts is important, such as with translucent or procedural rendering, then the block of surviving indices can be written out in wavefront creation order using `ds_ordered_count` [Advanced Micro Devices 2012]. Profiling determined that using ordered append to maintain vertex reuse across an entire mesh was usually not worth the cost, as work items of 256 triangles gives perfect vertex reuse. The factors contributing to the added cost are due to the way ordered append works under the hood, the size of the vertex cache, and what happens to vertex reuse when you start to remove parts of the mesh. If using ordered append, you can optimize it further through carefully tuned wavefront limits.

Figure 1.17 shows an overview of operations that the cull shader is performing on one triangle per thread across each work item.

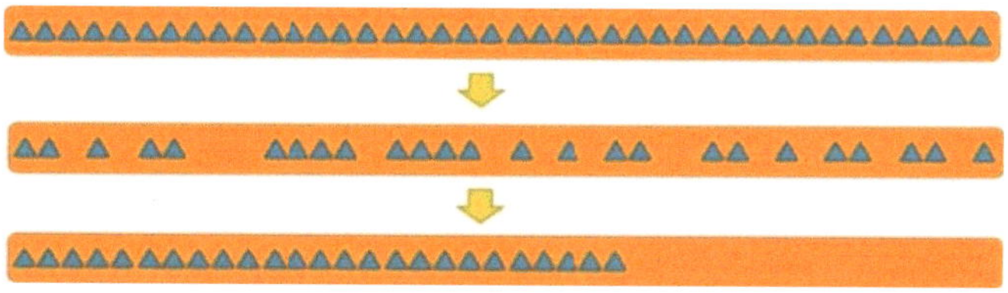

Figure 1.16. Triangles in a stream undergoing compaction after culling.

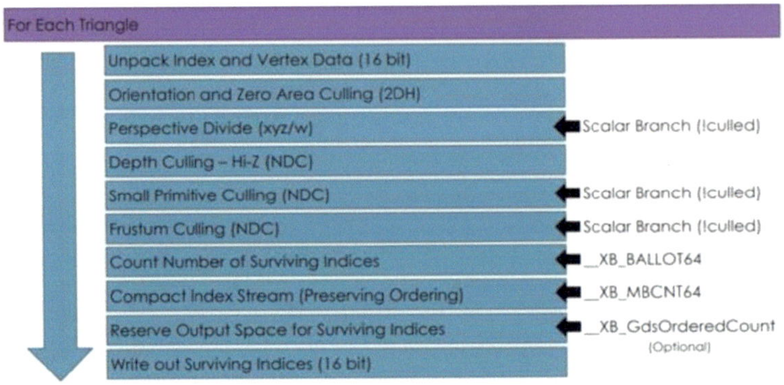

Figure 1.17. Overview of triangle cull shader operations.

Triangle data is unpacked, the various culling filters are executed, count/-compaction/reserve is performed, and then the indices are written out as 16-bit. Since compute cannot write out 16-bit types, the output buffer is first zeroed, the predicate & 1 is used on the thread id to determine low or high masking, and `InterlockedOr` is used on the output location. This cleverly uses the L2 cache as a write combiner.

Another important optimization to mention is that on consoles you can branch on a comparison with `ballot` to give the compiler a scalar branch uniformity hint in order to improve the generated code.

Without `ballot`, the compiler will generate two tests for most if statements. One is for the case where one or more threads enter the if statement, and the other is an optimization where the compiler will check to see if all threads did not enter the if statement, and if so the compiler branches over the if statement.

```
if (allNotEntering)
    Goto end;

if (threadEnters)
    modifyExecMask and execute if-statement
```

Listing 1.7. Typical compiler-generated conditional tests.

Really, this is just a single comparison test and the compiler essentially checks to see if all lanes had the same result, so the compiler is basically generating a ballot for you. This results in generated code that looks like Listing 1.7.

If you explicitly use `ballot` (or any/all/etc. which are high-level versions of `ballot`), or if you branch on a scalar value (i.e., `__XB_MakeUniform`), the compiler should only generate the single "if (allNotEntering) goto end;" part and skip the extra control-flow logic to handle divergence.

In the case of the culling work loop, `ballot` is used to force uniform branching and avoid divergence (including the slight code-gen hit), because there is no harm in letting all threads execute the full sequence of culling tests. If any thread needs to run that code, then all threads end up running it because of the SIMD being 64-wide.

There is a case where you should use divergent branching—if any of the culling tests involve memory fetches or LDS ops, it is worth masking those out, such as with depth Hi-Z culling.

1.7.1 Orientation Culling

On average, 50% of a mesh will be culled due to winding order. Therefore, we need a test which is as cheap as possible. One of the cheapest tests is the one shown in Listing 1.8 [Olano and Greer 1997], using the determinant of a 3×3 matrix with homogeneous coordinates [Blinn and Newell 1978]. This technique avoids clipping and projection, which includes quarter-rate reciprocal instructions coming from the perspective divide.

```
// Orientation and zero area (not small) test.
// Check the determinant of the 3x3 matrix of 2DH coordinates.
float det = determinant(float3x3(vertex[0].xyw,
                                 vertex[1].xyw,
                                 vertex[2].xyw));
bool cull = det <= 0.0f;
```

Listing 1.8. 2DH orientation and zero area test.

Using GCN specific optimizations, we can skip all the tests afterwards if winding order has already removed all the triangles within a wavefront. The direction of the determinant test is based on whether you are culling front- or back-facing triangles.

Figure 1.18. Back-face determinant test scene.

Figure 1.19. Results of back-face determinant test.

This particular test works under MSAA or EQAA conditions, as the zero area is not a small primitive test, but a degenerate triangle test—which any decent mesh pipeline should be removing offline, anyways.

Figure 1.18 is an example of the back-face determinant test applied to a character (Solas) from a particular view. Locking the current view, and then moving behind the character shows (in Figure 1.19) that all back-facing triangles have been removed, as expected.

When culling tessellated patches, it is also important to mention that the 2DH determinant test will not work correctly for back faces that displace into view. These faces would be culled pre-displacement, so you would lose a contributing portion of your silhouette (Figure 1.20).

For tessellated patches, we instead do back-face culling in view space with a dot-product bias that is determined by the max displacement amount.

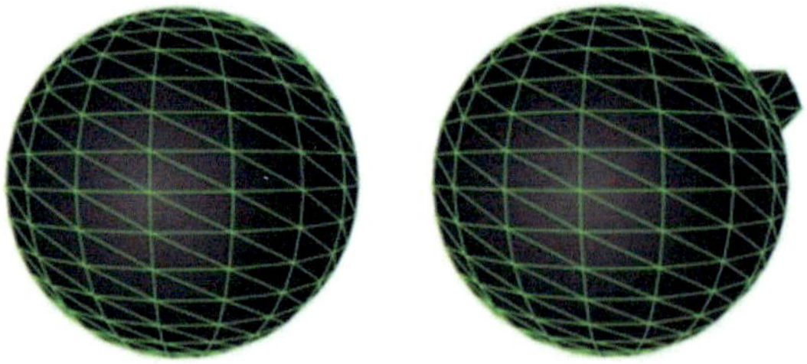

Figure 1.20. Back faces displacing into view.

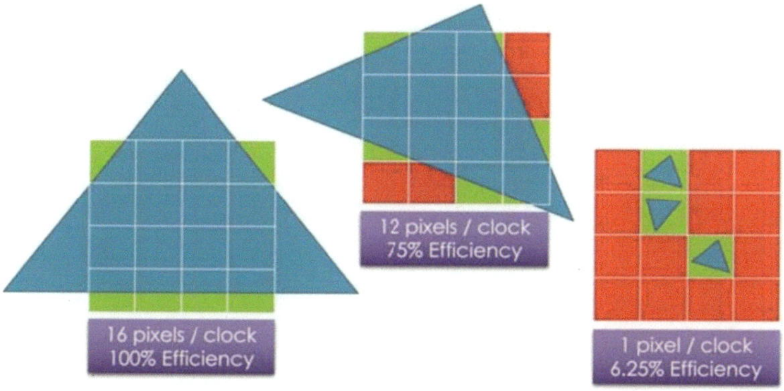

Figure 1.21. Small triangles are inefficient to rasterize.

1.7.2 Small Primitive Culling

Another effective filter is small primitive, or, culling triangles that do not generate pixel coverage. Each GCN rasterizer can read one triangle per clock and produce up to 16 pixels per clock. Because of this, small triangles are extremely inefficient to rasterize (Figure 1.21).

The left image in Figure 1.21 produces four quads, 16 pixels, at peak efficiency. The middle image produces four quads, but only 12 pixels are valid. It consumes 16 threads in the pixel shader though, due to helper lanes. Helper lanes still take time to pack and prepare, so they actually hurt your pixel rate. Efficiency in the middle image is lost due to partially filled quads, since the GPU shades in blocks of 2×2 pixel quads. The right image has become bound by hitting primitive setup limits.

Originally, a very exhaustive fixed-point hardware-precise small primitive filter was used, but later this was changed to the approximation you see below, for non-MSAA targets.

```
any(round(min) == round(max))
```

MSAA targets need to bias the test by enlarging based on sample count. If using custom-programmable sample points, a different solution will be needed. For MSAA, we need to essentially determine the maximum distance (in sub-pixels) between the pixel center and the outermost sub-pixel sample and use this to influence the test.

The general idea is to take a screen-space bounding box of a triangle and snap min and max to the nearest pixel corner. If the min and max snap to either the same horizontal or vertical edge, the triangle does not enclose a pixel center, therefore not contributing pixel coverage. In Figure 1.22(a), the triangle is not culled because it encloses a pixel center. In a simple case (Figure 1.22(b)), the triangle is culled because the min and max snap to the same location.

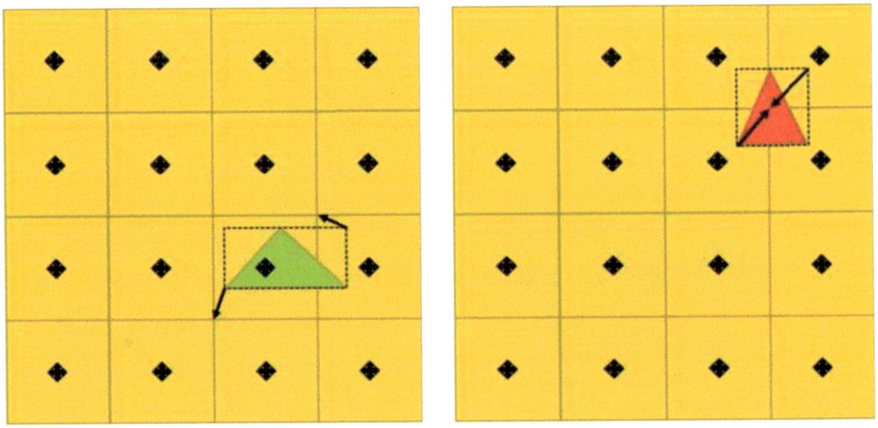

(a) (b)

Figure 1.22. (a) Triangle is not culled—no pixel coverage; (b) triangle is culled—min and max snap to same location

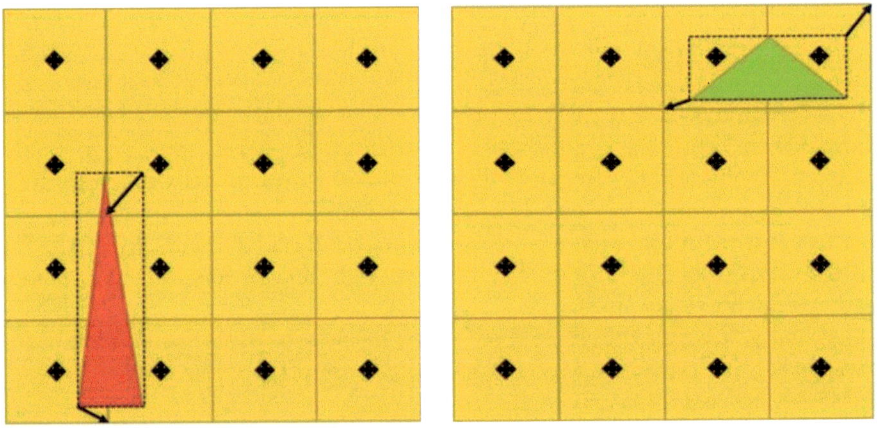

(a) (b)

Figure 1.23. (a) Triangle is culled; min and max snap to same horizontal coordinate; (b)Triangle is not culled; conservative test misses case.

In a more complex case (Figure 1.23(a)), the triangle is also culled. The min and max snap to different vertical coordinates, but to the same horizontal coordinate. This test is conservative, so there is a case where triangles should be culled, but are not, as shown by Figure 1.23(b). The bounding box min and max snap to different vertical and horizontal coordinates, yet the triangle does not enclose any pixel centers. Accounting for this case is not worth the cost, considering how cheap this test is.

Figure 1.24. Small primitive test scene.

Figure 1.24 shows the small primitive test applied to the character Solas, standing in the middle of the room, from a particular view. Locking the view, and moving over to him shows quite a number of sub-pixel triangles that have been removed with this filter (Figure 1.25). Notice quite a number of removed triangles from the hands, head, and highly detailed pelt over his back. This extra concentration of triangles is typically due to importance of fidelity during close-up cinematic shots during gameplay.

Figure 1.25. Results of small primitive test.

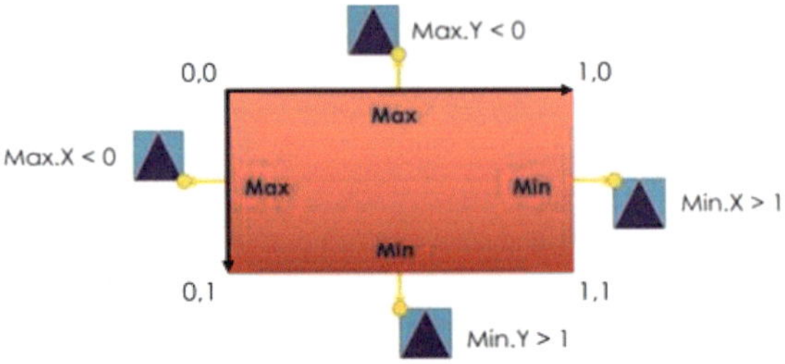

Figure 1.26. Fast frustum test.

1.7.3 Frustum Culling

The next per-triangle filter to cover is frustum culling. Most engines have whole-object frustum culling on the CPU, making per-cluster or triangle GPU frustum culling only effective when these objects intersect the planes. After the earlier culling filters, we now have post-projection vertices, and a huge budget of available ALU, so we do trivial frustum culling of four planes in four cycles (Figure 1.26), which still does provide some benefit in fringe cases, especially for composite objects which are made up of many parts.

Near- and far-plane culling is usually not worth the ALU for most games. Similar to back-face culling, it is important to mention that tessellated patches also require some form of tolerance values, in order to prevent incorrect culling of patches which tessellate from outside to inside of the view.

Figure 1.27 is an example of the frustum-culling filter; this is the current view with just frustum culling enabled. We have a mesh which survives CPU frustum culling, but there are still quite a lot of triangles that could be removed.

Figure 1.27. Frustum culling test scene.

Figure 1.28. Results of frustum-culling test.

After locking the view, moving backwards shows us how many triangles were removed using this filter (Figure 1.28).

1.7.4 Depth Culling

Another available triangle-culling approach is to do manual depth-testing [Hill and Collin 2011]. However, it is worth noting that directly reading depth for cluster- or triangle-culling is extremely scene-dependent due to availability and the quality of occluders at any given time. The general technique is to take the depth buffer and perform an LDS optimized parallel reduction [Harris 2007] (Figure 1.29), storing out the conservative depth min or max value for each tile.

In the initial implementation, a full z pre-pass was run that produced a 16×16 depth-tile grid (Figure 1.30), which was then tested against a screen-space bounding box of a triangle or cluster. If the box was fully contained within a single tile, a fast depth test was performed to reject it. This approach, while fast, would only remove a fraction of triangles; any occluded triangles that

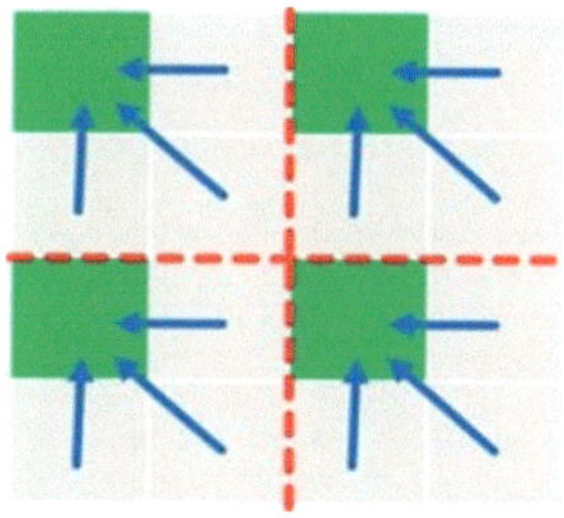

Figure 1.29. Depth reduction.

Figure 1.30. Generated depth tiles.

straddled a tile border would not be rejected. Modifying the filter to cull larger triangles spanning multiple tiles would be extremely expensive and not worth the cost.

Listing 1.9 shows a variant of parallel depth reduction which uses GCN lane swizzling to share data, bypassing LDS storage.

The DS_SWIZZLE_B32 instruction swizzles input thread data based on an offset mask and returns, without reading or writing DS memory banks.

Lane swizzle only works on 32 lanes, not 64, so we need to do a final combine which merges the first 32 lanes with the last 32 lanes. This is done with the read-lane instruction, allowing us to grab the reduced value from another lane

With a 16-bit ESRAM depth buffer already decompressed, this computation runs in approximately 41 μs on the Xbox One @ 1080p and is completely bandwidth bound. The result from this reduction is used for other parts of the rendering including compute light-tile culling.

```
float4 zQuad = g_linearZ.Gather(g_pointClamp (DTid.xy * 2 + 1) * g_rcpDim);

float minZ = min(zQuad.x, min3(zQuad.y, zQuad.z, zQuad.w));
float maxZ = max(zQuad.x, max3(zQuad.y, zQuad.z, zQuad.w));

// Use lane swizzling to share data, bypassing LDS

minZ = min(minZ, __XB_LaneSwizzle(minZ, 0x2F | (0x01 << 10)));
minZ = min(minZ, __XB_LaneSwizzle(minZ, 0x1F | (0x02 << 10)));
minZ = min(minZ, __XB_LaneSwizzle(minZ, 0x2F | (0x08 << 10)));
minZ = min(minZ, __XB_LaneSwizzle(minZ, 0x1F | (0x10 << 10)));

maxZ = max(maxZ, __XB_LaneSwizzle(maxZ, 0x2F | (0x01 << 10)));
maxZ = max(maxZ, __XB_LaneSwizzle(maxZ, 0x1F | (0x02 << 10)));
maxZ = max(maxZ, __XB_LaneSwizzle(maxZ, 0x2F | (0x08 << 10)));
maxZ = max(maxZ, __XB_LaneSwizzle(maxZ, 0x1F | (0x10 << 10)));
```

```
// Combine threads 0, 4, 32, and 36 to merge the four quadrants
minZ = min(minZ, __XB_LaneSwizzle(minZ, 0x1F | (0x04 << 10)));
maxZ = max(maxZ, __XB_LaneSwizzle(maxZ, 0x1F | (0x04 << 10)));
minZ = min(minZ, __XB_ReadLane(minZ, 32));
maxZ = max(maxZ, __XB_ReadLane(maxZ, 32));

if (GI == 0)
    g_minMaxZ[Gid.xy] = float2(minZ, maxZ);
```

Listing 1.9. GCN parallel depth reduction.

Another approach to depth culling is using a hierarchical Z pyramid [Greene et al. 1993], which starts at the resolution of the depth buffer and goes all the way to a single pixel. The first level of the pyramid is populated after depth laydown, similar to the depth-tiles method. After that, we populate the remaining mip levels in the pyramid through a custom downsample pass (Figure 1.31).

Figure 1.31. Depth pyramid example.

Each texel in mip level N contains the min or max depth of all corresponding texels in mip level $N - 1$. Culling can be done by comparing the depth of a bounding volume's longest edge with the depth stored in the Hi-Z pyramid. Because the pyramid goes down to a single level, we can very easily get a single mip level to fetch, instead of using multiple fetches to handle overlapping quads.

```
int mip = min(ceil(log2(max(edge, 1.0))), levels  1);
```

This is the approach used for the depth-based culling, except it has also been accelerated with HTILE.

GCN has a depth acceleration meta-data called HTILE [Advanced Micro Devices 2011] which accelerates regular GPU depth operations. Every 8×8 group of pixels has a corresponding 32-bit meta-data block. While this meta-data accelerates regular GPU depth operations, it can be decoded manually in a shader and used for early rejection of 64 pixels with a single test, or for any other relevant purpose.

HTILE is usually imprecise, and the bounds must be conservative. Additionally, the bounds can only grow until you "resummarize," where every depth value must be read in order to recompute the bounds.

On consoles, HTILE is used to give us conservative depth testing without having to decompress the depth buffer for testing in a shader, or disabling Hi-Z on subsequent depth-enabled render passes. We have a decompression compute shader which binds the HTILE surface as an R32 UINT texture, manually decodes the tile information, and produces a depth texture.

Figure 1.32. Visualized depth buffer of a scene.

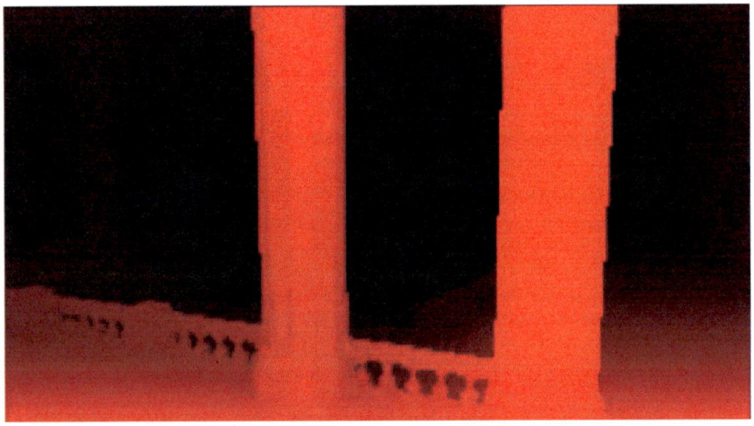

Figure 1.33. Visualized HTILE of a scene.

There are some complexities with using HTILE, but manual decoding or encoding can be a big performance-win in a variety of scenarios. Currently, HTILE is only directly accessible to console developers (see Figures 1.32 and 1.33).

When computing the first downsampled mip level of the Hi-Z pyramid, you can leverage the fact that the shader already read the input depth values. So that shader can also perform full and or half-resolution linearization of the depth values; we can also write out half-resolution HTILE. This has the benefit that other passes like particles can use Hi-Z culling against that mip level, without needing to resummarize the half-resolution depth buffer.

Since we need to build each HTILE meta-data block from 64 pixels, we cannot just use the already reduced 4 : 1 min and max values. We need to parallel reduce all pixels in an 8×8 tile to produce the correct min and max values for HTILE. You could do a parallel reduction in LDS, or you could take advantage of lane swizzling on GCN (shown in Listing 1.10).

```
// Compute the depth bounds
float minZ = depth;
float maxZ = depth;

// Compute depth tile bounds with wave-wide reduction
minZ = waveWideMin(minZ);
maxZ = waveWideMax(maxZ);

// Write HiZ and ZMask to half-res HTILE
if (GI == 0)
{
    uint htileOffset = getHTileAddress(Gid.xy, g_outTileDim);
    uint htileValue = encodeCompressedDepth(minZ, maxZ);
    g_htileHalf.Store(htileOffset, htileValue);
}
```

Listing 1.10. Lane swizzle HTILE generation.

Because each HTILE entry represents an 8×8 pixel block, we can use a wave-wide min and max operation across 64 depth values in a tile using lane swizzle (see Listing 1.11).

```
float waveWideMin(float val)
{
    val = min(val, __XB_LaneSwizzle(val, 0x1F | (0x01 << 10)));
    val = min(val, __XB_LaneSwizzle(val, 0x1F | (0x02 << 10)));
    val = min val, __XB_LaneSwizzle(val, 0x1F | (0x08 << 10)));
    val = min(val, __XB_LaneSwizzle(val, 0x1F | (0x10 << 10)));
    val = min(val, __XB_LaneSwizzle(val, 0x1F | (0x04 << 10)));
    val = min(val, __XB_ReadLane(val, 32));
    return val;
}

float waveWideMax(float val)
{
    val = max(val, __XB_LaneSwizzle(val, 0x1F | (0x01 << 10)));
    val = max(val, __XB_LaneSwizzle(val, 0x1F | (0x02 << 10)));
    val = max(val, __XB_LaneSwizzle(val, 0x1F | (0x08 << 10)));
    val = max(val, __XB_LaneSwizzle(val, 0x1F | (0x10 << 10)));
    val = max(val, __XB_LaneSwizzle(val, 0x1F | (0x04 << 10)));
    val = max(val, __XB_ReadLane(val, 32));
    return val;
}
```

Listing 1.11. Lane swizzle wave-wide min and max.

Rather than paying the cost of a depth read-back during a resummarize, we can manually encode HTILE during the downsample operation. HTILE encodes both near and far depth for each 8×8 pixel tile. Near depth is used for trivial accept, whereas far depth is used for trivial reject; anything in between these planes must do hi-resolution testing. If stencil is enabled, we have a 14-bit near value, and a 6-bit delta towards the far plane. If stencil is not enabled, min and max depth is encoded into two 14-bit pairs. The bottom 4 bits in both cases is z-mask, which we set to zero for clear.

The Hi-Z pyramid does not need stencil, so the encoding routine in Listing 1.12 is for the non-Hi-stencil format.

```
uint encodeCompressedDepth(float minDepth, float maxDepth)
{
    // Convert min and max depth to UNORM14
    uint htile = __XB_PackF32ToUNORM16(minDepth  0.5 / 65535.0,
                                       maxDepth + 3.5 / 65535.0);

    // Shift up minDepth by 2 bits, then set all four low bits
    htile = __XB_BFI(__XB_BFM(14, 18), htile, htile << 2);
    return htile |= 0xF;
}
```

Listing 1.12. HTILE encoding routine.

One problem with using depth for culling is availability. Many engines only have a partial Z pre-pass, or none at all. This restricts how early you can kick off asynchronous compute work. You need to wait for z-buffer laydown before performing the depth test for culling.

Frostbite™has had a software rasterizer for occluders since *Battlefield 3* (Figure 1.34) [Collin 2011], which is generated on the CPU for the upcoming GPU frame; the results of this operation can be used to load the Hi-Z pyramid prior to any related rendering passes, with no latency. In addition to loading the Hi-Z pyramid, you can also use your software raster to conservatively prime your HTILE buffer as if you had a full pre-pass! Without a software rasterizer or a full Z pre-pass, you can use a trick like reprojecting your previous depth buffer and testing with that.

Figure 1.34. Software occlusion raster.

Figure 1.35. Depth pyramid test scene.

Figure 1.35 shows the character Solas behind a pillar, and the results of the CPU-rasterized occlusion buffer in the top left. Using this buffer, a Hi-Z pyramid was constructed, and the triangles for Solas are being depth-tested against the appropriate mip level in this texture. Figure 1.36 shows the visualized occluder geometry used to produce the software occlusion buffer for this scene.

Figure 1.36. Visualized occluder geometry.

Locking the view, and moving to the other side of the pillar, we see the surviving triangles for Solas and what was rejected by Hi-Z culling (Figure 1.37).

Figure 1.37. Results of depth pyramid test.

1.8 Batch Scheduling

It is important to discuss how the batching is structured to make the overlap of culling and rendering efficient. In order to efficiently run all the culling filters against a scene and render the results, the batching had to be carefully architected. The number of triangles in a scene can wildly vary between game teams or even different views, and predictable memory usage is desirable.

We start with a fixed memory budget of N buffers $\times$ 128 k triangles, where N is large enough to get decent overlap between culling and render; N should be at least 4. Doing a dispatch, wait, draw, loop would be bad, as that would cause the CP to stutter. We want to go a couple of dispatches ahead of render to account for this efficiently (Figure 1.38).

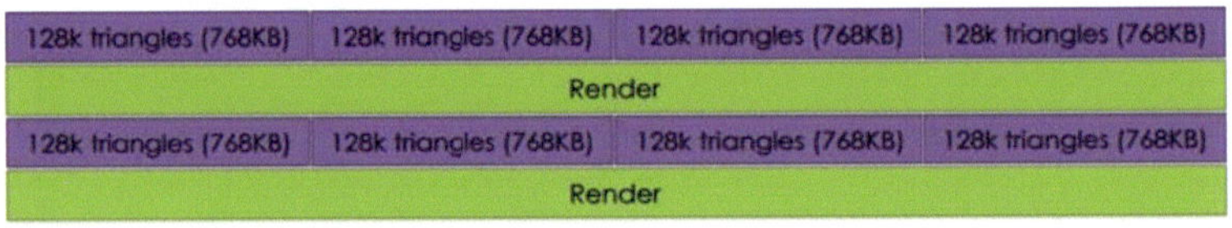

Figure 1.38. Fixed memory budget of batches.

Assuming 16-bit unsigned short, 384 k triangle indices is 786 Kb of memory. Four buffers is approximately 3 MB, which allows for up to a half-million triangles in flight. By sizing the buffers this way, and with careful scheduling, the data stays resident in the L2 cache when the vertex wavefronts execute.

In the example shown in Figure 1.39, we have four buffers, which gives us a total surviving triangle capacity of 512 k. We have to calculate output require-

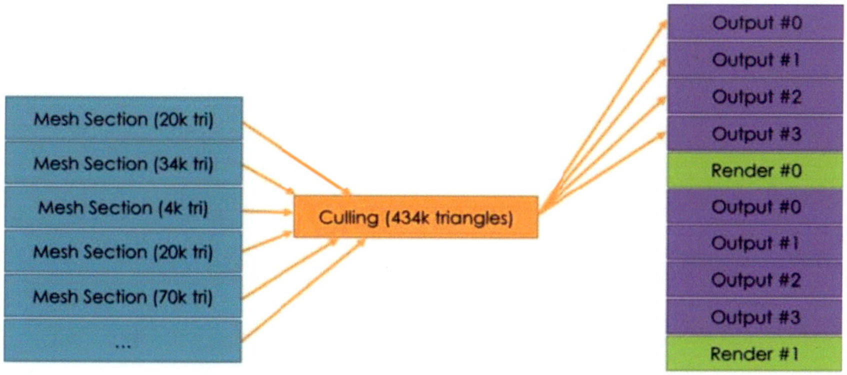

Figure 1.39. Batching within budget.

ments before culling, in case all triangles survive. An initial thought was to do a rough heuristic against 50% back-face culled, but certain projections could cause problems. You can see that culling is processing 434 k triangles, which fits well within our 512 k limit. Render #0 will occur, and then the next pass can reuse the output buffers. This leads into a more complex case.

In the example shown in Figure 1.40, the culling is processing more triangles than we have capacity for. When we determine that the buffers are exhausted, we can do a mid-dispatch flush of the rendering. This will free-up our output buffers for rendering the remaining triangles. Using triangle lists is nice, because we can trivially cut up a mesh without concern, as long as we maintain ordering for optimal vertex reuse, or translucent objects.

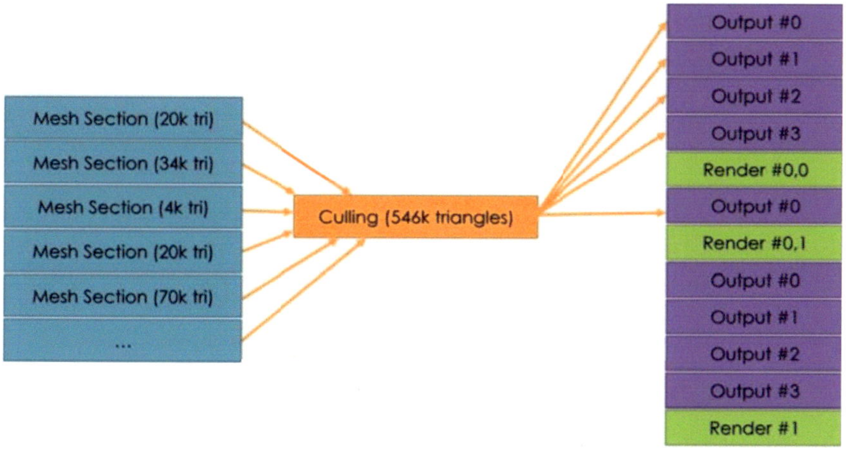

Figure 1.40. Batching over budget.

Overlapping culling and render wavefronts on the graphics pipe is great, but there is a high startup cost for the initial dispatch, when there is no graphics work to overlap (Figure 1.41).

Figure 1.41. Culling on graphics pipe.

Asynchronous compute to the rescue! We can launch the dispatch work alongside other GPU work in the frame, such as water simulation, physics, cloth, virtual texturing, etc. This can slow down some of the graphics pipe work a bit, but overall frame-time is faster. Just be careful about "what" you schedule culling to run with (Figure 1.42).

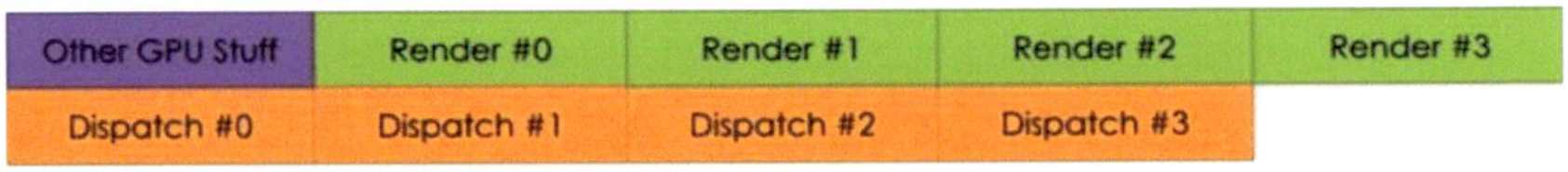

Figure 1.42. Culling on compute pipe.

You can use inexpensive wait on label operations to ensure that dispatch and render are pipelined correctly. On a PC, try to aim for fewer batches at a larger size, due to the inability of DirectX® 12 to issue efficient mid-command buffer fences.

In general, you want to schedule your asynchronous compute to happen at the same time as low-intensity rendering work, like a depth pre-pass or shadows. Use fences to bracket the dispatches so they do not start early or late on the GPU, and make sure to flush the asynchronous compute command buffer so it does not stall the GPU waiting on the auto-kickoff.

After that, you can use compute-shader limit APIs to restrict the total number of thread groups per CU allowed, or disable some CUs from either compute or graphics. You can also kick off asynchronous compute to do the work during the last stages of post-processing on the previous frame.

1.9 De-interleaved Vertex Buffers

Another architectural note is that the vertex buffers have been de-interleaved (Figure 1.43). This can be a substantial win on GCN architectures, and it also makes the task of compute mesh-processing much easier.

There are a number of reasons that de-interleaving your vertex data is beneficial. In terms of compute processing performance, having culling data like position in its own stream away from other attributes like texture coordinates, vertex colors, tangent space basis, etc. means that there is an almost never

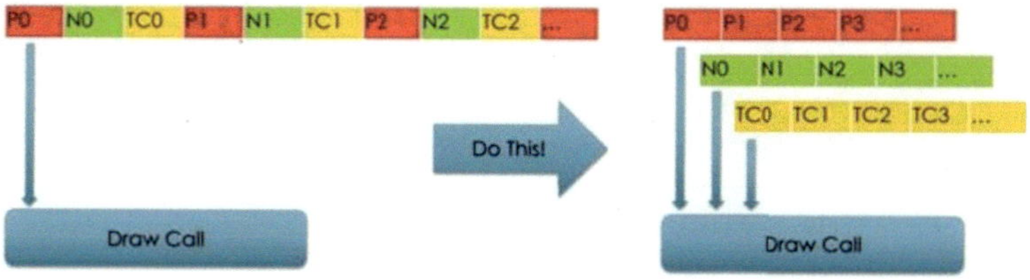

Figure 1.43. De-interleaved vertex buffers.

changing stride. The only time you would need to break batching would be 16-bit vs 32-bit precision.

Consoles and DirectX® 12 placement resources can be spanned across all the geometry data, meaning that with a constant stride and some pointer arithmetic to determine the right start vertex and index location for each draw, we can completely avoid binding varying buffers throughout rendering!

In addition to algorithmic benefits, de-interleaving your vertex data is more optimal for regular GPU rendering on GCN architectures, so there is really no excuse. The goal is to evict cache lines as quickly as possible. With interleaved data, the cache line needs to be kept between the first and the last read. With de-interleaved data and inlined fetch shaders, the wavefront fetches a cache line, consumes it, and the cache line is thrown away immediately. An additional benefit is that de-interleaving delivers faster processing on the CPU, as the data will be SoA instead of AoS, making it easier to process with SSE/AVX, etc., and the same advantage applies on the GPU.

If you want to be the most optimal across mobile, AMD, and other IHVs, it is common to at least have multiple interleaved streams of mutable vs immutable data, positions in their own streams (optionally with texture coordinates in the case of alpha tested shadows), skinning data, and other common data grouped together.

Another advantage of de-interleaved vertex buffers is that you can create separate index buffers per pass. A depth-only pass (like for culling) can have more vertex re-use than a full pass, because you often need to duplicate vertices for full rendering (same position but different texture coordinate, or same position but different normal).

1.10 Hardware Tessellation

Another interesting use-case for compute mesh-processing is to optimize hardware-tessellation GPU bottlenecks. There are a number of cases where hardware tessellation can be extremely beneficial, especially when you are looking at optimizing content creation, procedural algorithms, or offloading CPU level of detail to the GPU.

Figure 1.44. *Dragon Age*^{TM}*Inquisition* displacement mapping.

Tessellation is not for everyone, as there are games that cannot afford the overhead, but there are some strategies that can be used to improve performance when hardware tessellation is used, such as *Dragon Age*^{TM}*Inquisition* (Figure 1.44), and *Star Wars*^{TM}*Battlefront*.

When using tessellation, the goal is to produce vertex waves at peak rate per shader engine. If not, then you want the reason to be "pixel waves are not draining fast enough," i.e., the tessellation itself is not getting in your way. In a traditional hardware-tessellation pipeline (Figure 1.45), the hull shader would do the heavy lifting of calculating adaptive screen-space tessellation factors, as well as various patch-level culling techniques. The calculated factors would range between 0 and the max tessellation factor.

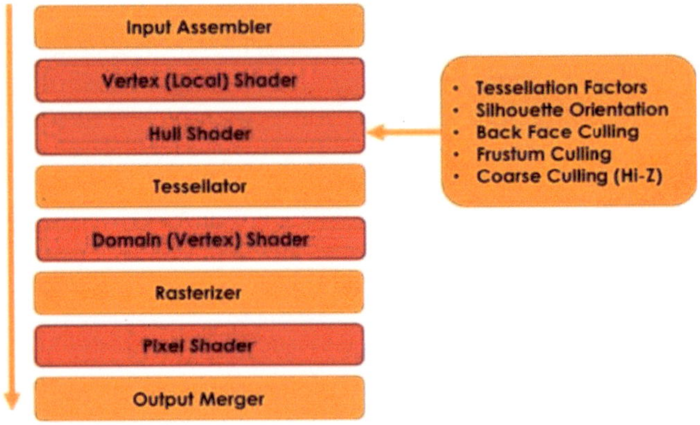

Figure 1.45. Hardware-tessellation pipeline.

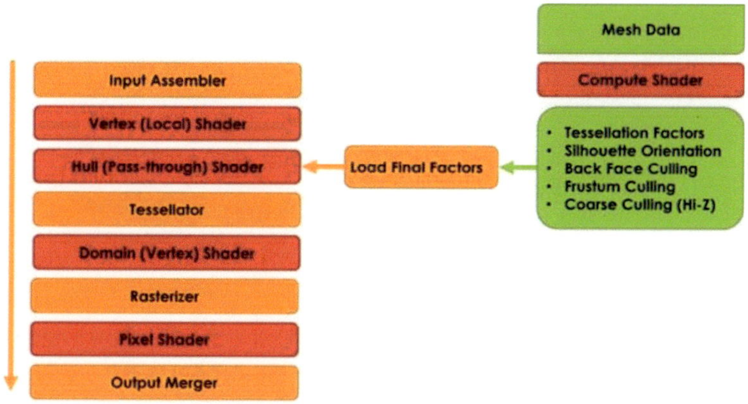

Figure 1.46. Offloaded tessellation factors calculation.

There are two main reasons why hull shaders are so bad and why we want to move the work over to compute. Hull shaders tend to have very few active threads out of the 64 per wave. One issue is that the GPU can only fit so much control-point data into LDS. The other issue is that the shader compiler implements the patch constant function in the case of three vertex triangle patches by turning off two out of the three active threads and only running code on the remaining thread. With these two problems, you are getting very low parallelism in what tends to be a very complex shader. In general, the recommendation for small tessellation factors is to load as much data as late as possible so it happens after expansion, i.e., in the domain shader.

A first step of optimization is to offload the work that the hull shader is doing, by moving these costly calculations to a compute dispatch earlier in the frame (Figure 1.46). The results are then stored into a factors buffer that the hull shader can index with `SV_PrimitiveId`. This optimization makes the hull shader stay active for the bare minimum amount of time, which is nice, but this method still suffers from high expansion bottlenecks and other inefficiencies. A factor of 0 would tell the hardware to cull the patch, and anything else would do a tessellated draw, including a factor of 1.

When doing initial profiling of tessellation on GCN, some overhead was expected, but it was shocking to find such a disparity between the cost of rendering a regular draw vs a tessellated draw with a factor of 1. Low tessellation factors would perform reasonably well, but high tessellation factors performed very poorly. Digging into it more, it turns out that vertex reuse is disabled at the vertex-shader stage and is instead enabled at the domain-shader stage when the tessellation factor is greater than 1. This equates to about three times more vertices! Additionally, these factor-1 draws suffer from the same parallelism constraints that were just mentioned.

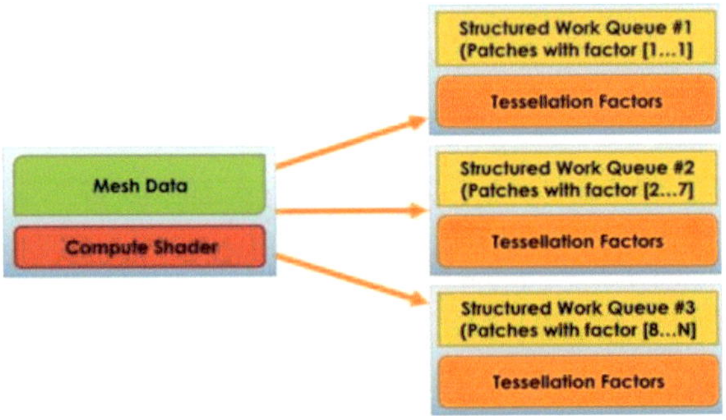

Figure 1.47. Compute tessellation work queues.

The improved optimization is to have a compute dispatch that, based on the compute tessellation factors, buckets the patches into one of three structured work queues (Figure 1.47). Culled patches with a factor of 0 are not processed further and do not get inserted to any work queue.

Patches with a factor of 1 get placed into a queue that will be rendered without tessellation. Patches with a factor of 2—7 get placed into a queue to be rendered with tessellation. Patches with higher factors get placed into a queue that will undergo coarse refinement prior to tessellation.

The general goal here is to produce small patches, so that we can parallelize more of the mesh across more CUs. All of the vertices heading into the domain stage need to be processed on the same CU, since tessellation-patch constants are stored in LDS, so the larger a patch, the less parallelism is achieved. The compute shader will do a coarse subdivision of the patch into four smaller patches and push them into the tessellation work queue with $\frac{1}{4}$ of the original tessellation factor (Figure 1.48).

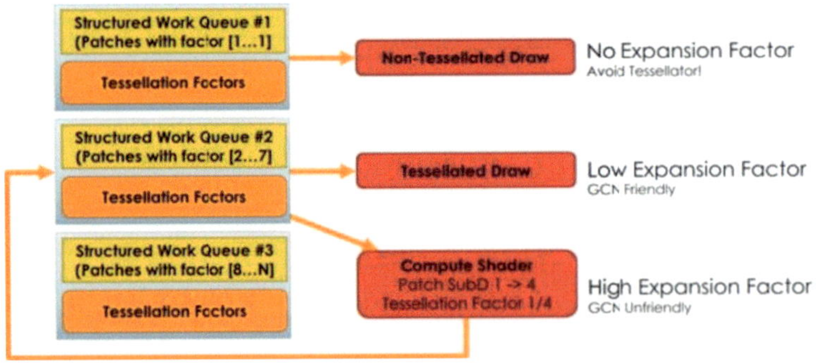

Figure 1.48. Compute tessellation pipeline.

One thing you need to handle is accounting for T-junctions between varying patch levels. Using an algorithm like PN-AEN [McDonald and Kilgard 2010] will give you triangle patches which include edge-adjacency information, which is helpful for solving this issue.

1.11 Performance

For the performance metrics, the test scene used is shown in Figure 1.49. There are quite a number of render passes, and with 171 unique PSOs, but the results shown are for a single g-buffer pass of 450 k triangles, rendered at 1080p on both platforms (without cluster culling or compute tessellation). For the Xbox One, the depth buffer and a few of the g-buffer color targets are in ESRAM, with everything else in DRAM.

Figure 1.49. Performance profiling test scene.

Aside from orientation culling, the other filters are very scene-dependent. If you have a lot of dense meshes, the small primitive filter can be very effective, especially in the case of dense shadow maps. If you have aggressive view culling on the CPU, or in the coarse cluster-culling pass, then the frustum culling may be less useful. However, once you have projected your vertices for the other filters, doing frustum culling is four cycles for four planes, so it doesn't hurt to leave it.

After orientation culling, the depth filter is the second most effective technique, but it is completely dependent on the quality of your depth buffer prior to culling. If you have a full z pre-pass, or can load it from software occluders or re-projected previous frame depth, then it may do wonders.

You will notice that for this scene, we have managed to cull enough that we are only left with 22% of the original triangle count. Now imagine feeding the

Processed	100%	443,429
Culled	78%	348,025
Rendered	22%	95,404

Table 1.5. Ratio of culled vs rendered triangles.

Filter	Exclusively Culled		Inclusively Culled	
Orientation	46%	204,006	46%	204,006
Depth	42%	187,537	20%	90,251
Small	30%	128,705	8%	37,606
Frustum	8%	35,182	4%	16,162

Table 1.6. Primitive culling amounts for the various filters.

Platform	Base	Cull	Draw	Total
XB1 (DRAM)	5.47ms	0.24ms	4.54ms	4.78ms
PS4 Std (GDDR5)	4.56ms	0.13ms	3.76ms	3.89ms
Fury X (HBM)	1.79ms	0.06ms	1.40ms	1.46ms

Table 1.7. Synchronous culling performance, no tessellation.

Platform	Base	Cull	Draw	Total
XB1 (DRAM)	5.47ms	0.26ms	4.56ms	4.56ms
PS4 Std (GDDR5)	4.56ms	0.15ms	3.80ms	3.80ms
Fury X (HBM)	1.79ms	0.06ms	1.40ms	1.40ms

Table 1.8. Asynchronous culling performance, no tessellation.

resultant culled index buffer into related passes, where we do not need to worry about the cost of culling.

Tables 1.5–1.8 are the performance figures for this scene, on both consoles and on an AMD Fury X on PC. Even with mesh data in DRAM, the Xbox One culling is slowest, yet needs barely any time at all to process one-half million triangles in a g-buffer pass. Synchronously, we are saving 15-30% of our rendering cost, and, asynchronously, we are saving a bit more. The draw and cull times get a little bit longer when running asynchronously, but you will notice that the overall cost goes down. This is due to some resource contention between compute and graphics. A shadow- or depth-pass would improve performance even further, likely by an additional 10–15%, but it is important to show the effectiveness of per-triangle culling even in a color pass with varying PSO changes.

Tables 1.9 and 1.10 are the performance figures when we add a complex tessellation expansion factor to all the triangles—specifically, a screen-space adaptive Phong tessellation with a factor no larger than seven. Here you will see a massive increase in initial rendering cost, due to numerous hardware bottlenecks. Because of this, our culling cost stays the same, as we are doing culling prior to tessellation, but the performance improvement to the final draw time is much higher, as the cost of rendering a surviving triangle is much more extreme. In

Platform	Base	Cull	Draw	Total
XB1 (DRAM)	19.3ms	0.24ms	11.1ms	11.3ms
PS4 Std (GDDR5)	12.8ms	0.13ms	8.08ms	8.21ms
Fury X (HBM)	3.35ms	0.06ms	1.46ms	1.52ms

Table 1.9. Synchronous culling performance, with tessellation.

Platform	Base	Cull	Draw	Total
XB1 (DRAM)	19.3ms	0.26ms	11.2ms	11.2ms
PS4 Std (GDDR5)	12.8ms	0.15ms	8.10ms	8.10ms
Fury X (HBM)	3.35ms	0.06ms	1.46ms	1.46ms

Table 1.10. Asynchronous culling performance, with tessellation.

this scene, synchronously culling saves between 40–80% of the rendering time, and, asynchronously, it saves a bit more.

1.12 Conclusion

Each instanced draw is unrolled into multiple draws, since each instanced draw needs its own culled index-buffer range. Instancing is primarily a CPU win, so the unrolling is not much of an issue for that under DirectX® 12 or Vulkan™, except for the unnecessary memory pressure of each instance reloading the same vertex data and less wavefront packing. However, this system is getting incredible L2$ hits for the instanced data, when running synchronously. With uninstanced data, profiling shows approximately 20 bytes of bandwidth usage per triangle, but with instancing due to the batch chunk size and near perfect L2$ residency, profiling shows approximately 1.5 bytes of bandwidth usage per triangle, which is excellent. So nothing needs to be done in the synchronous case, but the asynchronous case can be improved a lot.

An improvement to instancing would be to load the vertex data once into chunks of LDS for bandwidth amplification, as each instance would perform culling against LDS loaded data. It will also be important to further investigate careful tuning of wavefront limits and also CU masking.

It can be argued that traditional triangle processing in compute may not be the most effective use of the silicon, though aside from performance improvements, especially for shadow maps, this system serves as a platform for chaining other passes using the filtered index buffer for source triangles, instead of the unfiltered original index buffer. Additionally, the results from the culling can be resubmitted into subsequent passes from the same view, giving a performance amplification by skipping culling and reusing results.

In summary, small and inefficient draws are a problem. DirectX® 12 and Vulkan™provide an API to submit tons of draws at great performance from the CPU, but the GPU can still choke on these. Therefore, it is important to

Figure 1.50. AMD GPUOpen GeometryFX.

realize that compute and rasterization are friends; treat your draws as data and have both compute and graphics help each other out. You typically only want to use idle GPU resources to remove fixed-function bottlenecks; otherwise you may impact performance instead. Asynchronous compute is extremely powerful—be sure to schedule compute wavefronts alongside the rest of your frame, but do not forget that you can overlap compute and graphics work on the same pipe; many engineers do not realize this.

If you are interested in implementing something similar to this technology, you should look at AMD GeometryFX (Figure 1.50), released as part of GPUOpen. While not the exact same technology as discussed in this chapter, it serves as a great example on how to implement such compute-based triangle culling.

Acknowledgements

I would like to thank Johan Andersson, Christina Coffin, Mark Cerny, and the Frostbite Rendering team for their support of this research. I also want to thank the numerous people that offered guidance, ideas, improvements, support, and friendly conversation over a beer. Your help was very much appreciated! Thanks to Chris Brennan, Matthäus Chajdas (@NIV_Anteru), Ivan Nevraev (@Nevraev), Alex Nankervis, Sébastien Lagarde (@SebLagarde), Andrew Goossen, James Stanard (@JamesStanard), Martin Fuller (@MartinJIFuller), David Cook, Tobias "GPU Psychiatrist" Berghoff (@TobiasBerghoff), Christina Coffin (@ChristinaCoffin), Alex "I Hate Polygons" Evans (@mmalex), Rob Krajcarski, Jaymin "SHUFB 4 LIFE" Kessler (@okonomiyonda), Tomasz Stachowiak (@h3r2tic), Andrew Lauritzen (@AndrewLauritzen), Nicolas Thibieroz (@NThibieroz), Johan Andersson (@repi), Alex Fry (@TheFryster), Jasper Bekkers (@JasperBekkers), Graham Sellers (@grahamsellers), Cort Stratton (@postgoodism), Colin Barré-Brisebois (@ZigguratVertigo), David Simpson, Jason Scanlin, Mike Arnold, Mark Cerny (@cerny), Pete Lewis, Keith Yerex, Andrew Butcher (@andrewbutcher), Matt Peters, Sebastian Aaltonen (@SebAaltonen), Anton Michels, Louis Bavoil (@LouisBavoil), Yury Uralsky, Sebastien Hillaire (@SebHillaire), Daniel Collin (@daniel_collin).

Bibliography

Advanced Micro Devices, 2011. Radeon evergreen / northern islands acceleration. Evergreen Programming Guide. URL: http://developer.amd.com/.

Advanced Micro Devices, 2012. Southern islands series instruction set architecture. Reference Guide. URL: http://developer.amd.com/wordpress/media/2012/12/AMD_Southern_Islands_Instruction_Set_Architecture.pdf.

Barequet, G., and Elber, G. 2005. Optimal bounding cones of vectors in three dimensions. *Inf. Process. Lett. 93*, 2, 83–89.

Blinn, J. F., and Newell, M. E. 1978. Clipping using homogeneous coordinates. In *Proceedings of the 5th Annual Conference on Computer Graphics and Interactive Techniques*, ACM, New York, SIGGRAPH '78, 245–251.

Brainerd, W. 2014. Tessellation in *Call of Duty: Ghosts.* In *Advances in Real-Time Rendering in Games, SIGGRAPH Course*, ACM, New York.

Collin, D. 2011. Culling the battlefield: Data oriented design in practice. In *Game Developer's Conference.* URL: http://www.gdcvault.com/play/1014492/Culling-the-Battlefield-Data-Oriented.

Greene, N., Kass, M., and Miller, G. 1993. Hierarchical z-buffer visibility. In *Proceedings of the 20th Annual Conference on Computer Graphics and Interactive Techniques*, ACM, New York, SIGGRAPH '93, 231–238.

Haar, U., and Aaltone, S. 2015. Gpu-driven rendering pipelines. In *Advances in Real-Time Rendering in Games, SIGGRAPH Course*, ACM, New York.

Harris, M., 2007. Optimizing parallel reduction in cuda. http://docs.nvidia.com/cuda/samples/6_Advanced/reduction/doc/reduction.pdf.

Hill, S., and Collin, D. 2011. Practical, dynamic visibility for games. In *GPU Pro 2*, W. Engel, Ed. A K Peters, 329–347.

Lauritzen, A., Salvi, M., and Lefohn, A. 2010. Sample distribution shadow maps. In *Advances in Real-Time Rendering*, ACM, New York, SIGGRAPH 2010 course. URL: https://software.intel.com/sites/default/files/m/d/4/1/d/8/sampleDistributionShadowMaps_SIGGRAPH2010_notes.pdf.

Mah, L., 2013. The AMD GCN architecture: A crash course. AMD Developer Summit. URL: https://www.slideshare.net/DevCentralAMD/gs4106-the-amd-gcn-architecture-a-crash-course-by-layla-mah.

Mara, M., and McGuire, M. 2013. 2d polyhedral bounds of a clipped, perspective-projected 3d sphere. *Journal of Computer Graphics Techniques (JCGT) 2*, 2, 70–83.

McDonald, J., and Kilgard, M., 2010. Crack-free point-normal triangles using adjacent edge normals. Nvidia Report. URL: http://developer.download.nvidia.com/whitepapers/2010/PN-AEN-Triangles-Whitepaper.pdf.

OLANO, M., AND GREER, T. 1997. Triangle scan conversion using 2d homogeneous coordinates. In *Proceedings of the ACM SIGGRAPH/EUROGRAPHICS Workshop on Graphics Hardware*, ACM, New York, HWWS '97, 89–95.

VI

2

Real Time Markov Decision Processes for Crowd Simulation

Sergio Ruiz and Benjamín Hernández

Crowd simulations may aid in the analysis of different events related, for example, to disease propagation, evacuations or social evolutions. To support fast decision making, there is the need to develop algorithms and techniques to solve interactively fundamental problems such as navigation, agent-agent, and agent-obstacle collision avoidance.

Our observation is that an agent, while moving through an environment, solves a sequential decision problem to find a path that goes from its current configuration to a goal, constructing a set of additive rewards as it gets closer to its goal. This behavior can be described by a Markov decision process (MDP). However, classic planning such as A^* and its alternatives are commonly used solutions in video games; their performance is acceptable for static environments and when the amount of memory and characters allows it.

We are particularly interested in using MDPs to face a more general case where environment information may be incomplete, e.g., procedurally generated levels, and/or dynamically changing, but also in the case when having only one general solution will allow us to steer several hundreds of characters interactively.

2.1 Modeling Agent Navigation using a Markov Decision Process

A Markov decision process (MDP) is a tuple $M =< S, A, T, R >$, where S is a finite set of states, A is a finite set of actions, T is a transition model $T(s, a, s')$, and R is a reward function $R(s)$. A solution that specifies what an agent should do at any given state is a policy $\pi(s)$.

2.1.1 Problem Modeling

Considering a scenario for which the position of static obstacles is determined prior to the crowd simulation, a constrained, fully observable MDP can be evaluated in order to determine optimal navigation directions for groups of agents enclosed in cells, given that a 2D representation of the scenario is regularly partitioned in these cells that will be equivalent to the finite set of states S for the MDP. This set of optimal directions is the optimal policy (Π^*).

Therefore, from the formal definition of a MDP, $M =< S, A, T, R >$:

- S (finite set of states) is composed by every cell resulting from partitioning the navigable space.
- A (finite set of actions) is a set of actions representing an agent's available movement directions, e.g., forward, left, right, etc.
- T (transition model) is defined by the probabilities of taking a given action.
- R (reward function) are cells marked as points of interest (high-valued rewards), navigable space (medium-valued rewards), and obstacles (low-valued rewards).

After these definitions, we are ready to solve the MDP problem, so we want to find an optimal policy Π^*, i.e., a set of actions that maximizes the reward function R. Given a time step $t > 0$, for a given state or cell s, Π^* is calculated as

$$\begin{aligned} &\Pi_t^*(s) = \text{argmax}_a Q_t(s,a) \\ &Q_t(s,a) = R(s,a) + \gamma \sum_{j=0}^{|A|-1} T_{sj}^a V_{t-1}(j) \\ &V_t(s) = Q_t(s, \Pi^*(s)) \\ &V_0(s) = 0 \end{aligned} \quad , \tag{2.1}$$

where $Q_t(s,a)$ represents the value of taking action a—in this case moving towards direction a—from cell s, $V_t(s)$ represents the reward value of cell s at time t, $\gamma \in [0,1]$ is a future reward discount factor, and T_{sj}^a is the transition function, taking into account the probability with which an agent will choose state j from state s through action a.

To better understand how these set of equations work and setting a starting point to explain our parallelization approach, let's see an example consisting of a discretized 3×4 scenario, resulting in twelve states with a reward function, valued at -3 for navigable space, -100 for obstacles, and 100 for exits (Figure 2.1).

For simplicity, our agent can follow three actions 1) moving West, W, 2) moving North, N, and 3) moving East, E; thus, $A = \{W, N, E\}$; a reward discount factor $\gamma = 1$; a probability for T_{sj}^a of $p = 0.8$ when taking the current action a, and $q = 0.1$, otherwise. Finally we use an out-of-bound value of zero for rewards leading out of the scenario.

	1	2	3	4
a	-3	-3	-3	+100
b	-3	-100	-3	-100
c	-3	-3	-3	-3

Figure 2.1. A simple scenario where navigable space has a reward of -3, obstacles a reward of -100 and the exit a value of 100. The orange cell represents an agent's position.

Using Equation (2.1), we can compute the optimal policy ($\Pi_t^*(s)$) for cell $a3$. Considering $\Pi_t^*(s)$ and $Q_t(s, a)$ from Equation (2.1) and replacing s and a terms by $a3$ and actions from set A, we have

$$\Pi^*(a3) = \max\{Q(a3, E), Q(a3, W), Q(a3, N)\} \tag{2.2}$$

and,

$$\begin{aligned} Q_t(a3, E) &= R(a3, E) + \gamma[pR(a3, E) + qR(a3, W) + qR(a3, N)] \\ Q_t(a3, W) &= R(a3, W) + \gamma[qR(a3, E) + pR(a3, W) + qR(a3, N)] \\ Q_t(a3, N) &= R(a3, N) + \gamma[qR(a3, E) + qR(a3, W) + pR(a3, N)] \end{aligned} \tag{2.3}$$

Replacing the corresponding variables with their numerical values we obtain

$$\begin{aligned} Q_t(a3, E) &= 100 + 1.0 \times [0.8(100) + 0.1(-3) + 0.1(0)] \\ Q_t(a3, W) &= -3 + 1.0 \times [0.1(100) + 0.8(-3) + 0.1(0)] \\ Q_t(a3, N) &= 0 + 1.0 \times [0.1(100) + 0.1(-3) + 0.8(0)] \end{aligned} \tag{2.4}$$

From inspection of Equations (2.4), the action that maximizes the reward is $Q_t(a3, E)$, which corresponds to moving East to reach the exit.

From Equations (2.3), note that:

- For each cell or state, a similar set of equations is to be solved.
- The set of equations can be solved in parallel, if each cell knows the rewards from neighboring cells and out-of-bounds rewards.
- Probability variables p and q and rewards values $R(s, a)$ can be stored in arrays for each cell.
- Expressions in brackets can be solved by parallel reductions. A second parallel reduction using conditionals will solve Equation (2.2).

2.1.2 Algorithm

In the previous section we outlined a strategy to solve a MDP per-cell for crowd navigation. To extend this idea to a full space partition S, we propose the following steps, illustrated by the solution of the example shown in Figure 2.2.

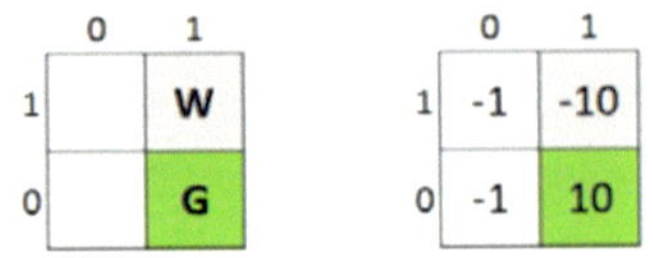

Figure 2.2. Example scenario to demonstrate boundary data collection. Possible actions are $A = \{W, S, E, N\}$ (cardinality $|A| = 4$), in that arbitrary order. For the left representation: W=wall, G=goal. The right schema represents the rewards function $R(s)$.

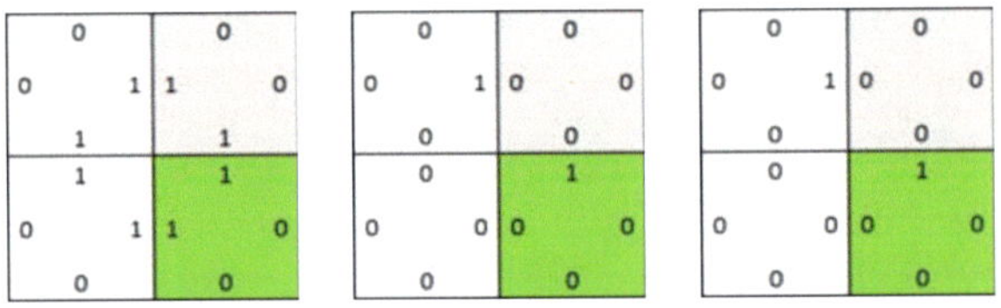

(a) In bounds (b) is wall (c) Ib-Iw

Figure 2.3. Cell boundary sampling example.

Offline processing. This step consists of capturing the geometric information of the spatial partition (discussed in Section 2.3.1) into data that is suitable for parallel computations, namely the scenario and MDP parameters; this also involves the creation of data arrays and the transition matrix T^a_{sj}.

1. Data collection at host. Consider for example the scenario shown in Figure 2.2. For each cell we sample boundary conditions as shown in Figure 2.3.

   1.1. *In-bounds vector.* For each cell, a 1 marks a valid movement option in terms of scenario boundaries, and 0, otherwise, as shown in Figure 2.3(a). The resulting vector, of size rows $*$ columns $*$ $|\text{A}|^2$, according to the arbitrary W, S, E, N order is in_bounds = $(0, 0, 1, 1, ..., 1, 1, 0, 0)$, repeating every $|A|$-tuple $|A|$ times, sampling the cells in the following order (cells coordinates are in form (row, column)): (0,0), (0,1), (1,0) and (1,1).

   1.2. *Is-wall vector.* For each cell, a 1 marks a wall in the corresponding action direction, and 0, otherwise, as shown in Figure 2.3(b). The resulting vector, of size rows $*$ columns $*$ $|\text{A}|^2$: $is\_wall = (0, 0, 0, ..., 0, 0, 0)$, repeating every $|A|$-tuple $|A|$ times. The difference vector $in\_bounds - is\_wall$ stores actual available actions for an agent discarding walls and out-of-bounds choices (Figure 2.3(c)): $in\_bounds\_is\_wall$ = $(0, 0, 1, ..., 1, 0, 0)$. We think of this structure as a sequence of rows $*$ columns matrices of dimensions $|A| \times |A|$ and compute their transpose over the secondary diagonal. The resulting *in_bounds_is_wall_trans* vector will be used to compute T^a_{sj}.

1.3. *Transfer to device.* The *in_bounds_is_wall* vector is uploaded to GPU memory along with the *in_bounds_is_wall_trans* vector to perform a fast computation of the transition matrix (Figure 2.4(a)).

1.4. *Vicinity vector.* Of size $\text{rows} * \text{columns} * |A|^2$, the function of the *vicinity* vector is to support the previous values update operation at the end of each iteration and it is generated as follows: construction of the *vicinity* vector samples cells analogously to the in-bounds routine, storing the $\text{rows} * \text{columns}$ value when the corresponding direction is out-of-bounds, or the index for the cell at a valid direction. Each W, S, E, N sampling is repeated $|A|$ times so that $vicinity = (4, 4, 1, 2, 4, 4, ..., 4, 4, 2, 1, 4, 4)$.

1.5. *Rewards vector.* Of size $\text{rows} * \text{columns} * |A|^2$, the *rewards* vector samples each available action $|A|$ times, storing a 0 value if the given direction is out-of-bounds, or the reward for the cell at a valid direction divided by $|A|$, so that

$$rewards = (0, 0, 0, 0, ..., -2.5, -2.5, -2.5, -2.5, ..., 0, 0, 0, 0)$$

for the reference example.

2. Data structures for the device.

2.1. *Auxiliary data structures.* Computation of the transition matrix requires auxiliary data structures as shown in Table 2.1 with values for the example in Figure 2.2. In general, the transition matrix computation requires $\text{rows} * \text{columns} * |\text{A}| * (|\text{A}| * 48 + 8) + 24$ bytes (3,224 bytes for our example).

2.2. *Auxiliary functions.* Three auxiliary unary parallel functions are used to fill the transition matrix with the probability of following or not the expected optimal path, and also to fill the diagonal vector, which is a sequence of $\text{rows} * \text{columns}$ diagonal matrices of dimensions $|A| \times |A|$, as shown in Listing 2.1. Note that in the listings, $NQ = |A|$.

2.3. *Transition matrix.* We apply parallel reduction and transformations from the CUDA Thrust library to run the code shown in Listing 2.2 which uses the functions in Listing 2.1 to compute the transition matrix. These steps correspond to Figure 2.4(a) to initialize the vector named *permutations* since it holds all possible weighted actions per cell. In our example, $permutations = (0, 0, 0, 0.2, ..., 0.2, 0, 0, 0)$.

STRUCTURE NAME	VALUE OR SIZE	TYPE
rows	2	int
columns	2	int
prob_f	0.2	float
prob_t	0.8	float
NQ (or $\|A\|$)	4	int
NQ2	NQ*NQ	int
indices_out_NQ	rows * columns * NQ	<int>
reachable_temp	rows * columns * NQ	<int>
in_bounds_is_wall	rows * columns * NQ2	<int>
in_bounds_is_wall_trans	rows * columns * NQ2	<int>
nqs_NQ2	rows * columns * NQ2	<int>
ones	rows * columns * NQ2	<int>
indices_NQ2	rows * columns * NQ2	<int>
reachable	rows * columns * NQ2	<int>
permutations (or T^a_{sj})	rows * columns * NQ2	<float>
temp_table	rows * columns * NQ2	<float>
diagonal	rows * columns * NQ2	<float>
diagonal_neg	rows * columns * NQ2	<float>
diagonal_T1	rows * columns * NQ2	<float>
full_T1	rows * columns * NQ2	<float>

Table 2.1. Data structures to compute the transition matrix.

```
struct false_prob : unary_function<float, float>{
  const float p;
  false_prob (float _p) : p (_p) {}
  __device__ float operator () (int reachable) const{
    float frc = (float)reachable - 1.0f;
    if (frc > 0.0f){
      return p / frc; // probabilities must sum 1
    }else{
      return 0.0f;
    }
  }
};

struct true_prob : unary_function<float, float>{
  const float p;
  true_prob (float _p) : p (_p) {}
  __device__ float operator () (int reachable) const{
    if (reachable > 1){
      return p;
    }else{
      return 1.0f;
    }
  }
};

struct index_diag : unary_function<int, int>{
  const int NQ; // NQ = |A|
  index_diag (int _nq) : NQ (_nq) {}
  __device__ float operator () (int index) const{
```

```
    int col = index % NQ;
    int row = ((index - col) / NQ) % NQ;
    if (row == col){
      return 1;
    }else{
      return 0;
    }
  }
};

```

Listing 2.1. Auxiliary transition matrix computation functions.

```
typedef device_vector<int>::iterator it;
fill            (nqs_NQ2.begin(),            nqs_NQ2.end(),         NQ);
sequence        (indices_NQ.begin(),         indices_NQ.end()         );
transform       (seq_indices.begin(),        seq_indices.end(),
                 nqs_NQ2.begin(),            indices_NQ2.begin(),
                 divides<int>                                         );
reduce_by_key   (indices_NQ2.begin(),        indices_NQ2.end(),
                 in_bounds_is_wall.begin(), indices_out_NQ.begin(),
                 reachable_temp.begin()                               );
repeated_range<it>
reachable_range (reachable_temp.begin(),     reachable_temp.end(),  NQ);
copy            (reachable_range.begin(),    reachable_range.end(),
                 reachable.begin()                                    );
// prob_f=0.2, prob_t=0.8
transform (reachable.begin(),                reachable.end(),
           temp_table.begin(),               false_prob(prob_f)       );
transform (seq_indices.begin(),              seq_indices.end(),
           diagonal.begin(),                 index_diag(NQ)           );
transform (ones.begin(),                     ones.end(),
           diagonal.begin(),                 diagonal_neg.begin(),
           minus<float>                                               );
transform (reachable.begin(),                reachable.end(),
           full_T1.begin(),                  true_prob(prob_t)        );
transform (full_T1.begin(),                  full_T1.end(),
           diagonal.begin(),                 diagonal_T1.begin(),
           multiplies<float>                                          );
transform (temp_table.begin(),               temp_table.end(),
           diagonal_neg.begin(),             temp_table.begin(),
           multiplies<float>                                          );
transform (temp_table.begin(),               temp_table.end(),
           diagonal_T1.begin(),              permutations.begin(),
           plus<float>                                                );
transform (permutations.begin(),             permutations.end(),
           in_bounds_is_wall.begin(),        permutations.begin(),
           multiplies<float>                                          );
transform (permutations.begin(),             permutations.end(),
           in_bounds_is_wall_trans.begin(), permutations.begin(),
           multiplies<float>                                          );

```

Listing 2.2. Transition matrix computation.

Modular iteration on device. See Figure 2.8 for a timeline overview, showing the modular MDP solution as a state machine corresponding to the following steps:

1. Upload to device. As shown in Figure 2.4(b) the *vicinity*, *rewards* and *prev_values* (initially a copy of *rewards*) vectors are uploaded to GPU memory.

2. Value iteration (Figure 2.4(c))

   2.1. *Previous policy vector update.* The vectors P, respectively, $prev\_P$ (of size rows $*$ columns each) store the current iteration policy, respectively, the previous iteration policy. At the beginning of each iteration a copy from P to $prev\_P$ updates the policies.

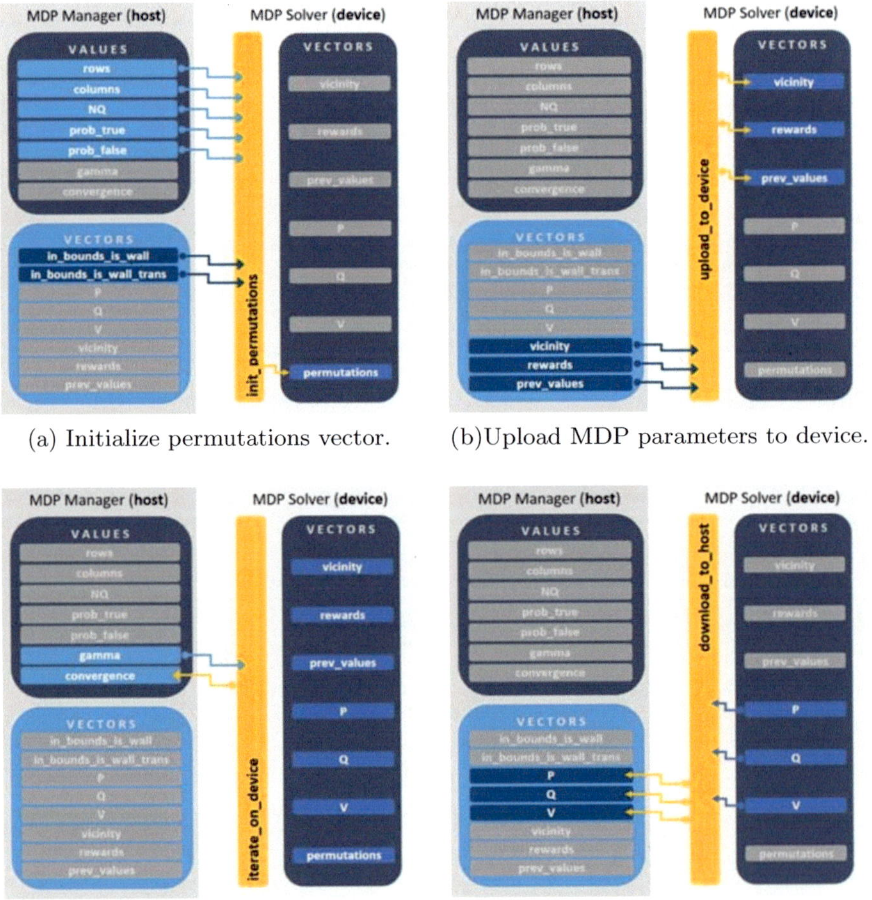

(a) Initialize permutations vector.

(b) Upload MDP parameters to device.

(c) Parallel value iteration.

(d) Download π^* to host.

Figure 2.4. MDP iteration detail.

```
transform     (permutations.begin(), permutations.end(),
               prev_values.begin(),  prob_tables.begin(), multiplies<float>);
transform     (prob_tables.begin(),  prob_tables.end(),
               discount.begin(),     prob_tables.begin(), multiplies<float>);
transform     (prob_tables.begin(),  prob_tables.end(),
               rewards.begin(),      prob_tables.begin(), plus<float>      );

fill          (nqs_NQ2.begin(),      nqs_NQ2.end(),       NQ               );
sequence      (indicesNQ2.begin(),   indicesNQ2.end()                      );
sequence      (indicesNQ.begin(),    indicesNQ.end()                       );
transform     (indicesNQ2.begin(),   indicesNQ2.end(),
               nqs_NQ2.begin(),      indicesNQ2.begin(),  dividex<int>     );
reduce_by_key (indicesNQ2.begin(),   indicesNQ2.end(),
               prob_tables.begin(),  ind_outNQ2.begin(),  Q.begin()        );
replace (Q.begin(), Q.end(), 0.0f, -100.0f);
```

Listing 2.3. $Q_t(s,a)$ computation.

2.2. *Computation of Q-values.* With the aid of a *discount* vector of size rows $*$ columns $*$ $|\text{A}|^2$ filled with the γ discount factor, and a temporary *prob_tables* vector of the same size, the Q vector of size rows $*$ columns$*|A|$ will store $Q_t(s,a)$ from Equation (2.1) after applying the transformations in Listing 2.3. Note that 0 values are replaced by -100 to ensure that the search for a maximum value skips these occurrences. $Q = (-100, -100, 40, -4, ..., -4, 40, -100, -100)$ in our example.

2.3. *Selection of best Q-values.* Performed by applying key-reduction over a zip-iterator as shown in Listing 2.4, where *seq_indicesQ*, *nqs_NQ* and *indicesNQ* are auxiliary vectors of size rows $*$ columns $*\,|A|$ each. For our example, $\textit{seq\_indicesQ} = (0,1,2,3,...,0,1,2,3)$, and $\textit{indicesNQ} = (0,0,0,0,...,3,3,3,3)$. After the key-reduction the V

```
device_vector<int>::iterator it;
maximum<tuple<float,int>> max_op;
for (it = seq_indicesQ.begin(); it < seq_indicesQ.end(); it += NQ)
    sequence (it, it + NQ);
fill                (nqs_NQ.begin(),       nqs_NQ.end(),       NQ          );
sequence            (indicesNQ.begin(),    indicesNQ.end()                 );
transform           (indicesNQ.begin(),    indicesNQ.end(),
                     nqs_NQ.begin(),       indicesNQ.begin(),  divides<int>);
ZipIterator firstIn  =
make_zip_iterator (make_tuple (Q.begin(), seq_indicesQ.begin())            );
ZipIterator firstOut =
make_zip_iterator (make_tuple (V.begin(), P.begin())                       );
reduce_by_key       (indicesNQ.begin(),    indicesNQ.end(),
                     firstIn,              indices_out.begin(),
                     firstOut,             equal_to<int>,      max_op      );
```

Listing 2.4. Selection of best Q-values.

vector will hold the best Q-values, and the P vector will store the corresponding indices for the current best policy. In our example, $V = (40, -4, -4, 40.5)$ and $P = (2, 0, 1, 1)$, i.e., $P = (E, W, S, S)$ is the current policy.

2.4. *Update of previous values vector.* The next value iteration towards π^* requires a vector holding the previous values in the directions W, S, E, N for each cell, with each $|A|$-tuple repeated $|A|$ times. Prior construction of the *vicinity* vector allows us to update the *prev_values* vector by mapping *vicinity* to *prev_values* using V as values:

```
gather (vicinity.begin(), vicinity.end(),
        V.begin(),        prev_values.begin());
```

but we require an extra index for V because *vicinity* values range from 0 to rows $*$ columns inclusive. We will establish that V is of size rows $*$ columns $+ 1$, and that its last value will be 0, with no effect for the rest of the algorithm. Then in our example, $prev\_values = (0, 0, -4, -4, ..., -4, -4, 0, 0)$.

2.5. *Check for convergence.* The condition to stop iterating values is a convergence in the recorded policy from one iteration to the next, so that if the count of zeroes in the parallel subtraction of vector *prev_P* from vector P equals rows $*$ columns, then we can guarantee that convergence is achieved and vector P holds π^*. In our example, a second iteration will yield: $V_2 = (9.3, -1.0, -1.0, 9.3, 0)$ and $P_2 = (2, 0, 1, 1)$. Since $P_1 = (2, 0, 1, 1)$ then $P_d = P_2 - P_1 = (0, 0, 0, 0)$ and $count(0, P_d) = 4$, so the process stops.

3. Download to host. As shown in Figure 2.4(d), the final (optimal) policy vector P is transferred to the host along with the final Q-values (Q) and best values (V) for verification.

In general, modular value iteration requires $4 * \text{rows} * \text{columns} * (5 + |A| * (4 + |A| * 6)) + 4$ bytes of memory space (1,876 bytes for our example).

2.1.3 Results

Results for the algorithm execution for the scenario shown in Figure 2.7 are reported in Table 2.2, showing a reduction of 87% in time over the generation technique for the *permutations* vector presented in [Ruiz and Hernández], by generating the vector entirely on the GPU with parallel transformations as shown in Section 2.1.2.

Time in milliseconds	[Ruiz and Hernández]	New method
Permutations vector	2501.373	322.337
Init CPU	142.583	142.197
Init GPU	2847.906	883.789
Iterations	1010.562	1013.704
Average iteration	3.4180	3.4190
Total MDP time	**4001.051**	**2039.690**

Table 2.2. Scenario University campus, 200 × 200 cells. GPU Titan Z (single GPU), Thrust v1.8, CUDA RC 8.0, Nvidia Driver 361.62.

2.1.4 Extensions

This algorithm is extended to provide a better navigation control under different situations as described below.

Agent Density. Non-congested routes will be used by agents when agent density per cell indicates it, i.e., instead of partially re-planning paths during the simulation, we propose to temporarily override the optimal policy π^* direction when the density threshold established for an agent is less than the actual density at the cell at which it points. When density information allows it, the agent will automatically regain optimal orientation even if the original path has been modified, by simply following once again the direction established by π^* [Ruiz and Hernández].

Multilayered Scenarios. The idea of multilayered scenarios is to guide agents using different "channels" of local navigation maps [Ruiz 2014]. Depending on the currently assigned channel for an agent, it can reach different goals, with different reward-penalty schemes. Multilayered scenarios are useful when modeling heterogeneous behaviors, i.e., different crowds with different goals.

Diverse terrain. Modeling different types of terrain is straightforward by using modified MDP reward values, e.g., the model could reward an agent walking over grass to reach its goal, but it could offer a greater reward to an agent walking over clear ground, as shown in Figure 2.7.

Different tile representations. In addition to using square tiles for space discretization, the MDP navigation algorithm can use hexagonal tiles reducing the action set A to six actions. Geometric representation of a hexagonal uniform tiling is translated into a matrix representation for array-based parallel computations [Ruiz and Hernández].

2.2 Crowd Rendering

Interactive crowd rendering involves several challenges that call for efficient solutions. First, crowd authoring should provide mechanisms to model and animate unique characters with the least amount of effort. Second, a compact representation of the crowd minimizes loading times and memory storage, but also it should support asset (models, animation rigs, textures) reuse. Finally, interactive frame rates can be achieved by a proper selection of the crowd's graphical representation and level-of-detail (LOD) techniques. Our crowd rendering engine was designed having these challenges in mind.

Our engine works in two main steps. The first step consists of data preparation and is performed only once. From a data set of virtual characters, we reduced, segmented, and labeled the virtual characters into three simpler body parts (head, torso with arms, and hips with legs and feet); labeling was manually generated to match and combine different body parts and generate new characters. Then, we generalized the rig and skinning information for each character gender, resulting in a unique rig and skinning, i.e., we encoded the rig and skinning data into the new characters UV space. Animation sequences were stored in auxiliary textures and additional textures (color, skin features, cloth patterns, displacement, etc.) were created to add visual diversity to the crowd.

The second step consists of applying view-frustum culling and discrete LOD on the GPU [Hernández and Rudomin 2011] to the characters' current positions and performing instancing with these assets to render the final crowd. Figure 2.5 shows a general diagram of the implementation after performing view-frustum culling, discrete LOD, and after loading assets into graphics memory. Charac-

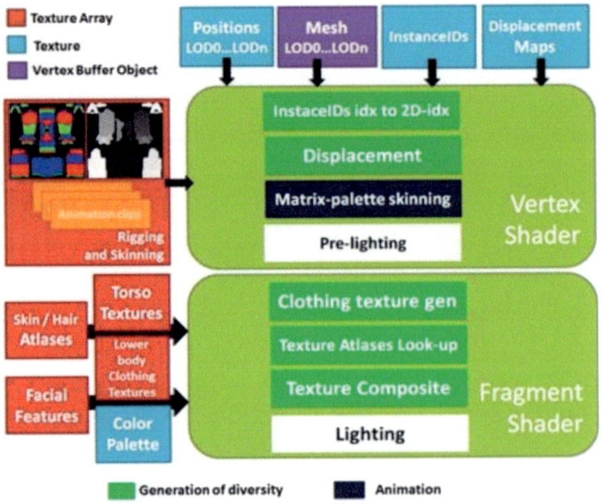

Figure 2.5.

ter positions and IDs (required for instancing) are stored in textures and LOD meshes in vertex-buffer objects. Rig and skinning information and different displacement maps are stored in texture arrays. Animation clips and all required textures for generation of diversity are also stored in texture arrays.

For a full explanation of the techniques in this section, the reader may consult [Hernández and Rudomin 2011] and [Ruiz et al. 2013]; [Beacco et al. 2015] article provides a comprehensive survey of real-time crowd rendering.

2.3 Coupling the MDP Solver with Crowd Rendering

MDP solution, navigation, collision avoidance, and crowd rendering are processed on the GPU, sharing parameters to achieve maximum performance, as shown in Figure 2.6. In the offline phase, scenario dimensions, discretization parameters, initial density, and agents positions are generated as vectors and then loaded to the GPU. Then, in the runtime phase, these data vectors are processed by the MDP solver to update the directional policy and also by the navigation and collision avoidance algorithms to update agents positions that in turn are the input for the crowd-rendering engine.

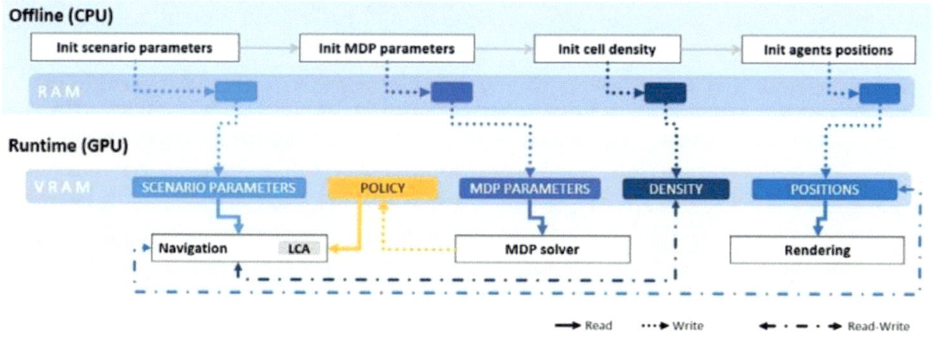

Figure 2.6. Method pipeline overview.

2.3.1 Offline Processing

For the case of navigation in a virtual scenario, discretization of two-dimensional pedestrian areas may be translated to the state space S (from the $< S, A, T, R >$ tuple) over which a MDP will determine optimal paths. We present the example of a college campus (Figure 2.7(a)) and its map as captured from Google Maps. At first we noticed that the map colors (Figure 2.7(b)) could establish pedestrian zones, but then realized that the actual walkable zones are more complex as they extend inside buildings and around urban equipment, so starting from the map

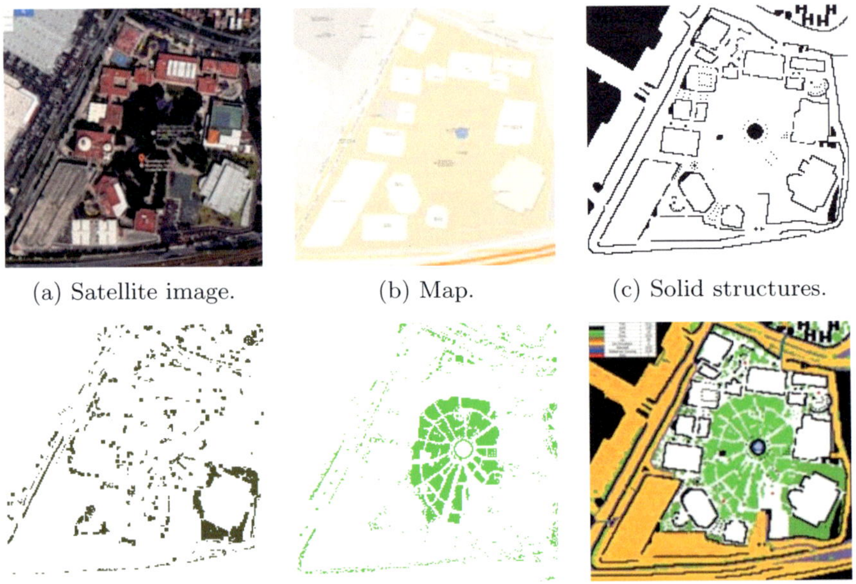

(a) Satellite image. (b) Map. (c) Solid structures.

(d) Grass. (e) Trees. (f) Combined texture.

Figure 2.7. MDP scenario discretization at 200×200 cells. The combined texture includes solid structures, grass, trees, and roads and pedestrian crossings.

and overlaying the satellite image, we proceeded to define solid structures and hence pedestrian areas for a 200×200 cell scenario (Figure 2.7(c)). In order to show that different terrain layers may modify the behavior of agents, we also mapped grass (Figure 2.7(d)), trees (Figure 2.7(e)), and roads and pedestrian crossings (Figure 2.7(f)) in the area. Encoded in a texture, this information stores all the required scenario and MDP parameters (Figure 2.6) for the simulation: width and height in cells, cell size, the state space for the MDP solution, and terrain types for the navigation algorithm.

2.3.2 Runtime Algorithm

In order to achieve an interactive frame rate while a change in topology is processed, our approach splits the MDP solution in stages over time as shown in Figure 2.8. A user-controlled change in scenario topology ($frame_{i-1}$) including addition or removal of an obstacle or exit, will trigger the MDP algorithm running interleaved with animation frames in sequence: *i)* update of the reward function $R(s)$ and initialization of data structures on the host ($frame_i$, Figure 2.4(a)); *ii)* uploading of scenario and MDP parameters to the GPU ($frame_{i+1}$, Figure 2.4(b)); *iii)* MDP iteration on the GPU towards optimal policy (one iteration per frame until convergence), achieved in c frames or stopped at a safety

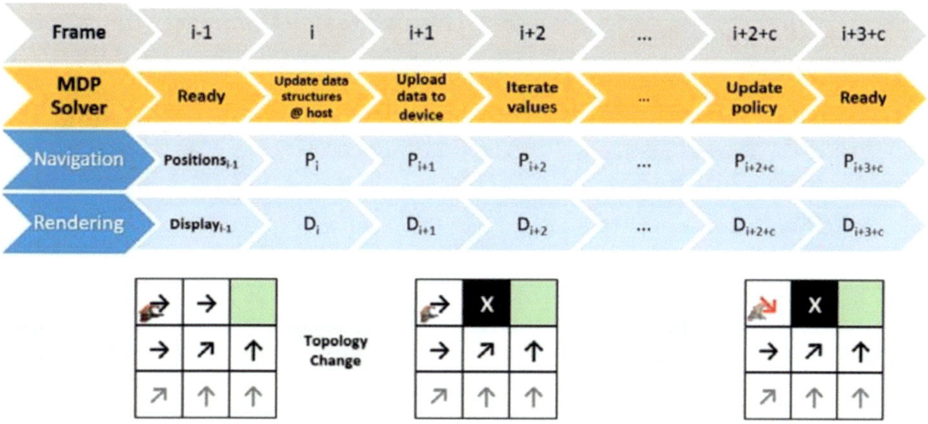

Figure 2.8. Split MDP iteration overview.

threshold ($frame_{i+2}...frame_{i+1+c}$, Figure 2.4(c)); *iv)* π^* update for the navigation algorithm when convergence is verified ($frame_{i+2+c}$, Figure 2.4(d)). To avoid host-device data transfer between iterations, device global memory is used to store the *permutations*, *vicinity* and *rewards* vectors (Section 2.1.2).

2.4 Results

To complement our solution and give a complete picture of the system performance, we included a local collision avoidance (LCA) method between characters based on cellular automata, using scatter and gather operations. The idea behind this is to direct agents toward (gather) and outwards from (scatter) the nearest cell marked by its MDP solution. This also allowed us to reuse the optimal policy as the base for a local navigation map. A detailed description of this LCA method is in [Ruiz 2014].

Performance for the coupled MDP solution method in different scenarios is reported in Table 2.3 and Table 2.4. We emphasize the relevance of the overhead that the MDP solution adds to the system. Following Section 2.3.2, timings from these tables are explained as follows:

Frame average reports rendering and navigation performance. *Frame avg. while iterating* adds to *Frame average* the "overhead" when MDP is being solved. So, for the Office scenario, this overhead is 1.711 ms per frame. The remaining fields break down the total MDP timing until optimal policy is reached.

Detailed rendering performance results are reported in [Ruiz et al. 2013] and [Hernández and Rudomin 2011]. Except for the Campus scenario, for the results reported, rewards of −10, −0.04, and 1, respectively, were assigned to obstacles, free space, and exits, respectively.

Time in milliseconds	Office (Fig. 2.9(a)) 780M	Office (Fig. 2.9(a)) Titan Z	Campus (Fig. 2.9(b)) 780M	Campus (Fig. 2.9(b)) Titan Z
Dimensions	60 x 60		200 x 200	
Iterations	187	177	211	213
Frame average	19.000	19.000	18.000	10.000
Frame avg. while iterating	20.711	22.347	27.791	14.188
MDP solution overhead	**1.711**	**3.347**	**9.791**	**4.188**
Init MDP vectors at host	47.000	15.660	547.000	83.970
MDP permutations vector	31.000	56.037	265.000	335.512
Upload to device	0.000	2.154	78.000	14.696
Total MDP iterating	330.000	367.975	848.000	807.888
MDP iteration average	1.765	2.091	4.019	3.793
Download to host	0.000	0.066	0.000	0.167
Policy update at host	15.000	2.954	156.000	13.496
Total MDP process	423.000	444.792	1894.000	1255.729

Table 2.3. MDP method performance for the Office and Campus scenarios.

Time in milliseconds	Town (Fig. 2.9(c)) 780M	Town (Fig. 2.9(c)) Titan Z	Maze (Fig. 2.9(d)) 780M	Maze (Fig. 2.9(d)) Titan Z
Dimensions	100 x 100		100 x 100	
Iterations	201	204	206	211
Frame average	17.000	9.000	17.000	10.000
Frame avg. while iterating	18.318	11.534	20.461	11.469
MDP solution overhead	**1.318**	**2.534**	**3.461**	**1.469**
Init MDP vectors at host	141.000	31.323	140.000	22.420
MDP permutations vector	63.000	129.115	78.000	70.756
Upload to device	15.000	5.505	31.000	4.095
Total MDP iterating	437.000	622.351	534.000	546.848
MDP iteration average	2.174	3.0517	2.592	2.592
Download to host	0.000	1.014	0.000	0.093
Policy update at host	47.000	5.078	47.000	3.625
Total MDP process	703.000	794.386	830.000	647.837

Table 2.4. MDP method performance for the Town and Maze scenarios.

For the Campus scenario, the following rewards were assigned: -0.01 for free space, -100 for solid obstacles, -10 for trees, -5 for streets, -0.02 for grass, -0.03 for sidewalks, -0.04 for pedestrian crossings and 1 for goals. Assignment of varied rewards allows us to simulate different kinds of terrain and priority for goals without additional computational cost for the navigation algorithm.

(a) Office

(b) Campus.

(c) Town.

(d) Maze.

Figure 2.9. Simulation scenarios. Arrows on the floor represent Π^*

The full system was tested in mobile (Windows 10) and desktop (Ubuntu 16) computers: **i)** Intel Core i7-4800MQ @ 2.70GHz CPU, GTX780M, Thrust v1.7, CUDA v7.0, Nvidia driver 368.81 **ii)** Intel Xeon CPU E5-2687W @ 3.10GHz, Titan Z (single GPU), Thrust v1.8, CUDA RC 8.0, Nvidia driver 361.62.

2.5 Conclusions

We presented a method to simulate crowds navigating in dynamic environments based on the GPU-implemented, real-time solution of Markov decision processes over a uniform grid. Different floor levels could be modeled by the multilayered scenario approach (Section 2.1.4), where stairs' entry points can be modeled as entrance/exits between stories; however additional changes should be done in the navigation algorithm so the agent can move in x-, y- and z-directions according to the stairs geometry.

Navigation paths estimated with the presented method are not limited by the number of agents, obstacles, or goals it can handle. Moreover, these obstacles and goals may have different priorities assigned to them without extra performance cost for the navigation algorithm.

Parallel solution of the MDP formalism was possible by formulating it in terms of transformation and reduction vector operations, thus segmenting the solution algorithm, differing it in steps interleaved with rendering, and taking advantage of the massive data parallelism in GPGPU computing to accelerate the solution time.

Acknowledgments

This research was partially supported by: CONACyT SNI-54067, Oak Ridge Leadership Computing Facility at the Oak Ridge National Laboratory, under DOE contract No. DE-AC05-00OR22725.

Sergio Ruiz would like to thank the Tecnologico de Monterrey IT & Computer Department for its support.

Bibliography

Beacco, A., Pelechano, N., and Andjar, C. 2015. A survey of real-time crowd rendering. *Computer Graphics Forum 35*, 8, 32–50.

Hernández, B., and Rudomin, I. 2011. A rendering pipeline for real-time crowds. In *GPU Pro 2*. A K Peters/CRC Press, Natick, MA, 369–383.

Ruiz, S., and Hernández, B. A parallel solver for markov decision process in crowd simulations. In *2015 Fourteenth Mexican International Conference on Artificial Intelligence (MICAI)*, IEEE Computer Society, Washington, DC, 107–116.

Ruiz, S., Hernández, B., Alvarado, A., and Rudomín, I. 2013. Reducing memory requirements for diverse animated crowds. In *Proceedings of Motion in Games*, ACM, New York, MIG '13, 55:77–55:86.

Ruiz, S. 2014. *A Hybrid Method for Macro and Micro Simulation of Crowd Behavior*. PhD thesis, Tecnológico de Monterrey. Available at https://www.researchgate.net/profile/Sergio_Ruiz7. doi:10.13140/RG.2.1.3897.1126.

About the Editors

Wessam Bahnassi is a software engineer and an architect (that is, for buildings, not software). This combination drives Wessam's passion for 3D engine design. He has written and optimized a variety of engines throughout a decade of game development. His latest shipped game was *Hyper Void*, a psychedelic 3D space-shooter full of visual effects, and its PlaystationVR DLC which simulates and renders natively at 120 FPS at 1440p.

Mark Chatfield is a graphics engineer at Visual Concepts, where he works on real-time rendering techniques and GPU optimization for the *NBA 2K* video game series. Prior to working in the video-game industry, he was the Lead Graphics Engineer at Maptek, where he focused on the core rendering technology powering a suite of products for the mining industry. He holds a Bachelor of Engineering (Software) (Honours) from Flinders University.

Carsten Dachsbacher is Full Professor at the Karlsruhe Institute of Technology. Prior to joining KIT, he was Assistant Professor at the Visualization Research Center (VISUS) of the University of Stuttgart, Germany, and post-doctoral fellow at REVES/INRIA Sophia-Antipolis, France. He received a MSc/diploma degree in Computer Science from the University of Erlangen-Nuremberg, Germany, in 2002 and a Ph.D. in Computer Science in 2006. His research focuses on real-time computer graphics, (interactive) global illumination, perceptual rendering, and visualization, on which he published several articles at various conferences and journals including SIGGRAPH, EG, EGSR, etc. He has been a tutorial speaker at SIGGRAPH, Eurographics, and the Game Developers Conference and reviewer for various conferences and journals.

Wolfgang Engel is the CEO of Confetti, a think-tank for advanced real-time graphics research and a service provider for the video-game and movie industry. Confetti worked in the last three years on many AAA IPs like *Tomb Raider*, *Battlefield 4*, *Murdered Soul Suspect*, *Star Citizen*, *Dirt 4*, *Vainglory*, *Transistor*, *Call of Duty Black Ops 3*, *Battlefield 1*, *Mafia 3*, and others. Wolfgang is the founder and editor of the *ShaderX* and *GPU Pro* book series, a Microsoft MVP, the author of several books and articles on real-time rendering, and a regular contributor to websites and the GDC. One of the books he edited, *ShaderX4*, won the Game Developer Front-line Award in 2006. Wolfgang is on the advisory boards of several companies. He is an active contributor to several future standards that drive the game industry.

Eric Haines is a Senior Principal Engineer at Autodesk, Inc., currently working on web-based 3D graphics. He is a coauthor of the book *Real-Time Rendering*, a founder of the *Journal of Computer Graphics Techniques*, and the designer of Udacity's free online course *Interactive 3D Graphics*, among other activities. He received an MS from the Program of Computer Graphics at Cornell in 1985.

Christopher Oat is the Technical Director at Rockstar New England where he works on real-time rendering techniques and performance optimizations for Rockstars latest games. Previously, he was the Demo Team Lead for AMD's Game Computing Applications Group. Christopher has published his work in various books and journals and has presented at graphics and game developer conferences worldwide. Many of the projects that he has worked on can be found on his website: www.chrisoat.com.

About the Contributors

Louis Bavoil is Principal Developer Technology Engineer at NVIDIA. He is a co-inventor of the HBAO algorithm and the creator of the HBAO+ library.

Jean Normand Bucci is director of Labs R&D deptartment at Eidos-Montral — Square Enix (https://ca.linkedin.com/in/jnbucci). During his previous experience as a well-rounded artist on big budget productions at Ubisoft Montréal ten years ago, Jean-Normand found his love for game technicalities which have helped him produce industry-leading game visuals. Having completed multiple massive productions in game development over varied positions, Jean-Normand has substantial experience in the world of art, technical direction, and research & development, all developing a strong management skill sets in the entertainment industry. He is currently managing a multi-disciplinary team to conceive and develop experimental new features in order to drive the industry forward. This work is shared across the Square Enix West division and its studios: Crystal Dynamics in California, Io-Interactive in Copenhagen, and Eidos-Montral, as well as through public appearance at major events. Always looking at improving his managerial skills, Jean-Normand is pursuing his training at the renowned HEC-Montréal University, towards a degree in Innovation and Creativity management. He is leading those different challenges, all while raising his family with supportive wife, Sarah, and two kids, Milo and Billie.

Stefan Buschmann studied computer science at the University of Braunschweig, Germany (2000–2007). In 2011, he joined the Computer Graphics Systems group at the Hasso Plattner Institute, Potsdam, as a research assistant and Ph.D. student. His research areas are 3D computer graphics, visual analytics, and spatio-temporal data visualization.

Felipe Chaves is a 3D artist focused on character modeling. He currently works at Black River Studios helping the team to find good artistic and technical solutions for 3D to be used on VR games. He's enthusiastic about both realistic and cartoon style, always trying to mix them to create a unique style.

Jürgen Döllner studied mathematics and computer science at the University of Siegen, Germany (1987–1992). He got his Ph.D. in computer science from the University of Münster, Germany, in 1996; he received his habilitation degree in 2001 also from the University of Münster. In 2001 he became full professor for computer science at the Hasso-Plattner-Institute at the University of Potsdam, where he is leading the computer graphics and visualization department.

Hawar Doghramachi studied dental medicine at the Semmelweis University in Budapest and received the doctor of dental medicine (DMD) title in 2003. After working for a while as a dentist, he decided to turn his lifetime passion for programming into his profession. After studying 3D programming at the Games Academy in Frankfurt, he has been working since 2010 as an engine programmer in the Vision team of Havok and then as a graphics programmer in the R&D team of Eidos Montreal. Currently he is working as a graphics programmer at Naughty Dog. He is particularly interested in finding solutions for common real-time rendering problems in modern computer games.

Alex Dunn, is a developer technology engineer for NVIDIA and spends his days passionately working toward advancing real-time visual effects in games. A former graduate of Abertay University's Games Technology course, Alex got his first taste of graphics programming on the consoles. Now working for NVIDIA, his time is spent working on developing cutting-edge programming techniques to ensure that the highest quality and best player experience possible is achieved.

Teofilo Dutra is a core tech engineer at Black River Studios, which is focused on developing mobile VR games/experiences. He obtained his Ph.D. in Computer Science from Universidade Federal do Cearà (UFC) in 2015 with an emphasis on crowd simulation. His research was mainly focused on simulating crowds where agents are endowed with synthetic vision.

Eric Heitz is a graphics researcher at Unity Technologies. He works on physically based rendering with a strong focus on shading and level-of-detail techniques. Eric got his Ph.D. from Grenoble University at INRIA in France.

Holger Gruen is a Technology Engineer at NVIDIA. He works with game developers to get the best out of NVIDIA's GPUs.

Benjamin Hernandez is a computer scientist in the Oak Ridge Leadership Computing Facility at the Oak Ridge National Laboratory. Before joining ORNL, he was a postdoctoral fellow at the Barcelona Supercomputing Center and full professor in the Computer Sciences Department at the Tecnologico de Monterrey in Mexico City. He provides advice to TITAN supercomputer's users to enable scientific discovery through the development and implementation of scalable visualization and data technologies. His research interests are in the intersection of interactive computer graphics, parallel programming, crowd simulation, and human computer interaction.

Stephen Hill is a Senior Rendering Engineer within Lucasfilm's Advanced Development Group, with a focus on physically based rendering. He was previously a 3D Technical Lead at Ubisoft Montreal, where he contributed to a number of *Splinter Cell* titles, as well as *Assassin's Creed Unity*.

Nathan Hoobler deeply appreciates the fusion of technical efficiency, mathematical rigor, and artistic vision that modern computer graphics requires. As an undergraduate he worked in the University of Virginia Graphics Research Group where he was fascinated by the invisible mechanisms that rendered the world around him visible. He has spent over a decade in the video game industry, most of it at NVIDIA in the Developer Technology group where he continues working to understand and recreate the everyday magic our eyes take for granted.

James Hughes works at Oculus on the PC SDK Graphics team. Prior to this, he was at Sarcos helping build the XOS2 robotic exoskeleton and at the Scientific Computing and Imaging Institute working on volumetric rendering. He has a B.S. in mathematics and enjoys working on the wide variety of geometric problems in graphics.

Edward Hutchins is currently a member of the Oculus PC SDK team. His past experience includes working at a number of Silicon Valley startups, founding NVIDIA's Tegra architecture team, and designing GPUs at GigaPixel and SGI. His love for all things computer-graphical started during the golden age of arcade videogames.

Felipe Lira is a graphics programmer experienced in mobile game development. He currently works at Unity Technologies as part of the graphics foundation team. He is enthusiastic about rendering, VR, engines and optimization.

Gareth Morgan has been involved in 3D graphics and game development since 1999. His career began at Silicon Graphics after which he worked at several games companies, including Activision and BAM Studios. For almost a decade, he researched sophisticated rendering techniques using Imagination Technologies' ray tracing Power VR GPUs. In 2014 and 2016, he presented at GDC, and his chapter on ray tracing was published in *GPU Pro 6*. Currently he is CEO of Axum Graphics, creating ground-breaking 3D content-creation tools using WebGL and other technologies.

Reza Nourai is currently Head of Graphics at Magic Leap, Inc., working on mixed reality rendering and performance. Prior to that, he spent years at both Oculus and Microsoft, delivering the Oculus Rift and the Xbox One. His expertise spans from core operating systems all the way up to real-time graphics and low-latency VR/MR algorithms and rendering.

Kleverson Paixão is a core tech engineer at Black River Studios where he is creating tools and optimizing (taming) VR games. He has experience in other fields of computing, but he's currently fine with code and graphics optimization.

Emil Persson is the Head of Research at Avalanche Studios, where he is conducting forward-looking research, with the aim to be relevant and practical for game development, as well as setting the future direction for the Avalanche Engine. Previously, Emil was an ISV Engineer in the Developer Relations team at ATI/AMD. He assisted tier-1 game developers with the latest rendering techniques, identifying performance problems, and applying optimizations. He also made major contributions to SDK samples and technical documentation.

Íñigo Quílez was born in and grew up in San Sebastián (a.k.a. Donostia), a beautiful city in the Basque Country, somewhere in Europe (Spain). He has worked at Tracasa, VRcontext, Pixar Animation Studios, and is currently at Oculus Story Studios. He is a co-creator of *Shadertoy* and enjoys writing articles and tutorials for his website at iquilezles.org.

Sergio Ruiz received his Ph.D. in Computer Science from Tecnologico de Monterrey, Mexico City Campus in 2014. His research area is in path planning for simulated crowds, his thesis, "A Hybrid Method for Macro- and Micro-Simulation of Crowd Behavior." After a research visit in 2013 working in crowd simulation at Barcelona Supercomputing Center in Spain, he is currently a full professor in the Computer Sciences Department at the Tecnologico de Monterrey in Mexico City, developing projects related to computer graphics for decision making.

Rahul Sathe works as a Senior DevTech Engineer at NVIDIA. His current role involves working with game developers to improve their experience on GeForce graphics. Prior to this role, he worked in various capacities in research and product groups for 17 years at Intel. He is passionate about all aspects of 3D graphics and its hardware underpinnings. He attended school at Clemson University and University of Mumbai. While not working on the rendering-related things, he likes running and enjoying good food with his family and friends.

Willy Scheibel studied computer science at the Hasso Plattner Institute / University of Potsdam in Germany (2008–2014). In 2014 he joined the Computer Graphics Systems group at the Hasso Plattner Institute as research assistant and Ph.D. student. His research areas are 3D computer graphics, GPGPU programming, and visualization of hierarchically structured data.

Jesus Sosa is an experienced art director/3D artist. Currently, he is the Creative Director at Dinosaur Games.

Wojciech Sterna has been working professionally in the games-and-around industry for a couple of years now. He was an intern at NVIDIA, engine/renderer programmer at Flying Wild Hog, and briefly at CD PROJEKT RED (among other tasks bug-fixing *Witcher 3: Blood and Wine*). He is now doing pretty exciting things at some VR startup in Warsaw, Poland.

Filip Strugar is a graphics software engineer at Intel Corporation where he works on research & development, application and optimization of graphics algorithms for GPUs and CPUs, as well as developer relations. Prior to this role, he worked within Sega Technology Group on engine development and technology support roles for games such as *Sonic* and *All-Stars Racing: Transformed*. Before Sega, he was part of the Rebellion's core team, helping develop engine features and graphics effects for *Alien Vs Predator* (2010) and other titles. Filip is still as passionate about game and software development as he was when he started working in the industry in 2002.

Marcus Svensson graduated with a master's degree in game and software engineering from Blekinge Institute of Technology. He currently works as a junior graphics programmer at Avalanche Studios.

Matthias Trapp studied computer science at the Hasso Plattner Institute / University of Potsdam in Germany where he received his Ph.D. in computer science. Currently he is leading the junior research group of the InnoProfile-Transfer-Initiative "4D-nD Geovisualization" at the Hasso-Plattner Institute / University of Potsdam in Germany. His major research areas are computer graphics, geovisualization, and software visualization.

Flávio Villalva is a VFX artist at Gameloft, Montréal. He graduated in Game Design from Universidade Anhembi Morumbi and has previously worked as tester, engineer, and tech art at Glu Mobile. He worked as VFX artist at Mobjoy, as well as at Black River Studios, where he started his studies about real-time shading and non-photorealistic rendering.

Graham Wihlidal is a senior rendering engineer on the Frostbite Labs team at Electronic Arts, researching and developing cutting-edge technology used in many hit games like *Battlefield 1*, *Mass Effect Andromeda*, *Dragon Age Inquisition*, and *Star Wars: Battlefront*. Prior to Frostbite, Graham was a senior engineer at BioWare for many years, shipping numerous titles including the *Mass Effect* and *Dragon Age* trilogies, and *Star Wars: The Old Republic*. Graham is also the author of *Game Engine Toolset Development* and specializes in low-level optimizations, engine architecture, GPU driver implementation, and console development.

KinMing Wong is an award-winning visual effects professional and the owner of artixels, a boutique visual effects software developer which focuses on plugin development for highend motion pictures. He has recently joined Professor TienTsin Wong's research group to pursue his Ph.D. degree. He works on photorealistic rendering problems with a strong interest in highperformance sampling and filtering techniques. He is also a computational artist with his works exhibited at SIGGRAPH and GRAPHITE (predecessor of SIGGRAPH Asia).

TienTsin Wong is a professor in the Department of Computer Science and Engineering at the Chinese University of Hong Kong (CUHK) and served as head of the committee advisory board of the Computer Game Technology Centre in the department. He has been coding in the computer graphics area for over 20 years, including writing publicly available codes, libraries, demos, and toolkits (please check his homepage http://www.cse.cuhk.edu.hk/~ttwong), as well as codes for all his graphics research. He works on GPU techniques, rendering, imagebased relighting, natural phenomenon modeling, computational manga, and multimedia data compression. He is a SIGGRAPH author and has published in *Computer Graphics Gems*, the *ShaderX* series and Game Developer Conference.

Made in the USA
Monee, IL
06 September 2026

62375914R00217